HISTORY BEGINS IN AFRICA

BY

MARY ACOSTA

Edited by
Kathleen E. Turner

Published by

BIRDS NEST PUBLISHING

PASADENA, CA

Birds Nest Publishing
366 N. Allen Avenue, Suite 245
Pasadena, CA 91106

To order this book, mail check or money order in US
dollars to:
Birds Nest Publishing
366 N. Allen Avenue, Suite 245
Pasadena, CA 91106

Current pricing and ordering information are available at
http://birdsnestpublishing.com/.

ISBN: 978-0-9842645-0-6
Printed and bound in the U.S.A.

Illustrations and Maps by Author
Cover Illustration by Author

Translations of citations from works in other languages are
those of the author unless otherwise indicated.

Dedication

To my sister, Kathleen, who helped when I thought help could not be hoped for.

Table of Contents

Dedication iii

Table of Contents v

List of Illustrations ix

Introduction xi

PART I 1

HISTORICAL BACKGROUND 3

  History 3

  Africa 4

  Begins 7

  Mesopotamia 7
    The Sumerian King List 7
    Late Uruk Trading Colonies 9
    Late Ubaid Pottery in Bahrain and Qatar 12

  Egypt 14
    Egyptian King Lists 14
    Naqada and Thinis 17
    The River Kingdom 18
    The Scorpion King Macehead 31
    The Great Land 35

THE PROCLAMATION ILLUSTRATED 37

  1. The Narrator and His Opponent 38

  2. The Hangings at Thinis 40

  3. A New Western Border for the River Kingdom 42

  4. Borders of the *Akuia* kingdom 44

Table of Contents

5. *Tiokenes* Rules West of the Nile 46

6. *Kaiaitos* and Elephant Land 48

7. The Great Chief of *Turanikum* (Eritrea) 50

8. The Elephant Lord 52

9. The Lord King of *Telad* 54

10. *Ataiokum* (Meroe) 56

11. *Uiriraskum* (Lasta) 58

12. From Cattle Land to the *Turo* Empire 60

13. *Testios*, the King of Scorpion Land 62

14. *Koloutios*, the Phoenician 64

15. *Tetu*, the Laguatan 66

16. An *Aunu* from the Land of Bes 68

17. The King of Suakin 70

18. The Captive *Melman* Lord 72

19. *Tueidunos*, the Phoenician 74

20. The Kingdoms of the Deep South 76

21. Victory in the North 78

22. *Melmanios*, King of Egypt, Arabia and Uruk 80

23. Thebes and the Dal Cataract 82

24. The Four Kings of *Akuikum* 84

25. The Enemy Lands 86

26. Decreed by Who and Where 88

ABOUT THE BOTORRITA III INSCRIPTION 91

The Bronze Plaque 91

The Writing System 99

Phoenician Origins.. 102

The Beginning of Writing.. 106

DECIPHERING THE TEXT: THE FIVE KEYS........... 113

The First Key: *KUM* 116

The Second Key: Hieroglyphic Placenames.............. 118

The Third Key: The Common Vocabulary................. 121

The Fourth Key: The Language Family..................... 151

The Fifth Key: The Logical Structure........................ 159

ATTACK ON THE BULL'S EYE................................ 168

Background.. 168

The Book of Invasions: Looking for a Date 174

Who is the narrator?.. 180

HISTORY LOST AND FOUND AGAIN...................... 181

PART II.. 183

WORKS CITED 185

GAZETTEER 203

APPENDIX A Grammatical Notes............................. 226

§1 Introduction... 226

§2 Phonology 227

§3 Pronouns 230

§4 Verbs... 234

§5 Nouns 243

§6 Adjectives 249

§7 Postpositions 254

Table of Contents

§8 Botorrita I-B Grammatical Notes............................ 258

APPENDIX B Botorrita III: Side by Side 261

GLOSSARY 279

INDEX 384

List of Illustrations

Map 1 Modern Kushitic Peoples Mentioned 4

Map 2 Late Uruk Colonies.. 11

Libyan Palette - Kingdom Side... 19

Libyan Palette - Cattle Land Side 21

Map 3 Cattle Land Kingdoms... 23

Map 4 *Melman* Egypt in I-B Period................................ 24

Map 5 Uruk Expansion Map... 25

Map 6 The Southern River Kingdom............................... 26

Map 7 The River Kingdom of *Terkinos*........................... 28

The Ubaid Style Vase from Hierakonpolis..................... 29

Royal Standards of Scorpion King Allies........................ 31

The Captive behind the Scorpion King............................ 33

The Lion Kingdom... 34

Madicenus Calaetus, Great Chaldean Lord 90

Map 8 Carthaginian Spain and North Africa 92

Table 1 Celtiberian-English Symbol Table..................... 99

Thoth, the God of Bureaucrats.. 108

The Symbol *KUM*.. 116

Table 2 Hieroglyphic Placenames in the Proclamation . 119

Map 9 Places in the Middle East.................................... 122

Map 10 Places in Egypt 127

Map 11 Places in Northeast Africa 132

List of Illustrations

Map 12 Greek and Libyan Places 138

Map 13 Places on the Arabian Peninsula...................... 142

Map 14 Places in the River Kingdom 156

Organization Chart of *Terkinos*' Empire 161

Organization Chart of Enemy Kings............................. 163

Map 15 Non-Kushitic Languages in the South............. 166

Map 16 Botorrita I-B 170

Table 3 Botorrita I-B, Text and Translation 171

Map 17 The Falcon Clan at War.................................... 174

Table 4 Book of Invasions Chronology 177

Map 18 World in the 3rd Millennium BC.................. 181

Map 19 World in the 4th Millennium BC.................. 182

Introduction

The purpose of this book is to translate the inscriptions found on two different bronze plaques in Spain. The first text is a Proclamation written by the ruler of an ancient and forgotten Red Sea empire. The second text is much shorter. It describes the events in a war in the eastern Mediterranean Sea. The Libyans fight against an alliance of Egyptians and Greeks.

The texts are very ancient. The first text can be dated to about 3236 BC. The second text cannot be dated so exactly, but it was probably written several centuries earlier. These texts are currently the oldest written original historical documents in the world. At least, they are the oldest documents that we can still understand.

Four sections are devoted to the first text, the longer of the two. The Historical Background describes what we know about events in the late 4th millennium BC. It shows how these new texts add to our knowledge.

Next is an illustrated free translation of the text. An ancient Red Sea emperor tells you his own story directly.

About the Botorrita III Inscription discusses what is known about the bronze plaques. It describes the writing system. It shows how the first text may be linked to the ancient Red Sea.

The fourth section describes how the texts were actually deciphered. The Five Keys are five major insights that revealed the meaning of the text. Each of these keys contributed to the final result.

Following these four sections, the Attack on the Bull"s Eye section translates the text on the second bronze plaque. This second text is written in the same language as the first text. It uses the same writing system. The section contains some historical background and two maps. It provides a side-by-side, bilingual translation.

A final section ends Part I of the book with a few concluding remarks.

Part II is a collection of various reference data. These two texts are both ancient and previously undeciphered. They contain priceless information for scholars in many fields. The reference section is intended to make this information more usable. It tries to make particular kinds of data easy to find.

Coming after the Works Cited is the Gazetteer. There are nearly 200 placenames in the texts. They provide contemporary geographical information for the Red Sea region in the late 4th millennium BC. Geographical information about the Red Sea is precious and rare in most historical periods. The texts provide unique documentation for some of the world's most ancient placenames.

Appendix A contains the Grammatical Notes. The words in the texts fall into two groups. The first group is the Common Vocabulary, about 80% of the words. Most of these words are foreign words for placenames, names of ethnic groups and titles. Words in the Common Vocabulary are discussed under the Third Key in the Decipherment section.

The second group is the Kushitic Vocabulary, about 20% of the words. These provide the actual grammar of the language. Every Kushitic word and grammatical particle is discussed in the Grammatical Notes. They are grouped into major categories by Noun, Verb, Postpositions, etc. Each word is discussed individually with examples from the texts. Every word in each of the texts is listed in the Glossary.

Appendix B provides the full text of the Proclamation. It gives this first, and longest, of the texts, in a side-by-side, line-by-line translation. The texts are thousands of years old. They are older than any other examples of Kushitic languages that have been found so far. The texts, the Grammatical Notes, and the Glossary are important resources for anyone studying Kushitic languages.

The Glossary is the first installment for a dictionary of this ancient language. It contains every word in both texts and an English translation. It gives references for information about the word and related variants.

Finally, there is an Index providing page numbers for major and minor topics not likely to be in the Grammatical Notes or the Gazetteer.

At no other place in this book do I mention the astonishment I felt at how complex the world already was a thousand years before the beginning of written history. Peek through the window yourself. See if what you find meets your expectations.

PART I

HISTORICAL BACKGROUND

History

Sometime around 3200 BC, the ancient city of Uruk in southern Iraq was destroyed. In the decades just before that, Uruk was still a great city, a world power. A newly deciphered, ancient text reveals an Imperial Proclamation. An ancient Red Sea Emperor from Africa led a large-scale struggle against Mesopotamian Uruk for control of the Red Sea.

The African leader, *Terkinos,* a southerner from Ethiopia, prevailed. In his Proclamation, he lists the enemies he hanged and his new provinces. The opposing leader was *Melmanios*. *Melmanios* was the second to the last King of Uruk. His efforts to expand Uruk had been putting increasing pressure on his neighbors in Africa. After *Terkinos* captured *Melmanios*, he had this proclamation engraved on a bronze plaque. His subjects could see that plaque in his summer palace, in the Keren Highlands of Eritrea.

Unlike archaeology, history depends on documents. It prefers official documents. A government in power should issue them. *Terkinos'* bronze plaque counts as a historical document, a primary source.

When the early chapters of the World History textbooks look at Africa, only Egypt appears. Only Egypt has all those ancient documents. They are carved and painted on the walls of very ancient tombs. *Terkinos'* bronze plaque will change that.

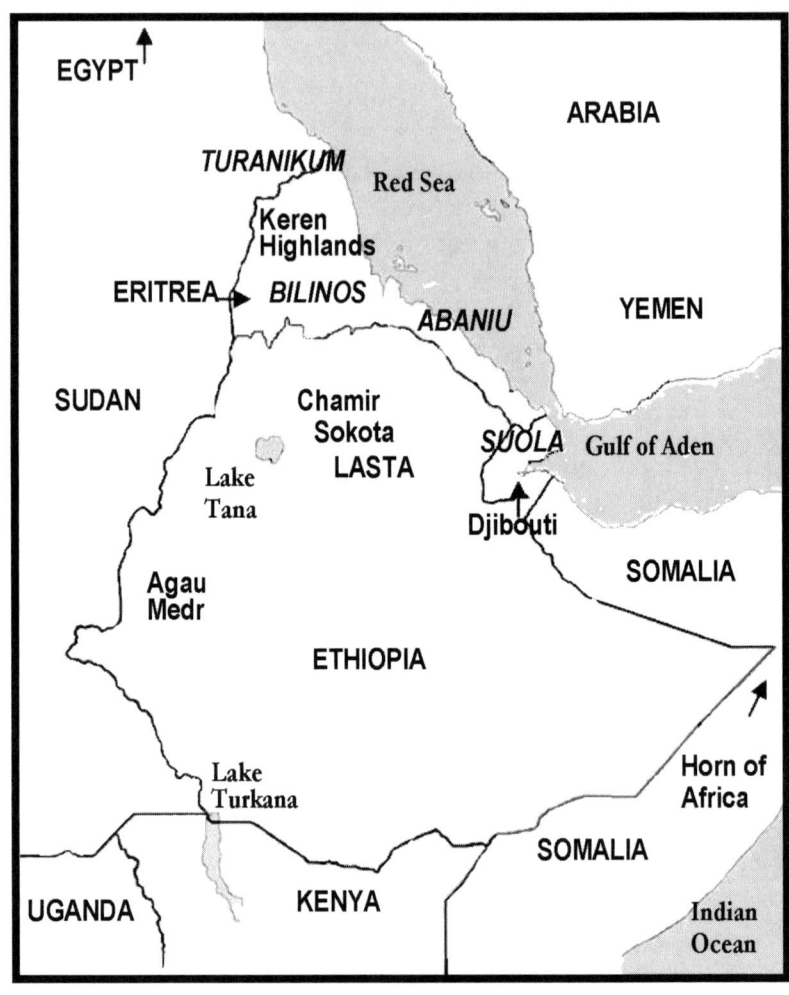

Map 1 Modern Kushitic Peoples Mentioned

Africa

The language of *Terkinos*' proclamation is a
Kushitic language.[1] Millions of people speak Kushitic

---

[1] Zaborski, "Cushitic Overview," 67-84; Bender, "Introduction," 2-5.

languages. You can hear them from the southern Egyptian border to the Horn of Africa in Somalia. The Proclamation mentions the names of some ancient peoples. Those names match the names of modern groups of Kushitic language speakers. We find the *Bilinos* (Bilin), the *Terkinos* (Bilin tribe, descended from Terqe), and the *Abaniu* (Afan / Afar). The *Akuia* (Agau) and the *Suola* (Somali) are names for large groups of peoples. These languages are spoken in Eritrea, Ethiopia, Djibouti and Somalia.

__Bilinos__ - Bilin / Bilen is spoken in the Keren Highlands of Eritrea. About four centuries ago, the Bilin people moved to Keren from Lasta, according to their traditions.[2] Lasta is in the Central Ethiopian Highlands.

Lasta is mentioned in the first line of the Proclamation. It says, 'A southerner from Lasta, I prevented the [would-be] conquering *Nouida* from going beyond the limits of their territory' (0.1).[3] The last line of the text mentions the Keren Highlands. It says, 'This was decreed for our provinces by *Terkinos* of *Turanikum* in the Keren Highlands of *Kustikum* (Eritrea)' (4.37-40).

In another part of the text, we read, 'The River Kingdom is ruled by the *Bilinos* of *Austikum*' (1.20-21). *Austikum* means 'Highland, plateau'. It is another name for the Lasta region, which is very mountainous.

__Terkinos__ - The *Terkinos* may have come from the Lake Turkana region on the southwest border of Ethiopia. In the Proclamation, some of the *Terkinos* were living in Lasta. The *Terkinos* seem to have combined with the Bilin there. Today, one of the two great tribes of the Bilin is the tribe of the Terqe-qur, the descendants of Terqe.

---

[2] Reinisch, *Die Bilin-Sprache*, 7.
[3] (0.1) refers to column and line number in the text in Appendix B.

Historical Background

The text mentions individual *Terkinos*, like the narrator ruling in *Turanikum*. There are also communities of *Terkinos* in Lasta, in Egypt, and in Yemen. The ethnic roots of the narrator lie among Kushitic-speaking peoples. He uses a Kushitic language to speak to us.

Abaniu - Afar / Afan is an East Kushitic language like Bilin. The people live in the Danakil region on the southern Red Sea coast.

Akuia - The *Akuia* of the text correspond to the ancient *Akhou* in Egypt. They are ancestors to the modern Agau in Sudan, Eritrea, Ethiopia and Somalia. The Agau / Agew language is part of a major sub-family of the Kushitic languages. The word *Akuia,* like the word Agau, means 'head or chief'. Agau is also the name of peoples, a province and a group of languages. Bilin and Afan are Agau languages, as is Chamir.

Chamir - In modern times, they speak Chamir in Lasta at Sokota. In the Proclamation, the name of the narrator is *Terkinos* of *Austikum*, the Sokotino. He is the *medukenos*, 'Great Chief' of Aqiq (2.12-15). The Chamir also call themselves the Kam or Cham. Kam appears in the text as the name of the fortress of *Kulu-Kam-ikum*.[4] Of all the Kushitic languages mentioned here, the Proclamation resembles Chamir and Bilin most closely.

Suola - Djibouti. People speak Somali dialects in that region. Somali is also a major sub-family of Kushitic. *Medukenos,* 'Great-Chief', mentioned above, compares to *madax-weyna*. This modern Somali word means 'President of the Republic', but is literally 'Great Chief'.[5]

The narrator begins by referring to himself as 'a southerner from Ethiopia'. The Kushitic language that he speaks is an African language. The subject matter is about

---

[4] Reinisch, *Die ChamirSprache*, vol. CV, 574-575.
[5] Ibid., *Die Bilin-Sprache*, 29. Bilin: *mad*, 'head'; Somali: *madax*, 'head, chief'; *weyna*, 'great'.

the new borders of his territories in Africa. He mentions the captive rulers that he executed in Africa. The decree is issued in Eritrea. These are strong reasons to believe this document was created in Africa.

Begins

What justifies an early date for this Proclamation? Ancient foreign placenames in the text lead us to Mesopotamia and Egypt. Both nations have ancient records. The evidence from Mesopotamia points to the Late Uruk period, 3500-3200 BC. The evidence from Egypt points to the PreDynastic Naqada II Period, 3500-3200 BC. It confirms and enhances the Mesopotamian data.

Mesopotamia

The Sumerian King List

In the beginning of the text, *Terkinos* says, 'to that Arab leader [held] captive in Scorpion Land, the Great King… has given his verdict' (0.1-1.5). The one great Arab leader in the text is the Lord of the *Kalaitos* (Chaldeans) of *Muturiskum* (Egypt, 𓄿𓃭𓈖). He is the king of Arabia, Chaldea and Uruk.

At this time, Egypt is divided into two pieces. A tiny corner in the northeast (Vulture Cobra Land) is ruled by the Chaldeans. The Berbers of Cattle Land rule the rest from the oases in Western Egypt.

This enemy Chaldean Lord rules an Egyptian Berber people called the *Melman*. The Somali word *meel* means 'place, land, location'. *Melman* would mean 'the locals, the native Egyptians'. An ancient Berber name for Egypt is *Ta Mera* (⎁⎍), 'The Land'.

Since our Chaldean Lord is a king of Uruk, we can look for him in the Sumerian King List. In this list of very ancient Mesopotamian rulers, the kings are divided according to which city had the kingship. In the list for Uruk, the second-to-the-last king was called *Melamanna*, 'the *Melman*', i.e., 'the Egyptian Berber'.[6] No other names resemble *Melamanna* in that list. Could an Egyptian faction have come to power in distant Uruk (in Iraq)? He only ruled for six years. The dates of his reign would be 3242 - 3236 BC. If *Terkinos* passed a death sentence on *Melamanna* in 3236 BC, he would have issued the Proclamation, announcing his verdict at that time.

In the Proclamation, we mostly read about this enemy lord by his titles. In just one place (1.27), we find a reference to territory taken from the kingdom of *Melmanios* of the River Kingdom.

Terkinos mentions another Sumerian when he describes the new borders of his empire. He has a hostile neighbor named *Kaiaitos*. On Terkinos' border is the fortress of *Atokum* (Aden). That fort was conquered by 'a lord of Bahrain and Qatar, *Kaiaitos*, from the nation of the Sumerian Land of Kish (*Kankaikiskum*)' (1.54-57).

The city of Kish (near Baghdad) was the ancient, traditional capital of Sumer. Sometimes, the kingship moved to other cities. For about 2,000 years, roughly from 5000 to 3200 BC, the kingship of Sumer was at Uruk (in southern Iraq).

According to the Sumerian King List, the last king of Uruk was *Lugal Kitun*.[7] He ruled for 30 years between 3236 and 3200 BC, just after *Melamanna*.

---

[6] Kramer, *The Sumerians*, 329.

[7] Kramer, *The Sumerians*, 329; Guisepi, "The Sumerian King List". Kramer shows the name as *Kidul* and Guisepi shows *Kitun* from a

Lugal is a title that means 'king'. K-Y-T is *Lugal Kitun's* actual name. This word appears in the cuneiform writing system. No writing system perfectly matches pronunciation. For that particular spelling, among the most likely pronunciations are - *Kīt, Kitt, Kayt* or *Kaiat*. *Kaiaitos*, in the Proclamation text, may be an African pronunciation of that name. In the Proclamation text, many personal names end in *-os*.

The point of all this is that *Kaiaitos* is *Lugal Kitun*, the last king of Uruk. *Kaiaitos* would also have been alive during the six-year reign of his predecessor, *Melmanios*. During the war between *Terkinos* and *Melmanios*, *Kaiaitos* is already the Lord of Bahrain and Qatar. He is not yet king of Uruk. In the Proclamation, we learn that he captured the fortress at Aden. However, his king, *Melmanios*, is captured and held captive in *Tirtanikum* (Scorpion Land) close by.

Being a hostile neighbor makes him a contemporary of our narrator. That is a second piece of evidence. It gives the Proclamation a date of some time within 42 years before 3200 BC, the year that Uruk was destroyed.[8]

Late Uruk Trading Colonies

Other details support this early date for the Proclamation. The trading colonies of Uruk were a notable feature of the Late Uruk Period. Those colonies spread across the Middle East. Archaeologists have found their ruins. The Late Uruk Period spans the three centuries before the city was destroyed. The Proclamation contains names and rulers for those Late Uruk trading colonies.

---

different copy of the list. Either would match because **t** and **d** are not distinct in the Proclamation writing system.

[8] Crawford, *Sumer and the Sumerians*, 18.

Terkinos mentions *Kabelaikiskum.* This is the 'Hill of Kish', or Byblos, in Lebanon. The early center of Byblos was a shrine built on a hill. *Kabelai* is similar to modern Semitic words for 'hill' like *gebel* and *jebel.* Many ancient documents, spread over thousands of years, confirm that some form of the word 'hill', (*gubla, guebla, kabela* and others,) was part of the name of Byblos. The name 'Hill of Kish', found in the Proclamation, tells us it was a Sumerian colony.

Terkinos also mentions *Ailokiskum* (Aila, Hebrew Eilat / Elath). *Kis(h)* in the name tells us this is another Sumerian colony. The ruins of Aila are near a resort at modern Eilat in Israel.

There are also clusters of *Arkanta* (Akkadian Arkaiitu, Urukites) at Thebes in Elephantine province, in Lower Nubia and at Thinis in southern Egypt.

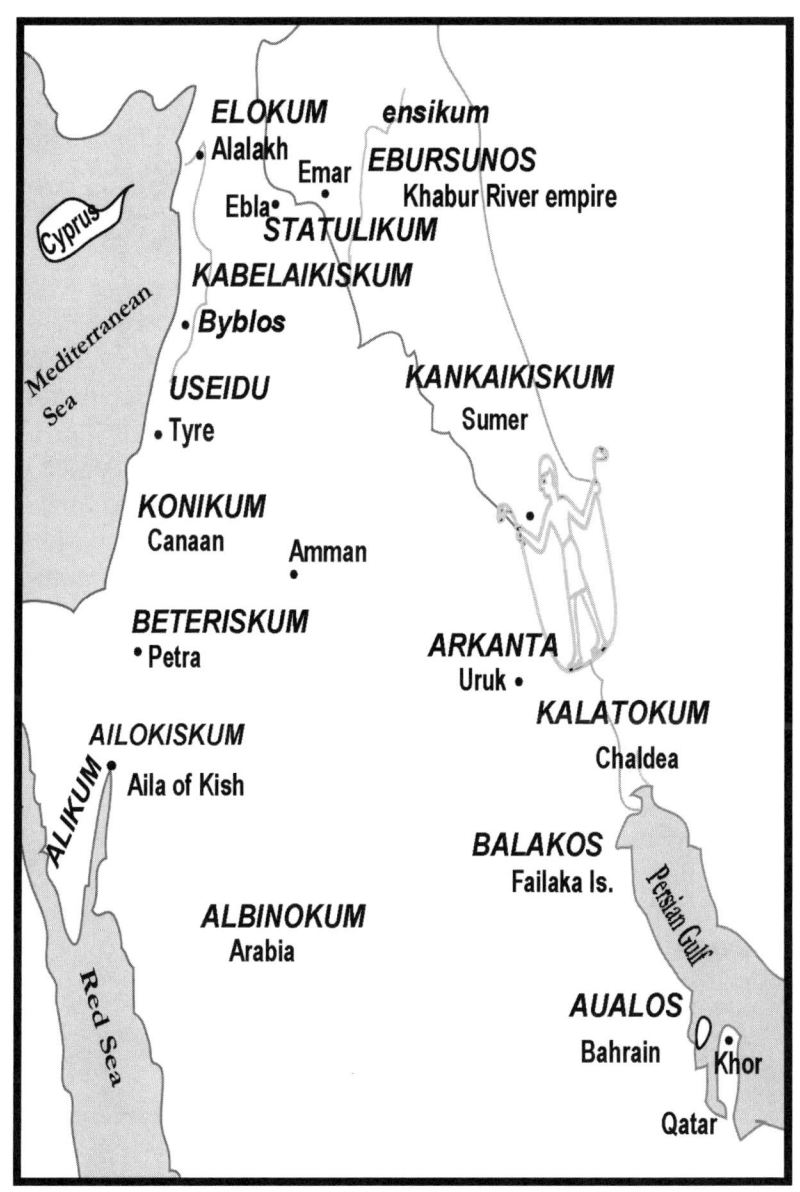

Map 2 Late Uruk Colonies

Historical Background

In the Proclamation, *Tueidunos* is an enemy lord, on *Terkinos'* new eastern border. *Tueidunos* was the Lord-King of the empire of the kingdoms of Uruk on the Khabur River (3.50-53). These kingdoms were north of Iraq, in Syria and Turkey. Archaeological excavations in the region have found remains of Late Uruk colonies.[9] *Tueidunos* was a Phoenician who also ruled Aila of Kish for Uruk.

Trading colonies in Africa are also mentioned. A Lebanese settlement of *Turaios*, people from Tyre from *Litanokum,* the Litani River, is at Kerma near the 3rd Cataract (3.56-58). *Koloutios*, the Phoenician, ruled the kings between the 1st and 2nd Cataracts on the Nile (3.5-11). We read about a border between Meroe and a settlement of Chaldeans in Eritrea (2.22-27).

Finally, in the list of *Melmanios'* titles, we see that he ruled the very busy commercial city of Coptus. Coptus was on the Nile Bend in southern Egypt. He also ruled the *Anu* people between the 1st and 2nd Cataract. He may have been an overlord of *Koloutios* (4.12-21).

The world of the Proclamation is very much a Late Uruk world. The Uruk trading empire is a major power. Many Uruk colonies are spread across the Near East. *Terkinos'* victory ends that predominance in Africa. The Phoenicians, from the Eastern Mediterranean coast, become his subjects. *Koloutios* is taken prisoner. *Tueidunos* continues as a Great King of Uruk in eastern Syria. *Melmanios* is taken prisoner, but *Kaiaitos* rules Uruk for another thirty-six years.

Late Ubaid Pottery in Bahrain and Qatar

Archaeologists often use pottery to date ancient sites. The Late Uruk period was characterized by Late

---

[9] Wyse and Winkleman, *Past Worlds Atlas*, 14.

Ubaid pottery.[10] This pottery developed locally in southern Iraq. It derived from the pottery of the Early Ubaid culture over many centuries.

Roaf, in *The Cultural Atlas of Mesopotamia*, shows a map of these pottery finds. It shows that archaeologists have found clusters of this pottery in Bahrain and Qatar.[11] Our Sumerian lord, *Kaiaitos*, was the Lord of Bahrain and Qatar. Apparently, he ruled over a region with close and stable cultural ties to the Sumerian home territory in Iraq. *Melmanios*, with his western Egyptian and Berber connections, is replaced after a very short six-year reign. *Kaiaitos*, from the eastern, Persian Gulf region, replaced him. *Kaiaitos* then rules for thirty-six years. It may have been more than just luck that his reign was longer and more stable.

The Mesopotamian timeline first crosses the Egyptian timeline in antiquity during the Late Uruk period. Among the Ubaid artifacts from Mesopotamia, there is a carved stone vase called the Warka Vase. (Warka is a modern name for Uruk). This vase resembles a carved stone vase found in Egypt at Hierakonpolis. Two vases in the same style are evidence for trade between the two regions at this time. Mesopotamian cylinder seals and some peculiar Mesopotamian 'nails' found in Egypt also point to interactions at this time.[12]

The picture from the Proclamation text confirms this view. We read of many *Arkanta* (Urukite) trading colonies. In addition to the *Arkanta*, the *Statulos* in Syria, the *Melman* in Egypt, the Arabs in Arabia, and the *Tirtanos*

---

[10] Roaf, *Cultural Atlas of Mesopotamia*, 53.
[11] Ibid.
[12] Bard, "The Egyptian PreDynastic", 265-288; Von der Way, "Indications of Architecture," 217-226; Honoré, "Earliest Cylinder-Seal Glyptic," 31-45; Watrin, "From Intellectual Acquisitions," 56ff. Watrin disagrees with Von der Way on the 'nails', but agrees strongly that there were interactions.

in Djibouti are all powerful kingdoms. They are interacting and competing. Many foreign placenames and ethnonyms in the text show that they were talking to each other.

Egypt

Egyptian King Lists

No other historical documents, other than this Proclamation, go back to the Late Uruk period. However, two documents that look back to this period are helpful. One is the Sumerian King List, mentioned above, for the early kings of Sumer. The other is the work of Manetho who gives us an ancient Egyptian king list.[13] Manetho was an Egyptian priest. He wrote in the 3rd or 4th century BC. His history was lost but passages from it are quoted in various later histories.

Manetho's history begins with the gods, then the *Akhou* in the PreDynastic period and then mortals. To the extent that we can check, the list of kings he gives for the mortals is not too bad. In his lists we find the kings of the Early Dynastic and Old Kingdoms (2950-2125 BC), the Middle Kingdom (2125-1539 BC) and the New Kingdom (1539-1075 BC).[14] Scholars have cross-referenced his list to the Palermo stone and the Turin Papyrus. They also provide lists of Egyptian kings.

The Palermo Stone records important events from the beginning of the First Dynasty. It extends to the end of the Fifth Dynasty of the Old Kingdom period. That would be from 2950 to 2325 BC.[15]

The Turin Papyrus is written in the Hieratic

---

[13] Manetho, *Manetho*, 5.
[14] Baines and Malek, *Cultural Atlas,* 36-37.
[15] Ibid.

14

Egyptian script. A temple document, it was compiled in the Nineteenth Dynasty in the New Kingdom period. Like Manetho, it goes back beyond the mortal kings of the Old Kingdom to the kings of earlier periods. It groups the kings into dynasties. It gives the number of years they reigned.

The Egyptologist Emery writes that the Turin Papyrus, like the Palermo Stone, is "a tragedy for archaeological research because of careless treatment".[16] Both wound up in pieces. Scholars have attempted to put them back together, but that has been the source of much uncertainty and debate. In the end, we come back to Manetho.

So far, evidence from Sumer dates the Proclamation to the Late Uruk period. Evidence from Egypt could provide confirmation. The Late Uruk period in Mesopotamia corresponds to the PreDynastic period in Egypt, before 2950 BC. That is before the first king of the first dynasty of the Early Dynastic Period. It is before written history begins in Egypt.

In Manetho's history, the *Akhou* (𓀀) are the kings that belong to the PreDynastic period. Modern scholars have cross-referenced some of the *Akhou* to the Sons of Horus, the Falcon Clan.[17] The Turin Papyrus mentions the *Shemsu Hor*, the Sons of Horus.

According to Manetho, the first king of the later Early Dynastic Period was a king of southern Egypt. He was notable for conquering northern Egypt. He created a united Egypt called *Mut-uris-kum* (𓅐 𓆓 𓈖). The word means Land (*Kum*) of southern Egypt protected by the Vulture goddess (*Mut*) and northern Egypt protected by the Cobra goddess (*Uris*, Latin uraeus). However, there are suggestions in various old documents that this was not the

---

[16] Emery, *Archaic Egypt*, 42.
[17] Manetho, *Manetho*, 5.

first *Muturiskum*. Long before this king, back in the days of the *Akhou*, the Falcon Clan from northern Egypt had already conquered southern Egypt. It had established an earlier *Muturiskum*.

In the Proclamation text, there are references to this early Falcon Clan and to the earlier *Muturiskum*. In Egyptian, 'Falcon Clan' translates as *At Kherui*. They lived in *Kheru An Kum*. This corresponds to *Karunikum* in the text. *Karunikum* is part of *Muturiskum* in the text.

According to Manetho, the *Akhou* ruled for thousands of years. Their first dynasty ruled for 1255 years. Then another line ruled for 1817 years. Then came thirty more kings of Memphis (in northern Egypt) who reigned for 1790 years. Ten kings of Thinis (in southern Egypt) ruled for 350 years. Finally, a fifth group of kings ruled for 5,813 years.[18]

In the Proclamation, the king of the *Terkinos* at Thinis rules southern Egypt up to the Swamp dwellers of the Harbor kingdom in the Delta in the north. When the king of kings executes enemy kings, he does so from Thinis. Could he have been one of the *Akhou*?

In Kushitic, the word *Akhou* might correspond to Agau, a word that means 'head, chief, and lord'. It was noted earlier that *Akuia* in the Proclamation corresponds to Agau. In the Latin histories that quote Manetho, they translate *Akhou* as 'heroes'. In Greek, they call them 'dead demi-gods'. In English, Waddell's colorful translation calls them "the Spirits of the Dead".[19] If those later *Akhou* Dynasties had Kushitic-speaking rulers, they would have written the histories that were passed on to the Old Kingdom. Manetho's *Akhou* may just be the old 'kings', known to later historians from the PreDynastic histories.

---

[18] Ibid.
[19] Ibid.

The references to *Toutinikum* (Thinis), *Muturiskum*, *Karunikum* and *Akuia* connect the Proclamation to the PreDynastic *Akhou* kings of Egypt.

Naqada and Thinis

When archaeologists look at southern Egypt in PreDynastic times, the Nile Bend is particularly interesting. Three significant sites in that region are Thinis, Naqada and Hierakonpolis. Some scholars interpret the remains as a competition between Thinis and Naqada. They think that Thinis conquered Naqada and absorbed Hierakonpolis.[20] The Thinite kings then went on to rule all of Egypt. Their royal tombs are at Abydos. Naqada is the modern name for their competitors. The center of the Naqada region was actually closer to Tukh. Tukh was known in ancient times as *Nubt*, an Egyptian word for gold.[21]

In the first sentence of *Terkinos'* Proclamation, he tells us that he prevented an invasion by the *Nouida* (0.1). The *Nouida* may have ruled over *Nubt.* In that case, the Proclamation may be describing the historic victory that the archaeologists have been suspecting. Naqada has three major phases with a, b and c subphases. They have supporting radiocarbon dates as follows:

Naqada I   a-b-c-4000 - 3500 BC.
Naqada II   a-b-c-3500 - 3200 BC.
Naqada III   a-b-c-3200 - 3000 BC.[22]

Late Naqada II would be the period closest to our other dates. Our narrator would be an *Akhou / Akuia* king. He would be the ruler of Thinis and Abydos, who defeated Naqada and its allies.

---

[20] Watrin, "From Intellectual Acquisitions," 72; Wikipedia Authors, "Protodynastic Period."

[21] Baines and Malek, *Cultural Atlas*, 110-111.

[22] Petrie Museum, "Chronology of the Naqada Period."

The Proclamation supports this view by mentioning 'the *Akuia* city of Abydos' (1.41-42). The king of kings hangs six of his enemies at Thinis (1.6-19). *Melmanios*, our narrator's opponent, was the ruler of the Egyptian city of Coptus on the Nile Bend (4.12-14). The city is quite close to Naqada and Tukh. He also had the Kharga Oasis, just to the west (1.26-27).

Archaeological evidence shows that cultural influence from Thinis and Abydos spreads north at this time (Late Naqada II).[23] In the text, a great block of territory is transferred to *Terkinos*. He says, 'I will extend the Harbor kingdom of the Swamp dwellers to the king of the *Terkinos* at Thinis' (2.51-53). That incorporates what was left of *Muturiskum* in the Delta into Thinis with the *Terkinos* in charge.

A more subtle connection may be the frequent depiction of boats. They are an important artistic motif during the Naqada period.[24] Central to the narrator is the kingdom of *Uiriaskum*, the (Nile) River Kingdom. Boats might be a symbol connected, not just to the Nile, but also to *Uiriaskum*, the River Kingdom that controls it.[25]

The River Kingdom

In the Proclamation, the narrator describes the River Kingdom. It stretches from the Mediterranean Sea far south to the entrance to the Red Sea. His empire also includes the Eastern Mediterranean coast nations. He has Israel, Lebanon and the provinces of Syria on the coast.

A representation of this River Kingdom appears on a PreDynastic Egyptian palette called the Libyan Palette. Eight kingdoms are depicted. We can compare the pictures

---

[23] Bard, "Emergence of the Egyptian State," 61-62.
[24] Midant-Reynes, "The Naqada Period," 54-55, 60.
[25] from *Uiriasku* 'the river'.

of creatures in the kingdoms on the palette with Egyptian hieroglyphics. The hieroglyphics give the pronunciations associated with the pictures. We can then match those pronunciations with the names of nations in the Proclamation. When we do, we find names of kingdoms for seven of them and an ethnonym for the eighth. The Libyan Palette shows us a picture of *Terkinos'* empire before he conquered it.

Libyan Palette - Kingdom Side

1) The Frog. The frog may represent the *Tirtouios* (Marsh people) of the Great Marsh region, the Sudd of southern Sudan. On the palette, they have their own kingdom. In the text, the *Tirtouios* are in *Turumokum*.

2) The Friends. Two partly visible figures are fighting or shaking hands. This might be *Turumokum* (Egypt

and Sudan, west of the Nile). The two figures would represent the Blue Nile and the White Nile. They merge at Khartoum. In the text, *Terkinos* takes *Turumokum* from Berber *Loukanikum* and hangs its commander.

3) The Phoenix or *bennu* bird (𓅣). In the Proclamation text, this is *Biniskum*, 'Phoenicia'. Phoenicia is a name for the eastern Mediterranean coast. It appears in the names of two officials. It is part of the name of a nation, the *Bini Rusku*.

4) The Baboon. *Bentikum* (Baboon Land, 𓃻 𓈙) was along the Red Sea coast in Eritrea. In the text, *Bentikum* is along the Red Sea where the modern Afar live, from the Buri Peninsula to Djibouti.

5) The Falcons. The symbols of the Falcon Clan (𓅂 𓅂) are for *Karunikum* in *Muturiskum* (northeastern Egypt).

6) The Scorpion. The Scorpion King of *Tirtanikum* is the ruler of southern Ethiopia. He rules the Strait at the entrance to the Red Sea. The name is a pun on Egyptian: *tchart*, 'scorpion', the Chercher mountains, and *tchertiu*, 'ancestor'. Puntland, thought to be an Ancestor Land, is in this region.

7) The Lion King. This Lion King is the king of Abyssinia (Lion Land). The word Abyssinia may come from Chamir: *abesa*, 'lion'.[26] In the Proclamation, we find the king of Ethiopia has the title *urkala*, 'lion' of *Austunikum* (Ethiopia) (4.31). *Urgula* is the word for 'Leo' in the Babylonian zodiac.[27]

---

[26] Reinisch, *Die ChamirSprache*, vol. CV, 583.
[27] Horowitz, *Mesopotamian Cosmic Geography*, 171.

Libyan Palette - Cattle Land Side

On the reverse side of the palette, we find images of *Loukanikum* (Cattle Land). The cattle, donkeys, sheep and olive trees were associated with Libya. The 'leg' hieroglyphic symbol meant Libya. Gardiner says, "It takes no great acumen to diagnose the cattle as booty, and the trees as yielding the much-prized Tjehnu (Libyan) oil."[28]

In this case, Gardiner and the scholars of his time may have been too quick. The top of the palette is broken off. On the piece that we have, there is no evidence on it at all that Libya was attacked.

The cattle are not booty but identifying symbols of *Loukanikum* (Cattle Land). The word comes from the Kushitic word *lukue* 'cattle'. It is a pun on the name of the *Laguatan* Berbers. The *Laguatan* lived in Phoenicia, in the oases in western Egypt, and around Barca in Libya.

The cattle with the olive trees tell us that the Berbers were at least members of this coalition / empire. However, one side is devoted entirely to them. At the time

---

[28] Gardiner, *Egypt of the Pharoahs*, 394.

this plaque was made, the Berbers may have been the rulers.

It seems far-fetched to think of the Libyans controlling Ethiopia. However, in the Proclamation, our Ethiopian narrator is taking a list of territories from the Berbers of *Loukanikum*. He would not be taking them if the Berbers had never had those territories in the first place.

His list begins at Klusma near Suez and goes down, far south, to the entrance to the Red Sea (2.44-49). Halfway to the Strait, the Barka River flows into the Red Sea below Suakin, in modern eastern Sudan. The Barka River is called the Loukanian River (2.3) in the text. Before *Terkinos'* victory, *Loukanikum* may have controlled most, if not all, of the kingdoms on this palette.

As you see, territories were moving back and forth between empires over time. A short history will help us keep things straight.

Taking the Libyan Palette, together with the two texts translated in this book, we can write a very short history of the PreDynastic Period. The two texts are referred to as the Proclamation text and the I-B text.

In the time of the Libyan Palette, Cattle Land has eight kingdoms: the seven kingdoms of the River Kingdom plus the kingdom of Phoenicia.

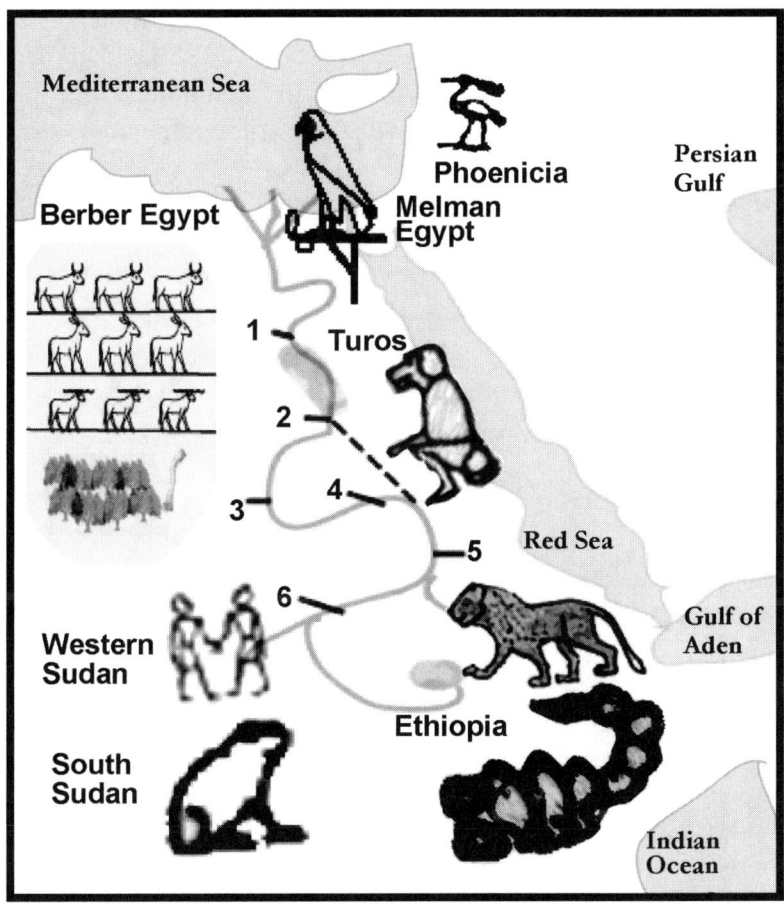

Map 3 Cattle Land Kingdoms

Historical Background

In the time of the Botorrita I-B text, the *Melman* Berbers (the Falcon Clan) have become independent of Cattle Land. The *Turos* of Baboon Land control the lands south of Egypt. *Turo* territory extends as far west as the Gebel Uweinat in western Libya. The *Melmunos* (Egyptian Berbers) take territories from the Libyan *Lubos* in the Eastern Mediterranean, and destroy cities on the island of Crete. They destroy the city of Tyre in Phoenicia. They establish a kingdom in Northwestern Arabia, defeating a local Scorpion Clan of *Tirtanos*. The Libyans destroy Barca and burn down cities in northern Egypt.

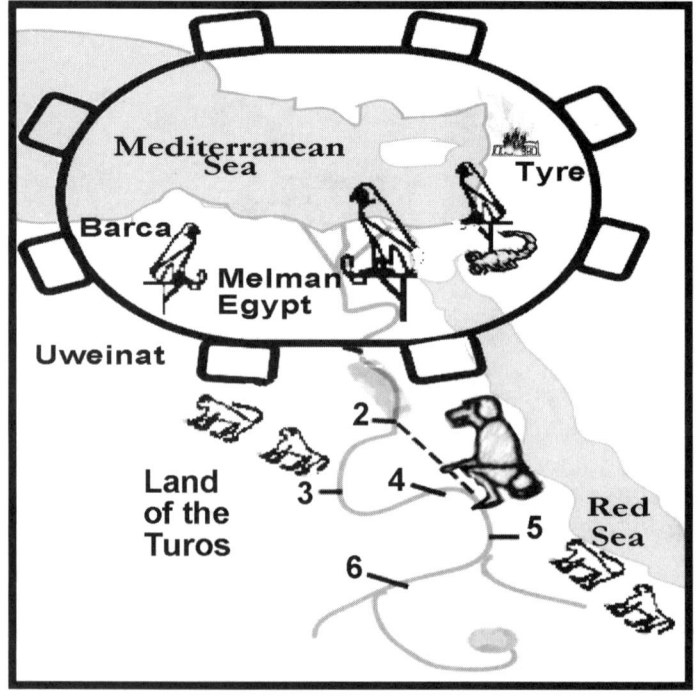

Map 4 *Melman* Egypt in I-B Period

During the time of the Uruk Expansion (3500BC to 3200BC), the Kingdom of Uruk ruled the East. Uruk ruled Iraq (Sumer, Uruk and Chaldea), eastern Syria and northern Arabia. These Chaldeans and *Arkanta* conquered the Egyptian *Melman* Berbers of the preceding period. They conquered the Eastern Mediterranean (Aila, Byblos, Ebla). They ruled the Falcon Clan in *Karunikum* (the northeast corner) in Egypt. The Berbers of Cattle Land had Western Egypt at this time. Cattle Land took control of much of Sudan. The Chaldeans and the Bedouin Antiu also controlled parts of eastern Sudan and Eritrea.

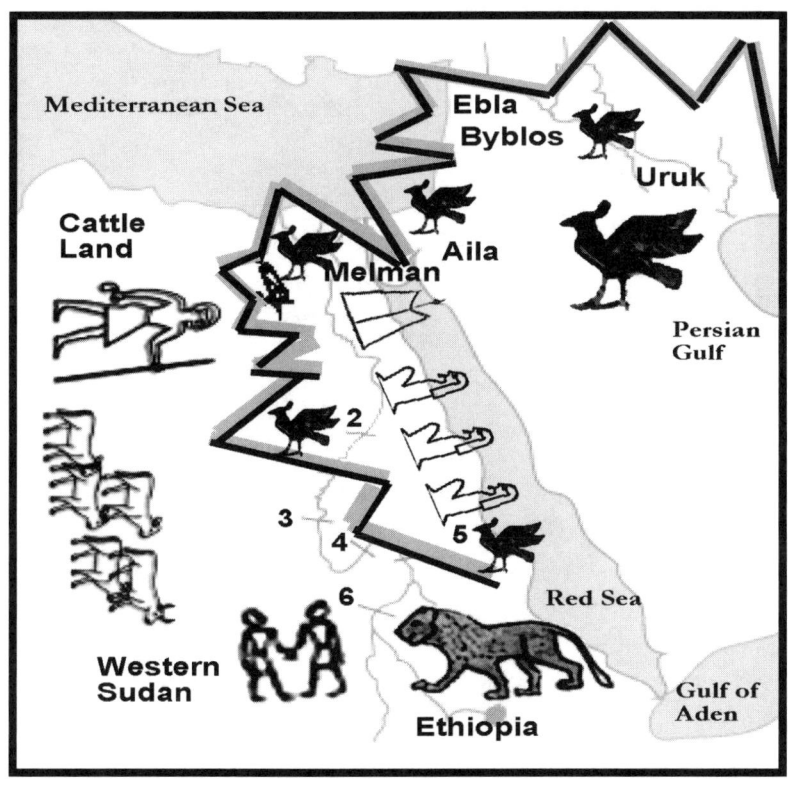

Map 5 Uruk Expansion Map

Historical Background

   Some time after the Libyan Palette, but before the Proclamation, the kings of the southern Kingdoms establish the Southern River Kingdom. They take control of what used to be southern Cattle Land, south of the 5th Cataract (2.40-42). Western Sudan, Southern Sudan, Somalia and Ethiopia become the Southern River Kingdom. The Proclamation narrator, *Terkinos* from Lasta in Ethiopia, is the ruler of the Southern River Kingdom.

Map 6 The Southern River Kingdom

Terkinos' Proclamation was written in 3236 BC, when the Africans from the Red Sea turned back the Uruk Expansion. Cattle Land was defeated. Its possessions were taken over and re-distributed by the narrator. His Red Sea *Turos* took control of all of the River Kingdom. They ruled the Eastern Mediterranean. Uruk and Sumer were pushed back, but they preserved their possessions in Arabia, eastern Syria and Iraq.

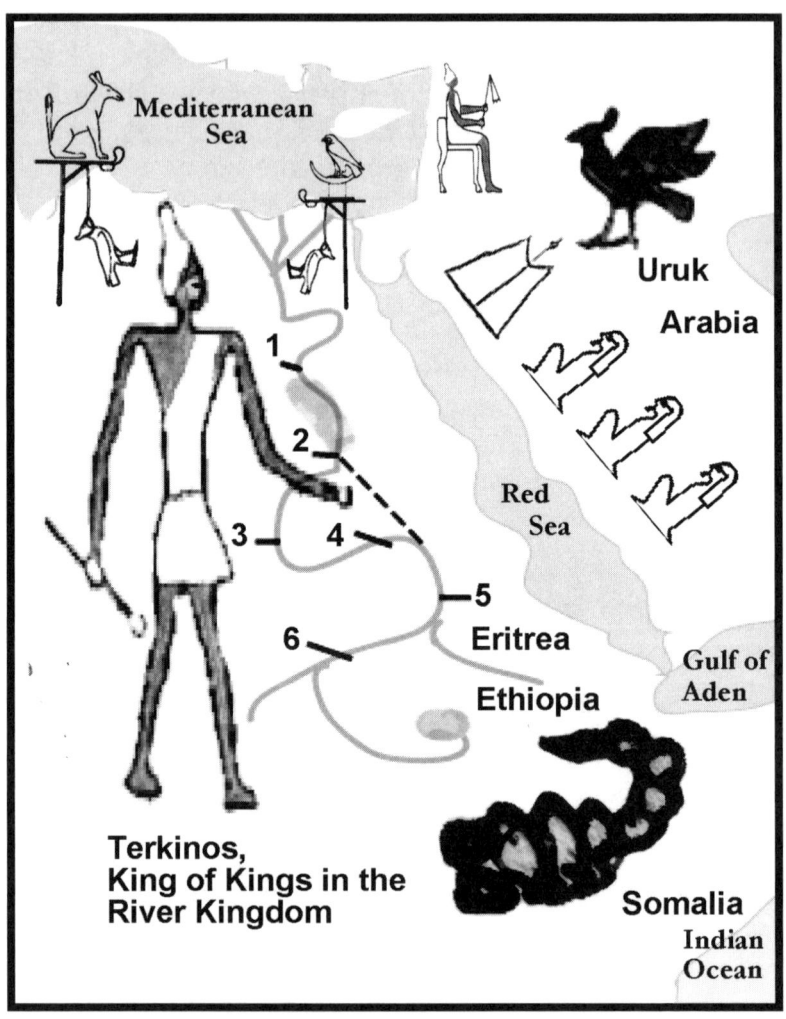

Map 7 The River Kingdom of *Terkinos*

One Enemy or Three and a Half

The Mesopotamian *Arkanta* (Urukites) are not a part of the Libyan Palette Coalition. In fact, we would expect them to be enemies of the Cattle Land peoples.

However, recall that there was a stone vase, possibly Ubaid in style, found at Hierakonpolis. It may tell us a little more about who the enemy *Nouida* were. It shines a light on who their allies may have been. This large vase has symbols of four nations on its sides.

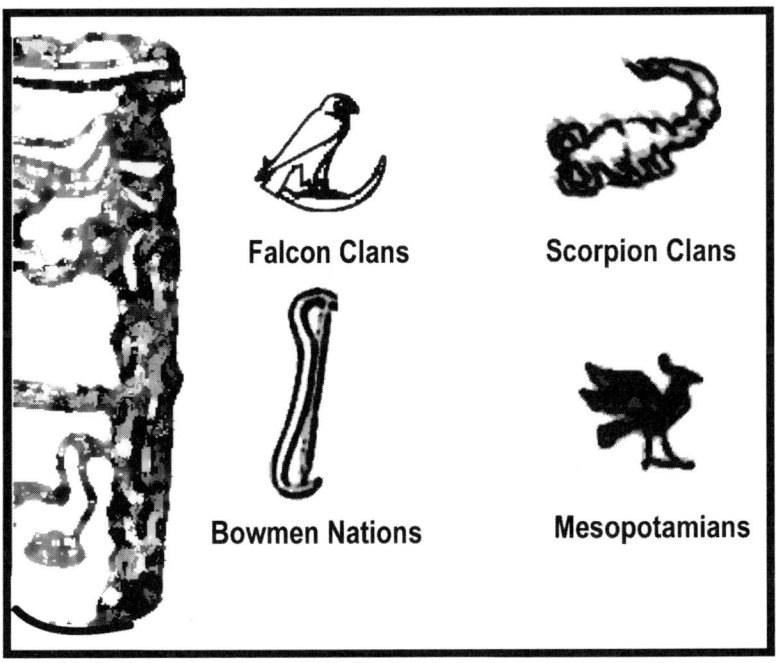

Falcon Clans   Scorpion Clans

Bowmen Nations   Mesopotamians

The Ubaid Style Vase from Hierakonpolis

1) Northern Egyptians, the Falcon Clan. (The Falcon on a crescent moon) corresponding to *Karunikum* (Heroonopolis) in *Muturiskum* (northeastern Egypt).

2) *Tirtanos*, Scorpion Clans. These Scorpion Clans are the ones in northwestern Arabia. They were conquered by the Egyptian Falcon Clan in I-B times. When Uruk conquered Egypt, these Scorpion Clans were conquered too.

3) Laguatan Berbers from *Loukanikum* (Cattle Land), the Bow. The *Nouida* of Naqada may also be Berbers. They may be the Nomida, the Numidians. There are also references to *unstibas*, 'rebel bowmen' and *steniontes,* 'the king of the bowmen'. The Berbers had a distinctive hairstyle with a feather sticking up. Hieroglyphs for bowmen and soldiers have this feather as well. They link the Bowmen to the Berbers (⚐).

4) Below the first three is a line. Below that is the fourth nation, a row of *Erkhēye* (lapwing birds). They are a pun on the name of the *Arkanta* of Uruk.[29]

Three of these four nations, Uruk, Falcon Clan Egypt, and the Berbers from the rest of Egypt are enemies of *Terkinos*. He executes their leaders and re-assigns their territories. The people he calls 'our Scorpion Clans' are *Terkinos'* allies in southern Ethiopia, not these enemies in Arabia. This vase may commemorate the signing of a new, possibly short-lived, alliance between Uruk and Naqada. The Laguatan Berbers of Barca in northwestern Libya, the *Melman* Berber Falcon Clans of northern Egypt and the Scorpion Clans in northwestern Arabia may have been allies of the Numidian Berbers of Naqada in southern Egypt. An alliance between Uruk and the Berbers would explain why *Terkinos* speaks of only one enemy, the *Nouida*.

---

[29] Ibid., 403.

The Scorpion King Macehead

The Scorpion King Macehead was found with the vase at Hierakonpolis. The hanging lapwings tell us that this Scorpion King is no friend of the *Arkanta*. Each member of his alliance has a lapwing hanging from its royal standard.

Royal Standards of Scorpion King Allies

The 'falcon-on-the-crescent-moon' (🦅) is a symbol for the northerners of *Karunikum*. The symbol *KUM* (◠) is the mountain-range land of Lasta in Lion Land / Abyssinia.

Below the *KUM* sign are two symbols for Seth, a red wolf. A red wolf, now on the Endangered Species list, is native to Eritrea and Ethiopia. Seth later became a religious figure in Egypt as Osiris' evil brother. The local god of Nubt (*Nouida*) of Naqada was Seth.[30] Seth may also have been associated with the red Berbers of Cattle Land. The Lowata / Laguatan controlled Barca (*Berkantikum* in the I-B text), the red city. It is in the Cyrenaica region of western Libya. A fine red dust lays on top of the soil. It gave a red tinge to clothing.[31]

Next to the *KUM* sign is a symbol for Anubis. This jackal god was associated with many places. To the right of that, is a fetish symbol (⊂æ⊃) associated with the god Min. Ancient Min cult centers were at Akhmim and Coptus, in Naqada territory.

The Falcon of the northeastern Egyptians, Min and the two Berber Seths on the Macehead should all have been allies of Naqada. The Macehead may tell us that the Berbers failed to unite in support of an alliance with their Chaldean enemies. That might put the time of the Macehead close to the defeat of the *Nouida* that *Terkinos'* Proclamation documents.

---

[30] Baines and Malek, *Cultural Atlas*, 111.
[31] al Idrîsî, *Description de l'Afrique*, 156.

32

The Captive behind the Scorpion King

Recall that *Melmanios* is that Arab prisoner held captive in *Tirtanikum* (Scorpion Land). The Macehead shows us just one, tiny, un-named, captive. Like *Melmanios*, he is a king of the *Arkanta*, watching his daughters pass by in chains.

The Lion Kingdom

The Proclamation text has its own point of view, but it fits in this world. Our narrator is a Lion King, not a Scorpion king. He is a southerner from Lasta, which is *KUM*, and Lion Land. He is not a friend of the *Arkanta*. He executes some of them and reassigns their territories. He is also not a friend of the Northern Falcon Clan. He executes the king of all of *Muturiskum,* (United Egypt) who rules the fortress of *Karunikum*. He decides the fate of 'that Arab leader held captive in *Tirtanikum* (Scorpion Land)'. He is also the enemy of *Loukanikum*, Berber Cattle Land. He executes Cattle Land rulers. He adds their territories to his empire.

In 3200 BC, the Uruk period ends when Uruk is destroyed. There would be little reason to struggle with the *Arkanta* after that date. Their neighbors would have no reason to form an alliance with them after 3200 BC. The Vase with the *Arkanta* Alliance and the Scorpion King Macehead with its hanging lapwings must date to sometime before 3200 BC, when the *Arkanta* were still interesting.

The narrator of the Proclamation is a contemporary of the last two kings of Uruk. That says he too must have lived before the destruction of Uruk.

The Great Land

One last PreDynastic Egyptian artifact shows connections with an *Akhou* Dynasty at Thinis. This green tile shows an image of an individual with the name in  hieroglyphs of *Te-r-a-neter* (Tera the god) or *Te-r-a-akhu* (tera+axe). The fourth glyph of the name is ambiguous. It could be either a godly banner or an axe for the sound 'akhu'.

Terakhu Profile

The archaeologist, Flinders Petrie, found the tile. He claimed that this king had a jaw with a steep angle, a feature that was hereditary. Petrie suggested that the Scorpion king on the Macehead had a similar steep-angled jaw. He found similar steep-angled jaws on bodies at Tarkhan, Egypt, a PreDynastic city that he excavated.

Petrie believed that all of the steep-jawed people were a PreDynastic people called the *Aunu*.[32] He guessed that the *Aunu* might be native to Egypt, or had perhaps originated from Lake Turkana. An interesting reference to the *Aunu* occurs in the Proclamation. Speaking of himself, the narrator says, 'this *Aunu* from the Land of Bes is now the Lord King of the kings of Alalakh in Northern Syria' (3.27-28). I understand that to mean 'this southerner has become a great king over the northerners'.[33]

The god Bes

---

[32] Petrie, *Making of Egypt*, 68-70; Manetho, *Manetho*, 5.
[33] The Egyptians regarded Bes as a southern god.

The image of Ter-akhu (perhaps, Teraku) on the tile might be an image of some great Terqe. He could be a god or a hero, one of the *Terkinos*. It could even be an image of the *Terkinos* narrating our text. The site of Tarkhan where Petrie found skeletons with that jaw appears in the proclamation as *Tarkunbiur* (Tarkun City). It was one of the places along the Red Sea ruled by the *Terkinos*.

The *Terkinos* could have originally founded that settlement as a trading colony. Petrie found the tombs of important individuals there. However, it was not a site with a lot of depth. Petrie guessed that it was abandoned when nearby Memphis rose to power at the beginning of the Old Kingdom.

Petrie found the green tile of *Tera-Neter / Ter-akhu* at Abydos, which is a short distance from Thinis. For millennia after this, Egyptians called this area *Ta-Ur*, the Great Land. That may originally have been just a flattering spelling for *Tur*, the Egyptian center of the *Turos* of *Turikum* and *Turanikum*. In the Proclamation, the region is part of *Abokum Turo*. *Abokum Turo* was one of five provinces in the River Kingdom. It included the Nile Valley east to the Red Sea. It extended from the Nile Bend to the Buri Peninsula in Eritrea. Our narrator, *Terkinos of Turanikum,* the king of kings, ruled from the Mediterranean Sea to Djibouti. Under his rule, it was indeed a Great Land.

So far, we have only talked about the Proclamation. In the next section, an illustrated, relatively free translation of the text will let you read it for yourself.

THE PROCLAMATION ILLUSTRATED

The Proclamation Illustrated

1. The Narrator and His Opponent

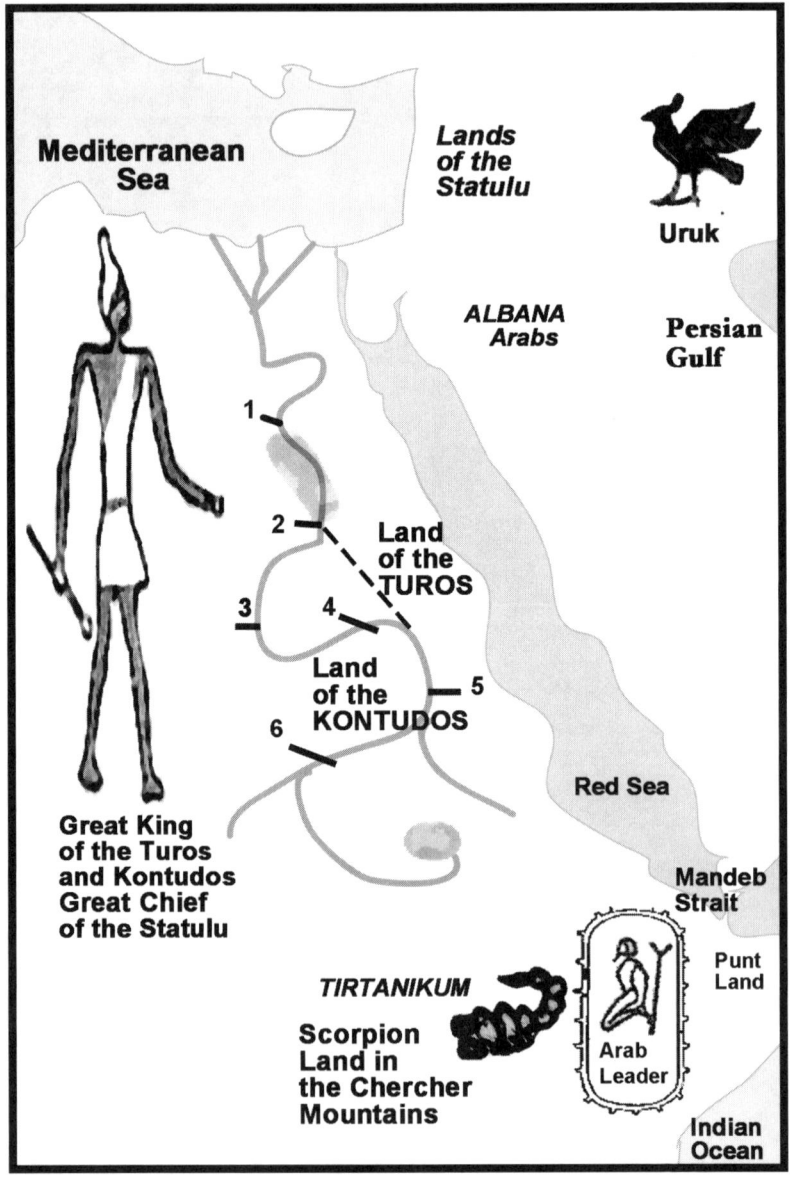

Mediterranean Sea

Lands of the Statulu

Uruk

ALBANA Arabs

Persian Gulf

1

2

Land of the TUROS

3   4

Land of the KONTUDOS

5

6

Red Sea

Great King of the Turos and Kontudos Great Chief of the Statulu

Mandeb Strait

TIRTANIKUM

Scorpion Land in the Chercher Mountains

Arab Leader

Punt Land

Indian Ocean

Translation Lines 0.1-1.5

'A southerner from Lasta, I have prevented the *Nouida* from conquering beyond the limits of their territory. I am the Great King of the *Turos* and the *Kontudos*, the Great Chief of the *Statulu*. I have given my verdict to that Arab leader held captive in *Tirtanikum* (Scorpion Land)'.

Note

The *Nouida* may be the Nomida, the Numidians. At this time they were in southeastern Egypt and Jordan. Later Numidians in North Africa fought with the Carthaginians against the Romans.[34]

All three of these titles say *Terkinos* is the Lord of territories he has recently conquered. His homeland, Lasta, is in the Central Ethiopian Highlands. He conquered the *Turos*, parallel to the 5th Cataract on the Red Sea coast. The *Kontudos* were in the Nile Valley around Napata at the 4th Cataract. His allies conquered the *Statulu* from the Chaldeans of Uruk.

Tirtanikum (Scorpion Land) was home to the *Tirtanos* (Scorpion Clans). The name may be a three-way pun between *Chart* (*Tchart*), a mythological scorpion, the Chercher Mountains and the Egyptian word *tchertiu* that meant 'ancestor'. The kingdom would have included Harar province in Ethiopia, the Chercher Mountains, and Djibouti. It would have included modern Punt Land on the Gulf of Aden. Some Egyptian stories link Punt Land to an ancient Ancestor Land. There were also *Tirtanos* in Yemen. They may have controlled the Mandeb Strait at the entrance to the Red Sea.

---

[34] Ibn Khaldoun, *Histoire des Berbères*, 511.

2. The Hangings at Thinis

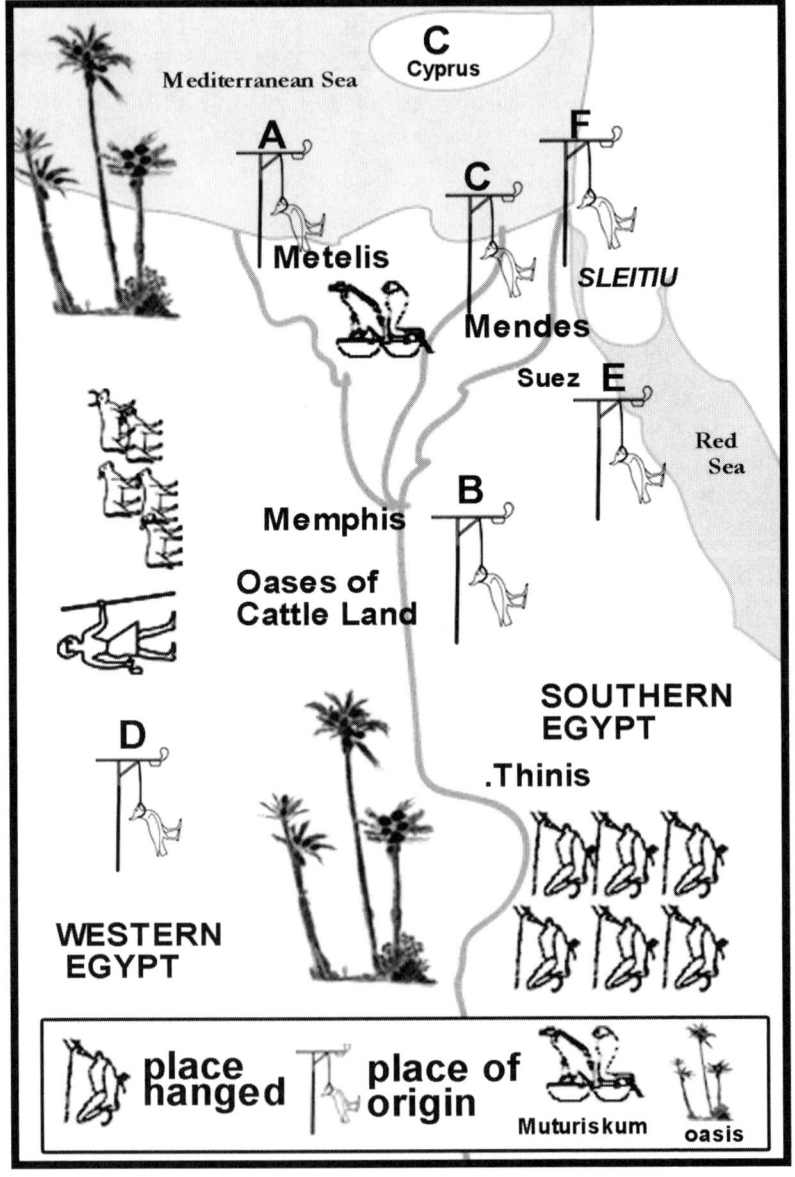

Translation Lines 1.6-1.19

'The Great King, our king of kings, has hanged these kings in Thinis.

A The king of the army of *Matulokum* (Metelis, Egypt) was from the River Kingdom.

B The king of Memphis.

C The chief of *Batokum,* (Mendes, Egypt), ruled the island of Cyprus.

D The king of the Shebka Empire was the commander of *Loukanikum,* Cattle Land.

E The king of the River Kingdom army.

F The king of all of *Muturiskum* (Vulture Cobra Land) had *Karunikum* (northeastern Egypt), of the Fort Sile people. The empire of this Great King extended to *Batokum* (Mendes)'.

Note

Three of the executed kings would have a claim on Egypt. The current ruler of most of Egypt was **D**, a king based in the oases of Western Egypt. The ruler of what was called Egypt, Vulture Cobra Land, at this time, was **F** in northeastern Egypt. Memphis had been an ancient capital of Egypt. Its king, **B**, might also have had a claim.

The word *Loukanikum* comes from the word *lukue* for 'cattle'. It is a pun on Laguatan, the name of a confederation of Berbers in Phoenicia, Egypt and Libya.

'Shebka' is a geological feature in North Africa. It is a flat plain, which becomes a marsh or a shallow lake after a rain. Oases are often dependant on shebka. Berber peoples often have names that mean 'people of the shebka'.

3. A New Western Border for the River Kingdom

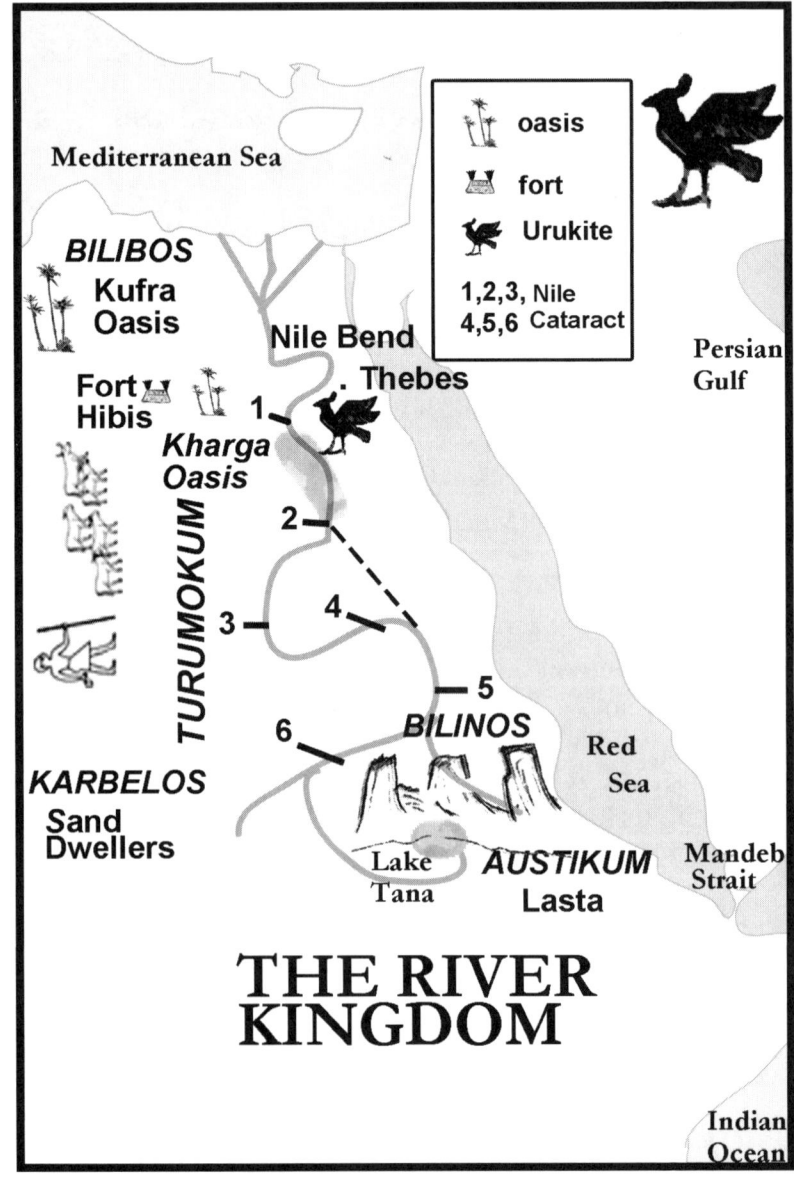

Translation Lines 1.21-1.28

'*Uiriaskum,* the River Kingdom, is ruled by the *Bilinos* of Lasta. A new province, *Turumokum*, that will be part of their River Kingdom ends at Fort Tjamet. It begins in the land of the *Bilibos*. This new region includes Fort Hibis in *Melmanios*' kingdom. It begins from the *Karbelos* (Sand dwellers) of *Turumokum* (on the edge of the Sahara Desert in western Sudan)'.

Note

Uiriaskum is the River Kingdom, formed from *uirias-ku*, a word that means 'the river'. It includes all of the territory along the Nile from the Mediterranean Sea to Lake Tana where the Blue Nile begins. It extends beyond that to Djibouti near the Mandeb Strait. East to west, it stretches from Yemen to the western border near the Kufra Oasis in Libya.

The southerners defeated *Loukanikum*, the Berber empire of Cattle Land. *Turumokum* (Egypt and Sudan, west of the Nile) was roughly the western half of the old River Kingdom. Here, the narrator and his allies are annexing *Turumokum*. They are making its western borders the new western borders of their River Kingdom of *Uiriaskum*. Their new western borders are near the western borders of modern Sudan, on its borders with Libya and Chad.

A piece of *Melmanios*' kingdom in the west is included here in *Turumokum*. That is Fort Hibis in the Kharga Oasis, just west of the Nile Bend.

4. Borders of the *Akuia* kingdom

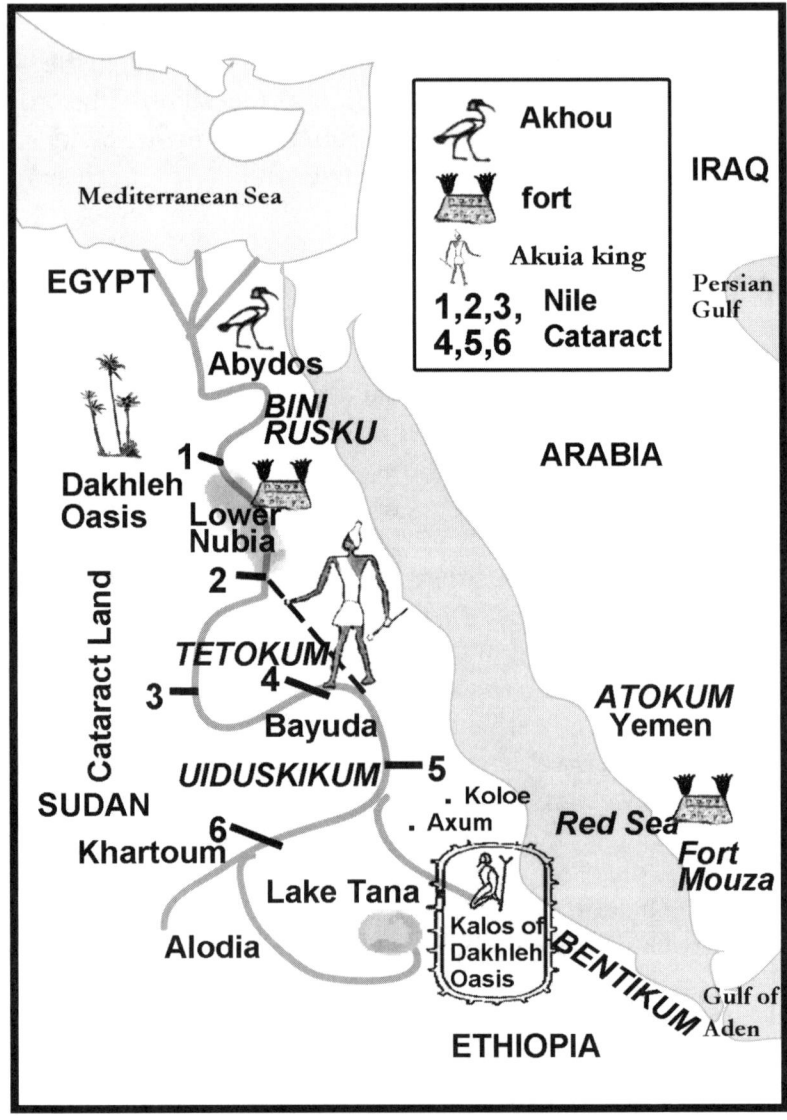

Translation Lines 1.29-1.42

'Below the prince of this district, the kings of the *Akuia* kingdom rule *Tetokum* (River Land). In *Uiduskikum* (Bayuda at the 5th Cataract), they rule as far as Fort Mouza in the eastern district of the king of Sana'a in Yemen. The Great Lord over these princes is the ruler of the Southern River Kingdom. [He now rules] from Lower Nubia where the *Bini Rusku* [have] the noble citadel of the island kingdom. He rules as far north as the *Akuia* city of Abydos in Egypt. To the south, Alodia is as far as he rules in Cataract Land.
In Cataract Land, *Kalos*, from the Dakhleh Oasis, was one of the kings of Cattle Land. This Great Chief of Cattle Land is now held at the fortress of Axum'.

Note

Here again, the Berbers of Cattle Land (under *Kalos*) are losing territory. The *Akuia* (Agau) people of the narrator now have all the territory along the Nile from the 1st to the 6th Cataract. Old and new together, their territories stretch all the way down to Alodia, which is just below Khartoum. *Tetokum* and *Uiriaskum* both mean 'River Kingdom'. They may represent, respectively, a Berber and a Kushitic name for the Nile Valley.

The territory of the *Bini Rusku* may have been just east of Aswan. At the 1st Cataract, there are several islands with ancient ruins.

The *Akuia* already had the territory south of the 5th Cataract, the Southern River Kingdom. The new territory is north of there. They also acquire new territory, probably from Naqada, in southern Egypt, between Lower Nubia and Abydos.

5. *Tiokenes* Rules West of the Nile

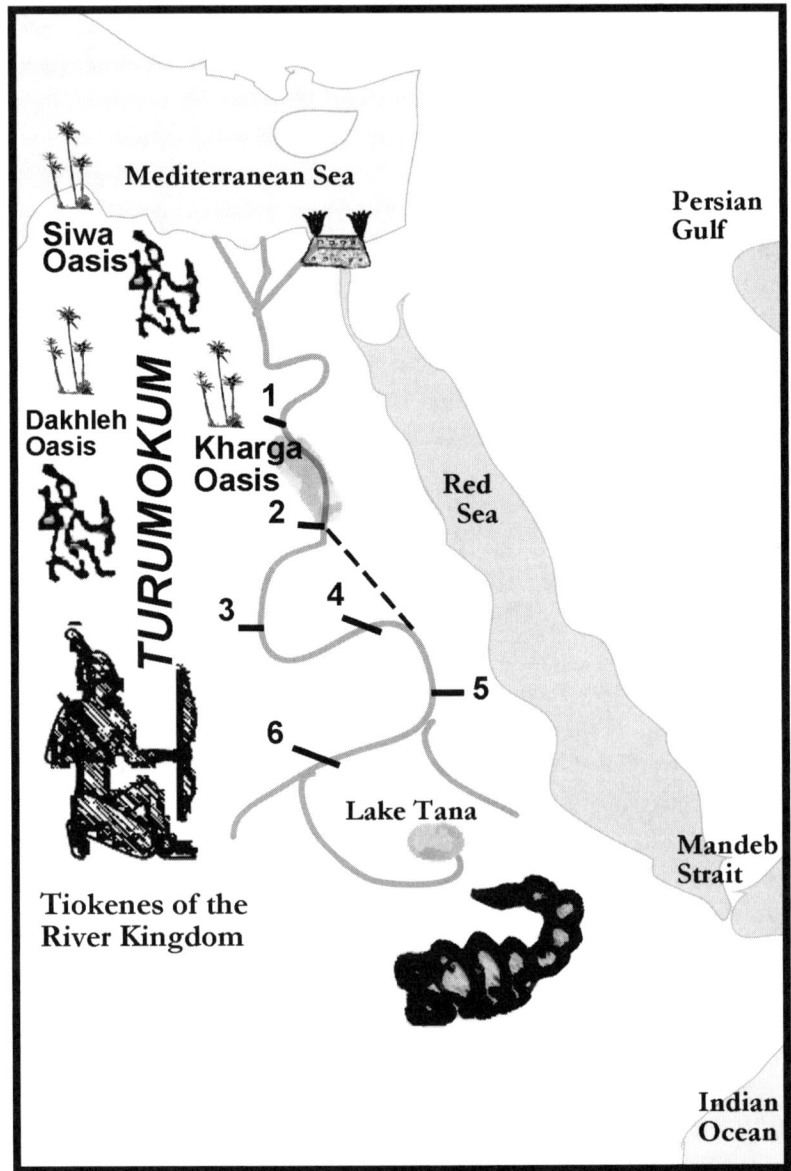

Translation Lines 1.48-1.52

'From the Northern Lands of the Fort Sile people to the
River Kingdom with its rebel archers, *Tiokenes* of the River
Kingdom rules. He is the Great Lord of *Turumokum*, the
lands west of the Nile. He rules as far as the First Lord of
the Great Kings of our *Tirtanos* (Scorpion Clans)'.

Note

The Numidian Berbers at Naqada made that Vase
Alliance with their Chaldean enemies. Some of the other
Berbers may have disagreed. *Tiokenes* appears to have been
a king or official of the old Berber River Kingdom who
was allied with the southerners. If so, as we can see, he was
rewarded handsomely.

6. *Kaiaitos* and Elephant Land

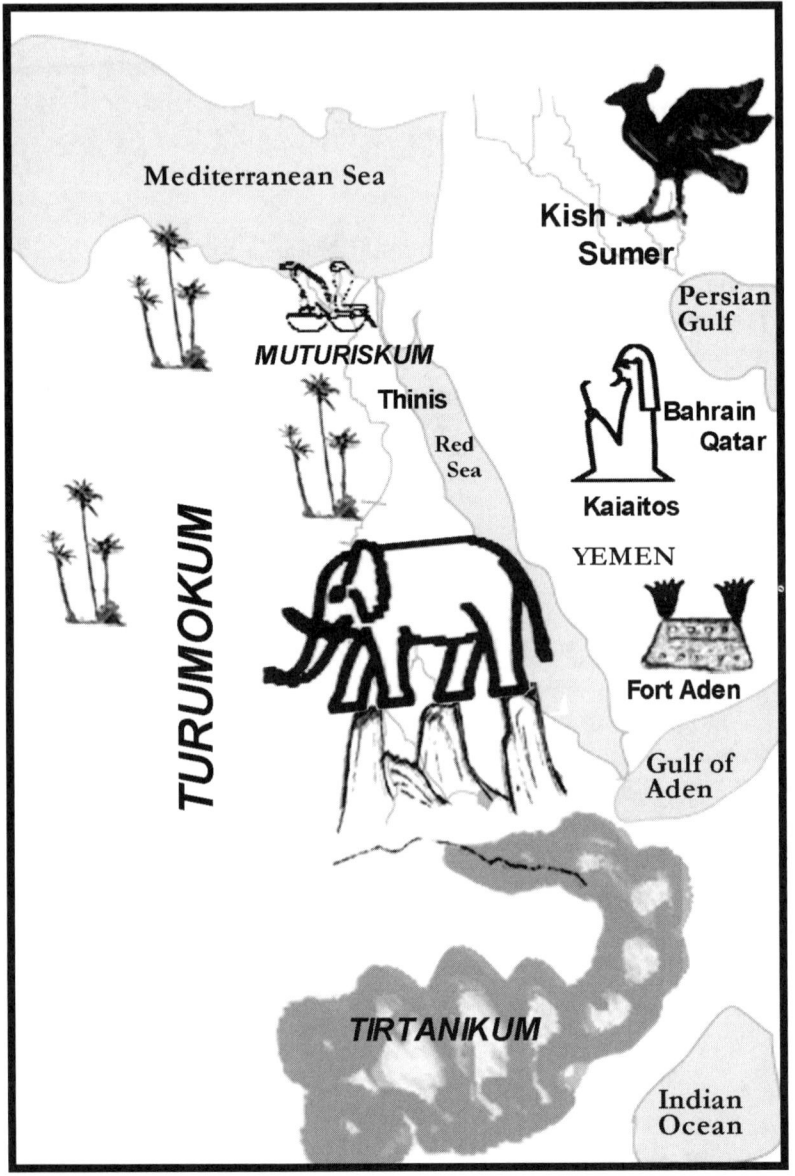

Translation Lines 1.53-2.3

'The River Kingdom begins at Fort Aden. That fortress was conquered by the Lord of Bahrain and Qatar, *Kaiaitos*, of the Sumerian nation of Kish. I have excluded Muturiskum (northeastern Egypt) from Elephant Land. However, Elephant Land stretches west to the Nile river border with *Turumokum.*
The Great Chief of *Turo* Elephant Land rules the borderland with the Cattle Land Berbers as far as the southern Scorpion Clans'.

Note

Notice that the Sumerians are conquering far to the south of their base in Iraq. Fort Aden would have been a strategic place for trade.

On the Libyan Palette, Elephant Land was not a separate kingdom. It replaces northern Baboon Land.

Petrie found a PreDynastic image in relief of an elephant on hills at Coptus.[35]

At this point, we have the three main regions in *Terkinos'* northern River Kingdom: *Muturiskum, Abokum, and Turumokum. Muturiskum* is northeastern Egypt. *Abokum* is Elephant Land, the Nile Valley itself, and the territories east of the Nile. *Turumokum* is west of the Nile.

The borderland is the region on the former northern border of the Southern River Kingdom, the area north of the 5th Cataract.

---

[35] Petrie, *The Making of Egypt*, 58 #91.

7. The Great Chief of *Turanikum* (Eritrea)

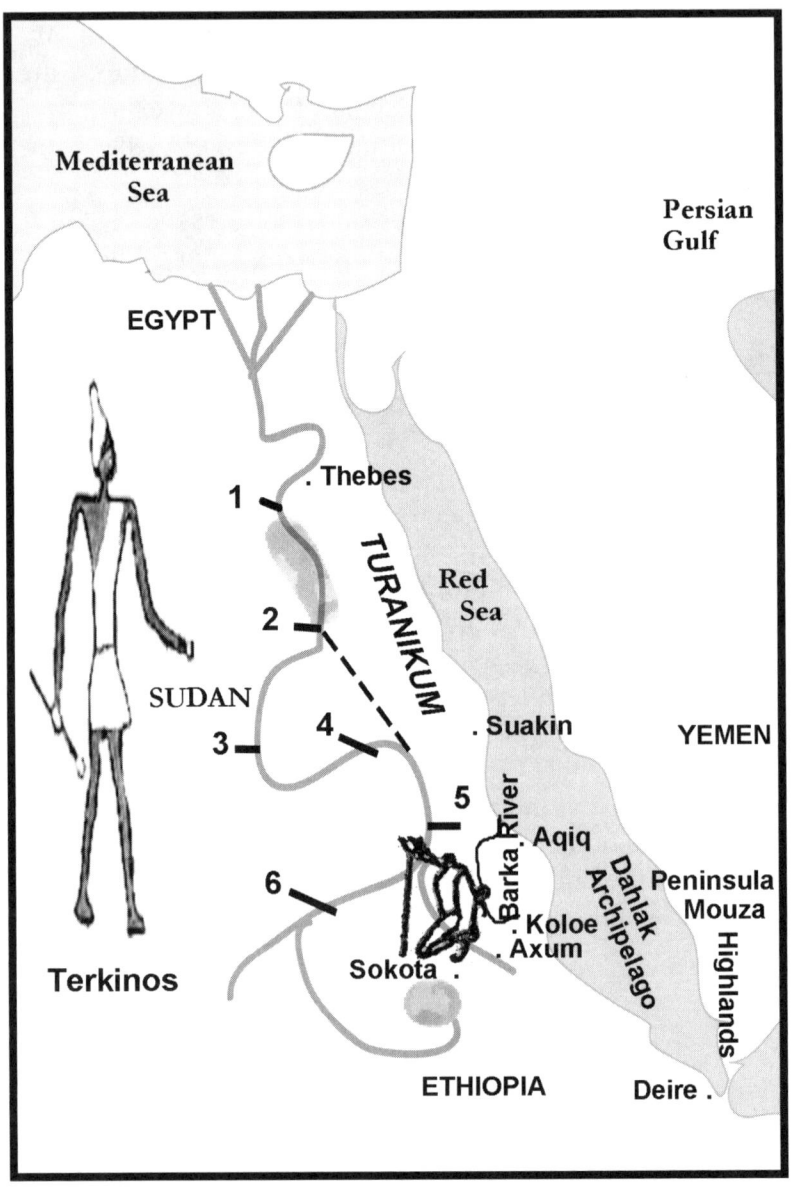

Translation Lines 2.3-2.14

'On the *Loukaniko* River, the Great Chief of *Turanikum* is the king of the Southern River Kingdom. His territory extends to the princes of Mouza in the Al Jazirah, 'peninsula', off the Highlands in Yemen. It stretches from the gates of Thebes in Elephant Land, down to Fort Koloe of Kam where the chief was hanged.
The islands of the Dahlak Archipelago are under the chief of *Tirilokum* (Deire) who is under the Great Chief of Aqiq, *Terkinos* of Sokota from Lasta'.

Note

    Akikum (Aqiq) and *Turanikum* (Ptolemais Theron), may be different names for the same place. Both are near the mouth of the *Loukaniko* (Barka) River where it flows into the Red Sea. In that case, *Terkinos* of Sokota is the Great Chief of Aqiq. He is also the Great Chief of *Turanikum*, and our narrator.

    We read earlier (1.44-49) that *Kalos,* the Great Chief of *Loukanikum,* was held at the fort of Axum. Axum was a metropolis, a collection of towns and suburbs. Close by, Koloe was a huge, strategically located fort. It may have been part of metropolitan Axum. *Kalos,* the previous ruler of *Tetokum,* could have been held at Koloe and executed there.

    Aqiq and the Barka River were important for the Berbers, the Chaldeans and the *Akuia.* The *Akuia* make it their administrative center when they conquer it.

8. The Elephant Lord

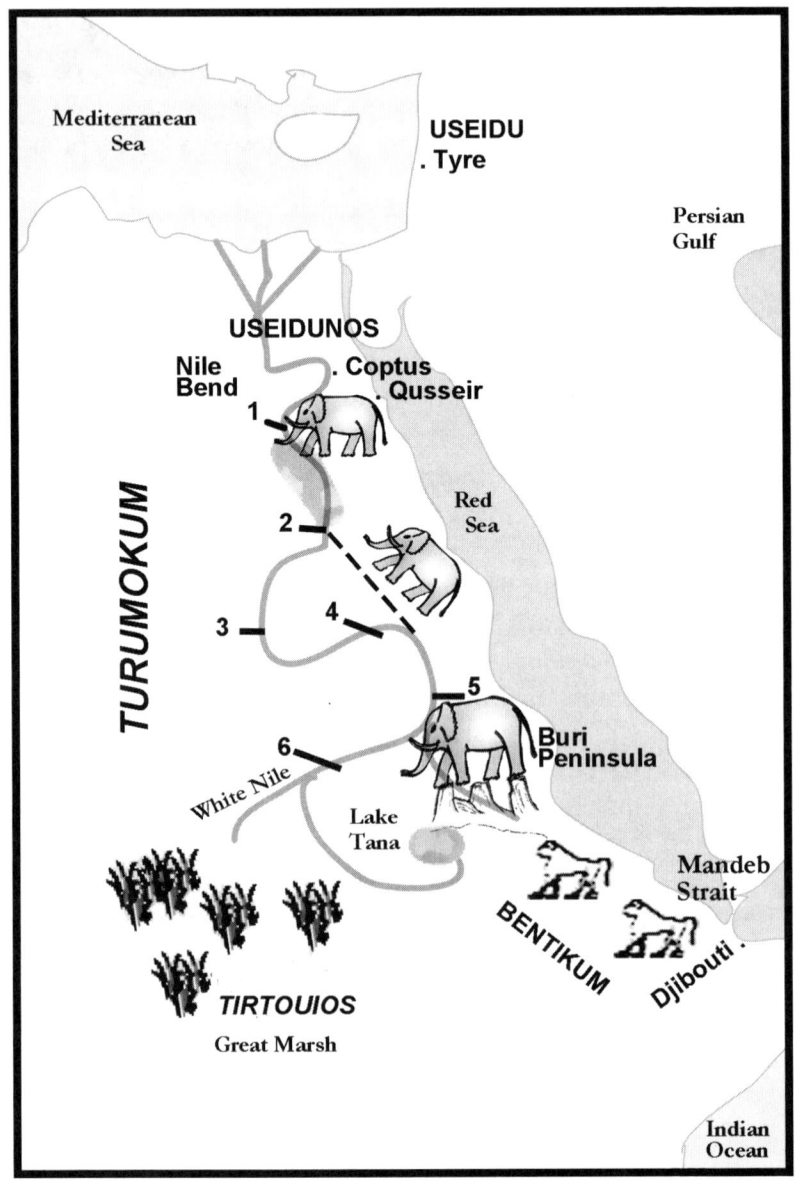

Translation 2.15-2.17

'The king who rules from the Lebanese *Useidunos* in Elephant Land, to the *Tirtouios* (Marsh peoples) of southern Sudan is the *elaukos* (Elephant Lord). He rules *Bentikum* (Baboon Land) from the middle of the Red Sea coast'.

Note

Tirtouios comes from *tirto*, 'all' and *uios*, 'waters' in order to get 'Marsh people', from the Sudd. The Sudd is a marshy region where a network of rivers comes together to feed into the White Nile.

The *Useidunos* (people from *Useidu* in Phoenician Lebanon, but living in Egypt) are probably linked to the Phoenician *Bini Rusku*. They lived east and southeast of the Nile Bend. The Nile Bend area had many cities. It was an important commercial center because of a nearby port on the Red Sea at Qusseir.

Elau is a Berber word for 'elephant'. As *elaukos*, he is the 'Elephant Lord' of *Abokum*, an Egyptian word meaning 'the Elephant Kingdom'.

The 5th Cataract is roughly parallel to the middle of the western Red Sea coast. Our narrator is from *Turanikum* near the 5th Cataract. Baboon Land begins south of the Buri Peninsula and extends to Djibouti. It is part of the Southern River Kingdom. East of the Nile River, Elephant Land extends from the Nile Bend to Baboon Land. Here we learn the White Nile where the *Tirtouios* live is the border between Elephant Land and *Turumokum*.

9. The Lord King of *Telad*

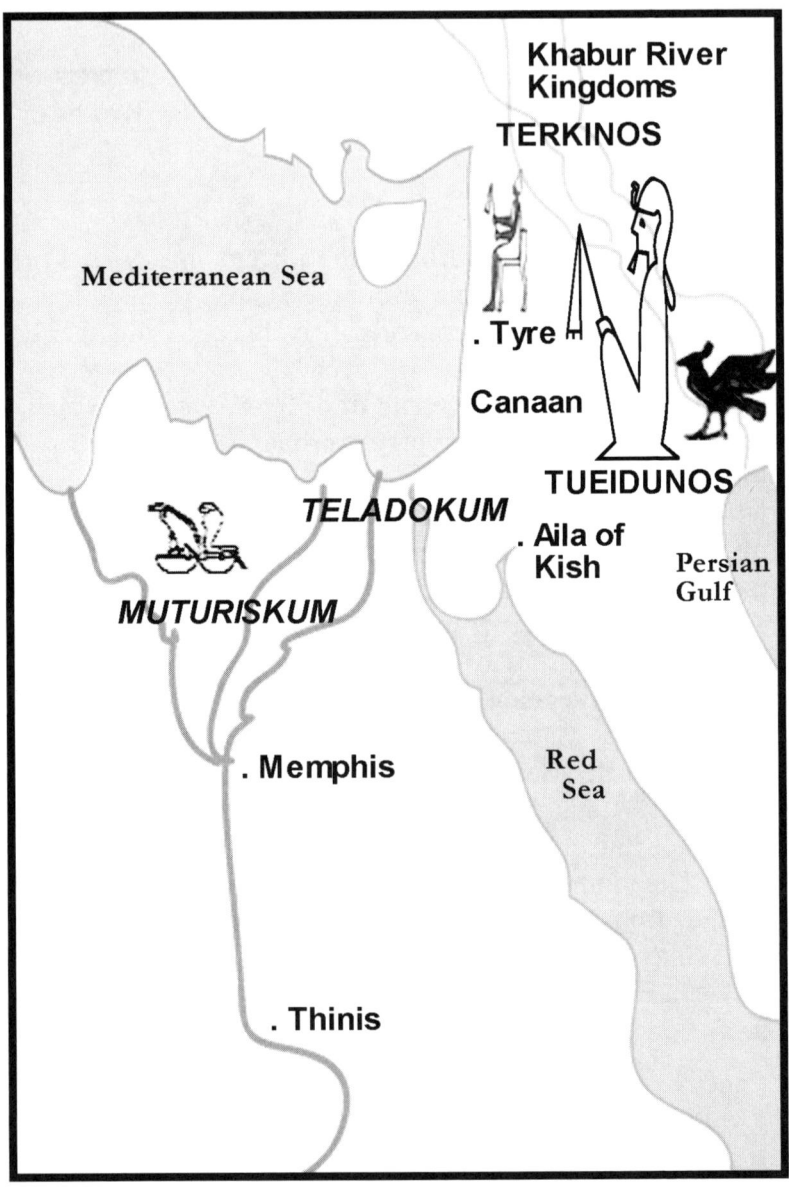

Translation Lines 2.18-2.22

'One of the kings of *Muturiskum* (Egypt), *Terkinos* of *Telad* (Tjel, or Deled) is the chief of the Tyre region in Canaan. His territory extends as far as *Tueidunos*, the Great chief of all the kings'.

Note

     Tueidunos rules the Khabur River valley in Eastern Syria (3.50-57). His western border is at Aila of Kish. West of there, the territories along the Eastern Mediterranean now belong to *Terkinos,* the narrator. *Terkinos* of *Telad* is perhaps a cousin, the local ruler of Tyre in Canaan. Canaan is one of the Eastern Mediterranean territories that were conquered.

10. *Ataiokum* (Meroe)

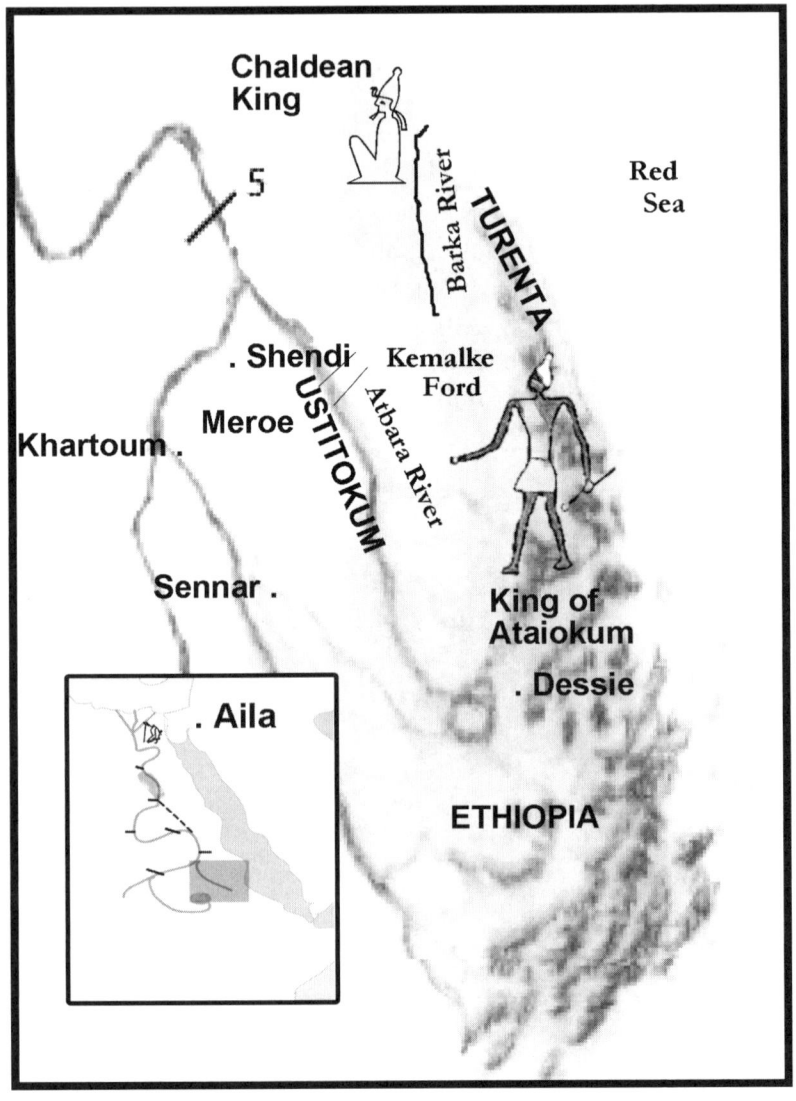

Translation Lines 2.22-2.34

'His kingdom begins from Aila of Kish in Jordan. It extends
to the kingdom of those who were hanged (in northeastern
Egypt). It goes down to *Ustitokum*, (*Astitokum*, Atbara
River Land), in the region of southern *Turenta*. This king of
Ataiokum (Meroe), in the district of the Kemalke Ford,
rules as far as the kings of the southern kingdoms. Those
kings have become kings of the River Kingdom. They rule
over the districts of Western Shendi in Meroe, over *Tais*
(Dessie) and the Basa in the River Kingdom. They rule up
to the territory of the king of the *Kalaitos* (Chaldeans)'.

Note

 The king who rules from Aila down to Meroe is our
narrator. Here we learn that he is the king of *Ataiokum*. He
is ruling over those new territories in Eastern Sudan. Here
he gives his allies in the Southern River Kingdom new
titles, and possibly, new territory.

 For another reference to the Chaldeans of *Kustikum*
(Eritrea), see the discussion of *Melmanios* (4.12 -21). This
Chaldean colony in Eritrea appears to have endured.
Munzinger in a map drawn in the middle of the 19th century
shows the *At Gultane*, a tribe of Chaldeans, along the Barka
River. They live north and northwest of the Keren
Highlands.[36] Reinisch in his late 19th century texts reports
Kelau and *Kelauti* along the Barka River in the stories in
his Bilin texts.[37] Note also the reference to the Barka River
as the *Loukaniko* River (2.3-2.5).

---

[36] Munzinger, *Über die Sitten und das Recht der Bogos*, Map.
[37] Reinisch, *Texte der Bilin Sprache*, 18.

11. *Uiriraskum* (Lasta)

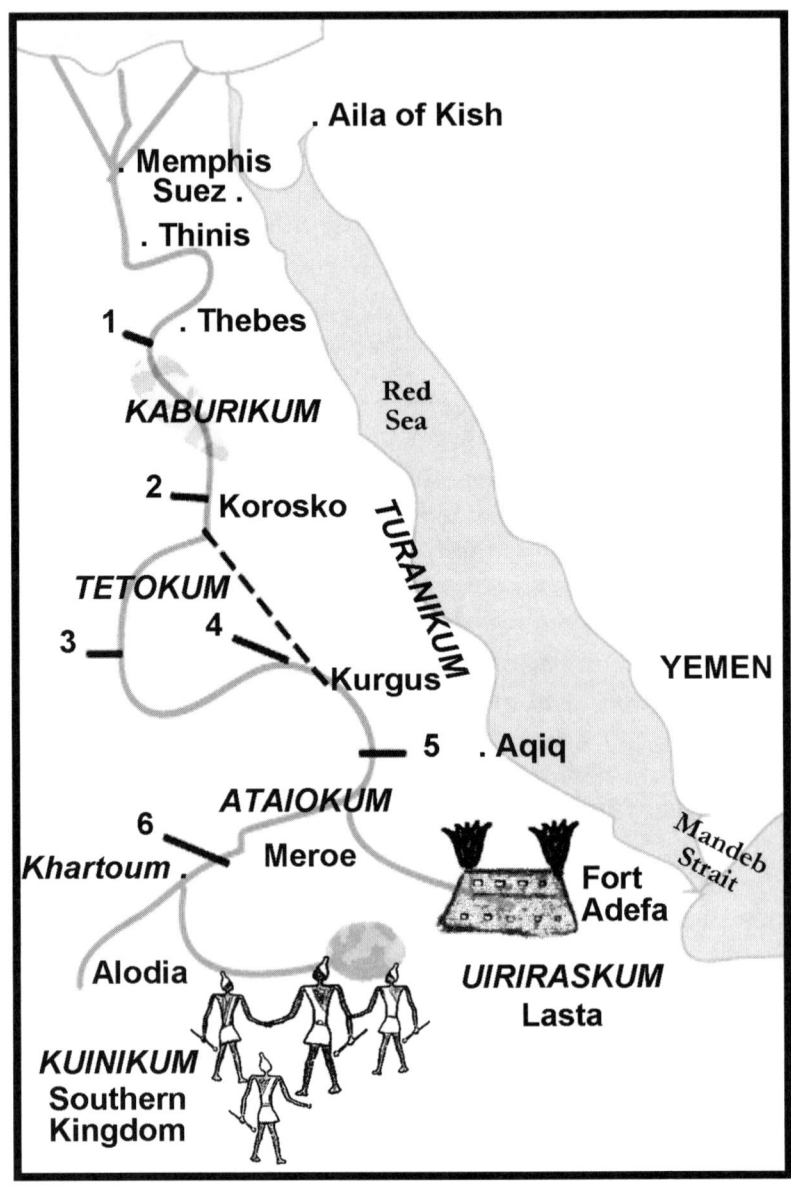

Translation Lines 2.34-2.43

'In *Uiriraskum* (Lasta region), those *Ataiokum* (Ethiopian) princes of mine below *Kaburikum* (Lower Nubia) now rule the territories along the road from Korosko to Kurgis. That road passes through *Tetokum*. They rule down to the birthplace of the rivers near Lake Tana. In the River Kingdom, the kings at Fort *Atauikum* (Adefa, modern Lalibela), [already] have all of *Kuinikum* (the Southern Kingdom). [They have now taken] all of the [former] territories of *Loukanikum* (Cattle Land)'.

Note

    Uiriraskum corresponds to Warawar and Urvuar. Those are names for the Lalibela region, which is part of Lasta. An ancient name for the city of Lalibela is Adefa. Fort *Atauikum* (Fort Adefa) may be an earlier form of this name. In the 13th century AD, the Agau speaking, Kushitic Zagwe kings made Lalibela their capital. They claimed it was the seat of the ancient Kushite kings.[38] This passage provides a little support for that claim. It describes a situation where the princes and kings cluster at the royal court located at Fort *Atauikum*.

    Notice that the kings at Fort Adefa already had all of the Southern River Kingdom, below the 5th Cataract. In section 4, we read that the territories in the Cataract region taken from *Kalos* would be added to that. That gave them all of the territories north to the Nile Bend in Egypt. In the next section, we begin to talk about territories east of Suez that have been conquered.

---

[38]Munro-Hay, *Ethiopia*, 22, 23.

12. From Cattle Land to the *Turo* Empire

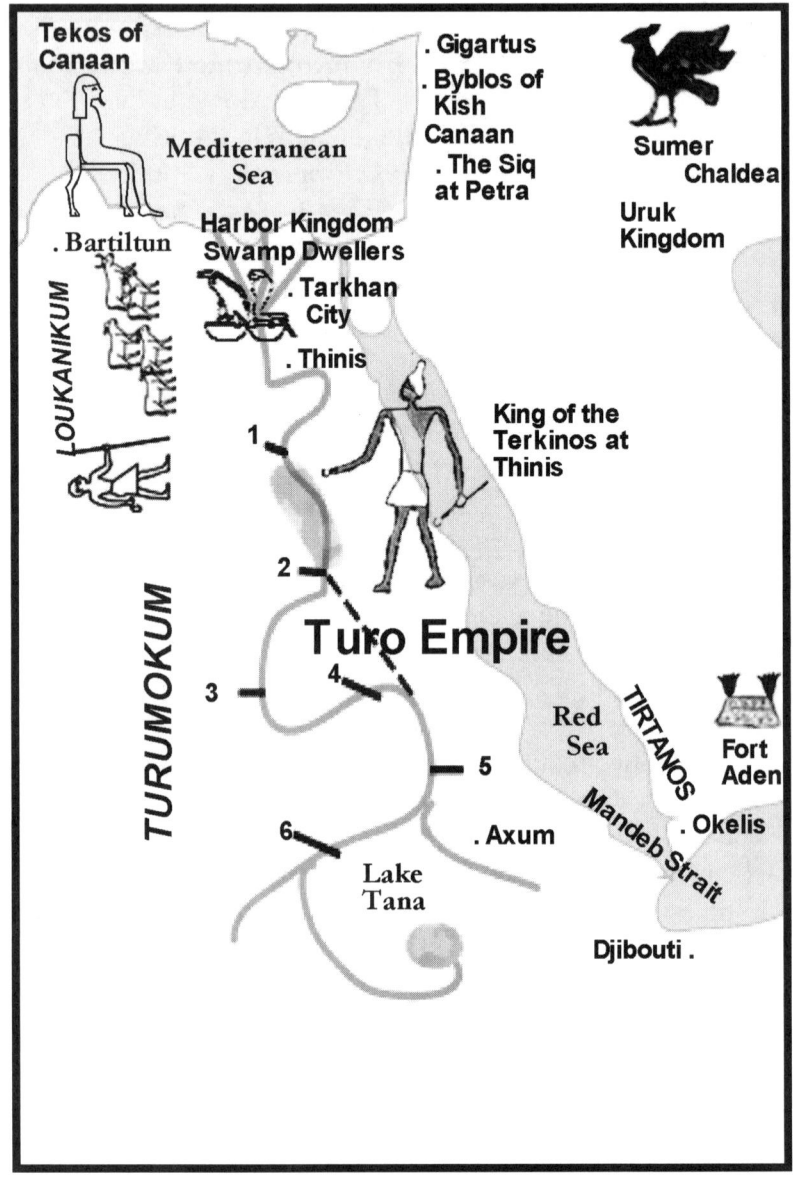

Translation Lines 2.44-2.57

'From the eastern border of Klusma (east of Suez), we took territories from Tarkhan City to the people at the Mandeb Strait in the *Tirtano* region of Yemen. Territories at the Siq at Petra were taken from the [former] commander of *Turumokum*, *Tekos* of Canaan. He was the lord of the leaders at *Bartiltun* in Egypt. His territories stretched as far as the boundaries of our king.

I am extending the Harbor kingdom of the Swamp dwellers down to the king of the *Terkinos* at Thinis. From the kings of Ocelis at the Mandeb Strait to Gigartus near Byblos in Lebanon, all are now clan territories of our kings of the *Turo* Empire'.

Note

    Tekos is described above as 'the lord of the leaders at *Bartiltun*'. *Bartiltun* was probably the capital of *Loukanikum*, where the court was.

    Muturiskum (Vulture Cobra Land) was not part of *Abokum* (Elephant Land) (1.57-59). Here the narrator extends the Harbor Kingdom in the Egyptian Delta region to Thinis. It sounds like he is making *Muturiskum* a part of *Toutinikum* (Thinis). However, the name *Muturiskum* endured. A compressed version survives in the word *Misr*, the modern name for Egypt.

    Terkinos has the Eastern Mediterranean. The text mentions Byblos and Petra. He also has Ocelis in Yemen, right at the Strait. It is not so clear that he conquered Arabia. Certainly, *Melmanios*, the chief of Arabia, is a prisoner. However, Sumer is still *Terkinos'* enemy. *Kaiaitos* ruled Uruk for another 36 years after *Melmanios'* reign ended. His conquest of Fort Aden may have preserved Uruk's control over part, if not all, of Arabia.

13. *Testios*, the King of Scorpion Land

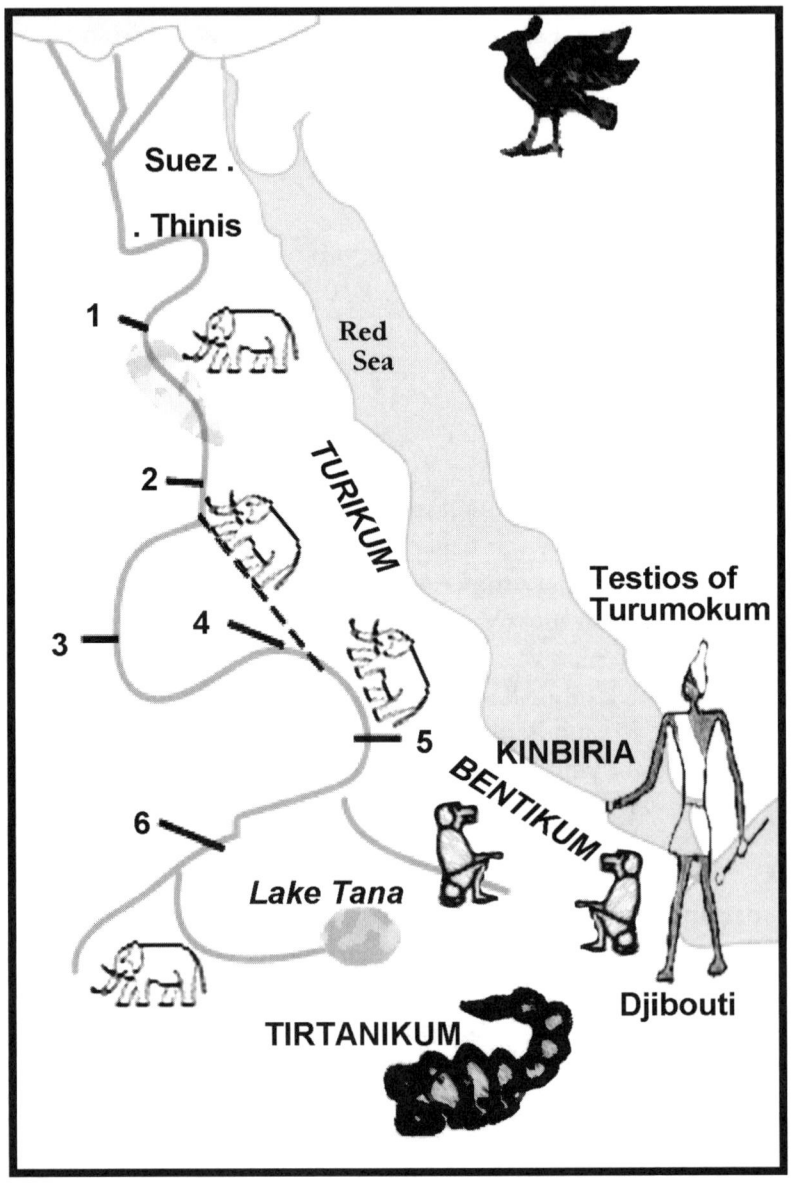

Translation Lines 2.58-3.5

'The province of *Bentikum* (Baboon Land) extends up to the borders of the *Akuia* Empire in Elephant Land. It begins from the territories of the king of Djibouti, *Testios* of *Turumokum*. From the king of Scorpion Land in the River Kingdom, it extends to *Kinbiria* (the Buri Peninsula), south of the border of the king of *Turikum*'.

Note

     Notice that *Testios* from *Turumokum*, the king of Djibouti, is also the king of *Tirtanikum* (Scorpion Land). His territories begin on the border of *Bentikum*.

     Turikum is very ancient. In this text, this is the only place it is mentioned. Apparently, at this time, it overlaps with Elephant Land. The southern boundary of *Turikum* here is *Kinbiria*, the Buri peninsula. The southern boundary of Elephant Land goes down to Fort Koloe. That would be in the same region near modern Qohaito. *Bentikum* at this time corresponds roughly to modern Dankalia in Eritrea.

14. *Koloutios*, the Phoenician

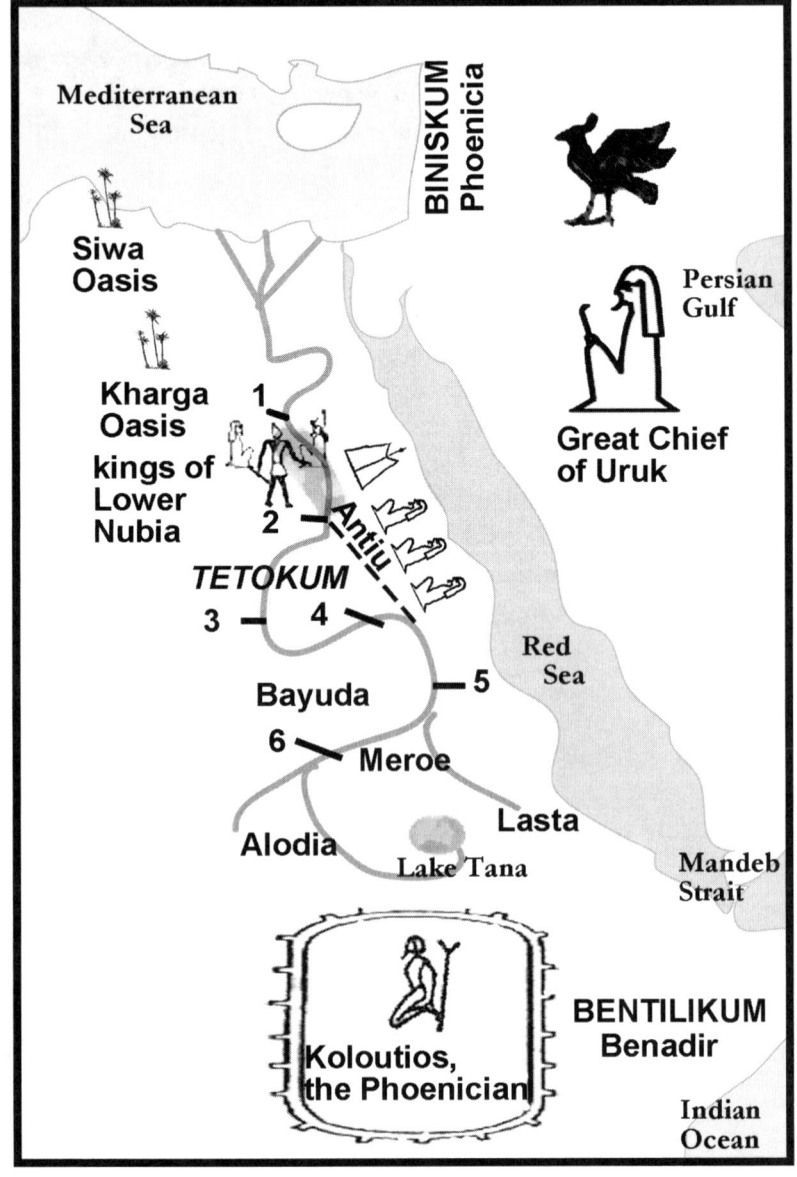

Translation Lines 3.5-3.11

'In *Austunikum* (Ethiopia), *Koloutios*, the Phoenician, is one of the kings [held] at Fort *Bentilikum*. He was the Lord of the Antiu in the *Melman* part of the River Kingdom. *Koloutios* ruled over the kings of *Kaburikum,* as far as the Great Chief of Uruk'.

Note

The Antiu were the people of the Antat, between the Nile and the Red Sea. Egyptian hieroglyphs for the Antiu feature tents and sometimes Bedouin dress.

Fort *Bentilikum* was near Mogadishu, in Benadir, the Indian Ocean coast of Somalia.

Lower Nubia, the region between the 1st and 2nd Cataracts on the Nile, was controlled by Uruk. It is called *Kaburikum* (the Springs of Horus). In the discussion of the boundaries of the *Akuia* kings, it is called *Babokum*, Wawat, a name for Lower Nubia (1.36-42). *Koloutios'* former territory is now part of the new region that those *Akuia* kings will be ruling.

The region is part of Elephant Land. It was inhabited by the *Babos*, people now subject to *Kainu* (3.55-4.3). The *Anu* were identified as living in the same area and may be related to the *Babos* (4.12-15). *Melmanios*, who is also a prisoner now, ruled the *Anu*. Formerly as the king of Uruk, he was probably *Koloutios'* overlord.

15. *Tetu*, the Laguatan

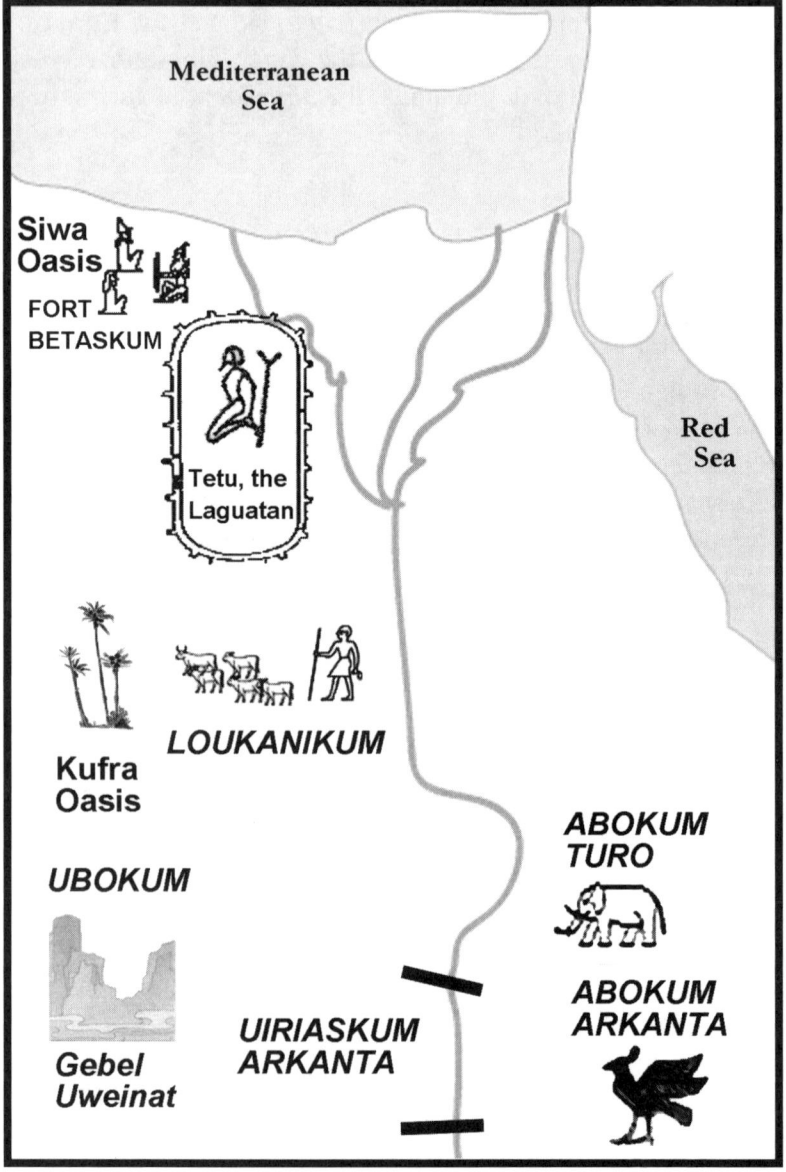

Translation 3.12-3.21

'In Elephant Land of the *Arkanta* (Urukites), a king of Cattle Land, the conquered kingdom, was held at Fort *Betaskum,* (Um Ebeida), by the *Melman* kings at the Siwa Oasis. He was the commander of *Ubokum*, (the Gebel Uweinat), outside of the conquered empire. He is *Tetu,* the Laguatan, who was a king on the border. His kingdom was between the River Kingdom and the region in the River Kingdom controlled by Uruk'.

Note

The Gebel Uweinat is west of *Abokum Arkanta* (Lower Nubia), a region east of the Nile formerly controlled by Uruk. The *Melman* kings who captured *Tetu* may have been allies of *Tiokenes* who fought for the south.

16. An *Aunu* from the Land of Bes

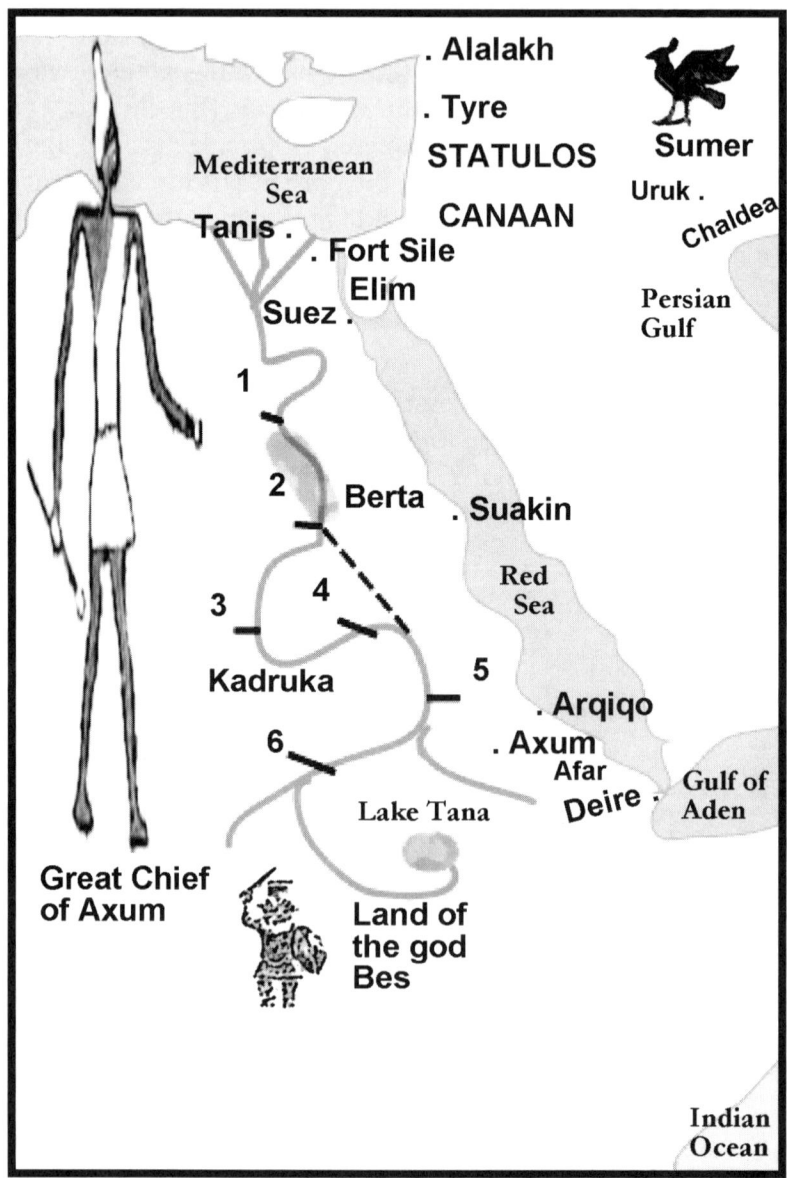

Translation Lines 3.21-3.34

'I am over all of the Western Land in this empire we have conquered. As the first Lord of the royal domain at Axum, I am the foremost chief in both directions. I rule as far as the Afar in the south and the Berta in the north. As the Great Lord of Suakin in Sudan, I rule over the *Statulos* (Canaanites) of Canaan. This *Aunu* from the land of Bes is now the Lord King of the kings of Alalakh (in Syria). As the Great Chief at Axum, I rule from Elim in the *Akuia* Sinai up to the court of the Deire people at the Mandeb Strait in the River Kingdom. I rule as far as Kadruka (near the 3rd Cataract) in the west. From there I rule up to the Mediterranean Sea coast at Tanis over the Sile-ites'.

Note

In this list, the narrator controls Northeastern Africa from the Mandeb Strait to the Mediterranean Sea. He also has the Eastern coast of the Mediterranean Sea. Notice that he does not mention Arabia or places on the eastern coast of the Red Sea.

17. The King of Suakin

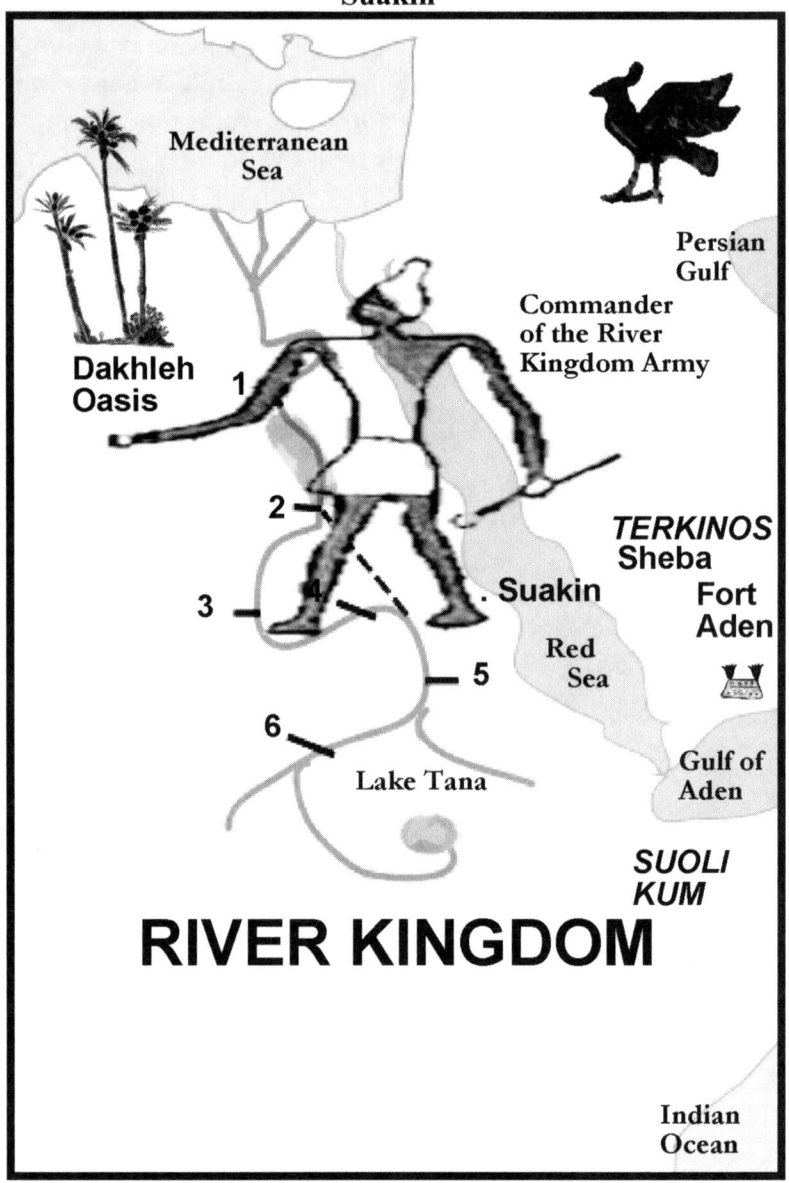

Translation Lines 3.35-3.40

'The new commander of the River Kingdom army is the king of Suakin. He is at the court of the lord of *Suoli Kum*, 'Somalia'. His domain is from the ruler of the Dakhleh Oasis to the *Terkinos* of the desert lands of Sheba in southern Yemen'.

Note

    The old king of the army of the River Kingdom was hanged. In the list of hangings, he was captive E (1.6-19).

    This king of Suakin was a noble at the court of *Testios*, the Scorpion King, in Djibouti.

18. The Captive *Melman* Lord

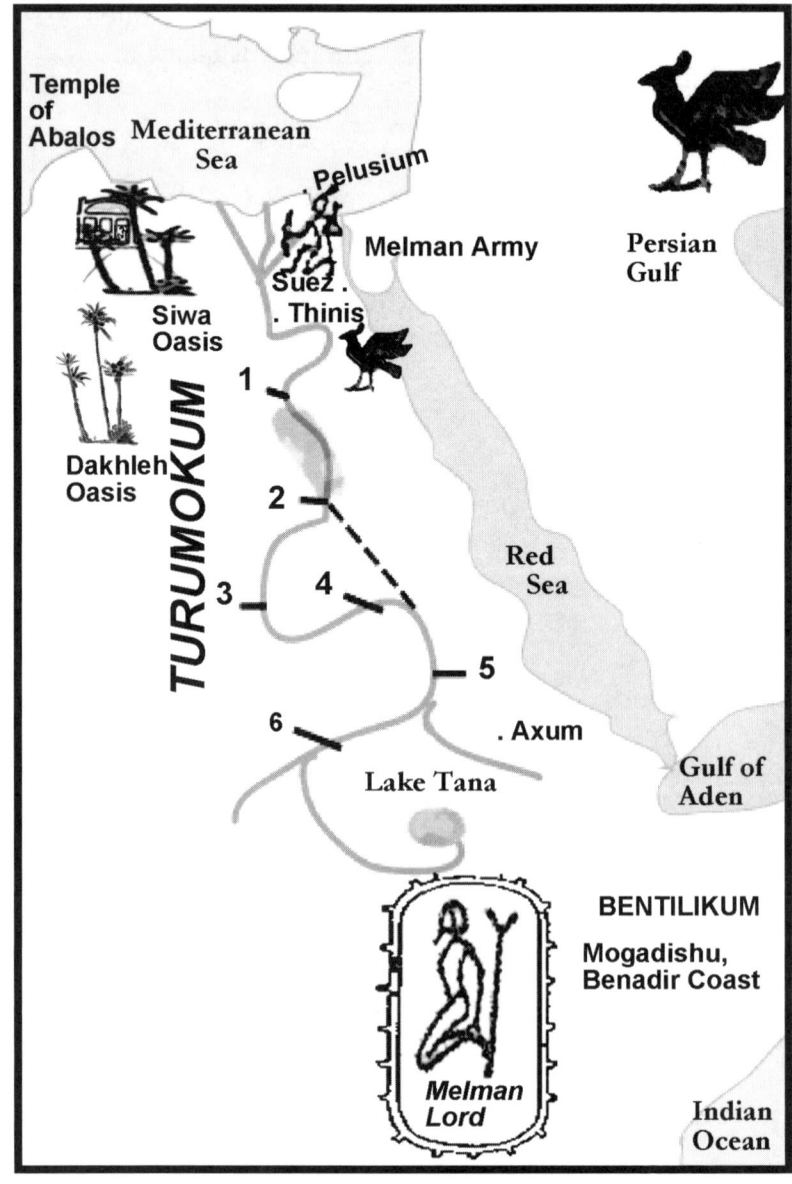

Translation Lines 3.41-3.50

'The first Lord of the Dakhleh Oasis is the *Melman* Lord.
He is held at the central fortress of *Bentilikum* (Benadir
region around Mogadishu). He ruled the *Arkanta* at Klusma
(Suez), those who were within the borders of Thinis. He
ruled the army of the (defeated) *Melman* Empire. His
territory stretched from Klusma (Suez) up to the temple of
Abalos (Apollo), the Most High.
In *Karunikum* (northern Egypt) he ruled from the kings of
Pelusium to the princes of *Turumokum* (west of the Nile)'.

Note

This *Melman* Lord is a second prisoner from the
Dakhleh Oasis. *Kalos*, held prisoner at Axum, was a lord of
Cattle Land in Cataract Land. This Lord belonged to
Muturiskum and to the Falcon Clan. He had authority over
the *Melman* army at Suez, up to the temple of Apollo at the
Siwa Oasis. *Bartiltun,* the Cattle Land capital, is quite close
to the Siwa Oasis.

19. *Tueidunos*, the Phoenician

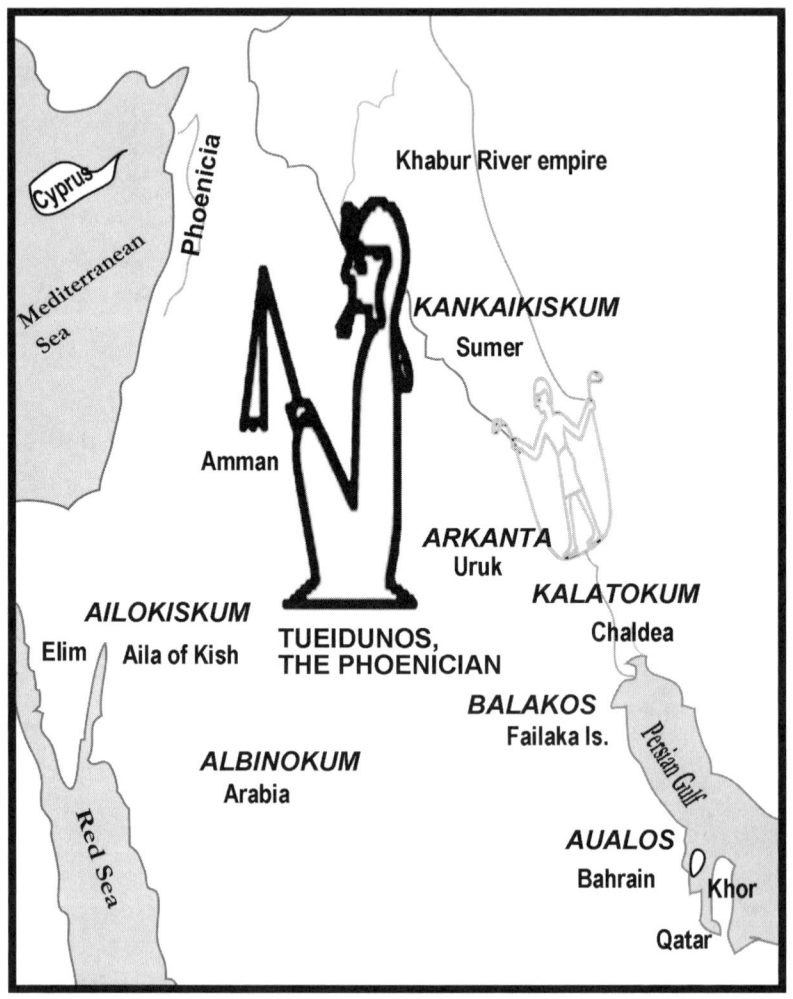

Translation Lines 3.50-3.55

'*Tueidunos,* the Phoenician, is the Lord King of the Khabur River empire of Uruk kingdoms. *Tueidunos* rules the *Suros*, Syrians, at Aila of Kish, from *Alikum* (Elim in the Sinai) up to *Ama* (Amman, in Jordan).

Note

    Tueidunos is a Phoenician (from Lebanon) and a client king of Uruk. He has two territories here: Eastern Syria and Jordan.

    Recall that *Koloutios*, another Phoenician, is a prisoner in the fort at Mogadishu. *Terkinos* has just conquered Phoenicia from the Mesopotamian Chaldeans. It is no surprise to find Phoenicians among the enemies and prisoners.

20. The Kingdoms of the Deep South

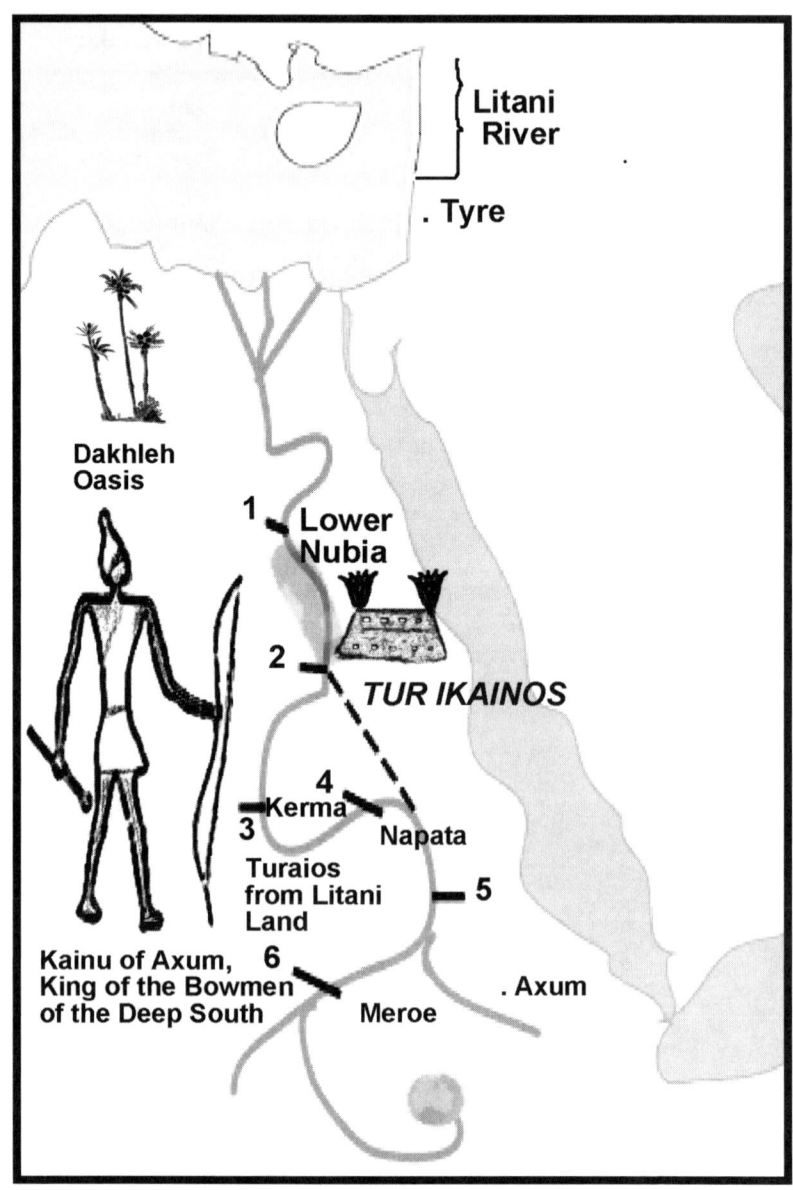

Translation Lines 3.55-4.3

'In the River Kingdom, *Kainu*'s kingdom begins from south of the Lower Nubians. It goes down, in the River Kingdom, to the Lebanese *Turaios* from Litani Land who settled in southern Kerma. Still in the River Kingdom, it extends to *Kari,* (the Napata district, at the 4th Cataract). These territories of the River Kingdom's Deep South are ruled by *Kainu* of Axum. He is the king of the bowmen at the southern town of the *Tur-ikainos*'.

Note

This section describes the lands between the 2nd and 4th Cataracts as the 'Deep South'. That would suggest that the old Berber River Kingdom's southern border was at the 5th Cataract. That may have been its border just before *Terkinos*' conquests. In other places, he tells us that the River Kingdom now extends much further south. It extends to the Gulf of Aden and to Alodia, south of the 6th Cataract.

The *Tur-ikainos* are the people of the *Tur*, 'citadel', at Iken at the 2nd Cataract.

21. Victory in the North

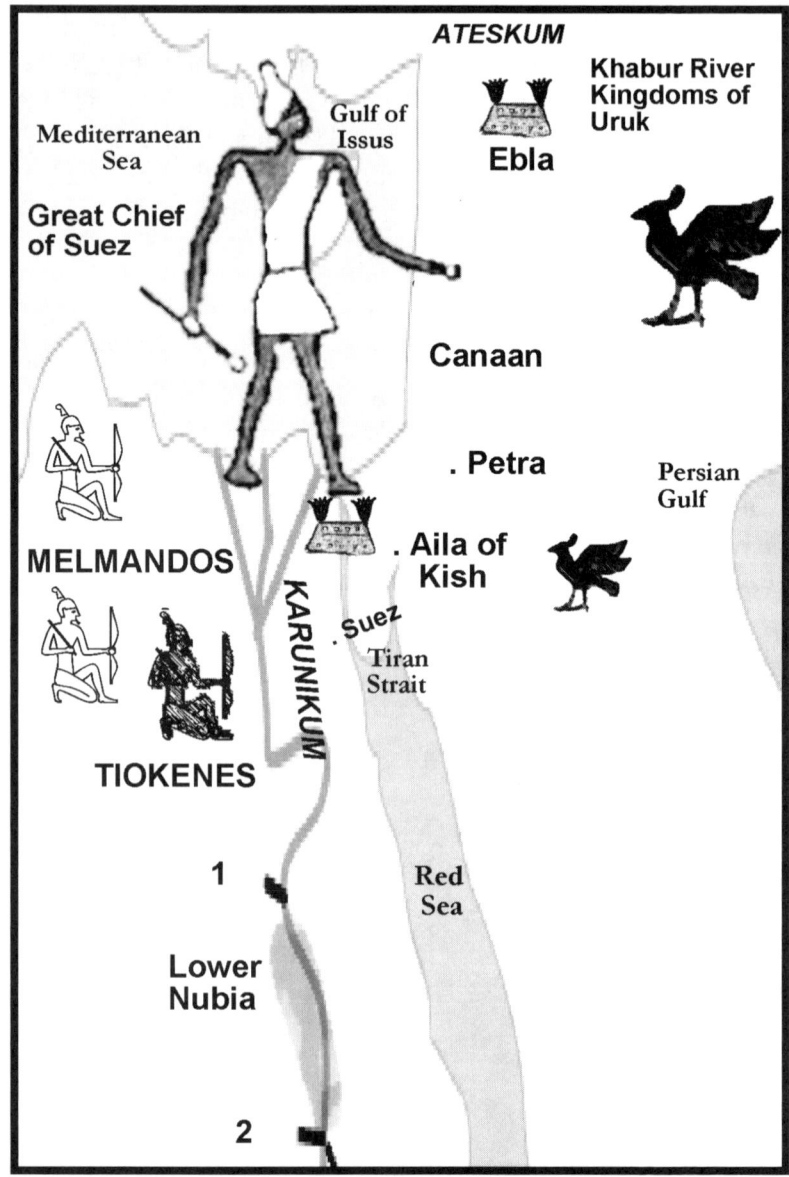

Translation Lines 4.4-4.11

'The *Melmandos* lcd by *Tiokenes* conquered the Chaldeans of *Mturiskum* (Metcher / Egypt). The Chaldeans were defeated at the fortress of *Karunikum* (Northeastern Egypt) and at the royal fortress of Ebla.
In *Makeskokum* (the Northern Lands), as a result, I became the Great Chief of Suez. I am now the king from the middle of the Tiran Strait in the Red Sea to the Gulf of Issus in Edessa'.

Note

It appears that *Tiokenes* from the Old River Kingdom became an ally of the southerners. Here he leads an army of *Melman* against the Chaldeans. Clearly, not all of the *Melman* Berbers were part of the Vase Alliance. We read earlier that he was the new Great Lord of the lands west of the Nile (1.50-2.1). Apparently, his victory allowed *Terkinos* to become the Great Chief of the *Statulu* in Canaan and Syria.

Makeskokum, the Northern Lands, may be linked to *Tamehu*, a Berber word meaning 'the northerners'. It is an ancient name for Berber peoples in this region.[39]

---

[39] Nesmenser, "The Temehu Tribes of Ancient Libya."

79

22. *Melmanios*, King of Egypt, Arabia and Uruk

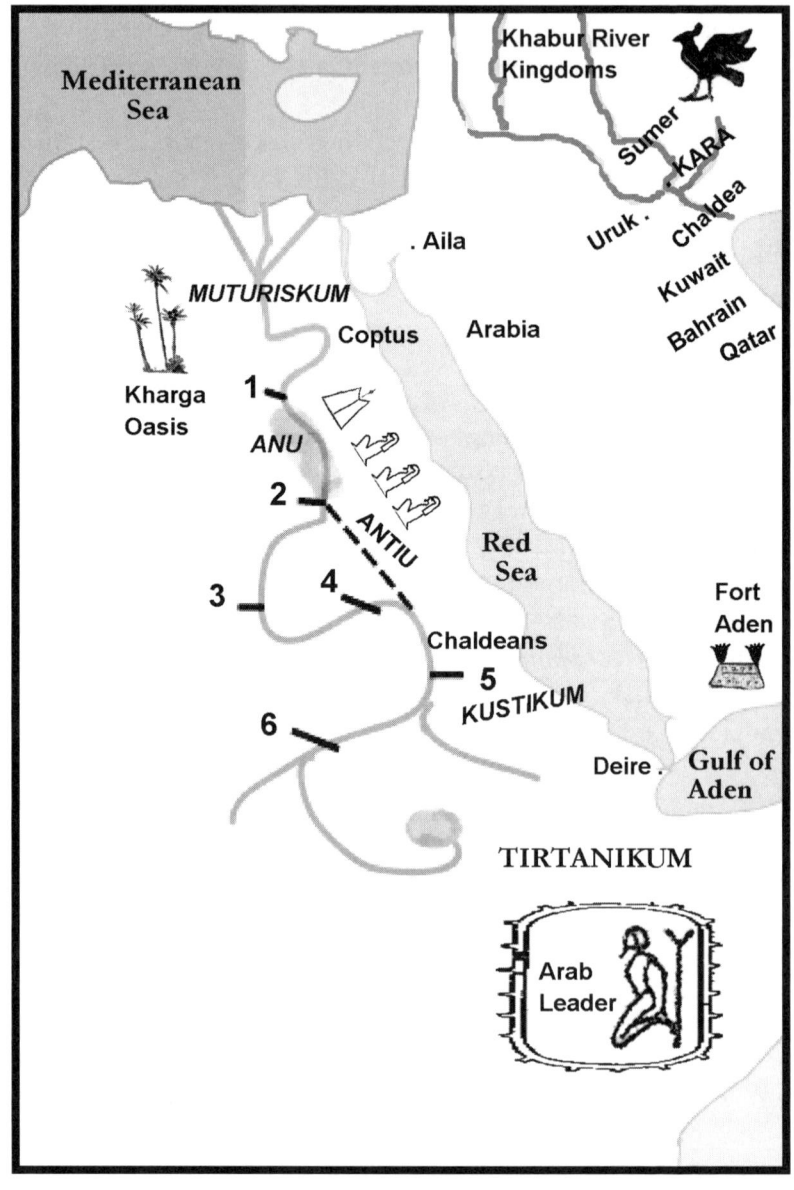

Translation Lines 4.12-4.21

'One of the Chaldeans of *Kustikum* (Eritrea), the Lord of the Antiu of Eritrea, ruled Coptos on the Nile Bend in Southern Egypt. He was Lord of the *Anu* people in Lower Nubia in the River Kingdom.
This chief of the Chaldeans of *Muturiskum* ruled Arabia. He ruled the province of Failaka (in Kuwait). He ruled Charax Spasinu of Chaldea . He ruled the kingdom of Uruk of the kings of Arabia'.

Note

    This tells us several things: The Chaldeans under *Melmanios* controlled the northeastern corner of Egypt that included Fort Sile. The area under Chaldean control included *Albinokum*, western Arabia, in addition to Canaan and Lebanon. Uruk, under *Melmanios*, was part of the territory of the kings of Arabia.

    Since *Melmanios* is the king of Uruk, he is also the King of Sumer. That means *Tueidunos*' territories in eastern Syria come under him. *Kaiaitos*' territories in Bahrain, Qatar, and at Fort Aden are also part of his empire.

    Melmanios is also the Arab leader held captive at Deire in *Tirtanikum* (0.1-1.5).

23. Thebes and the Dal Cataract

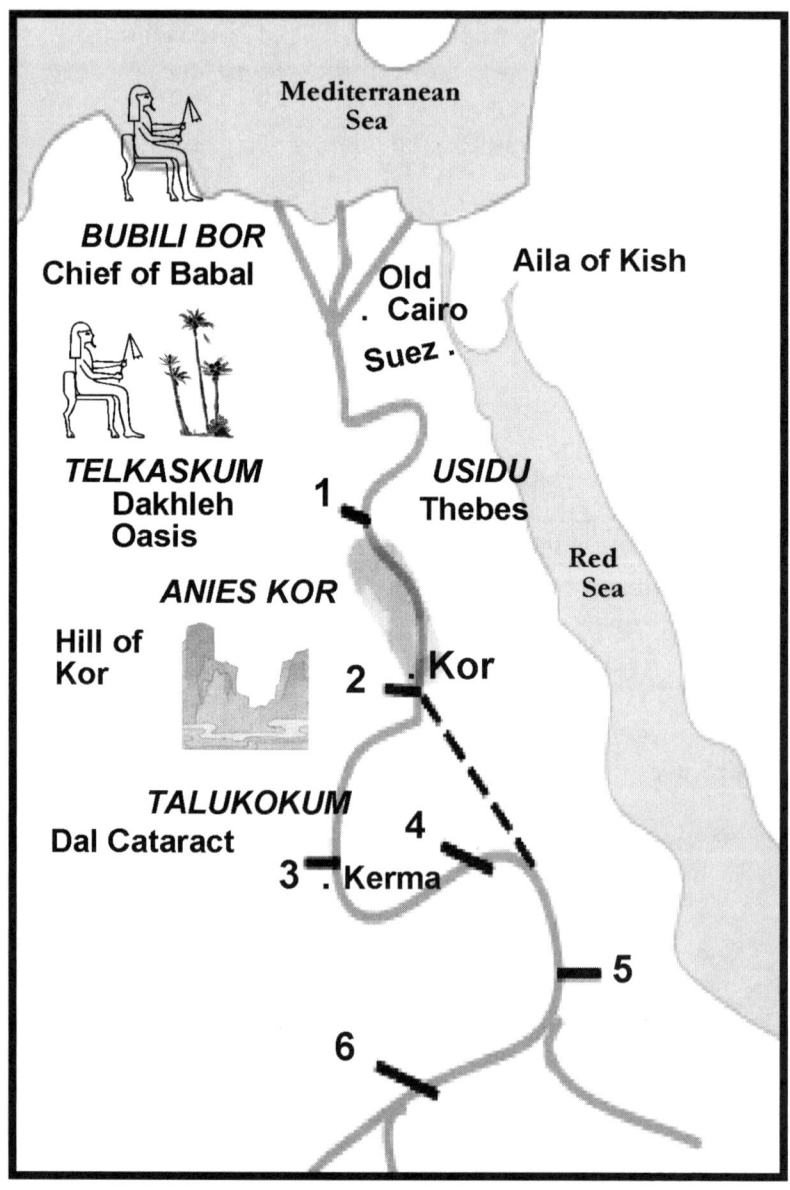

Translation Lines 4.22-4.27

'The Chief of Babal (Old Cairo) in the River Kingdom rules Thebes in the River Kingdom.
One of the kings of the River Kingdom from the Dakhleh Oasis rules *Anieskor* (Mount Kor or modern Gebel Sheikh Suleiman). He rules the Dal Cataract kingdom up to the border with Kerma'.

Note

　　Anies, meaning 'hill, mount', occurs frequently in placenames in Saudi Arabia. The name *Anieskor* may be a legacy from the time when Lower Nubia was controlled by Uruk.

24. The Four Kings of
Akuikum

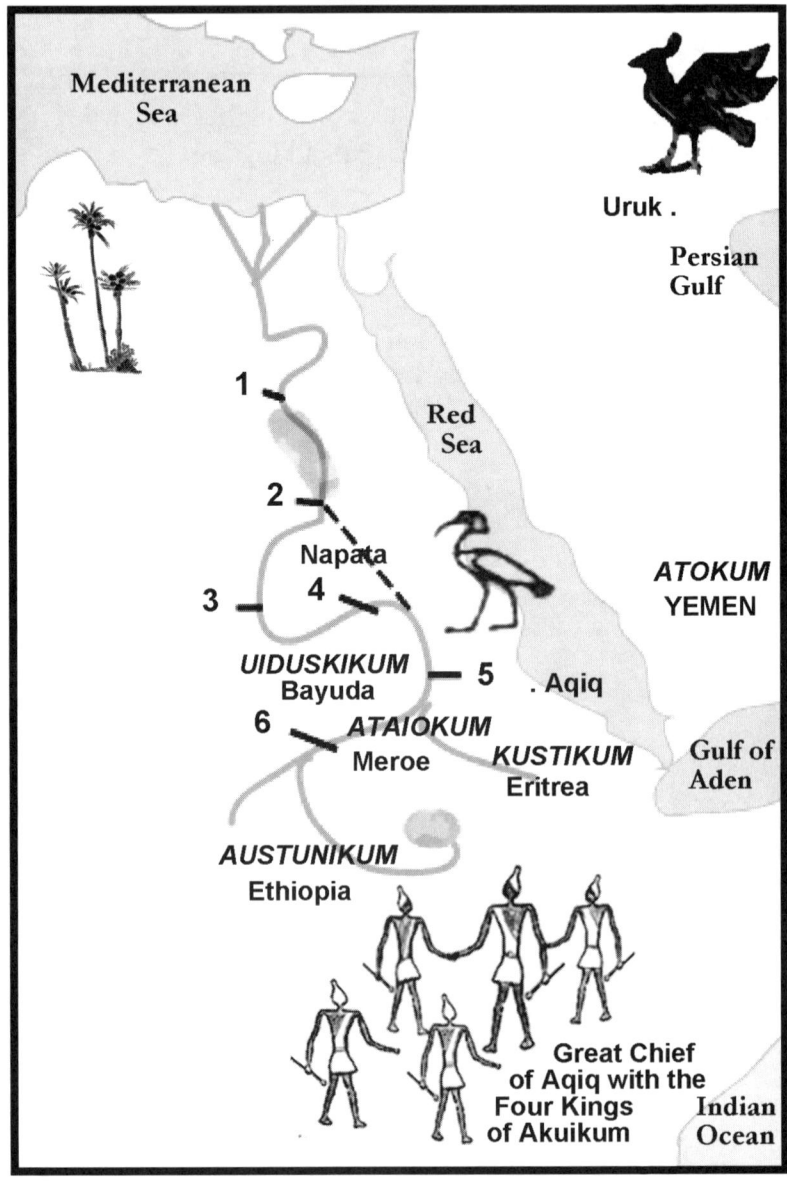

Translation Lines 4.28-4.33

'The lords of *Akuikum* (Agau Land) are under the jurisdiction of *Terkinos* from Sokota, the king of Aqiq. They are: the leader of Napata, the Lion of Ethiopia, the lord of Meroe, and the Great King of Eritrea'.

Note

This section tells us who the *Akuia* were. They were the lords of the *Akuia* (Agau) lands. The people there spoke Kushitic languages, like the language of the text. Their principal home regions were Ethiopia, Eritrea, Meroe and Napata. The king of Aqiq is their overlord. At this time, he is one of the *Terkinos* from Sokota in Lasta.

On the Libyan palette, Lion Land had three client kingdoms, plus their lion overlord. Since that time, the *Akuia* have taken Napata and Aqiq from the Berbers. The *Akuia* now have four client kingdoms, plus the overlord at Aqiq.

25. The Enemy Lands

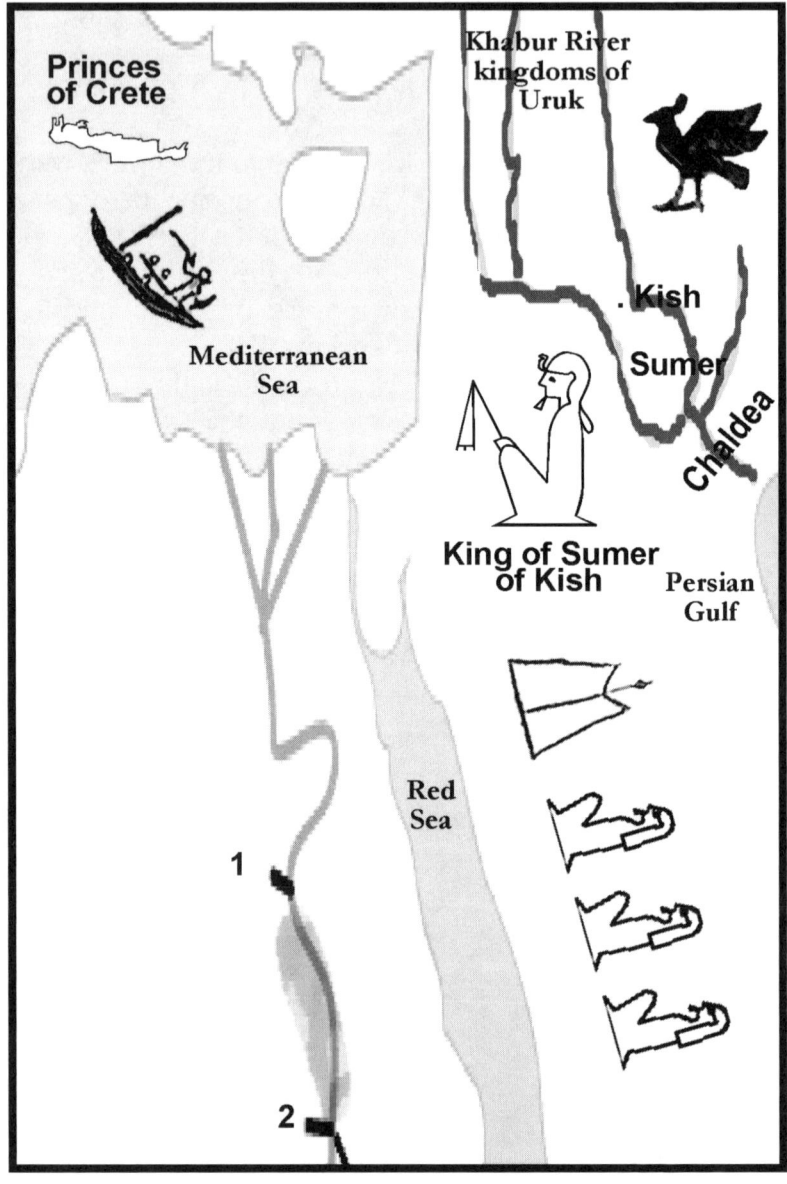

Princes of Crete

Khabur River kingdoms of Uruk

Mediterranean Sea

. Kish

Sumer

Chaldea

King of Sumer of Kish

Persian Gulf

Red Sea

1

2

Translation Lines 4.34-4.36

'The evil lords of the enemy lands are: the king of
Kankaikiskum (Sumer of Kish) and the princes of
Kuedontikum (Kydonia in Crete)'.

Note

In the Late Uruk period, the king of Uruk is the
King of Sumer. At this time, the King of Uruk is also the
king of the Arabs, the Antiu and the Chaldeans.

The Berbers of *Loukanikum* (Cattle Land) have
been defeated. They are not listed here. Egypt and the
Eastern Mediterranean are occupied. The borders have been
adjusted. The leaders were executed or imprisoned.
Perhaps, the Berbers no longer seem like a threat.

Except in Kydonia, Crete at this time may be the
last outpost of the otherwise defeated enemy Berbers.

26. Decreed by Who and Where

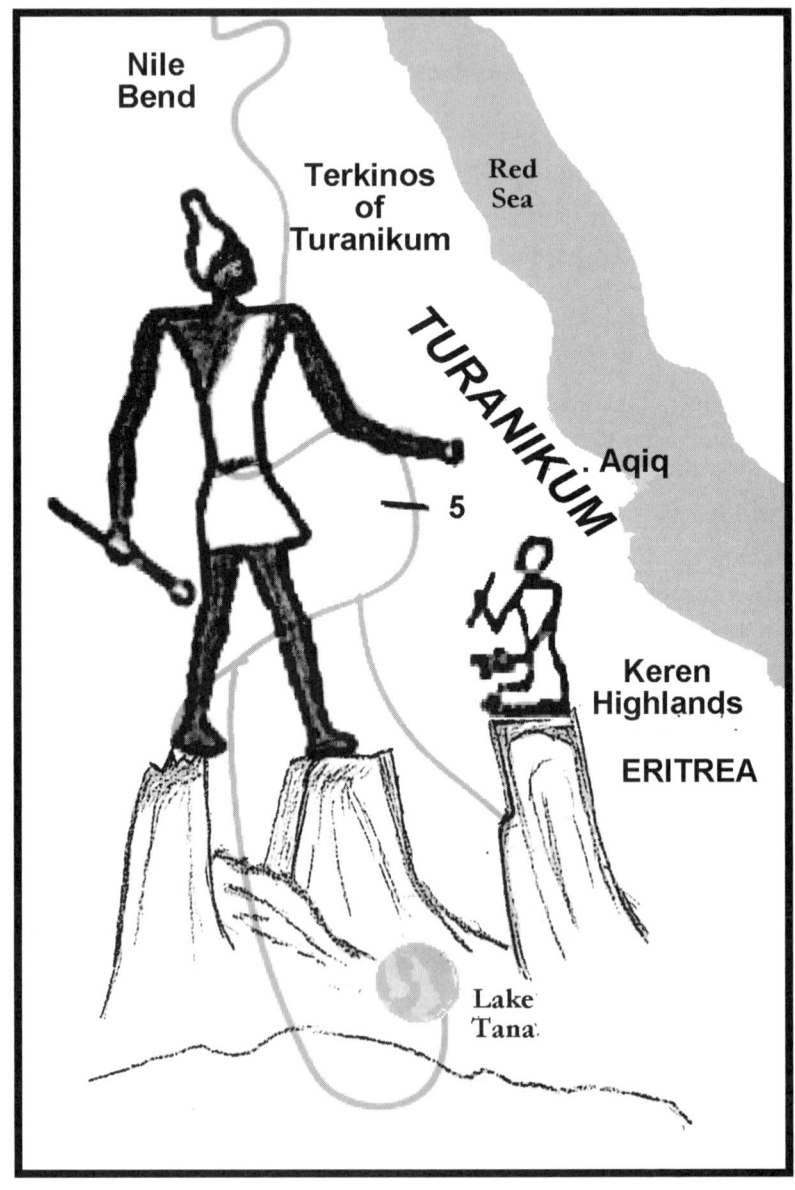

Translation Lines 4.37-4.40

'For our provinces by king *Terkinos* of *Turanikum,* this was decreed at *Kustikum* (Eritrea), in the Keren Highlands'.

Note

Aqiq was the capital of *Turanikum*, the administrative center of *Akuikum*. Like the other cities on the Red Sea coast, it has a hot, humid, tropical climate, particularly in the summer. People who can afford to often have summer homes at Keren in the cooler Highlands.

Madicenus Calaetus, Great Chaldean Lord

ABOUT THE BOTORRITA III INSCRIPTION

The Bronze Plaque

The bronze plaque that contains *Terkinos'* Proclamation is at the Museum of Zaragoza in Spain. The archaeologist M. Antonia Diaz Sanz found the plaque in 1992 at Botorrita. The site, Cabeza de las Minas, is about 20 kilometers southwest of Zaragoza in northeastern Spain. This region, including Zaragoza and Botorrita, was part of the Carthaginian province of Celtiberia under Hannibal. Based on coins and early documents, Spanish scholars believe the town near the site was called Contrebia Belaesca in Greek and Roman times.[40]

Many other Iberian inscriptions use the writing system used on the plaque. These inscriptions were found all over the Peninsula. Most were found in the east and southeast. There are several different versions of the Iberian writing system.

A couple of the symbols used at Botorrita differ from those used elsewhere. Only a few of the Iberian inscriptions have been translated. They were mostly short inscriptions on tombstones with texts in both Latin and Iberian. Even without a translation, scholars believe that the language of the Botorrita III plaque is different from the language of most Iberian inscriptions found elsewhere. Botorrita III is the bronze plaque with the Proclamation.

---

[40] Untermann and Wodtko, *Monumenta Linguarum*, 561-565, 576.

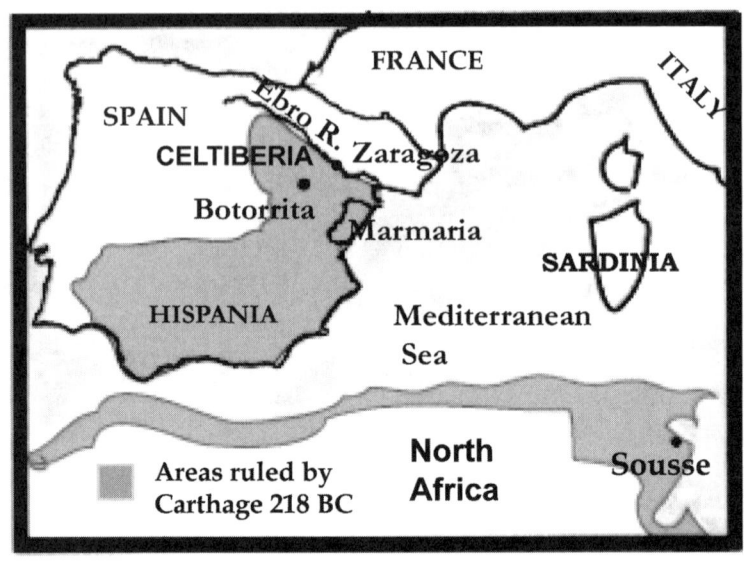

Map 8 Carthaginian Spain and North Africa

Scholars also found a bronze plaque in Latin. It identifies the nearby town as Contrebia Belaesca. The plaque refers to a dispute over water usage in 87 BC. The dispute was between the city of Zaragoza and the *Sosinestana civitas* (citizens from the Land of Sousse / Hadrumetum, that is, Berber North Africans, formerly citizens of Carthage). Names of the officials involved were 'clearly Celtiberian'. A number of coins were also found at Botorrita. One of the coins read: *contebakom bel*. The language is similar to that in Botorrita III. Based on the plaque in Latin and the coins, scholars have tentatively assigned a date of 87 BC to Botorrita III. They have classified the language as Celtiberian.[41]

The Iberian and Celtiberian inscriptions from the Iberian Peninsula have been collected, photographed and hand-copied in a collection called *Monumenta Linguarum*

---

[41] Ibid., 561-562.

Hispanicarum. The comments above summarize and translate their description of the items found at Botorrita.[42]

There is a huge gap in time and place between what is known about the place where the bronze plaque was found and the world in which that plaque was originally created.

To bring the world of the text a little closer to Spain, we need to talk about the *Melman.* The name *Melman* for Egyptian Berbers dropped out of use a long time ago. In Strabo, 1st century AD, we can still find a reference to the *Marmaridae* in Western Egypt. The Byzantine historian, Corippus, also mentions the *Marmaridae* as Laguatan Berbers in the 6th century AD.[43]

They appear in one of the earlist histories written in Spanish, Alphonso the Wise's 12th century *First General Chronicle.* Among the nations that supported Pompey against Caesar in 49 BC, are "those from Libya and the sands of Africa. From those countries came the peoples that are called *marmaricas*".[44]

About this time, al-Idrisi, in his geography of El Andalus, Moslem Spain, mentions a province called *Marmaria*, corresponding roughly to the modern Spanish province of Castellon.[45] The North African Berbers who ruled El Andalus may have named *Marmaria* three or four centuries earlier, closer to when they first invaded in 719 AD.

They may have wished to preserve the memory of a still earlier pre-Roman kingdom. The dispute over water rights at Botorrita with the 'citizens of the land of Sousse' tells us there was a settlement of Berbers in the Botorrita region in 87 BC. They may have been a remnant of the

---

[42] Ibid., 561.

[43] Mattingly, "The Laguatan", 101.

[44] Menéndez Pidal, *Primer Crónica*, 79.

[45] al-Idrisi, *Description*, 211-212, 233.

Carthaginian colony of Celtiberia, defeated by Rome in the Punic wars.

A possible step in bridging the gap in time is to look to the Irish histories. One place to start is the *Book of Leinster*. It contains an early copy of the Irish *Book of Invasions* and some potentially very early stories. While some scholars claim the *Book of Invasions* may be part myth, a comparison to the Botorrita plaques reveals interesting correlations. Another place to look is at the genealogies of Irish families.[46]

The Irish count the Iberians among their ancestors. They have stories about them that may go back to the Bronze Age. In the *Book of Invasions*, they write about the Milesians. Their Milesians may correspond to the *Melman* in the Botorrita III text. The Milesians who wrote the *Book of Invasions* were a family of scribes descended from Fenius Farsaid. He was a powerful official at the court of Tur (*Turikum*). He established a school for scribes and bureaucrats. Tur Nebroith (the Lord of *Turikum*) made him the king of Sokota. His eldest son inherited the kingdom of Sokota. His younger son, Nil or Mil, went to Egypt.[47] Fenius' grandchildren fought over the succession to the throne of Sokota. After being defeated, the descendants of Mil returned to Egypt where they prospered.[48] Many centuries later, when a king Tures, linked to their ancient enemies, came to power in Egypt, the Milesians left Egypt and went to Spain.[49] In Spain, Eber and Eremon, sons or descendants of Mil, son of Bile, assembled a force and invaded Ireland. They became the first of approximately 160 Milesian kings of Ireland. Their rule spans about 36

---

[46] Best, Bergin, and O'Brien, *Book of Leinster,* 2, 6, 12, 14, 54, 56; Meyer, "*Über die Älteste Irische,*" 42, 45.

[47] Best, Bergin, and O'Brien, *Book of Leinster,* lines 100-112.

[48] Ibid., lines 173, 221.

[49] MacAlister, *Lebor Gabála Érenn*, vol. I, 200-201.

centuries, from roughly 3000 BC until the Danes and Anglo-Saxons invaded in the 5th and 6th centuries AD.[50]

Among the Irish stories, our *Melmanios*, the King of Sumer, shows up as *Concho bur*, that is, as *Kankai Bur* (Sumerian Lord). *Conchobur* appears in a whole series of Irish stories called the Ulster Cycle. Were you wondering whatever became of 'that Arab leader held captive in Scorpion Land'? There is a story in the Ulster cycle about the death of Conchobur. "Conchobur went aside alone to let the women see what a splendidly fine handsome fellow he was.... It was Cet (Ket, ?Kaiaitos) who encouraged him to go. Cet knew full well that Conchobur would be walking into an ambush....On the brink of the Ford of Daire da Baeth it was that Conchobur fell."[51]

Ath Daire Da Baeth may mean the Long Ford at Daire. Certainly, the Mandeb Strait is a good bit wider than a river ford. All the same, the town of Deire in Scorpion Land is right there on its western bank.

The Ulster Cycle has other interesting stories that address our questions. They do not entirely answer them, but no one else is talking to us. The Irish story of the birth of Conchobur tells us he was the child of *Neith*, an Egyptian Berber war-goddess, who was raped by *Cathbad*, an Arab war-god, a Chaldean fortune-teller.[52] Yet another story tells us he succeeded his stepfather to become the King of the East.

Only the Irish treat any of these stories as history. Even for them it is a struggle. However, the Irish history explains how *Terkinos*' Proclamation could have turned up in Spain. *Terkinos* may be the king of their old enemies, the *Turos*. His victory may have persuaded them to leave. All those references to the *Melman* in the Proclamation may

---

[50] Ibid., vol. VI, 1.
[51] Meyer, *The Death Tales*, 7
[52] Basset, *Le Dialecte de Siyouah*, 59.

have sounded like death sentences and notices of eviction to the Milesians.

Conversely, the Proclamation's bronze plaque gives concrete evidence about the Milesians. It confirms that they did indeed come to Spain from Egypt, carrying priceless historical documents with them. The king of Egypt had invited their ancestor, Nil / Mil, to Egypt because he was an expert in the language of Sokota.[53] They would have been able to read the Botorrita III text. It may be written in that language.

An ancient name for Egypt - Ta Mera / Ta Mela (⊔⊓) might explain why the Irish remember these people as the Milesians. Perhaps they were the Melesians - the Egyptians.

Do we need the Milesians to explain how an African Proclamation traveled from Egypt to Spain? Surely, any plunderer could have carried a bronze plaque from Egypt to Spain at any time. No personal interactions with the Spaniards need have occurred. However, the evidence tells us there were personal interactions and for many centuries.

A coin was minted in 87 BC. It used the Proclamation's 3200 BC language to say *kontebakom bel* - '[issued] by the Lord of Conteba Land'. The Spanish scholar, Carlos Jordán Cólera, at the University of Zaragoza, has documented numerous 'Celtiberian' texts on metal, on stone, on coins, on ceramics.[54]

Not all of his examples belong to the same language as that of the Botorrita III text. Some belong to a different language family. Still, many of his examples are clearly related. Coins only began to be used, anywhere in the world, in the 6th century BC. They were first introduced by a king of Lydia in Turkey.

---

[53] MacAlister, *Lebor Gabála Érenn*, vol. I, 192-193.
[54] Jordán Cólera, "Celtiberian," 823-850.

Several coins in Jordán Cólera's document show words and suffixes used in the Late Uruk period on the Red Sea. For three thousand years, those words continued to be used in Spain. They were used in the same way, with the same meaning until the development of coinage and beyond.

Eleven of the coins show the suffix -*kos* meaning 'lord'. For example, *arkaili-kos,* 'the Lord of Argaela' [has issued this coin]. In the Botorrita III text, *antio-kos* means 'Lord of the Antiu'.

The Antiu were very, very ancient enemies of the Egyptians. They were the people of the Antat, the region between the Nile and the Red Sea. The early kings of the Old Kingdom began a yearly ritual. They called this ritual 'Smashing the Antiu'.[55] In the Botorrita III text, the Antiu are still flourishing, still powerful, unSmashed.

We can lay the *antio-kos* from the Proclamation next to the *arkaili-kos* and *kalakorikos* and *kueliokos* from coins minted in the 6th century BC or later. We see these words in an ancient writing system. They use the same suffix for some 3,000 years. Remarkable! More than remarkable, if you are trying to explain how it occurred.

In another example, the Lord of the *Kalaitos* of *Mturiskum* was one of the Great chiefs, *medukenos,* referenced in the Botorrita III text. *Calaitos* shows up on inscriptions on stone at Peñalba in Spain on Jordán Cólera's list. A Latin inscription for *Madicenus Calaetus* appears on a funerary stele with the image of a warrior on horseback.[56]

People, who spoke the language of the Botorrita III text, lived in Spain for a very long time. They venerated the old heroes. They preserved some understanding of the old written language. The random act of a plunderer dropping a

---

[55] Breasted, *Ancient Records of Egypt*, 159. See Palermo Stone, #104.

[56] Rose, "Text and Image in Celtiberia," 166-169.

About the Botorrita III Inscription

bronze plaque in a foreign land will simply not account for
the range of texts and the periods to which they belong.

The Writing System

Table 1 Celtiberian-English Symbol Table

P	a	I	ba
ϟ	d̲	ʎ	be
⌐	e	Γ	bi
И	i	*	bo
⌐	l	□	bu
Y	m	⋀	ka
И	n	⟨	ke
H	o	⟋	ki
φ	r	X	ko
M	s	☉	ku
↑	u	X	ta
		⬦	te
		Ψ	ti
		Ш	to
		⬓	tu

The Proclamation is written in a version of the Iberian Writing System. An alphabet-syllabary, this system is part alphabet, part syllabary. Note the alphabetic symbols in the left column above. The symbols for syllables are in the right column. It resembles the Phoenician system although most of the symbols are different. The conventional view is that it evolved like most other alphabets from the Phoenician system. That system first appears around 1400 BC.

A different, and, I believe, better explanation comes from Flinders Petrie, an eminent British archaeologist.[57] In the years before World War II, Petrie excavated a large number of major Old Kingdom and PreDynastic sites in Egypt.

Petrie noticed and published 'pot marks'. The 'pot marks' were symbols on pottery shards found at many of his sites. He is known among archaeologists for developing a system of dating archaeological sites. In his system, the pottery was essential in establishing correct dates for his sites. It was used to establish the correct sequence of materials found at the site. Because of that, he and his teams examined, classified and documented the pottery they found very carefully.

These 'pot marks', Petrie believed, were part of a super-set of symbols. Those symbols were used for writing down many languages, among them the Iberian texts.[58] Each language would choose the subset appropriate to its needs.

He believed the 'pot-mark' symbols were older than, and not related to, the Egyptian hieroglyphs. The pottery with 'pot marks' that he found at PreDynastic sites was older than 3000 BC. That convinced him that their writing system must be older than the Phoenician system, where the earliest text does not appear until 1400 BC. However, he claimed that the Phoenician system was related. As with many other languages, the Phoenicians had selected symbols from the original superset to create their alphabet.

Petrie wrote many books documenting his excavations. He often makes the case for the 'pot marks'

---

[57] Petrie, *Making of Egypt*.

[58] Ibid., 83; Ibid., *Formation of the Alphabet*; Ibid., *Royal Tombs of the Earliest Dynasties*, 47; Ibid., *Royal Tombs of the First Dynasty*, 32.

that I have summarized. Books by Petrie like *The Formation of the Alphabet* and *The Making of Egypt* make the case directly. They lay out the evidence clearly, with tables, cross-references and many examples.[59]

Petrie used his pottery fragments to show the 'pot-mark' writing system was used on offerings and merchandise. It identified gods and artisans. What he lacked was a long text in a language that was understandable. The *Terkinos*' Proclamation, found about 50 years after his death, is a kind of 'smoking gun'. It proves that Petrie was right. It provides an example of an entire proclamation, written in PreDynastic times. The Proclamation uses a subset of the 'pot-mark' writing system. That subset, we know, is also a variant of the Iberian writing system.

One difference between the Botorrita script and scripts more closely related to Phoenician may be of interest here. Most of the scripts base the letter **R** on the symbol ᚱ *ras* 'head'. It shows a head with the face turned to one side.

The Botorrita symbol for *R* ᚠ seems to be the Egyptian glyph 𓁷 *'hr'*. It shows a head facing forward. A short vertical line below it, called the stroke determinative, indicates that the symbol stands for the object, which it depicts.[60] In this case *hr* would mean 'face' or 'on, over'.

Terkinos' scribes may have selected the Egyptian symbol for *'hr'* to represent an **R** that had a voiceless, whispering quality, like the **R** in modern Somali.[61] However, to do that, the writers would need to be familiar with both sets of signs, so they could select the symbols that best met their needs. They would have needed to know what a voiceless Somali **R** sounded like. In the

---

[59] Ibid., *Formation of the Alphabet*; Ibid., *Making of Egypt*.
[60] Gardiner, *Egyptian Grammar*, 34.
[61] Appendix A, §2.4.

Proclamation's world of 3236 BC that would have been true. That later scribes in Spain would have known both systems is more doubtful. That they would have felt free to substitute symbols among ancient languages known only from texts is even more doubtful.

Phoenician Origins

The Proclamation sheds new light on the origins of the Phoenicians. They were living in Lebanon when the Greeks wrote about them. The new information from the Proclamation may clarify how the two writing systems, Iberian and Phoenician, are related.

The Botorrita III text is not just a chapter in the history of Lasta. It is not just a story of Lion Kings and Scorpion Kings, although it is that. It is also an important document for Phoenician history. That may explain why the text was preserved over such a long period.

Some of the Phoenicians may have spoken this language. Some may have been able to read it. Many would have valued its account of their ancient history.

How were the linguistic and cultural patterns in the inscriptions in Jordán Cólera's list preserved?[62] We do not know the whole answer. However, we know a few things.

In the I-B text the *Melmunos* attack the Phoenicians of Tyre. The Irish *Book of Invasions* describes the same event as an attack by the children of Nemed, the Numidians, against the Phoenicians of Tyre. Still later, in the Botorrita III text, a Phoenician kingdom in the Eastern Mediterranean including Lebanon is called *Biniskum*. The Phoenicians of Tyre were the allies of the Numidian *Nouida* / Nomida on the Nile Bend and at Petra. Both were conquered by *Terkinos* and his southerners.

---

[62] Jordán Cólera, "Celtiberian," 749-850.

At Ebla in Syria in the 1970's, archaeologists found a text dating to around 2300 BC. The text is from the Old Kingdom period, not quite a thousand years after *Terkinos*. It mentioned a couple that made a trip to their ancestral home of *Bin-ash-ki* to perform a ritual.[63] That may have been a trip to *Biniskum*.

A thousand years after that, in the reign of the Egyptian king Sethos I, 1290-1279 BC, the Amarna tablets describe his invasion of the Eastern Mediterranean. His route passes the *Takhsi*. These Libyan colonists were in the mountains just east of Beirut and Byblos in modern Lebanon.[64]

Again in the thirteenth century BC, the Merneptah stela, describing another Egyptian victory in the Eastern Mediterranean, says, "Desolation is for *Tekhenu*...Plundered is the Canaan with every evil."[65] The reference to *Tekhenu*, like *Takhsi*, and *Tekos of Canaan* in Botorrita III refer to Libyan Berbers, people from Taucheira in western Libya. They live in Canaan among the ancient Phoenicians.

By about 1100 BC, we know Phoenicians had trading colonies in Spain. Later, Phoenicians from Tyre established a colony at Carthage. All around Carthage in Tunisia and eastern Algeria was the kingdom of the Numidian Berbers, cousins, if not descendants, of their old neighbors in Phoenicia. Still later, the Carthaginians, including those North African Numidians, occupied part of Spain for several centuries. This continued presence would have preserved old texts. A language familiar to them would have been used on new artifacts, like coins.

During the Punic Wars between Rome and Carthage, there was fighting in Spain. The shrine / archive

---

[63] Archi, Piacentini, and Pomponio, *ARES II*, 179.

[64] Pritchard, *Atlas of the Bible*, 47.

[65] Ibid., 50.

About the Botorrita III Inscription

that had preserved the Botorrita III Proclamation until then may have been destroyed during those wars. In the *Monumenta*, they suggest it may have been a little later, during the war between Caesar and Pompey.[66]

In the world of the Botorrita III text, the Phoenicians play many roles. Prominent prisoners of war and kings of enemy kingdoms have Phoenician names. Some have Phoenician origins like *Koloutios of Biniskum* and *Tueidunos of Biniskum*. We read about Phoenician settlements in Africa by the *Turaios* of *Litanokum* and the *Useidunos* of Elephant Land.

The Greek-Roman-Turkish geographer, Strabo wrote that the Phoenicians came originally from the Red Sea. He was at least partly right. Three thousand years before Strabo, we find Phoenicians on the Red Sea and in Lebanon.

Carthage was a Phoenician colony. The name of the father of Dido, a famous queen of Carthage, was *Matgenus,* a name, perhaps a title. It resembles the Botorritan title, *medukenos,* and the Somali title, *madax-weyna*.[67] No doubt, he too was a Great Chief.

What is relevant here is that the text reveals Phoenicians who were major actors in kingdoms in Syria, in Egypt, and in Africa as far south as Kerma and Mogadishu. They lived in the same provinces as the *Terkinos*. They had the same rulers. They may have had a common trading language. Such a language would have had common conventions for recording events and documenting transactions. The two writing systems (Iberian and Phoenician) would resemble one another. They would reflect common experiences and values that date from this time.

---

[66] Untermann and Wodtko, *Monumenta Linguarum*, 563.
[67] White, *Ships of Tarshish*, 4, 28, 92.

This does not really differ from the conventional view. What differs is the claim about which writing system was earlier and just how much earlier. I am saying that the Botorritan version of the Iberian writing system used for the Proclamation is very early. It is much earlier than the writing system found in any of the Phoenician texts that have been preserved.

One additional note on a people called the *Bini Rusku*, (possibly, 'the Phoenician *Rus*'). In the Proclamation, they inhabit a territory in southeastern Egypt. Their territory would have been roughly from the Egyptian border to the city of Abydos (1.38). Within that territory, later placenames recall an ancient Phoenician presence. There are placenames like Phoinikon and Ras Benas.

An Old Kingdom inscription describes a battle in this region (near Qusseir) between the *Hr-rusku* and the Egyptian king.[68] *Bini Rusku* in the Proclamation shows us that the name of this people was *Rusku*, 'the Rusha' or 'the Rus'. *Hr-Rusku* would have meant 'Overlord of the *Rus*'. That raises the possibility that the *At-Rusku*, or tribe of the *Rus*, may be the forbearers of the *Et-Rusku*, i.e., the Etruscans. This may be the earliest reference to them.

Bonfante quotes Dionysius of Halicarnassus (1st century BC) as saying that the Etruscans called themselves the *Rasna* or *Rasenna*.[69] *-ana*, and *-na* are plural suffixes used on other names in the Botorrita III text.[70] The text has *albana* for 'Arabs' and *lesana* for 'lands'.

The hereditary kings of the Etruscans were the Tarquins. Their name resembles that of our imperial *Terkinos*. Instead of Terqe, their ancestor is Tarchnas.

---

[68] Lepsius, *Nubische Grammatik*, 87. Contains Pepi, 6th Dynasty, Old Kingdom inscriptions; Krall, *Beiträge zur Geschichte der Blemmyer*, 23.

[69] Bonfante, *Etruscan*, 6, 13.

[70] Appendix A, §5.4, §8.3.

About the Botorrita III Inscription

The homeland of the Etruscans was Turhenia. Strabo notes, "For the Turhenni, who chiefly infested our [Mediterranean] sea, were followed by the Cretans, who succeeded in the haunts and piratical practices of the former people." This puts the Turhenni in the eastern Mediterranean before the rise of the Cretans. However, the Cretans are already mentioned in the Botorrita III text as enemies. That pushes this piratical competition back into the fourth millennium BC, to the period of the Botorrita III text. The Turheni are now in the same places at the same time with the same competitors as the Turani of *Turanikum*.[71] Turhenia is *Turanikum*, written with *hr*, that whispery, voiceless, Botorritan **R**.[72] The point is relevant here because the Etruscan writing system resembles the other two writing systems, Phoenician and Iberian. Scholars suspect it may be related to both of them.

This would not necessarily be the beginning of these writing systems. They may already have been old in the Late Uruk period. All three would trace back to a common place (the Red Sea) at the same time (late 4th millennium BC). At that time, all three would have been subject to a similar cultural and commercial environment.

The Beginning of Writing

The Proclamation forces us to change our account of the beginning of writing. Standard texts tell us the Mesopotamians invented writing. Writing, they say, begins with the cuneiform system of writing in the 4th millennium BC. However, that is no longer early enough to count as the beginning.

The Proclamation shows that the *Terkinos'* alphabetic system of writing already existed at that time as

---

[71] Strabo, *Geography of Strabo*, 197.
[72] Appendix A, §2.4.

a separate system. Writing must have been invented before, perhaps long before, the 4th millennium BC.

Petrie, for example, insists that the Pot Mark writing system is separate from, and much older than the hieroglyphs.[73] However, he notes that no one knows when, where, or who invented the hieroglyphs. They appear elegant and fully developed in the first examples that archaeologists have found from the PreDynastic period. There is rock art, showing many of the hieroglyphic symbols, in the Sudan that goes back to 7000 BC.

Baboons and Bureaucrats

In the text, the province of 'Baboon Land' is just south of *Terkinos'* imperial capital at Axum. Where you have empires and imperial governments, you have bureaucrats. For the Egyptians, the god of scribes and bureaucrats was Thoth, in the form of a baboon. A number of images found in Egypt show Thoth as a baboon inspiring the scribe below him who is writing busily.[74] Thoth, as a scribe, is also the master of the law, the god of contracts and of diplomats.

Perhaps these images preserve a tradition that scribes came from *Bentikum*. They might reflect the period we read about in the Proclamation. Bureaucrats from Baboon Land were sent north to the Nile Bend in *Abokum Turo* to help administer an empire that had just expanded.

---

[73] Petrie, *Making of Egypt*.
[74] Oakes and Gahlin, *Ancient Egypt*, 268, 372; von Dassow, ed., *Egyptian Book of the Dead*, 133.

About the Botorrita III Inscription

Thoth, the God of Bureaucrats

We know that Aramaic was spread all over the Middle East. It reached to Central Asia and India, including an early text of the Christian Bible. Before Aramaic, in the first half of the Third Millennium, scribes all over the Near East wrote in Akkadian. Perhaps the tradition of an official and international scribal language originated in *Bentikum.*

Fenius Farsaid

I have already mentioned the story of Fenius Farsaid in the Irish *Book of Invasions*.[75] If, as I believe, the Milesians carried the Proclamation with them to Spain when they left, that puts a very early date on the parts of the Milesian history that were already written before they left for Spain. In fact, most of the *Book of Invasions* would have been written before the Proclamation, before 3236 BC. Fenius Farsaid and the students at his scribal school would be using writing in an organized way for

---

[75] MacAlister, *Lebor Gabála Érenn*, vol. I, 192-193.

administrative purposes for many centuries before the late 4th millennium BC.

The Botorrita plaques are original sources. As texts they are four thousand years older than any copy we have of the *Book of Invasions*. The copies we have of the *Book of Invasions* are no longer written in the original writing system. However, they tell us about the world in which the Botorrita texts were written. In some cases, the stories in the *Book of Invasions* must be older than either of our texts.

An Ancestral Writing System

The Celtiberian writing system that the Botorrita III text uses is an appropriate writing system for the East Kushitic language of the text. The second, I-B, text may have been written more than a thousand years earlier. It used the same language and the same writing system. However, the set of symbols used in these two texts was designed to be a writing system for a slightly different language, a language closer to Somali.

I suspect that in the original language, *ba, be, bi, bo, bu, ka, ke, ki, ko, ku* and *ta, te, ti, to, tu* were common and important grammatical function words. Each one had a dedicated symbol in the Celtiberian writing system. The symbol would have been a kind of shorthand used for frequent words. For example, the suffix *-ku* (☉), means 'the'. To write *uiriasku*, 'the river' you just add a single symbol, ☉ to the end of *uirias*, 'river'.

In Somali, the syllables *ba, be, bi, bo, bu* are used to mark focus and emphasis, sometimes new information, like an indefinite article ('a, an'). The syllables *ka, ke, ki, ko, ku* and *ta, te, ti, to, tu* are used for definite articles ('the'), demonstrative adjectives ('this, that') and postpositions for words like 'to' and 'in'. The Botorrita III text has the *k-* and *t-* series but lacks the *b-* series used for focus. The original language, the one the writing system was designed for, should have been a language closer to Somali, perhaps spoken in *Tirtanikum*, Ancestor Land. However early the dates for Fenius Farsaid and the language of Sokota, documents in this 'Somali' language for which the writing system was designed will be even earlier.

A Hieroglyphic Loan

At least one of the 'Egyptian' hieroglyphs seems to be a loan glyph from Kushitic to Egyptian. That is the

mountain range sign *KUM* (◠◠), an ancient name for Lasta. Lasta supplied the picture, the pronunciation and both the literal meaning, 'mountain range', and the pun that gives the abstract meaning 'kingdom, country'. For many centuries, the Egyptians used *KUM* as a semantic marker. It marked placenames, but was not pronounced.

Kum is discussed further in the next section of this book, but for now, consider this question. How could such a loan word, a word that for many centuries was not even pronounced, have become attached to so many of the placenames in Egyptian? This loan word may have been the normal suffix for placenames in the Kushitic language of those scribes from *Bentikum*. They would have done most of the writing in the governments of the later *Akhou* dynasties. Perhaps they established scribal traditions that the scribes who came after them preserved.

So far, we have assumed that we can easily read the Botorrita III text. We just needed to clear up a few loose ends in thinking about what it says.

Some people think the language of the Botorrita III text is 'Celtiberian'. The language they call 'Celtiberian' is not a Berber language, spoken by Numidians around Carthage. Their 'Celtiberian' is a mostly undeciphered,

Indo-European language. An Indo-European language may yet be found among the Iberian texts. It is reasonable to think that an ancient text found in Europe would be in a European language. However, Spain is ancient. It has had one foot in the north and one foot in the south since long before our records began. For these two Botorrita texts, we need to look to the south.

DECIPHERING THE TEXT: THE FIVE KEYS

The description of how the text was deciphered is organized around five Keys. The actual decipherment took years and was often messy. However, for a reader with these five keys, all those locked doors should open easily.

First Key

The first key, or crucial insight, was that *Kum* was a placename marker.

Second Key

The second key builds on that. It recognizes that *Kum* is ᗰ, the placename marker in Egyptian. That makes it possible to recognize important, and ancient, Egyptian placenames that are mentioned in the text.

Third Key

The third key looks at the Common Vocabulary. As much as 80% of the vocabulary in most languages are foreign words. Words for placenames, names of foreign peoples, titles of foreign rulers and foreign personal names are particularly likely to be foreign words.

Egyptian provides many ancient words in the text, but there were also words from ancient Sumer, like *kankaikiskum*. This name for Sumer was forgotten, even in Iraq, by the 1st millennium BC, if not earlier. The

113

Deciphering the Full Text: The Five Keys

Proclamation mentions places in the Ancient Near East, like the narrow gorge, called the Siq, leading to the city of Petra in Jordan. There are also words like *Ataiokum*, which resembles the word Ethiopia, which belong in the Red Sea region.

Fourth Key

The fourth key is grammar. You can make a map if you have many placenames, but you need grammar to understand, or even recognize, sentences. Was there an invasion? Who invaded whom? Who is the enemy? Who are allies? Without grammar, even a wonderful map will take you nowhere.

Writers often identify themselves in the beginning or at the very end of a text. Using the placenames from the third key, we see that Lasta in Ethiopia is mentioned in the beginning of the text. The Keren Highlands in Eritrea is mentioned at the very end.

Kushitic languages are spoken in Lasta and in the Keren highlands. Those languages, Bilin and Chamir, have many grammatical features that can be recognized in the language of the text. All three languages are AFTER languages. They have Postpositions, not Prepositions. (Some of their postpositions are used in the text.) The verb comes at the end of the sentence.

By studying the grammar of these, and other, Kushitic languages, it became possible to recognize and translate sentences in the text.

Fifth Key

The Fifth Key is the logical structure. What was the purpose of all these lists of rulers and territories? Using maps and organization charts, we see that rulers have been executed and are being replaced by new rulers. The new boundaries of provinces are described. The word *teudesi*, 'decreed' tells us we are dealing with a decree or a Proclamation. Our narrator has defeated his enemies. He is announcing new rulers. He describes the boundaries of the new territories in his empire.

Step by step we use these keys to assemble all the pieces and we translate the text. A voice that has been silent for 5,000 years speaks to us.

The First Key: *KUM*

The Symbol *KUM*

For the Botorrita III text, the word and suffix *kum* is in several ways the key to enlightenment. Out of 518 words in the text, there are 88 with the suffix *kum*. In several Kushitic languages, *kum* means 'mountain range'. In Bilin, the word is *qum*.[76] In Dhasanac, the word is *gum*.[77]

Egyptian is not a Kushitic language, but the Egyptian hieroglyph shown above is the glyph that marks

'countries, kingdoms'. The symbol ⌒⌒ looks like a drawing of a mountain range. It was the name of Lasta in PreDynastic times. Lasta is deservedly famous for its rows and rows of mountain ranges. Large pots with this sign show up on PreDynastic sites in Egypt.[78]

In Middle Kingdom Egyptian, this hieroglyph affected the meaning but was not pronounced. We can see that it was once pronounced '*kum*' in Egypt because in a few words it does not act as a placename marker. Instead, it tells us what those words sounded like. It tells us that the

---

[76] Reinisch, *Die Bilin-Sprache*, 93.
[77] Sasse, "Dasenech," 203.
[78] Hoffman, *Egypt Before the Pharaohs*, 292.

sound q-m / qum / qem is part of how those words are pronounced. There you can see that the phonetic value was *qum* for:

q-mau, 'miners, woodcutters',

q-m-ḥ, 'to see, to look', and

q-m-ḥ-u, 'leaves, leafwork'.[79]

We also know that someone was pronouncing *kum* as a placename marker because it was exported to other languages. In Sumerian cuneiform, *kum,* written *ki-ma,* is a common placename marker, not as common as native *ki,* but hardly rare. The Sumerian name for 'Ur' is Uriash<u>kum</u>.

In Latin, we find *cum,* pronounced *kum.* If you look through a Latin or bilingual version of *Caesar's Commentaries on the Gallic War*, you can find *Britanicum,* 'land of Britain', alongside *Britania,* 'Britain', plus *Gallicum* and *Gallia, Illyricum* and *Illyria,* and many others.[80]

Among the *Nart* stories from the Caucasus region, there is a story about the wonderful kingdom of *Gum.* The *Nart* hero, Soslan, encounters a man from the mountain of *Gum.* When Soslan searches for Gum, "he passes seven mountains. At the eighth mountain, that was the mountain of *Gum.*"[81]

One of the most curious exports is the English idiom 'kingdom come', as in 'blown to kingdom come'. That sounds like a relic of a time when speakers of English were used to hearing long lists of kingdoms, all ending in come / *kum.* Any old, unspecified kingdom was 'some kingdom come'. All of this, taken together, leads me to suspect that the 88 words ending in *kum* are placenames, names of kingdoms and countries.

---

[79] Budge, *Egyptian Hieroglyphic Dictionary*, 771.
[80] Caesar, *Commentaries on the Gallic War*, 45, 197, 219, 226, 376.
[81] Dumézil, ed., "Soslan et l'Homme du Pays de Gum," 78-81.

The Second Key: Hieroglyphic Placenames

One natural question at this point is: Do any of the Botorrita III placenames correspond to Egyptian hieroglyphic placenames? Indeed, they do.

Table 2 below provides 20 examples. These are some of the easy ones that can mostly be recognized as matches by looking at the pictures.

Abo in Egyptian means 'elephant'. The Egyptians could write this with an elephant symbol ( ) or they could spell it out *a-b-u* and add the elephant for clarity. The province of Elephantine ( ) can be written *Abokum*, which is how it appears in the Botorrita III text or with training wheels as *a-b-ABU-u-KUM* as in the table below.

We mentioned above that an ancient name for Egypt, going back to the Old Kingdom and the *Akhou* before them, was *Muturiskum,* written just like that, four times, in the Botorrita III text. In hieroglyphics, it is written , Vulture (*Mut*), Cobra (*Uris*, uraeus), Land (*kum*).

In the following table, upper case glyphs are semantic determiners. They affect the meaning, but they were not normally pronounced in Middle Kingdom Egyptian. Except for *KUM*, the Botorrita III text does not pronounce them either. Most Romanizations and translations are from Budge.[82] Comments not from Budge are in parentheses.

---

[82] Budge, *Egyptian Hieroglyphic Dictionary*. Note that Budge uses **tch** for English **ch.**

Table 2 Hieroglyphic Placenames in the Proclamation

BOTORRITA	EGYPTIAN HIEROGLYPH	ENGLISH
ⲣ ⲭⲛ̇ⲟⲩ a-bo-i-o-ku-m	A-b-jo-u-KUM	Abydos, Egypt
ⲣ ⲭⲟⲩ a-bo-ku-m	A-b-ABO-u-KUM	Elephantine Egypt
ⲣ ⲟⲛⲟⲩ a-ku-i-ku-m	A-ḫ-au-u-KUM	Aḥau, (Agau Land)
ⲣ ⲅⲛ̇ⲟⲩ a-l-bi-n-o-ku-m	A-l-b-i-no-u-KUM	Arabia
ⲣ ⲙ̇ⲟⲩ a-to-ku-m	Aa-b-tio-KUM	East Land (Aden)
ⲣ ⲧⲙⲩⲟⲩ a-u-s-ti-ku-m	Ḥ-s-t-KUM	foreign land (Lasta)
ⲓ ⲙ̇ⲟⲩ ba-to-ku-m	Baṯ-t	Mendes, Lower Egypt
ⲝⲛ̇ⲩⲟⲩ be-n-ti-ku-m	B-n-ti-KUM-BENTI	Baboon Land
ⲗⲟ ϥⲛ̇ⲟⲩ ka-bu-r-i-ku-m	Q-b-ḫ-u-QEBḪ-Ḫeru-KUM.	Lower Nubia, (Springs of Horus)
ⲗ ϥ ⲅⲛ̇ⲟⲩ ka-r-bi-l-i-ku-m	Ḫ-a-r-b-u-KUM	Sand kingdom, Sheba, Himyar (Charibael)

119

ka-r-u-n-i-ku-m	Heru-An-KUM	Heroonopolis, (Eye of Horus)
ku-l-u-ka-m-i-ku-m	K-a-a-m-KUM	Kaam (Koloe in Kam)
ku-s-ti-ku-m	K-a-sh-t-i-KUM	Kush (Eritrea)
m-a-ke-s-ko-ku-m	Mh-t-AH	Meh - north (Northern Land)
m-u-tu-r-i-s-ku-m	Mut-Uris-KUM	Egypt
s-a-m-i-ku-m	S-m-KUM-SEMUI	Siwa Oasis (in Cattle Land)
te-i-u-a-n-ti-ku-m	Ta-imn-t-KUM	the West Te Amenti
ti-r-ta-n-i-ku-m	Ti-r-ti-r-KUM	Terter (Chercher Mountains, Ethiopia)
	tcha-r-t-TCHART	Mythological scorpion
to-u-ti-n-i-ku-m	To-t-n-no-u- -TN-KUM	Thinis (ancient capital)
u-i-r-i-r-a-s-ku-m	wr-r-sh-MR-KUM	Uererash (Warawar, Lalibela).

The Third Key: The Common Vocabulary

The Botorrita III text has 518 words. 80% of those are placenames, ethnonyms (names of ethnic groups), and titles. Here, as in many languages, such words are foreign words. For us, that helps a lot. It allows us to find many of these words in ancient hieroglyphic and cuneiform texts. We can deduce where we are (Northeastern Africa and the Middle East) and when (the Late Uruk period, 3500-3200 BC).

Many examples of likely foreign words from these categories are given below. (Words marked by * are from the shorter I-B* text. It is translated later in this book.) Note that this vocabulary is coherent. The placenames are not widely nor randomly scattered. They form meaningful subsets. The placenames cluster in ways that are relevant to ancient and on-going patterns of interaction in the region. This is just a sample to let you see how many there are and the patterns they make. All of the words in both texts, plus citations for references and for maps, are in the Glossary.

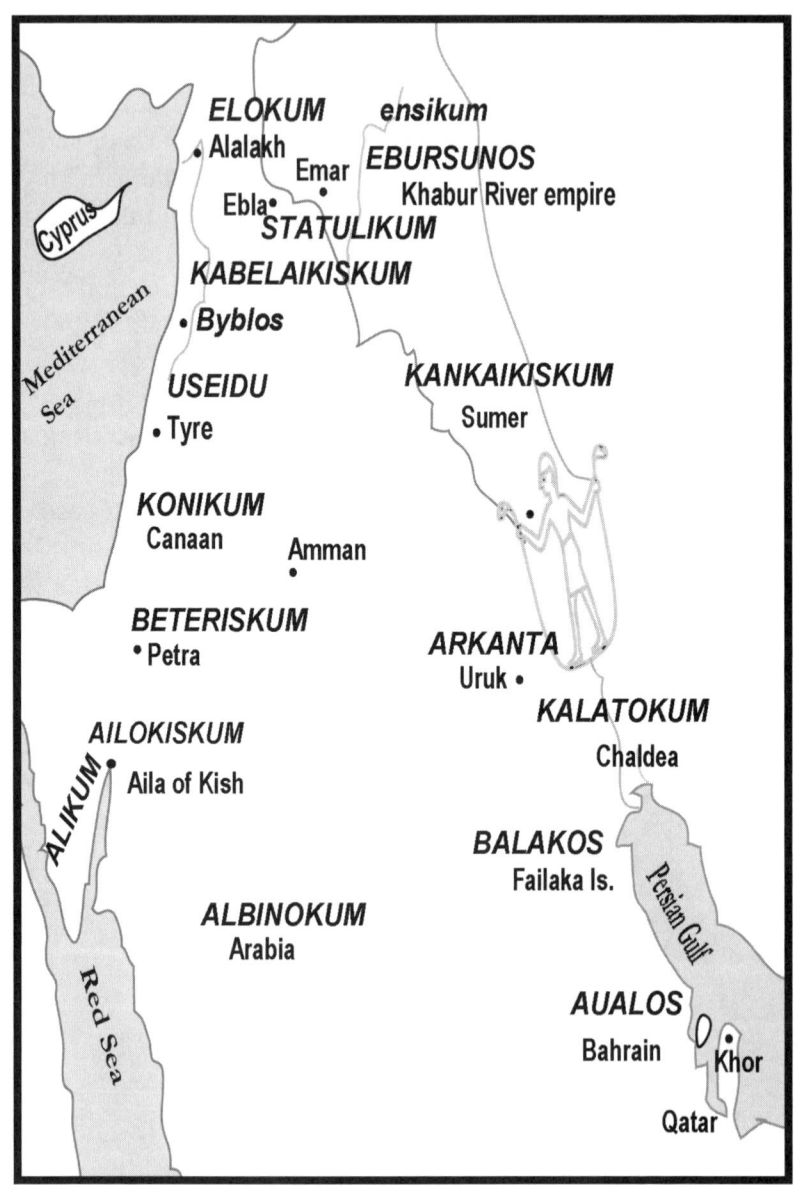

Map 9 Places in the Middle East

1 Placenames and Ethnonyms

1.1 Mesopotamia, Syria, Lebanon, Jordan, Israel, Turkey

Patterns: Many places with ties to Kish, to Uruk and to Chaldea at this time suggest multiple Late Uruk colonies. The Eastern Mediterranean is a battleground. In the I-B text, the Eastern Mediterranean, including Canaan and Lebanon, is controlled by the Libyans down into Northern Arabia. Between the texts, the Chaldeans conquer the region. Then the Red Sea *Turos* defeat the Chaldeans.

   1.1.1 (*burdu*) *Abilikum* - the Fort of Ebla, Syria. In Botorrita III, Chaldeans here are conquered by the *Turos*.
   1.1.2 *Aiankum Tauro** - 'Eye of the Bull'. It includes Cyprus, and Eastern Mediterranean coastal cities. It was ruled by Libyans, then Chaldeans, then *Turos*.
   1.1.3 *Ailokiskum* - 'Aila of Kish' was a colony of Uruk. Its ruins are near Aqaba, Jordan, near a resort at modern Eilat in Israel.
   1.1.4 *Ama* - Amman, Jordan. It was ruled by the Khabur River lord, who is a vassal of Uruk.
   1.1.5 *Arkanta* - a loan translation. It resembles an Akkadian name, *Arkaiitu,* for the Urukites from Uruk in Sumer. In Kushitic languages, the verb *arka,* 'to know', gives it the meaning 'those who know, the wise ones, the wise guys'. In Egyptian, it is *r-kh-y-t,* 'wise ones, fortune-tellers'. It is a pun on the Egyptian word for 'lapwing', *Erkhēye',* those hanging birds on the Scorpion king macehead. Also *mailikum Arkanta* for the kingdom of Uruk and

mailikinokum Arkanta for kingdoms of the
Arkanta.

1.1.6 *Ateskum* - kingdom at the Gulf of Issus with
name similar to Edessa.

1.1.7 *Balakos* - Failaka Island, Kuwait. It was ruled
by the lord of Uruk.

1.1.8 *Beteriskum* - Petra, Jordan.

1.1.9 *Biniskum* - Phoenicia was a name for the
Eastern Mediterranean coast. *Biniskum*
appeared as a client kingdom of Libyan
Loukanikum on the Libyan Palette. However, in
Botorrita III, *Tueidunos* of *Biniskum* is a client
king of Uruk, while *Koloutios* of *Biniskum,* the
former Lord of the Antiu*,* is held prisoner by
the *Turos* at a fortress in Mogadishu.

1.1.10 (*ensikum*) *Ebursunos* - the Khabur River
Empire of the kingdoms of Uruk left ruins at
Tell Brak, Syria.

1.1.11 *Elokum* - Alalakh, Syria. It was taken from
the Chaldeans by the *Turos.*

1.1.12 *Esueiku* - the Gulf of Issus in *Ateskum* was the
northern border of the Chaldean territory
conquered by the *Turos.*

1.1.13 *Kabelaikiskum* - 'The Hill of Kish', is an
ancient name for Byblos, in Lebanon. It was a
colony of Uruk.

1.1.14 *Kalaitos* - Chaldean. See also *Kara
Kalatokum* (Chaldea). Note also Berber *kaldi,
geldi* meaning 'empire'. Chaldeans were in
southern Iraq, Lower Nubia, in Egypt, Eritrea
and the Eastern Mediterranean.

1.1.15 *Kankaikiskum - Kankai* is 'Land, particularly
Sumerian land'.[83] -*kis*- 'Kish, the ancient

---

[83] Hayes, *Manual of Sumerian Grammar*, 60-61, 64, 68-69, 248.

capital of Sumer' makes this 'Sumerian Land of Kish'.[84] This is a very ancient name for Sumer.

1.1.16 *Kara Kalatokum* - was in the vicinity of Charax Spasinu in Chaldea. This was the later Roman province of *Characene*.

1.1.17 *Konikum* - Canaan was a Libyan colony, then under the Chaldeans, then conquered by the *Turos*. The narrator, as the Great Lord of Suakin, rules the *Statulos* of Canaan.

1.1.18 *Kortikos* - was the Lord of Khor, capital city of Qatar, which was under Sumer.

1.1.19 *Sikeia* - the Siq at Petra, Jordan (*Beteriskum*). The Siq is a narrow ravine at the entrance to the city.

1.1.20 *Statulikum** - Astata, with ruins at Emar in Syria, was a large empire with its base in Syria.

1.1.21 S*uros* - people from the salt flats, from the desert, living between Elim in the Sinai and Amman in Jordan. They were ruled by the Khabur River lord, a vassal of Uruk. The word is from *shur*, 'salt'.

1.1.22 *Turaios* - an ethnonym, someone from the city of Tyre, in Lebanon.

1.1.23 *Useidu** - Ushu, the mainland part of Tyre in Lebanon was the Libyan city destroyed by Egyptian *Melman* (Berbers) in I-B.

1.1.24 *Useidunos* - people of *Useidu*. They had other cities in the *Aiankum Tauro* that were attacked by the Greeks in I-B. In Botorrita III, they have a colony in southern Egypt.

---

[84] Appendix A, §2.3.

1.2 Egyptian

Patterns: Egypt is unusually small at this time, but its role is central. The ruler of all of the forces united under Uruk is *Melmanios*, an Egyptian Chaldean. His name says he is an Egyptian Berber. *Terkinos* takes him prisoner. *Terkinos* calls the *Melman* kingdom in northern Egypt 'our captured empire'. The Cattle Land Berbers had Egypt west of the Nile. They also had and lost large territories in Sudan.

Pre-conquest in southeastern Egypt, several great powers seem to have had their own settlements. *Melmanios* had Coptus and the Kharga Oasis. The Phoenicians had settlements. *Terkinos'* people were at Abydos and Thinis. Lower Nubia was ruled by Uruk. The Numidian *Nouida* were also in this region.

In the war, the Egyptians were great losers and great winners. The Egyptian Lord over all of Uruk was captured. Their country was occupied by a new set of conquerors. However, the new rulers unified the country and shining centuries in Egyptian history come just after this time.

Even for the *Melman,* the outcome was mixed. Allies of the southerners like *Tiokenes* did well. For others, life was hard. The Milesian scribes fled to exile in Spain.

No record of *Melmanios* has been found in Egypt. In Iraq, they remember only his name and that he ruled Uruk for 6 years. Only in Ireland is he still remembered. However, what the descendants of those *Melman* refugees remember would surprise him greatly.

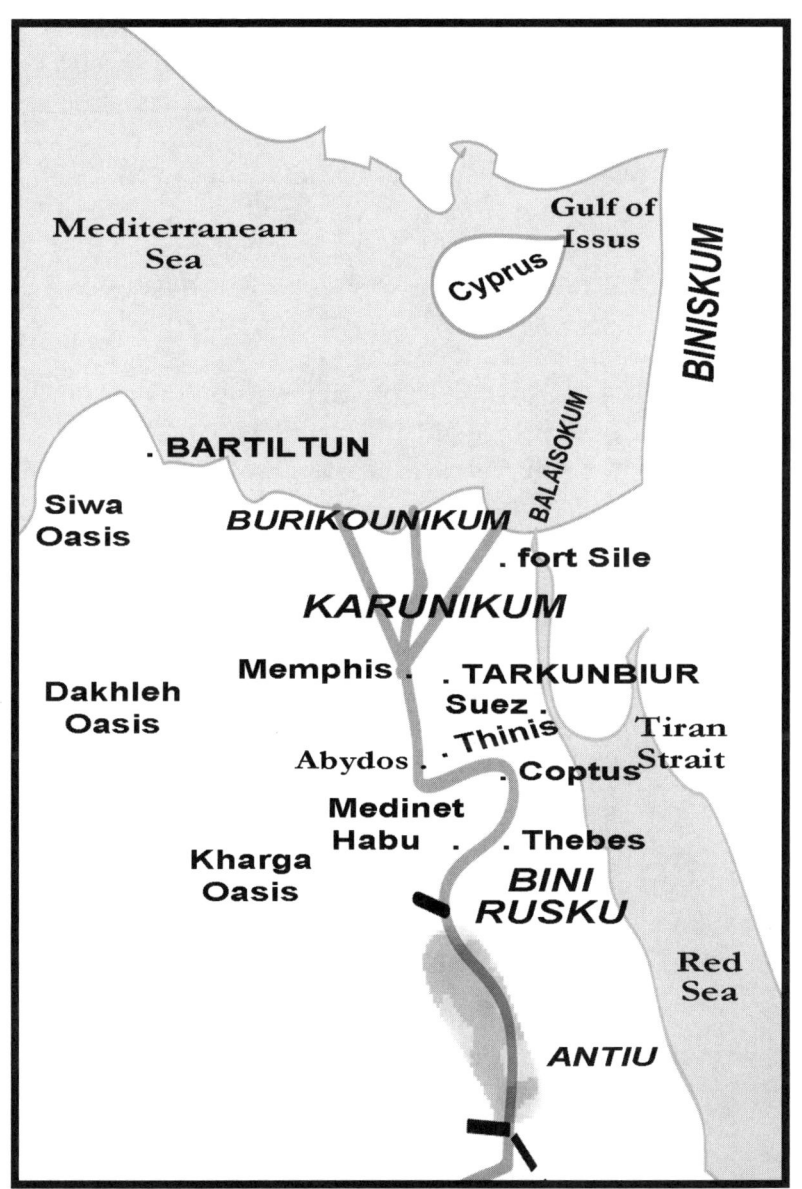

Map 10 Places in Egypt

1.2.1 *Aboiokum* - Abydos is near Thinis in southern Egypt. Some of the *Turo* kings, PreDynastic kings of the last *Akhou* Dynasty at Thinis, are buried here.

1.2.2 *Abokum* - Elephantine, southern Egypt. *Abokum Turo,* Elephant Land, is the territory between the Nile Bend in Egypt and the Buri Peninsula in Eritrea. It replaced and absorbed *Abokum Arkanta,* which was controlled by Uruk.

1.2.3 *Antio-kos* - the 'Lord of the Antiu'. The Antiu were people of the Antat, the region between the Nile and the Red Sea. The Egyptians had a festival called 'Smashing the Antiu' in remembrance of their ancient enemies. In the Proclamation, the Antiu were in *Abokum Arkanta*, the *Melm* (Berber) regions of the River Kingdom and in *Kustikum* (Eritrea). They were ruled by *Melmanios*, the Great King of Sumer, as overlord of *Koloutios*, the Phoenician.

1.2.4 (*burdu*) *Auikum* - (fort) Hibis, in the Kharga Oasis, ruled by *Melmanios*.

1.2.5 *Balaisokum* - Pelusium is in northeastern Egypt on the Mediterranean coast. The *Melman* Lord, held captive at Mogadishu, ruled *Karunikum* from Pelusium to the princes of Western Egypt.

1.2.6 *Bartiltun* - Baretoun. The Roman name was Latin Parætonium. It meant 'the walls, that is, 'the ruins'. The modern name is Mersa Matruh, a western Egyptian port. The lord of the leaders of *Loukanikum* had his court here.

1.2.7 *Batokum* - Mendes, Egyptian *Ba-tet*. Shrine of Osiris as *Ba*, a ram-headed god. On a middle branch of the Nile Delta, in Botorrita III, this was the western border of *Muturiskum* (United Egypt). The king of *Batokum*, who also ruled Cyprus, was hanged at Thinis.

1.2.8 (*burdu*) *Betaskum* - the fort at Umm Ebeida was at the Siwa Oasis.

1.2.9 *Burikounikum* - the Harbor Kingdom was in the Delta on the Mediterranean Sea.

1.2.10 *Ensikum skirtunos* - the captured empire.

1.2.11 *Kabutu* - Coptos, on the Nile Bend in Egypt, was important for trade on the Red Sea. It was ruled by Uruk.

1.2.12 *Kalisokum* - Klusma, 'the beach', is also written Qulzum. It is near Suez. Under the *Turos*, the Great Chief of Klusma (Suez) rules *Karunikum* and the Eastern Mediterranean as far north as the Gulf of Issus on the Turkish border.

1.2.13 *Karunikum* - *Kheru An,* the eye of Horus, Heroonopolis. It included Fort Sile at modern el Qantara in Egypt. It may also have included the Suez region. *Karunikum* was part of *Muturiskum* (United Egypt) which extended to Mendes in the middle of the Nile Delta. The *Turos* took the Eastern Mediterranean by defeating the Chaldeans at Fort *Karunikum* and at the royal fortress of Ebla in northern Syria.

1.2.14 *Matulokum* - Metelis, Egypt, was near modern Damanhur. It was on the western branch of the Nile in the Delta. Its king was hanged at Thinis by the *Turos*.

1.2.15 *Melm, melman, melmando, melmandos, melmanios, melmu*, melmunos** - From Somali: *meel*, 'place, location, land'. *Melm* and its derivatives may all be words that mean 'local, the locals'. In Egypt, 'the locals' should be Egyptians. The *Melman* were probably

Egyptian Berbers. They were powerful in western Egypt where we find the *Marmaridae* in Roman times. They were also in Suez and seem to have had towns far to the south along the Nile. Both the Sumerian name, *Melamanna*, and its Botorrita III version, *Melmanios*, should mean something like 'one of the *Melman*'

1.2.16 *Mturiskum* - Metcher was a name for Egypt, taken from 'the double wall' of Egypt. These were fortifications in the Sile region on the northeastern border. The *Turos* defeat the Chaldeans of *Mturiskum* when they take the Eastern Mediterranean coastal region.

1.2.17 *Muturiskum* (🦅🦶〰️) - United Egypt, the Land of Upper and Lower Egypt. Both before and after Botorrita III times it was a name for all of Egypt, as we know it in modern times. However, in the Botorrita III text, the king of *Muturiskum*, before the *Turos* hanged him, ruled *Karunikum*, which had Fort Sile. His kingdom extended up to Mendes in the middle of the Nile Delta.

1.2.18 *Nouida* - Numidian Berbers in southern Egypt around the Nile Bend. They may have had political connections to the Nabataeans at Petra in Jordan. They are the named enemy in the Botorrita III Proclamation. They may be the people of Naqada.

1.2.19 *Raiokum* - Mit Rahina was the ancient city of Memphis. The *Turos* hanged the king of *Raiokum* at Thinis. Manetho's Third Dynasty of the *Akhou* once had its capital at Memphis.

1.2.20 *Tarkunbiur* - 'Tarkun City', Tarkhan, Egypt. Petrie excavated a PreDynastic site here.

1.2.21 (*burdu*) *Teiuantikum* - the fort of the Western Land was also called (fort) Tjamet and Medinet

Habu. It was across the river from Thebes in southern Egypt.

1.2.22 *Telkaskum* - the Dakhleh Oasis, in western Egypt. *Kalos*, the Great Chief of Cattle Land, held at Axum, was from here. The First Lord of *Telkaskum* is the *Melman* Lord. The Turos hold him at Mogadishu.

1.2.23 *Toutinikum* - Thinis, the capital in southern Egypt of the Fourth Dynasty of the PreDynastic *Akhou*.

1.2.24 *Usidu* - Thebes in southern Egypt was called *Waset* in Egyptian.

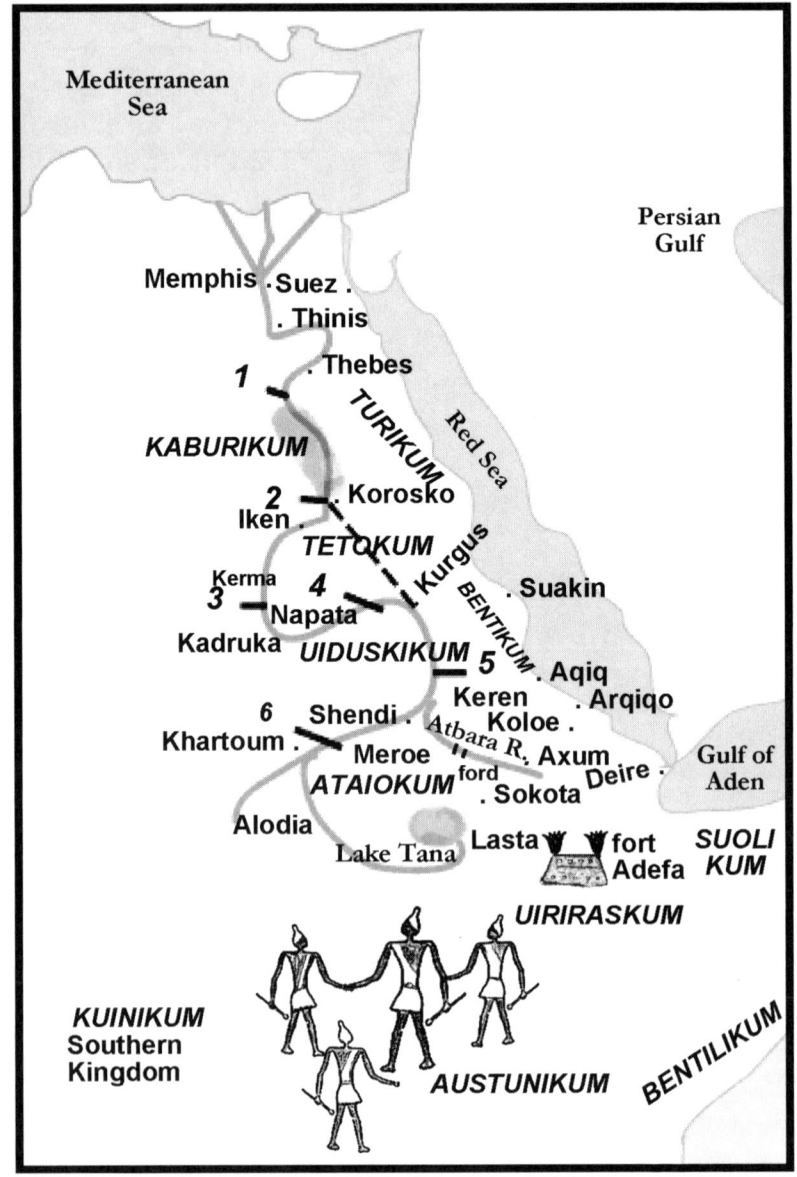

Map 11 Places in Northeast Africa

1.3 African: Sudan, Ethiopia, Eritrea, Djibouti

Patterns: If you compare the Proclamation to the accounts of ancient travelers, *Terkinos* seems to have conquered all the interesting places in the region. Traders and other travelers in the west would follow the Nile, stopping at the major river ports, ruled by his kings. They might decide to bypass the Cataracts by taking the Korosko-Kurgus road, which his kings control.

In the east, travelers sail down the Red Sea from Klusma (the beach) near Suez, stopping at major seaports that he controls, such as Suakin, Aqiq, Ptolemais Theron and Arqiqo. The main route between the Red Sea and the Nile goes from Arqiqo, past his fortress at Koloe, to his capital at the Metropolis of Axum. Just beyond Axum, the Takazze River flows into the Atbara River below the Kemalke Ford, where he rules as king of *Ataiokum*. The Atbara flows into the Nile just south of the 5th Cataract. Ethiopian kings of his hang out at the court of Adefa in Lasta, his own homeland, not far from the source of the Blue Nile.

- 1.3.1 *Akikum* - is Aqiq, a Red Sea port. The narrator is the Great Chief of Aqiq.
- 1.3.2 *Akuikum* - means 'Kingdom of the Agau'. *Akuikum* is ruled by the king of *Akikum* (Aqiq). It includes *Uiduskikum* (Napata), *Austunikum* (Ethiopia and Somalia), *Ataiokum* (Meroe), and *Kustikum* (Eritrea). These are the four main kingdoms of Kush in later centuries.
- 1.3.3 *Alu* - Alodia, the region south of Khartoum between the Blue and White Nile.

1.3.4 *Araiokum* - Cataract Land, from Nubian *ar-e, arr-e*, contains the cataracts of the Nile. The Roman historian, Pliny, mentions the *Aithiopes aroteres* 'the Ethiopian cataracts'.

1.3.5 *Ataiokum* - Incense Land, from *ataio*, 'incense'. The name corresponds to the word 'Ethiopia'. The territory associated with the name is more like Meroe. It is a little further west, and more Nile-centric, than modern Ethiopia. In Egyptian, *atyob,* as well as *atef,* mean 'incense'. The second form appears in *Adefa* (an ancient name of Lalibela), capital of Lasta, in the Central Highlands of Ethiopia.

1.3.6 (*burdu*) *Atauikum* - (fort) Adefa, modern Lalibela, was a fortress near the birthplace of the Nile.

1.3.7 *Austikum* - the 'High Land', Egyptian *Hastikum,* a name for the Lasta region, in Ethiopia.

1.3.8 *Austunikum* - Highlanders' Land was in Ethiopia. It included *Bentilikum* (Somalia).

1.3.9 *Bentikum* - Baboon Land was Dankalia, along the southwestern Red Sea coast (2.58-3.5). It extended from the Buri Peninsula in Eritrea to Djibouti.

1.3.10 *Bentilikum* - the Benadir region. From *Bandar*, meaning 'port'. The Benadir region extends along the Indian Ocean coast of Somalia, including the area around Mogadishu.

1.3.11 *Bilinos* - the Bilin / Bilen, or *bilinux* were the rulers of the River Kingdom. In modern times, they live in the Keren Highlands of Eritrea. Their original homeland is in Lasta in Ethiopia. The *Terkinos*, people of the narrator, are a sub-group of the *Bilinos*.

1.3.12 *Elkueikikum* - *elku* means 'king' so this is 'the royal domain'. The word is preserved in Arqiqo, a port city on the mainland across from the island of Massawa, a port on the Red Sea, in Eritrea.

1.3.13 *Eskutino* - is someone from Sokota in Lasta, Ethiopia.

1.3.14 *Kadarokum* - Kadruka, is south of Kerma on the Nile, in Sudan.

1.3.15 *Kalmiku* - was the Kemalke Ford on the Atbara River.

1.3.16 *Kares* (*ruaku*) to *Korkos* - the villages of Korosko and Kurgis are two ends of a famous desert road that bypasses the Cataract region on the Nile.

1.3.17 *Kari* - was the district around Napata, Sudan.

1.3.18 *Kaukirino* - is a name for the Keren Highlands in Eritrea, from *Kau*, 'highlands, stony rock walls', and *kiriŋo*, 'stony'.

1.3.19 *Kuinikum* - the South Land. It is the kingdom called 'Kueneion' in the Periplus. The name is related to Somali: *koonfer*, 'south'.

1.3.20 (*burdu*) *Kulukamikum* - (fort) Koloe of Kam may be among the ruins of a large fortress at modern Qohaito, Eritrea. This may be the fortress of Lion Land on the Libyan Palette.

1.3.21 *Kurmilokum, Kurmiliokum* - was Kerma, Sudan.

1.3.22 *Kustikum* - is a name for the Gash River region in Eritrea.

1.3.23 *Lestera* - 'a person from Lasta'.

1.3.24 *Suaikinokum* - Suakin is a Red Sea port in Sudan.

1.3.25 *Suola* - was Djibouti (Zeyla).

1.3.26 *Suolikum* - could be Djibouti, or Somalia.

1.3.27 *Talukokum* - the Dal Cataract region in Sudan.

1.3.28 *Tirilokum* - is the region around Deire 'the neck', an ancient town on the western side of the Mandeb Strait, opposite *Ukulikum* (Ocelis, Akila) on the eastern side.

1.3.29 *Tiriu* - were the people of Deire, a town mentioned by Strabo.

1.3.30 *Tirtanikum* - was in the Chercher Mountains and Harar Province. It also included Djibouti. At times, it controlled much of the eastern Red Sea coast.

1.3.31 *Tirtanos* - the people of *Tirtanikum*.

1.3.32 *Tirtobolokum* - *tirto*, 'all', and *bolo*, 'city', so 'all cities or metropolis'.[85] This was Axum, a city in Ethiopia.

1.3.33 *Turanikum* - Ptolemais Theron is on the western Red Sea coast, at or near Aqiq.

1.3.34 *Turikainos* - *tur*, 'fort, citadel', *ikain*, 'Iken, Aken'. This is modern Mirgissa near the 2nd Cataract.

1.3.35 *Turikum* - was a name for the coastal plain of the western Red Sea coast, the *Troglodutike* of the Periplus. This latter term may be an ancient distortion of *Turo Keldi*, 'coastal empire'.

1.3.36 *Turos* - were the people from *Turikum*.

1.3.37 *Turumokum* - Egypt and Sudan, west of the Nile. Umm Durman, the mother of fortresses, is near Khartoum in Sudan, where the White and Blue Nile streams merge.

1.3.38 *Uiduskikum* - is the Bayuda region at the 4th and 5th Cataracts. It includes Napata.

---

[85] Huntingford, *Periplus*, 90. Periplus, in Greek, refers to '*ten metropolin ton Axomiton*' speaking of 'the Metropolis of the Axumites,' referring to Axum in modern Ethiopia.

1.3.39 (*aureiaku tuateres*) *Uiriaskum* - the birthplace of the [Blue Nile and Atbara] streams of the River Kingdom is east of Lake Tana in Ethiopia.

1.3.40 *Uiriraskum* - Lalibela, Lasta, was also called Urvuar and Warawar, in Ethiopia.

1.3.41 *Ustitokum* - This may refer to the Atbara, ancient *Astabara,* a branch of the Nile. The Kemelke Ford (*kalmiku*) is on the Atbara.

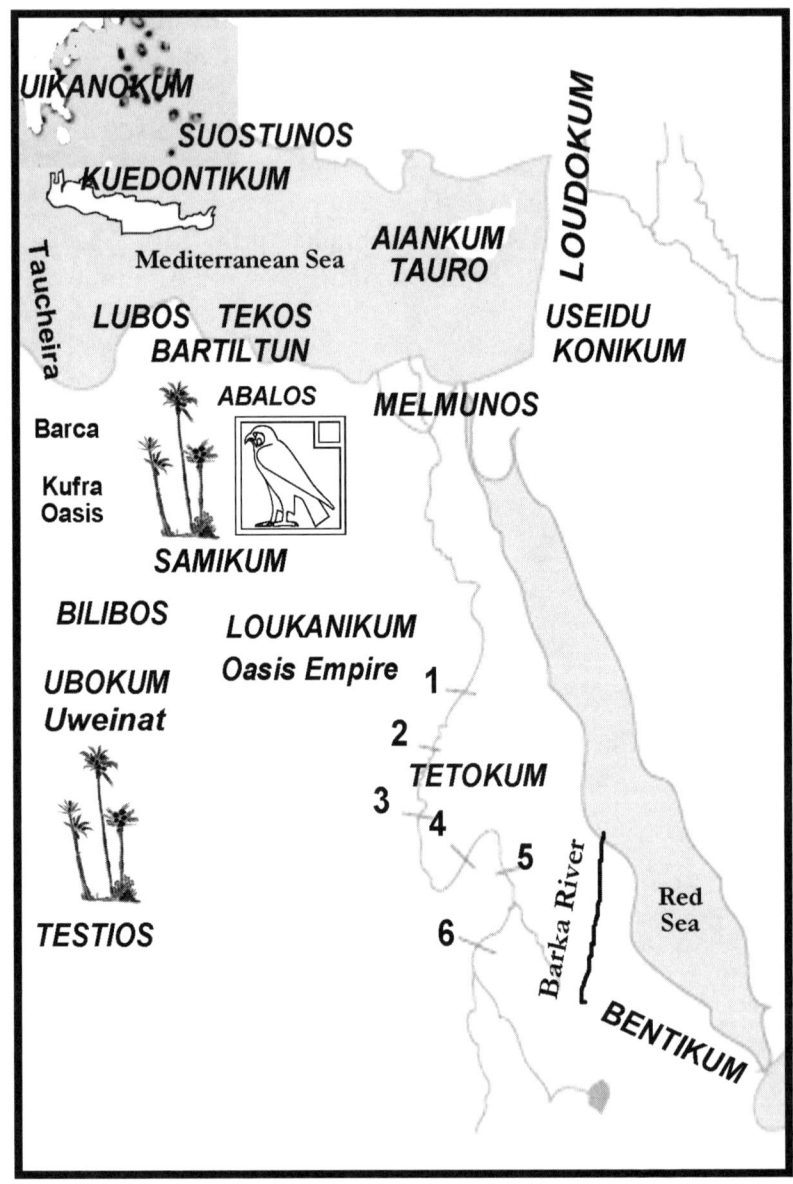

Map 12 Greek and Libyan Places

1.4 Libyan and Greek

Patterns: The placenames of Libya and Greece do not just cluster meaningfully. They tell us things that are new.

The I-B text, unexpectedly, mentions the Achaeans and the Mycenaeans, names for Greeks known from Homer's *Iliad*. In that I-B text, all four of the cities of Crete (Knossos, Gortyn, Lyttus, *Kuedontikum*, 'Kydonia') are Libyan. The Greeks and Egyptians attack the Cretan cities as part of a war with the Libyans. Barca in the Cyrenaica region in western Libya is part of *Melman* Egypt. The Libyans burn it down. Then they burn down all the cities of Egypt down to the Gebel Uweinat. Geography does not tell the whole story but it helps.

In I-B, Egyptian Berber *Melman* conquer the Eastern Mediterranean from the Libyans. Crete is probably still Libyan in Botorrita III times. The princes of Crete are mentioned in the list of abominable lords of enemy lands.

The Libyan Empire was large and powerful. One way to recognize ancient Berber peoples in North Africa and in Egypt is to recognize words for oasis and shebka. They appear repeatedly in their ethnonyms.

1.4.1 *Abalos* - near *Usama Abalos*, [the town / temple] of Apollo, the Most High. Apollo was the [Holy] Son in a family of North Star gods. Three thousand years after this Proclamation, Alexander the Great visited the famous oracle of Apollo near the Siwa Oasis in western Egypt.

1.4.2 *Aiankum Tauro** - was Cyprus, Eye of the Bull Land. It included Crete and the Libyan cities of the Eastern Mediterranean coast, *Esokum*, *Loudokum*, and *Useidu*.

1.4.3 *Akainad** - 'by the Achaeans', the Greeks.

1.4.4 *Alasku* - 'the island', is Cyprus, which was called *Alashiya* in ancient texts.

1.4.5 *Atokum* - meaning 'East Land' and referring to Aden and modern Yemen, from the Berber word *adhou, ado* meaning 'wind, east wind'.

1.4.6 *Bartiltun* - the capital of *Loukanikum* (Berber Egypt). *Tekos* (below) held court as lord of the leaders there.

1.4.7 *Berkantikum** - Barca, the red city, is in modern northwestern Libya. In I-B, when it was part of *Melman* Egypt, the Libyans destroyed it.

1.4.8 *Katunos* - 'Swamp dwellers'. Another ancient Berber people in Egypt were called the *Meshwesh* or *mShausha*. That was also a name that meant 'Swamp dwellers'.[86] *Shausha* is a form of the word for 'shebka', a geologic feature, in North Africa, which is a flat plain, often high in salt. After a rain, the plain becomes a marsh or a shallow lake. *Gaedel*, a name in the Irish documents for the Milesians, when they lived in the Egyptian Delta, also meant 'Swamp dwellers'. Note also *Sekanos* below.

1.4.9 *Kounesikum** - Knossos on Crete.

1.4.10 *Kuedontikum* - Kydonia, a city in Crete. Strabo comments that the name of the city was used as a name for Crete. In Botorrita III, the princes of Kydonia are enemy lords from an enemy land.

1.4.11 *Letikum** - Gortyn on the Lethaeus River in Crete.

---

[86] Basset, *Le Dialecte de Syouah*, 2-3.

1.4.12 *Loudoukum** - was in Laodikea (modern Latakia) a modern province of Syria.

1.4.13 *Loukaniko* River - is the Barka River that flows into the Red Sea near Aqiq, south of Suakin. The Chaldeans of *Kustikum* (Eritrea) may have lived along this river. The region was claimed by the Berbers, before it was conquered by the *Akuia*.

1.4.14 *Loukanikum* - Cattle Land from Chamir: *lukue*, 'cattle'. This empire included most of Egypt and territories in Sudan. The name may be a pun on the name of a Berber alliance such as the Laguatan who fought with the Romans, and even later with Napoleon.

1.4.15 *Lubinad** - 'by the Libyans'.

1.4.16 *Lubos** - Libyans.

1.4.17 *Sekanos* - an ethnonym for Cattle Land Berbers, someone from the Seko (shebka) empire.

1.4.18 (*ensikum*) *Seko* - a shebka empire of North Africa. It was an Oasis Empire. The king of this empire, a commander of *Loukanikum*, was hanged at Thinis.

1.4.19 *Suostunos**- the *Suostunos* of Mycenae were people of the Cyclades Islands just north of Crete. They were often ruled from Samos, so *S[a]mostunos*.

1.4.20 *Tetokum* - Berber: *that*, 'river'. *Tetokum*, 'river land' stretched from the 1st to the 6th Cataract, and east to the seacoast.

1.4.21 *Ubokum Turo*- the Uweinat in Libya, southwest of Egypt, controlled by the *Turos*.

1.4.22 *Uikanokum** - was Mycenae in Greece.

1.4.23 *Ukontad** - 'by the Mycenaeans' who were from *Uikanokum**.

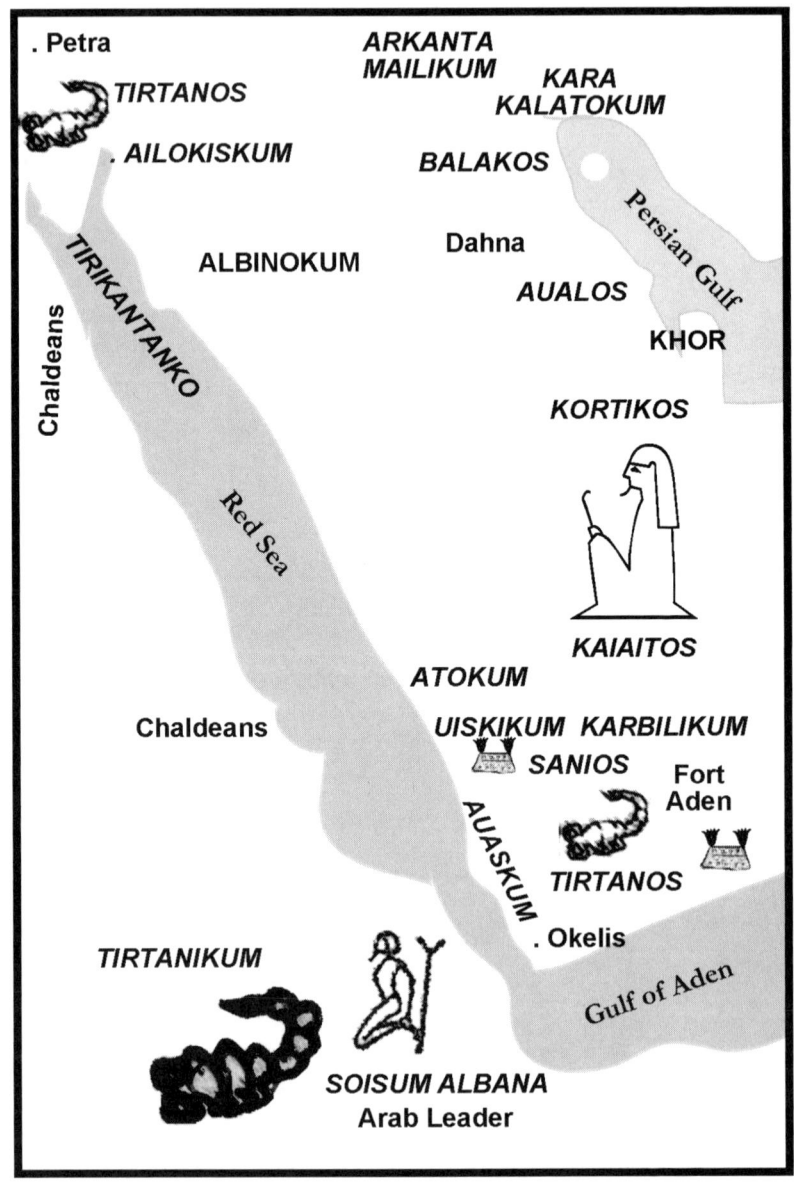

Map 13 Places on the Arabian Peninsula

1.5 The Arabian Peninsula

Patterns: Compared to early texts from Egypt or even
from Mesopotamia, the two Botorrita texts are unusually
rich in references to the Arabian Peninsula. Our maps show
us that the Arabian Peninsula has (at least) three regions.
1. *Albinokum* in the northwest has links to the Eastern
Mediterranean and to the old Libyan Empire, perhaps to
Petra and the Nabataeans as well. The I-B text mentions
some *Tirtanos* (Scorpion Clans) in this region. The Antiu
on the western Red Sea coast may have had links to people
in this region as well.
2. *Ad Dahna*, in the northeast, is a region with strong ties to
Iraq and the Persian Gulf. This is the land of *Kaiaitos* in the
text, of the *Tuatha De Danaan* in the *Book of Invasions*.
The text mentions Chaldeans at Coptus in Egypt, in Lower
Nubia and in Eritrea. Those "Chaldeans" may have come
from southern Iraq. Some may just be coming from Arabia.
3. *Atokum* is the south, (Yemen means 'south'). There were
native Yemeni like the *Sanios* and the *Kasilos*. However,
we also see references to *Terkinos* and *Tirtanos* in Yemen
who have relatives living in Ethiopia and Somalia.

> 1.5.1 *Albana* - Arabs. See also *albinokum.* In
> Botorrita III, the leader of the *Albana* is held
> captive in *Tirtanikum* (Scorpion Land), perhaps
> near Djibouti. He may have been captured
> during the battle for Fort Aden.
> 1.5.2 *Albinokum* - Arabia. The *eladuna albinokum,*
> kings of western Arabia, are the rulers of
> Arabia, Uruk, Chaldea and Sumeria in the
> Botorrita III text (4.16-21).

1.5.3 (*burdu*) *Atokum* - is (fort) Aden, Aden in modern Yemen. This fort was conquered by the Lord of Bahrain and Qatar, *Kaiaitos*, from the Sumerian Land of Kish.

1.5.4 *Atokum* - is East Land, Aden. All references are to southern parts of the Peninsula.

1.5.5 *Aualos* - were people of Bahrain.

1.5.6 *Auaskum* - is the Highlands region in the Habashat region in Yemen.

1.5.7 *Balakos* - Failaka Island in Kuwait.

1.5.8 *Karbilikum* - 'Desert Land' is Sheba and Himyar. An ancient name was Charibael / Kharibael.

1.5.9 *Kasilos* - an ethnonym, for people from Al Jazirah, Yemen, on the coast due west of Sana'a. Somali / Arabic: *gazira, jezira,* 'peninsula, island'.

1.5.10 *Nouantubos** - the *Nouida* and / or the Nabataeans, ancestors of Roman era people of Jordan and northern Arabia. Greeks conquer them in I-B. *Terkinos* has Petra, a later capital of Nabataea, in Botorrita III. The people of the Carthaginian city of Numantia in Spain may have been later cousins.

1.5.11 *Sanios* - people of Sana'a in Yemen.

1.5.12 *Tirikantanko* - 'from the middle of the Tiran Channel'.[87] It is near the Gulf of Aqaba.

1.5.13 (*burdu*) *Uiskikum* - (fort) Mouza is in the eastern district of the Sana'a people of Yemen.[88]

1.5.14 *Uiskikum* - is Mouza in Yemen.

---

[87] Appendix A, §7.1.1.
[88] Appendix A, §6.6.

2 Titles

2.1 Semitic

2.1.1 *bilir* - 'of the lord' from Semitic: *bel, baal.*

2.1.2 *bilo-nikos* - 'lord-king'.

2.1.3 *bilos-ban* - 'evil lord' from Egyptian: *ban,* 'evil, abominable'.

2.1.4 *Bubili-bor* - Babal lord, lord of Old Cairo. For *bor,* see *buria* next.

2.1.5 *buria* - 'lord', in Kassite, a Mesopotamian people, who were not necessarily Semitic. In Basque, *buru* is 'head, chief'.

2.1.6 *mel, mailikum, mailikinokum* - 'king, kingdom, kingdoms'.

2.1.7 *or-bilos* - 'great lord' from Egyptian: *or = wr* which means 'great'.

2.1.8 *sekontios* - 'commander'.

2.1.9 *turtunad* - 'court' or 'of the vizier, chief official', from Assyrian: *turtanu,* 'chief official of the court'.

2.1.10 *turtunta* - 'the vizier, the chief official, the controller' from Assyrian: *turtanu,* 'chief official of the court'.

2.1.11 *urkala* - 'lion' from Babylonian: *ur.gu.la,* 'Leo, the constellation Leo'.

2.1.12 *usama* - 'the most high'. It is a title for a god, from Arabic: *'azim, 'azama,* in *Usama Abalos,* '[Town] of Apollo, the Most High'.

2.2 Egyptian

2.2.1 *ekarbilos* - the 'leader-lord', from Egyptian *heq*, *heqa*, 'leader'.

2.2.2 *kentisku* - 'the foremost one', Egyptian: *khentis*, 'before, upstream, in front of'.

2.2.3 *kenti-sum* - 'foremost leader', is from Egyptian: *kenti*, 'foremost', Amharic: *shum*, 'leader'.

2.2.4 *niskekue* - 'near the king'. *niske* means 'king' from Egyptian *nesu*, 'king', which corresponds to Mesopotamian: ensi, 'governor, client king'. The Botorrita III text has *ensikum*, 'kingdom, empire'. Note also Kassite: *nishakku*, 'mayor, chief seer, high priest'.

2.2.5 *stena, stenu* - 'king', from Egyptian: *s-t-n* (⚘ ◯ 〰 𓏏), 'king of Upper Egypt'.

2.2.6 *sten-iontes* - 'king of the bowmen', *iont*, 'bow'. See also *unstibas*, 'rebel bowmen'.

2.2.7 *tama* - 'lord' from Egyptian: *T-m, T-ma*, 'god, lord, sky god'.

2.2.8 *uiroku* - 'the great [lord]' from Egyptian: *wr*, 'great', with the Kushitic definite article - *ku*.[89]

---

[89] Appendix A, §6.6.

2.3 Libyan and Greek

> 2.3.1 *ekar-bilos* - title of the Cattle Land ruler at
> *Bartiltun.* 'lord of the leaders' is composed of
> Egyptian: *heqa*, 'leader', Semitic: *bilos*, 'lord',
> and Kushitic: *-r*, genitive.
>
> 2.3.2 *ekar-bilos* - if it meant 'lord of the horsemen',
> might be related to Mycenaean: *e-qe-ta*, 'the
> Follower, officer leading a military unit', 'lord
> of the Followers' instead of, or in addition to
> Egyptian: *heqa*, 'leader'.[90] More contexts
> would be needed to be certain.
>
> 2.3.3 *koitina, koitinas, koitu*, 'that king, to that king
> (dative), kings' from Amharic: *geta*, 'lord,
> master, owner', Chamir: *gutya, gueta*, 'king',
> Mycenaean: *lawa-getas*, 'commander, leader of
> the army'.[91]

2.4 African

> 2.4.1 *bilo-nikos* - 'lord king' from Ge'ez and
> Amharic: *negus*, 'king'. Note also Basque:
> *nagusi*, 'owner, head, and boss'.
>
> 2.4.2 *eladuna, eladuno, eladunos* - 'lords' from
> Ge'ez: *Ella Allada,* 'lord of lords'.
>
> 2.4.3 *elku, elkua, elkinos, elkueid, elkuanos* - are
> from Amharic: *alaqa*, 'chief, leader, boss'.
> Notice also the city of *Elkueikikum.*

---

[90] Chadwick, *Decipherment of Linear B*, 106. From tablets found at
Pylos.
[91] Ibid., 112.

2.4.4 *elu* - from Ge'ez : *Ella*, 'he who, lord', Allah.

2.4.5 *-kos* - the suffix means 'lord, owner', as in *antio-kos, korti-kos, elau-kos*, perhaps from Nubian verb: 'to have, to own' and Nubian: *ko*, 'lord, owner'. The suffix is also found in *basilis-kos*, 'client king' in a Blemmye testament written in Greek, and on Celtiberian coins.

2.4.6 *koitina, koitinas, koitu* - 'that king, to that king (dative), kings', from Amharic: *geta*, 'lord, master, owner', Chamir: *gutya, gueta*, 'king'.

2.4.7 *likinos* - 'princes, kings, archbishops' from Ge'ez : *liq*, 'king, prince, chief'.

2.4.8 *medukenos* - 'great chief', from Somali: *madax ka weyna*, 'head the great'.

2.4.9 *miduku* - 'the first' from Somali: *mid*, 'one' and Somali: *-ku*, 'the'. This may be a native Kushitic word, but *mid* has a very limited distribution alongside two other words for 'one'. It may be a loan word.

2.4.10 *retu-k-enos* - 'great-king', 'great man', Shilluk: *Reth*, 'Divine King', Egyptian: *retu*, 'man, person', plus Kushitic: *-ka*, definite article, plus Somali: *weyn*, 'great'. The Shilluk speak a Nilo-Saharan language. They live in Southern Sudan, near the Shilluk River. Collins reports they have distinctive rituals surrounding the Divine King or *Reth*.[92]

---

[92] Collins and Tignor, *Egypt and the Sudan*, 17.

3 Personal Names

3.1 *Kaiaitos - Lugal Kitun / Kidul*, the last king of Uruk in Sumer. This name is known from the Sumerian King List.

3.2 *Kainu of Tirtobolokum - Kainu* of Axum.

3.3 *Kalos of Telkaskum - Kalos* of the Dakhleh Oasis.

3.4 *Koloutios of Biniskum* - Koloutios, the Phoenician. *Kolodi* is the Nubian word for 'seven'. In Roman families, children were named by birth order; Quintius would be the fifth child. Perhaps *Koloutios* was the seventh child.

3.5 *Melmanios of Uiriaskum - Melmanios* of the River Kingdom, *Melamanna*, the second to the last king of Uruk in Sumer. This name is known from the Sumerian King List.

3.6 *Tekos of Konikum - Tekos* of Canaan, one of the Tjekker / Takhsi (from the Libyan colonies) of Canaan. Someone from the Libyan city of Taucheira.

3.7 *Terkinos of Turanikum - Terkinos* of Aqiq (4.38), the Narrator of the text. He is also called *Terkinos of Austikum the Sokotino*, which is *Terkinos* of Sokota in Lasta. Great Chief of Aqiq.

3.8 *Terkinos of Teladokum - Terkinos* of Tjel.

3.9 *Testios of Turumokum - Testios* of Turum Land, from the Tibesti Mountains, West of Egypt. *Ta Sty* in hieroglyphics, the Land of the Bow. The Scorpion King, i.e., the king of Scorpion Land.

3.10 *Tetu of Loukanikum - Tetu,* the Laguatan.

3.11 *Tiokenes of Uiriaskum - Tiokenes* of the River Kingdom.

3.12 *Tueidunos of Biniskum - Tueidunos,* the Phoenician.

So far, the Common Vocabulary has told us where we are and when. Many titles let us know we are talking about rulers and their territories. The placenames and ethnonyms let us identify the major actors: the Red Sea Turos, the Arabs, Uruk, Egypt and the Berbers. To understand the role of the Eastern Mediterranean, we need Grammar from the Fourth Key in the next section.

The Fourth Key: The Language Family

Narrowing the Search

We know from the Common Vocabulary that the text is very ancient. We would like to place it in a language family. That would give us a rough idea of what the grammar might be like. Most of the languages with which we would compare it are more modern. They were first recorded hundreds or thousands of years after our text was written.

One strategy to deal with that gap is to focus on word order. In language families where word order is important, it is usually very stable. Scholars have focused on four features in particular, based on data from many languages.[93]

1) Word order in the sentence.
   a) Verb Subject Object. In Egyptian, Celtic, Hebrew, Arabic and Berber, they say 'Conquered *Tiokenes* the Chaldeans'.
   b) Subject Verb Object. In English, this is '*Tiokenes* conquered the Chaldeans'.
   c) Subject Object Verb. In the Kushitic languages and the language of the text, '*tiokenes kalaitos litu*', '*Tiokenes* the Chaldeans conquered'.
2) Prepositions (as in English) compare to Postpositions (as in Kushitic languages and the language of the text). English and the Berber languages say, '**to** that Arab leader [held] captive in *Tirtanikum*'. The Kushitic languages and the language of the text say, 'leader Arab-that [held]

_____
[93] Greenberg, "Some Universals", 108-110.

captive in *Tirtanikum* **to**' (0.1-1.1), *'soisum albana skirtunos Tirtanikum **l**'*.

3) <u>A</u>N (adjective precedes noun, as in English, 'that-<u>Arab</u> leader') or N<u>A</u> (adjective follows the noun, as in some Kushitic languages and the language of the text, *'soisum <u>alba</u>-na'*, 'leader <u>Arab</u>-that'.

4) N<u>G</u> (when one noun is the possessor (G) and the other noun is the possessed (N), the noun possessed (N) precedes the possessor noun (G). In English, N<u>G</u>, 'the sister of the <u>bride</u>', compares with <u>G</u>N, 'the <u>bride's</u> sister'. English is unusual in having both orders. Most languages just have one. Egyptian and the other Berber languages have N<u>G</u>. The Kushitic languages and the language of the text have <u>G</u>N. *'<u>statulu</u> medukenos'*, 'the <u>Statulu's</u> Great Chief'.

In the Common Vocabulary, there are many Egyptian words, some Berber words, and many words familiar to us from Hebrew and Arabic. However, those languages are structurally BERBER languages with Verb-Subject-Object, <u>pre</u>positions, N<u>A</u> and N<u>G</u>.

We also see many references to Kushitic peoples in the text. We have placenames in the Kushitic traditional homelands. That makes it reasonable to check if the language of the text is a Kushitic language.

Structurally, the Kushitic languages are a good fit. They are Subject-Object-Verb, with <u>post</u>positions, and <u>G</u>N. On adjectives, some are N<u>A</u>, some <u>A</u>N. Afar is both. The Kushitic languages have borrowed many words from both Semitic and Egyptian. They have had ancient and continuing contacts with those peoples. So both the grammatical structure and the diversity in the Common Vocabulary match well with the language of the Botorrita III text.

The scholar Greenberg also looked at word order in common noun-proper noun pairs.[94] He predicted that if a common noun precedes a proper noun ('Lake Michigan' versus 'Reelfoot Lake'), then it is likely that the language will be GN. In the Botorrita III text, the language is GN. There, it is also true that a common noun like 'fort' precedes the placename. An example is *burdu Karunikum*, 'Fort *Karunikum*'.

In fact, the Botorrita III text uses the 'Lake Michigan, or Mr. Smith' model for noun phrases that have the form 'title proper noun'. An example with a title is *stena Muturiskum*, 'a king [of] Egypt'.

Greenberg compared many languages. He grouped them using features that described their basic word order. In his system, the features we described above for the language of the Botorrita III text define Group 24.[95] In that group, along with Nubian and Basque, we have the Kushitic languages, Somali and Afar. The Kushitic languages Chamir and Bilin are in Group 23. Chamir and Bilin have all of the same features except one. They put the adjective before the noun, instead of after it. Kushitic Afar is in both Group 23 and Group 24, because it allows both AN and NA. In the Botorrita III text, possessive adjectives can be AN or NA. All the other adjectives are NA.

Nubian, a Nilo-Saharan language, is spoken in the Nile regions just south of Egypt. It is also in Group 24. Where Nubian differs from Kushitic, it also differs from the language in the Botorrita III text. There are a few Nubian contributions to the Common Vocabulary. You will see them in the Glossary. Still, the grammar of the text is Kushitic, not Nubian.

Basque is also in Group 24. The Celtiberians lived near the Basque homelands in Spain. Basque was not used

---

[94] Ibid., 89 (Universal 23).
[95] Ibid.

to translate this text. The Common Vocabulary of Basque has a long European history. It is very different from the Common Vocabulary we find in the Botorrita III text. Where grammatical patterns in Basque are similar, or appear to be relevant, they have been mentioned.

In modern times, the Bilin, the ancient rulers of the River Kingdom, live in the Keren Highlands. *Terkinos* originally issued his Proclamation there. According to the traditions of the Bilin, their ancestors came from Lasta.[96]

Reinisch's grammars of Bilin and of Chamir compare the two languages directly.[97] He tried to document how they had evolved since the Bilin moved away from Lasta to Keren. He noted that in his time, they were no longer mutually intelligible. However, there were still many parallels structurally and in the vocabulary.

It turns out that it is possible to use the grammars of Bilin and Chamir to translate the Botorrita III text. Using a grammar of modern French to translate Voltaire would be easier. However, it is not nearly as difficult as you might expect. Much in the ancient language of Lasta has been preserved.

The Grammatical Notes in Appendix A give a word for word analysis of each Kushitic morpheme in the text. Taken together they provide a grammar for the language of the text.

I have also referred to two other Kushitic languages: Somali and Dhasanac. Bilin and Chamir are East Kushitic languages. Somali belongs to its own sub-family. Some of the Somali dialects are spoken in the *Tirtano* regions of Djibouti and Harar. Those regions were part of the River Kingdom. The *Tirtanos* have many relationships with the narrator's tribe of *Terkinos*. I could not assume that Somali

---

[96] Reinisch, *Die Bilin-Sprache*, 7.
[97] Ibid.

would be irrelevant in doing a translation. In fact, valuable insights into the text were gained from looking at Somali.

Dhasanac is classified as a Lowland East Kushitic language. It is spoken north and northeast of Lake Turkana.[98] The *Terkinos* may have originated from that region, albeit long before the Botorrita III text was written. Dhasanac is spoken the furthest away from the coast among these languages. I hoped it would be a little less susceptible to Semitic influence. I turned to them several times, hoping to find what the original Kushitic form might have looked like. Two of the Dhasenac pronouns ('I' and 'our') appear in the Botorrita III text.

In other respects, the text resembles the East Kushitic languages most closely. However, this is a time of Kushitic prominence. Leaders speaking a Kushitic language rule a large empire centered on the Red Sea. The languages spoken may not have been East Kushitic so much as a blend of several dialects. The language in the text may have been a kind of regional trade language. It had a Kushitic base and many loan words from trading partners.

---

[98] Tosco, *Dhasanac Language*, 1.

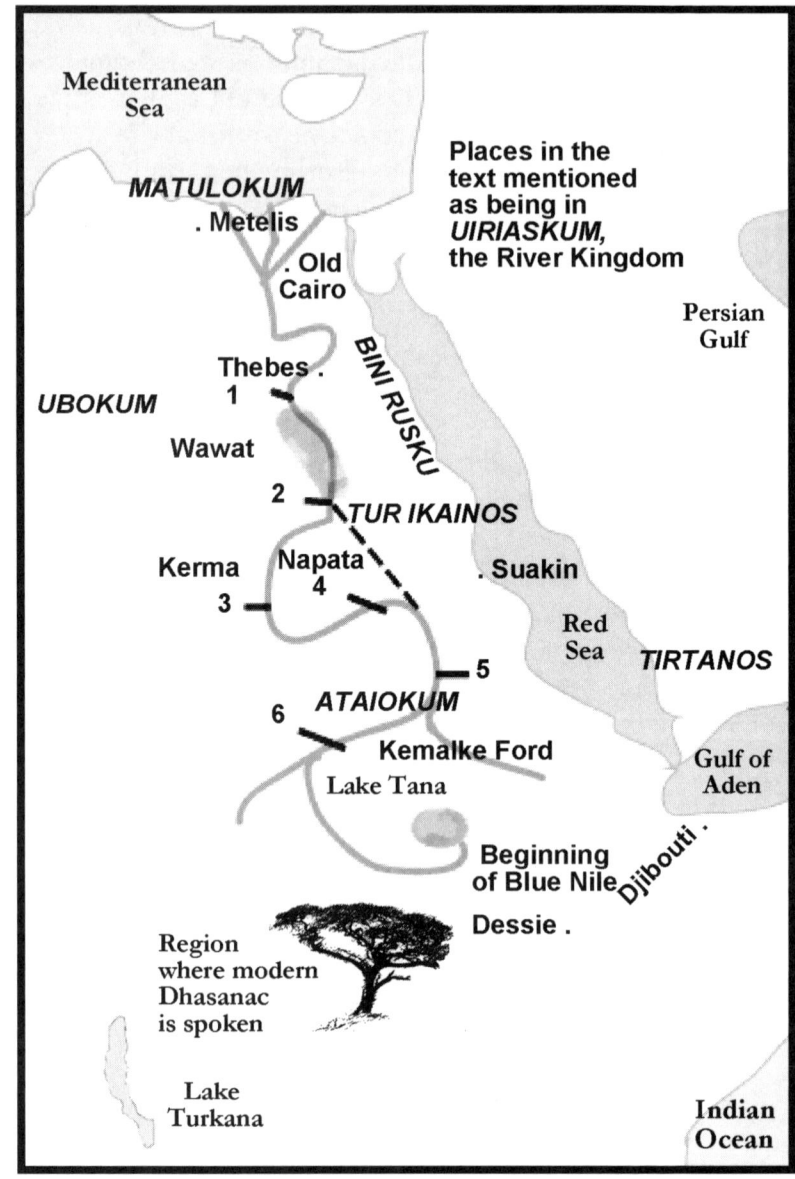

Map 14 Places in the River Kingdom

As I worked on the text, I began to realize that Lasta was the ancient homeland of an important kingdom. Many arrows pointed to Lasta:

1) The narrator of the text is 'a southerner from Lasta'.

2) *Austikum* is the Lasta region on the High Plateau of Ethiopia. The *Bilinos* of *Austikum* rule *Uiriaskum*, the River Kingdom.

3) *Austunikum* (Highlanders' Land) and *Ustitokum* (*Astitokum* - Atbara River Land) refer to other parts of the Ethiopian region that includes Lasta. They cover overlapping, but not identical, parts of that region.

4) Lasta is the kingdom where the Blue Nile begins (*aureiaku tuatereskue*, 'down to the birthplace of the streams') (2.39-40).

5) Abyssinia means Lion Land and is another old name for Lasta. *Absa / Abisse* means 'lion' in Chamir.[99]

6) The Chamir told Reinisch the name of their homeland was *Kam*, as in *Kulu-kam-ikum* in the Botorrita III text.

7) When we discussed the Egyptian Predynastic period earlier, we saw evidence from pottery and from the Scorpion King mace-head, that there was an ancient kingdom called *KUM*. Its symbol was the mountain range glyph. Gardiner, a British Egyptologist, argued that, instead of *KUM*, the mountain range glyph should be pronounced *Has* or *Hasti*.[100] However, I suspect that 'Hastikum' is a way of writing *Austikum* (the High Land, the Plateau). *Austikum* is another name for *Kum*, a description of where it is, what it looks like.

---

[99] Reinisch, *Die ChamirSprache*, vol. CV, 583.
[100] Gardiner, *Egyptian Grammar*, 488.

> *KUM*, I believe, is a hieroglyphic pun on *Kam*. (A picture of a mountain range, *kum*, represents a kingdom in the mountains, *Kam / Kham*.) Inscriptions from later kings of Axum, north of Lasta, mention them fighting with a neighboring people called the *Has* or *Hasti*.
> Dialects in the broader Agau sub-family of Kushitic languages differ between those languages and dialects that pronounce an initial H and those that do not.[101] Bilin adds a 'u' to some words, but Chamir leaves out the 'u'. I believe these dialectical differences explain the difference between *Austikum* and 'Hastikum'.

8) In the Bible, Noah has three sons, Shem, Ham (*Kham*) and Japheth.[102] *Kham* appears to be the legendary ancestor of the ancient, but very real, people of *Kham*.

I mostly avoid giving this language a name, anywhere in this book. Nowhere does the narrator tell us what he calls the language he is speaking. However, if we accept the relevance of the Irish *Book of Invasions*, we can christen it. In that case, we would call it *Skota* or 'the language of Sokota'. That was the language that Fenius Farsaid went to *Turikum* to learn.

By a coincidence that is entirely accidental, Reinisch tells us about the Ethiopian who worked with him to help him learn and document Chamir. He was a very capable young man named Birru from Sokota in Lasta.[103] I have already pointed out that Chamir, as documented by Reinisch and Birru, resembles the language of the Botorrita III text very closely.

---

[101] Appendix A, §2.5.
[102] Genesis 10:1 (New International Version).
[103] Reinisch, *Die ChamirSprache*, vol. CV, 574-575.

The Fifth Key: The Logical Structure

The Organization Chart

Embedded in the Botorrita III text, we can see an organization chart. Without the hangings, the Botorrita III text resembles a corporate restructuring notice. A large corporation would send out a notice like this after a hostile takeover.

After the first batch of hangings, the text says, 'the River Kingdom is ruled by the *Bilinos*. The provinces of the River Kingdom are...' (1.20-22). What follows is a long list of provinces, kingdoms, and their leaders. This list consumes most of the text.

We can create an organization chart of that list, with the narrator, *Terkinos* of *Turanikum*, over all. Let us begin with a list of his titles.

Titles of the Narrator

0.1	one of the southerners of Lasta
1.2-3	the Great King of the *Turos* and *Kontudos*
1.4	the Great Chief of the *Statulu*
1.5	the King, the Great Lord
1.6	our King of Kings
1.60	the Great Chief of *Abokum Turo*
2.4	the Great Chief of *Turanikum*
2.5	the king of the Southern River Kingdom
2.17	the Elephant Lord
2.25-26	the king of *Ataiokum* (Meroe)
2.51-52	King of the *Terkinos* at Thinis
3.21-22	over all of the Western Lands, the First Lord in the Royal Province (*Elkueikikum*) of *Tirtobolokum* (Axum)
3.24-25	the foremost chief in both directions as far as the Afan people [in the south] and the Berta people [in the north].

3.26	From Suakin, [he is] the Great Lord of the *Statulos* of Canaan.
3.27	An *Aunu* from the land of Bes
3.28	the Lord-King of the Kings of Alalakh in Syria
3.29-34	the Great Chief at *Tirtobolokum* (Axum) from Sinai to the Mandeb Strait to Kadruka below the 3rd Cataract on the Nile, to Tanis in our conquered empire on the Mediterranean Sea
4.40	*Terkinos of Turanikum*

1) Since he is the King of the *Terkinos* at Thinis, he has the province of Thinis. He has the *Terkinos* of Southern *Atokum* (Yemen). His cousin, *Terkinos* of *Teladokum* (Tjel) at Tyre is also subject to him.
2) As the Great Chief of Aqiq, he rules the four kingdoms of *Akuikum* (Agau Land). We can add a fifth territory for *Tirilokum* (Deire) (2.12). Under Deire, we need a single territory for the Dahlak Archipelago (2.13).
3) As the Great Lord of Suakin, the King of Suakin reports to him, but indirectly. This king is the commander of the River Kingdom army. He is at the Somali court so he reports directly to *Testios*.
4) As the Great King of the River Kingdom,
   a) he rules *Muturiskum* (Vulture Cobra Land), in northeastern Egypt and Thinis.
   b) As the Great Chief of *Abokum Turo* (Elephant Land), he rules the lands east of the Nile. He also rules the Lebanese trader settlements there. He is the Elephant Lord who rules Baboon Land.
   c) *Tiokenes* of the River Kingdom reports to him. *Tiokenes* rules Western Egypt. He also has Western and Southern Sudan.
5) As the king of the Southern River Kingdom, *Testios of Turumokum* who rules Djibouti is subject to him.

Terkinos speaks of 'our *Tirtanos*' (1.52). *Tirtanikum* (Scorpion Land) may also be subject to him, perhaps part of *Testios'* kingdom (2.58-3.5).

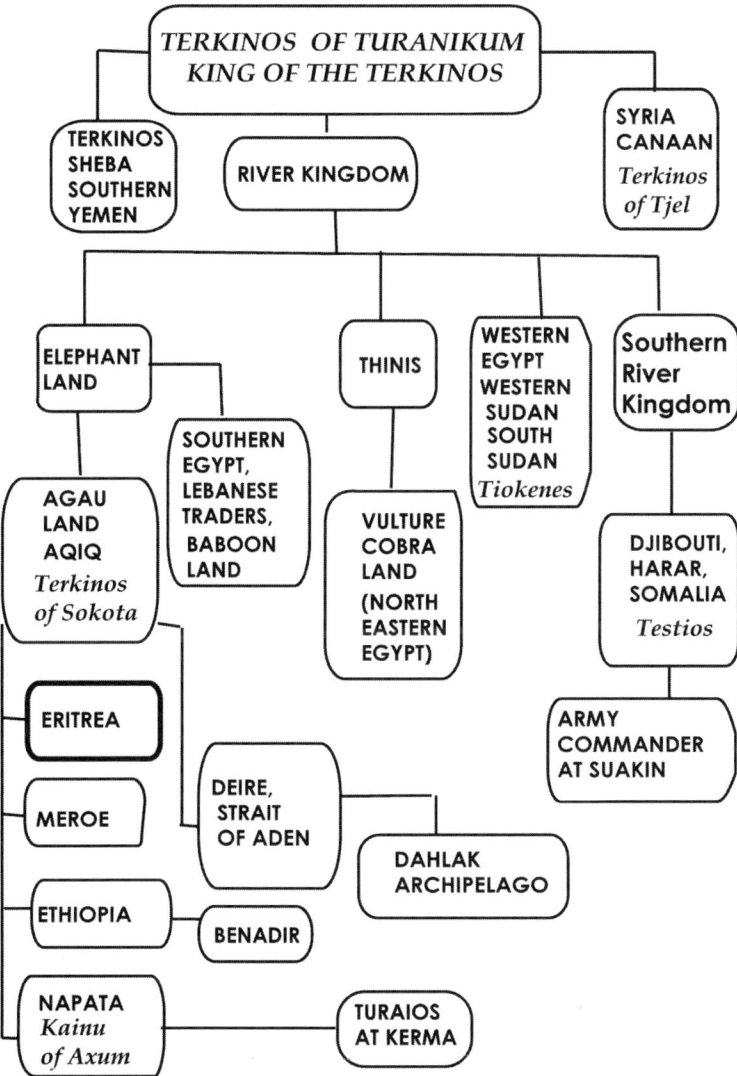

Organization Chart of *Terkinos'* Empire

161

The Abominable Lords of the Enemy Lands

Terkinos also gives us a list of the abominable kings of the enemy lands. There are just two of them, the king of *Kankaikiskum* (Sumer) and the kings of *Kuedontikum* (Crete). This lets us distinguish neighbors from hostile neighbors.

The list of abominable kings of enemy lands does not mention the names of these enemies. It may assume that everyone knows that the king of Uruk in the Late Uruk period <u>is</u> the king of *Kankaikiskum* (Sumer). That means that *Melmanios*, who is the King of Uruk, should be the king of *Kankaikiskum*. That would make him an abominable enemy. He is neither a vassal nor a potential ally. Reporting to *Melmanios* is *Tueidunos*, the Lord King of the Khabur River Empire of Uruk kingdoms.

At the time of the Proclamation, *Melmanios* is probably still alive, but not for long. The king of kings speaks to him, but only to pronounce the verdict. After *Melmanios*, *Kaiaitos* from Qatar and Bahrain becomes the king of Uruk and *Kankaikiskum*.

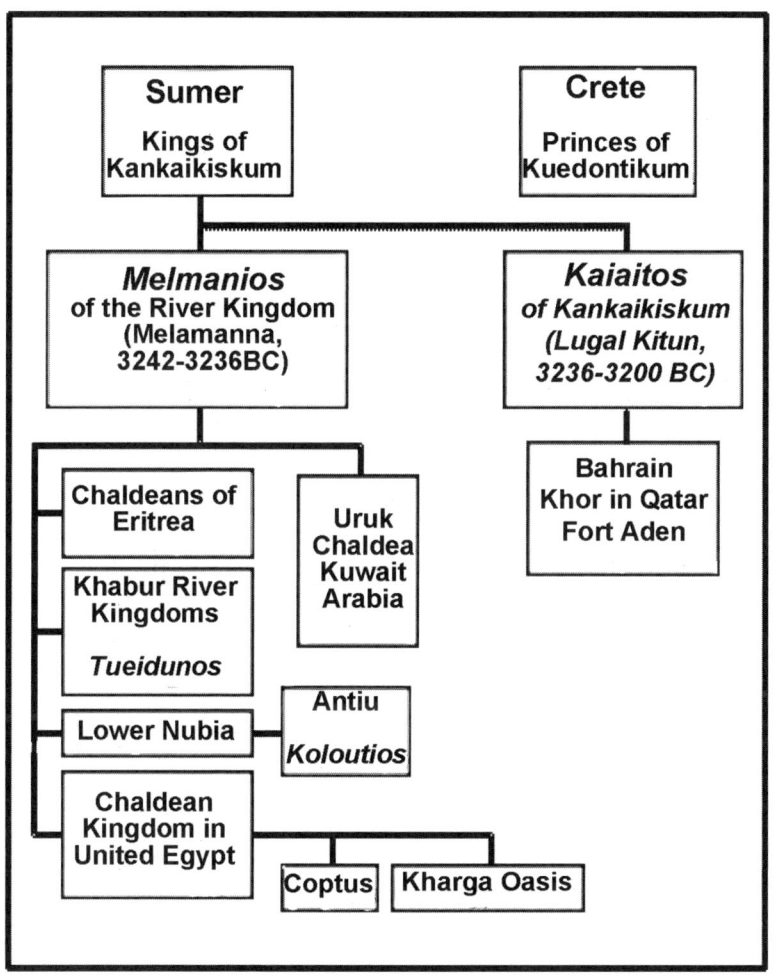

Organization Chart of Enemy Kings

The Capital of the Empire

The capital of this Red Sea Empire was *Tirtobolokum*, the Metropolis. (*Tirto*, 'all' and *bolo*, 'city', gives the meaning 'all cities' or 'metropolis').

The Periplus tells us that Axum was called the 'Metropolis of the people of Axum'.[104] *Tirtobolokum* falls under our narrator, *Terkinos* of *Turanikum*. The text calls him '*the first lord of Tirtobolokum*' (3.22-25). In modern times, Axum is near the border between *Kustikum* (Eritrea) and *Austunikum* (Ethiopia), but in Ethiopia.

The *Terkinos* also had provincial capitals, Thinis in Egypt and Aqiq in *Akuikum*. The later rulers in Thinis built very elaborate tombs for their dead in nearby Abydos.

The full Botorrita III text with a side-by-side, line-by-line translation is in Appendix B. It follows the Grammatical Notes. At this point, you are ready to read this first text. You know the subject matter and the vocabulary. Appendix A will provide the grammar. If you need more information, the lists and tables in Part II will tell you or provide a place to look.

We can also apply these insights to the language of the second text, the one called Botorrita I-B. You can read a translation in the next section, Attack on the Bull's Eye. That new text has more surprises. It opens a second window. You see a new view of yet another part of the ancient world.

---

[104] Huntingford, *Periplus*, 90.

Non-Kushitic Languages in the River Kingdom

The main focus of the Proclamation is on the Kushitic peoples of the River Kingdom and on their empire. Evidence for non-Kushitic peoples is of two kinds:

1) Special vocabulary words, 'loan words'. The best example of this is the word *Reth* from the non-Kushitic Shilluk people. Their word for 'Divine King' may have influenced the word *retukenos* 'Great king' that we find in the Proclamation. Mostly, this approach is difficult because the Proclamation is so old. It becomes hard to distinguish who was the original lender.

2) Evidence of links to Cattle Land for people speaking the Group 1 languages. Berber languages are Group 1 languages. Word order in the Group 1 languages is Verb-Subject-Object, Noun Genitive, and Noun Adjective. They have prepositions.

One of these Group 1 languages is Ge'ez , used widely in Ethiopia for many centuries. It is still the language for the religious documents of Christian Ethiopians. Before Proclamation times, the Loukanians at Aqiq on the Barka River (2.3) may have spoken Ge'ez. Ge'ez titles are used in the Proclamation. That suggests early use of Ge'ez as an administrative language.

Other African languages in Group 1 are Turkana, Masai, Lotuko, Nandi and Didinga. In modern times these languages are spoken in southern Sudan. They are spoken in the border regions between Sudan and Ethiopia. The people are traditionally cattle herding people. Some of these languages are also spoken in Kenya and regions further south.

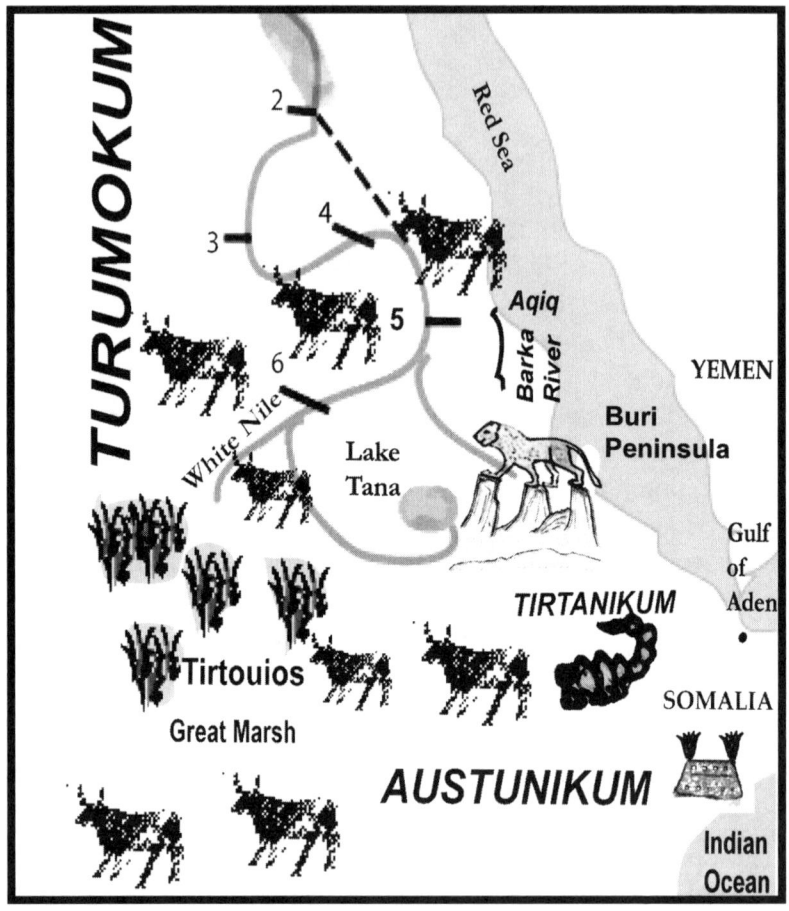

Map 15 Non-Kushitic Languages in the South

In ancient times, the people in southern Sudan and those on the Sudanese-Ethiopian border would have lived in the Southern Kingdoms of Cattle Land as we see them on the Libyan Palette. On the maps, they would have lived in *Austunikum, Turumokum, Tirtanikum* and among the *Tirtouios* on the White Nile. They would have been subjects of *Terkinos,* when he ruled the Southern River Kingdom.

166

Some of these non-Kushitic languages also have vocabulary that suggests contact with the Kushitic languages. In Nandi, a medicine man is an *Orkoiyat*, recalling both Kushitic Chamir: *arqata* 'fortune teller' and the non-Kushitic stargazing *Arkanta* of Uruk[105]

---

[105] Wikipedia Authors, "Nandi People".

ATTACK ON THE BULL'S EYE

Background

On a map, the Eastern
Mediterranean shore takes the shape of a
bull's head in profile. Just where the eye of
the bull would be is the island of Cyprus.
The ancients knew this and called Cyprus
Aian - a Semitic word for 'eye'. *Aiankum
Tauro* means 'Eye of the Bull Land'. *Tauro*
refers to the 'bull', the constellation
Taurus.

The Bull's Eye

**AIANKUM
TAURO**

Actually, it is a little more complicated than that.
For thousands of years, off and on, Cyprus was part of
Cattle Land, a Berber kingdom. The Berbers controlled
large areas in North Africa. They had colonies on the
Eastern Mediterranean shore. They controlled big port
cities like Tyre and Byblos. We are looking here at the
northern part of the world we saw on the Libyan Palette. In
the I-B text we are about to translate, *Aiankum Tauro* refers
to the Libyan / Berber colonies on the Eastern
Mediterranean shore plus Crete and Cyprus.

Aian was also used to mean 'the most important city
or region'. In that sense, it was used as a name for the Suez
Canal region of Egypt.[106]. It included the region along the
coast road north to Gaza. A line of forts was there,
beginning with Sile. [107]

---

[106] Brugsch and Seymour, *History of Egypt*, 252.
[107] Pritchard, *Atlas of the Bible*, 50. Contains a map of the line of forts.

The Egyptian name was *Kheru An Kum*

(🦅 ⬭ ᨒ), 'The Eyes of Horus Land'. The sun (the
falcon) and the moon (the crescent moon) were the eyes of
Horus.

The *Sleitiu* (Fort Sile people) from this region
turned up in the Botorrita III text several times. They are
usually in, or associated with, *Karunikum*, a Botorritan

spelling for *Kheru An Kum* (🦅 ⬭ ᨒ).

In the I-B text, it appears that *Aiankum,* by itself,
refers to *Kheru An Kum* in northeastern Egypt. It is
controlled by the *melmunos*. They are Egyptian Berbers
who have become independent of Libya. They are now
challenging its dominance. *Aiankum Tauro* refers to the
places that are still Libyan colonies, particularly Tyre on
the coast of modern Lebanon.

So, in this I-B text we are about to read, the *Lubos*
(Libyans) control the Lands of the Bull's Eye in the Eastern
Mediterranean. Their opponents, the Egyptian *Melmu,*
control Egypt and the Barca region in modern,
northwestern Libya. The Egyptians attack the cities of the
Bull's Eye. They conquer the Eastern Mediterranean. They
have Greek allies from Mycenae. The Achaeans and
Mycenaeans also attack the Libyan cities, including those
on Crete.

The text is short. If you have a map, the story is
pretty straightforward.

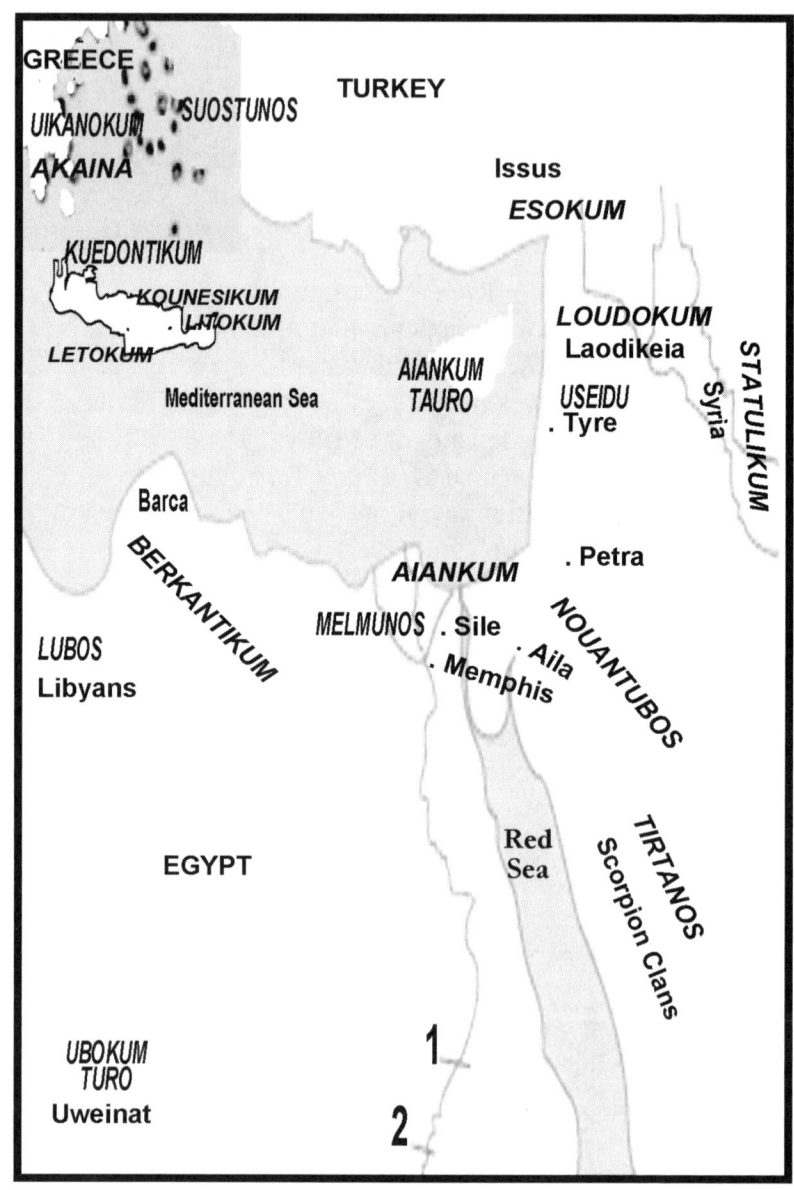

Map 16 Botorrita I-B

Table 3 Botorrita I-B, Text and Translation

1. *lubos kounesikum melmunos bintis letontu litokum* 2. *abulos bintis*	1. Knossos (in Crete) of the Libyans was destroyed by the *Melmunos* (from Egypt) extending to Lyttus (in Crete) 2. where they destroyed the towns.
melmu baraudanko lesunos bintis 3. *letontu ubokum turo bintis lubinad aiu*	The plundered *Melmu* land (Egypt) that was destroyed, 3. extended to the *Turo* Uweinat. It was destroyed by the Libyans.
berkantikum 4. *abulos bintis*	The town of Barca (in modern Libya, but under the Egyptians then), 4. the Libyans burned it down.
tirtu aiankum abulos bintis	They burned down all of the towns in *Aiankum* (northeast Egypt).
abulu loudokum 5. *useidunos bintis akainad*	The *Useidunos'* (Lebanese) cities in *Loudokum* (Laodikea, Syria) were destroyed by the *Akaina* (Achaeans, Greeks?) which extended [the fighting] to

letontu uikanokum suostunos 6. *bintis*	5. *Uikanokum* (Mycenae) where the *Suostunos* were burned out.
tirtanos statulikum lesunos bintis nouantubos 7. *letontu*	6.They (the Greeks) destroyed the land of the *Tirtanos* (Scorpion Clans) of *Statulikum* (Syrian empire) 7. reaching down to the *Nouantubos* (people in Jordan and Northern Arabia).
aiankum melmunos bintis useidu aiankum tauro	*Melman* (Egyptian) *Aiankum* destroyed *Useidu* (Ushu / Tyre) in the *Aiankum Tauro* (Lebanon).
8. *tis abulu aiankum tauro bintis* *letontu letikum abulos bintis* 9. *ukontad letontu*	8. Those cities of the *Aiankum Tauro*, which were destroyed. included the town of *Letikum* (Gortyn on the Lethaeus River in Crete). It was destroyed 9. by the *Ukonta* (Mycenaeans), including
esokum abulos bintis	the town of Issus, which they [also] destroyed.

As you can see, Egypt was quite large at this time. It stretched to the modern southwestern Egyptian border at Gebel Uweinat. Egypt included Barca in the Cyrenaica region of what is modern western Libya.

With assistance from the Greek Achaeans and Mycenaeans, the Egyptians conquer the Libyan port city of Tyre in Canaan. It appears that they seize control of the Eastern Mediterranean. They even conquer a part of northwestern Arabia.

Lines 6-7 provide that reference to Scorpion Clans in northwestern Arabia, mentioned when discussing the Vase Alliance. *Statulikum* was a Syrian Empire based in northern Syria. It could have stretched as far south as Jordan and northwestern Arabia. The *Nouantubos* are likely to have been there around Petra in southern Jordan. There were other *Tirtanos* (Scorpion Clans) near the Mandeb Strait in southern Yemen. However, these *Tirtanos* should have been in the north, nearer to the other places mentioned in the text. The Bible mentions a placename where the border of Edom (Jordan) begins, called the Scorpion Pass.[108] As I understand the text, the Greeks and Egyptians have destroyed a part of northwestern Arabia where some of the Scorpion Clans were settled.

If that brought northwestern Arabia under Egyptian Berber control, it might help us understand some of the later events. In Botorrita III, it would help us to understand how Uruk could have had a ruler with a name that meant 'Egyptian Berber'. This Egyptian Berber ruled the Egyptian *Melman*, the Arabs, the Chaldeans, Sumeria and the *Arkanta* of Uruk. Later history tells us that the Arabs, the Chaldeans and the nearby region around Uruk have shared many adventures and disasters. Missing was a link to the Egyptians and the Berbers.

---

[108] Numbers 34:4, Joshua 15:3, Judges 1:36 (NIV).

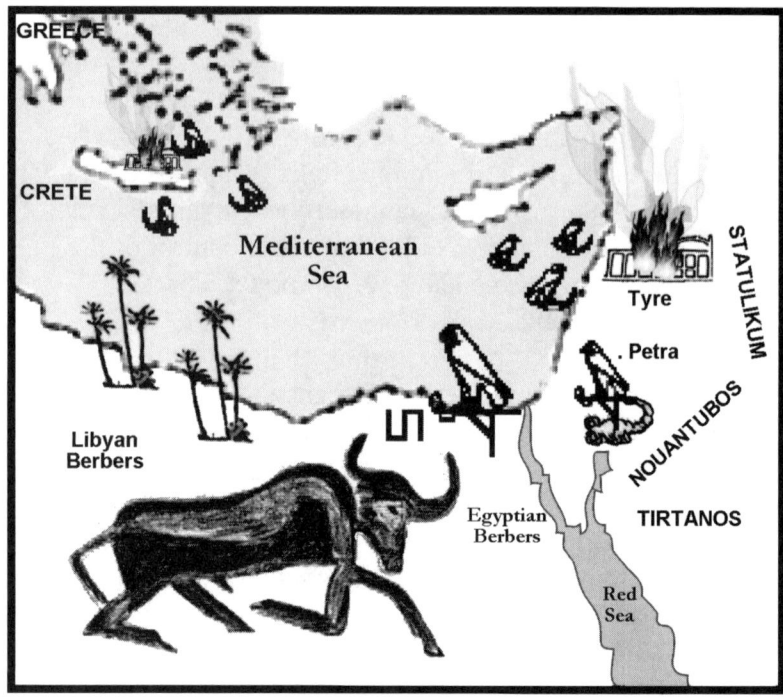

Map 17 The Falcon Clan at War

The Book of Invasions: Looking for a Date

The *Book of Invasions* has six separate histories. They are 1) *Caesra*, 2) *Partolan*, 3) *Nemed*, 4) *Fir Bolg*, 5) *Tuatha de Danaan*, and 6) *Milesians*. The book was compiled by the Milesians, a scribal family descended from Fenius Farsaid. The histories overlap in time, so the 6th book, their family chronicle, begins during the same time as *Caesra*. The family history continues in Egypt until the end of the time of the *Tuatha de Danaan*. *Terkinos'* rise to power sends the *Melman* Milesians into exile. At that point, their story follows them into exile to Spain and later Ireland.

The second history, *Partolan*, tells of the establishment of a large Libyan Empire. This sounds like the time of the Libyan Palette.

The third history, *Nemed*, tells a story very much like the I-B text we just read. Nemed may be the ancestor who gave his name to the *Nouida* (Nomida) and the *Nouantubos*, the Numidians and the Numantians.

Under Nemed, Egypt was independent of Libya. They conquered from Aian to Semne (*Samikum*, the Siwa Oasis). Nemed died of the plague in the Numidian land of Aila in the Litani river region.[109] In the I-B text, we found the *Nouantubos* near Aila.

After his death, the children of Nemed in Egypt conquered the city of Tyre with Greek allies against the Canaanites.

Thirty thousand over the sea, thirty thousand went by land. They went to take Tyre.
They destroyed Canaan and its clans.[110]

In addition to the history in the *Book of Invasions*, the siege of Tyre, also known as the battle of Moytura, is a notable event in several old Irish stories. The Irish remember that their ancestors defeated *Tor* (Tyre). However, after they had destroyed the city and divided up the spoils with the Greeks, things took a turn for the worse.

Not long afterwards, the Lord King of Deled (?*Teladokum*) led a fleet against the men of *Herind* (*Karunikum* in Egypt) from Cetne (?*Kuedontikum*, Cydonia in Crete).

A fleet of 60 ships went hunting the people down.
Of the men of *Herind* in that battle on the sea,
no one was left but one boat with 30 strong men.

---

[109] Best, Bergin, and O'Brien, *Book of Leinster*, lines 615-620, 630-631.
[110] Ibid., lines 639-641.

They left the bodies of the dead outside, covered up, for fear of the plague. The plague killed so many of the *Bitiach* (Lower Egyptians) that the total age of ten women who survived was 60. Some of the leaders sought refuge in Edom (in modern Jordan) with Herdoman, the Arab leader.

Others went to Greece in the thousands. The Greeks attacked them in their mountains wherever they saw them.

Hard was the lot of those who left. Greater still was the suffering of those who stayed.[111]

We are looking at the *Book of Invasions* here to help us date the I-B text. However, trying to put dates on events in the *Book of Invasions* is not for the faint of heart. The absolute dates are almost all corruptions / additions by European scholars in the Middle Ages.

Those scholars assumed that the history of the world began with Adam 6,000 years ago. All events had to be squeezed into those 6,000 years. Their additions are mostly not helpful.

Some of the relative dates in the book may be old. Dates for how long a dynasty lasted may still be reasonable. We use the date of the Proclamation, 3,236 BC, as an absolute date. Then we use those relative dates to work our way back to the time of Nemed, even to the time of Partolan. That gives us the Table of Events below. See the references to MacAlister for issues and variations in these durations.

---

[111] Best, Bergin, and O'Brien, *Book of Leinster*, lines 641-653. These lines are shortened and simplified as translated here.

Table 4 Book of Invasions Chronology

Year Event Started	Event	Years Until Next Event
4978 BC	Partolan establishes Libyan Palette empire. It lasts 550 years.	550
4428 BC	Turos defeat Libyans. After Partolan's defeat, *Herind* is a wasteland for 300 years.	300[112]
4128 BC	Nemed establishes Melman Berber Numidians in Egypt.	400[113]
3728 BC	Siege of Tyre. The seed of Nemed were in Herind for 630 years.	230[114]
3498 BC	Fir Bolg conquer Egypt 230 years after the siege of Tyre. They rule 31 years.	31[115]
3467 BC	Eochaig mag Eirk, Lord of the Accadians of Uruk, conquers the last of the Fir Bolg kings. He rules for 10 years.	10[116]
3457 BC	After him, the Tuatha de Danaan, the Uruk Expansion, rule *Herind* for 221 years.	221[117]
3236 BC	*Turos* under *Terkinos* defeat Uruk and the Numidian descendants of Nemed.	

---

[112] MacAlister, *Lebor Gabala Erenn*, vol. VI, N 81.
[113] Ibid., N 82.
[114] Ibid., N 79, 82, 84, 85.
[115] Best, Bergin, and O'Brien, *Book of Leinster*, lines 877-886.
[116] Ibid., lines 886-890.
[117] MacAlister, *Lebor Gabala Erenn*, vol. VI, N 79.

In *Partolan*, MacAlister has several references to a line that says, "Partolan took *Herind*. He dwelt there 550 years till the *Cynocephali* drove him out."[118] *Cynocephali* is a Greek word that means 'baboons, dog-headed creatures'. MacAlister doubted that this Greek word was in the original. It probably was not, but it may be a copyist's translation of a word that was there. Maybe, he wanted to say 'the people of Baboon Land drove him out'. He did not want to say, 'the baboons drove him out'.

Baboon Land was the western Red Sea coast, the land of the *Turos*. The reference to *Ubokum Turo* (I-B 3, Map 16) confirms that, much later, in Nemed's time, the *Turos* still controlled northern Sudan. The Libyans destroy all the towns in *Aiankum* (Egypt) up to the Egyptian border with the *Turos*. To me that sounds like the line from the *Book of Invasions* is probably correct, in spite of that Greek word.

It also says that it probably was not Nemed who originally defeated the Libyan Empire. That conquest was made by the *Turos*. Three hundred years later, Nemed moves in, perhaps from Jordan, and begins conquering kingdoms in northern Egypt.

In the archaeological record, there is evidence in the Dead Sea region (c. 3800 BC) that trade with Mesopotamia and with Egypt was passing through Jordan.[119]

The *Book of Invasions* is written in Gaelic. The language of the I-B text is still Kushitic. The writing system is the same as Botorrita III. Who would be using the *Akhou* language of Sokota in Egypt so early? I suggested earlier that perhaps the language of Sokota was carried north by the *Terkinos*. They could have introduced the language when they strengthened their Imperial presence at

---

[118] MacAlister, *Lebor Gabala Erenn*, vol. VI, N 83.
[119] Watrin, "From Intellectual Acquisitions," 67.

Thinis. However, here, we have a document written, perhaps, in 3728 BC, long before *Terkinos* and his Proclamation. We do not really know the story of how or why that would have happened. It is possible though that the language of Sokota was adopted very early in that long *Akhou* period. In that case, we find it in the time of Nemed and again in the time of *Terkinos*, because it is still in use.

That would explain another part of the puzzle. Historians like Manetho call the whole period for all five Egyptian dynasties the Time of the *Akhou*. In the *Book of Invasions*, it appears that the southerners only rule Egypt during part of that time. Northerners and local Egyptians rule Egypt in the times of *Partolan*, *Nemed*, the *Fir Bolg* from the Balkans and the Chaldean *Tuatha De Danaan*. So why is the whole period an *Akhou* period?

Perhaps the administrative language was the language of Sokota during the whole period. When later historians looked in their archives and libraries, the documents for this whole block of time would be in the language of Sokota. Later Egyptian documents used a different writing system. The difference would have been obvious at the first glance.

The *Akhou* may still have been a major power throughout this long period. The fate of Partolan's empire reminds us that even a large action by the *Akhou*, like ending an empire, could leave us with very little evidence. However, the amount of direct control they exercised in Egypt does appear to have varied.

Who is the narrator?

The narrator might be one of the Egyptian *Melman*. Recall that this inscription is engraved on a bronze plaque. That would not be a likely medium for announcing breaking news.

If he is looking to the north to *Aiankum*, to the west to *Berkantikum*, to the southwest to *Ubokum* and to the east to the *Tirtanos of Statulikum*, he could be in Memphis. Memphis was an important city for the *Melmunos*. It was sometimes their capital.

His sympathies are not with those who destroyed the 'plundered' *Melmu* lands of Egypt. It seems unlikely that he has given us the Libyan version of this war. This could be the Egyptian version, a press release.

Our narrator writes in the elegant and official language of Lasta. He is stlll blissfully unaware of those reinforcements on the way from Crete. He cheerfully documents the king's successful and entirely justified campaign against the Libyans.

HISTORY LOST AND FOUND AGAIN

We have now translated two lost historical texts. These stories have been added to what may seem like a rich historical treasury.

Does this matter? It might, at least, to some of us.

Without these texts, history begins in the 3rd Millennium BC. The map below shows the world through the eyes of History. It marks places where we have documentary evidence from and about that place at the beginning of history. If you look carefully, you can find the only two small spots, one in Egypt and one for Sumer in Mesopotamia. These two regions have documented stories that go back as far as the 3rd Millennium BC.

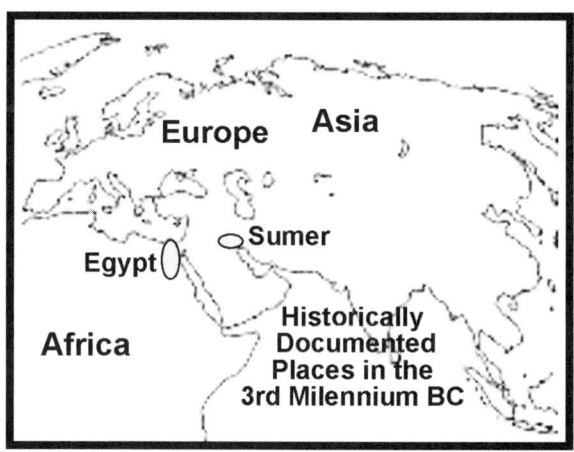

Map 18   World in the 3rd Millennium BC

The two texts from Botorrita move the starting point for history further back in time, roughly a thousand years further back in time, to the 4th Millennium BC. They provide documentation for a center of civilization on the Red Sea. They give us stories, people and placenames for a large area, all around the Red Sea. They confirm the antiquity of the stories in the *Book of Invasions*.

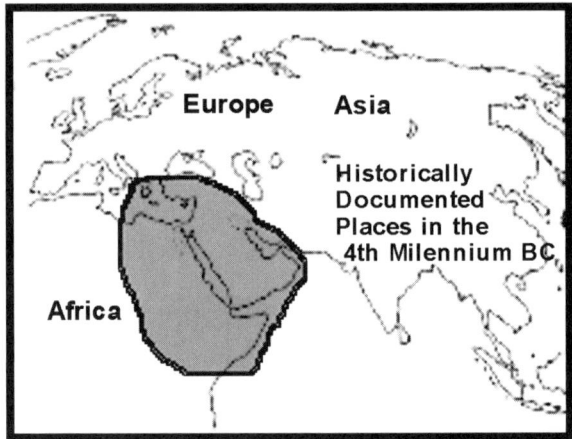

Map 19 World in the 4th Millennium BC

All of those placenames mentioned in these texts now have a history that goes back to at least the Late Uruk period. All those ethnonyms are the names of groups who are ancestors of people living in the world today. Many of them are still living in the regions around the Red Sea. To the extent that we can unravel their stories, they belong to all of us.

PART II

WORKS CITED

Abdel-Massih, Ernest T. *A Reference Grammar of Tamazight: A Comparative Study of the Berber Dialects of Ayt Ayache and Ayt Seghrouchen.* Center for Near Eastern and North African Studies. Ann Arbor: University of Michigan, 1971.

Algaze, Guillermo. *The Uruk World System: The Dynamics of Expansion of Early Mesopotamian Civilization.* Chicago: University of Chicago Press, 1993.

al Idrîsî, Muhammad. *Description de l'Afrique et de l'Espagne.* Arabic text with French translation by R. Dozy et M. J. de Goeje. Leiden: E. J. Brill, 1866. http://books.google.com/books?id=ltUOAAAAQA AJ. (Accessed January 31, 2010).

Archi, Alfonso, Paola Piacentini, and Francesco Pomponio. *ARES II. I Nomi di Luogo dei Testi di Ebla.* Rome: Missione Archeologica Italiani in Siria, 1993.

Autenrieth, Georg. *A Homeric Dictionary.* Norman, OK: University of Oklahoma Press, 1958.

Baines, John and Jaromir Malek. *Cultural Atlas of Ancient Egypt.* Rev. ed. New York: Checkmark Books, 2000.

Balkan, Kemal. *Die Sprache der Kassiten.* Kassitenstudien, vol. 37, no. 1. Translated by Fr. R. Kraus. New Haven, CT: American Oriental Society, 1954.

Gazetteer

Bard, Kathryn A. "The Egyptian PreDynastic: A Review of the Evidence." *Antiquity of Man: Exploring Human Evolution, Gender and Social Organisation.* Reproduced from the *Journal of Field Archaeology* 21, no. 3 (Fall 1994): 265-288. http://www .antiquityofman.com/EgyptianPredynastic.html. (Accessed September 30, 2009).

————. "The Emergence of the Egyptian State (c. 3200-2686 BC)." In *The Oxford History of Ancient Egypt,* ed. Ian Shaw, 61-88. Oxford: Oxford University Press, 2000.

Barraclough, Geoffrey, ed. *Atlas of World History.* Ann Arbor, MI: Borders Press/Harper Collins, 2003.

Basset, René. *Le Dialecte de Syouah.* Publications de l'École des lettres d'Alger. Bulletin de correspondance Africaine 5. Paris: Ernest Leroux, 1890.

Bender, M. Lionel. "Introduction". In *The Non-Semitic Languages of Ethiopia*, ed. M. Lionel Bender, 1-25. Committee on Ethiopian Studies, ed. John Hinnant, no. 5. East Lansing, MI: Michigan State University, 1976.

Best, Richard I., Osborn Bergin, and Michael A. O'Brien eds. *The Book of Leinster, formerly Lebar na Núachongbála.* vol. I. Dublin: Dublin Institute for Advanced Studies, 1954.

Bingen, Jean, Adam Bülow-Jacobsen, Walter. E. H. Cockle, Hélène Cuvigny, Lene Rubinstein, and Wilfried van Rengen. *Mons Claudianus Ostraca Graeca et Latina I (O. Claud. 1 à 190).* Cairo, Egypt: Documents de fouilles de l'Institut Français d'Archéologie Orientale, 1992.

Bliese, Loren. "Afar." In *The Non-Semitic Languages of Ethiopia*, ed. M. Lionel Bender, 133-165. Committee on Ethiopian Studies, ed. John Hinnant, no. 5. East Lansing, MI: Michigan State University, 1976.

Bonfante, Larissa. *Etruscan: Reading the Past*. Berkeley, CA: University of California, 1990.

Breasted, James Henry, ed. *Ancient Records of Egypt*. vol. 1, *The First Through the Seventeenth Dynasties*. Translated by James Henry Breasted. Chicago: University of Chicago Press, 1906.

Brinkman, John A. *A Political History of Post-Kassite Babylonia, 1158-722 BC*. Analecta Orientalia, no. 43. Rome: Pontificium Institutum Biblicum, 1968.

Brugsch, Heinrich Karl and Henry Danby Seymour. *A History of Egypt Under the Pharaohs Derived Entirely from the Monuments*. 2nd ed. Translated by Philip Smith. London: John Murray, 1881.

Brugsch, Heinrich Karl. *Dictionnaire Géographique de l'Ancienne Égypte*. Leipzig, Germany: J. C. Hinrichs, 1879-80. Reprint, New York: Georg Olms Verlag, 1974.

Budge, E. A. Wallis. *An Egyptian Hieroglyphic Dictionary*. vols. I, II. London: John Murray, 1920. Reprint, New York: Dover Publications, 1978.

Caesar, Julius. *Caesar's Commentaries on the Gallic War*. Books I-VII,1st ed. Translated by Frederick Holland Dewey. New York: Translation Publishing, 1918.

Calassanti-Motylinski, Gustave-Adolphe de. *Grammaire, Dialogues et Dictionnaire Touaregs*, ed. René Basset. Algiers: Pierre Fontana,1908.

Gazetteer

Chadwick, John. *The Decipherment of Linear B*. 2nd ed. New York: Cambridge University Press, 1995.

Collins, Robert O. and Robert L. Tignor. *Egypt and the Sudan*. Englewood Cliffs, NJ: Prentice-Hall, 1967.

Cornell, Tim and John Matthews. *Atlas of the Roman World*. New York: Facts on File, 1987.

Crawford, Harriet. *Sumer and the Sumerians*. Cambridge, United Kingdom: Cambridge University Press, 1991.

Dougherty, Raymond Philip. *The Sealand of Arabia*. Yale Oriental Series: Researches, ed. H. Milford, vol. 19. New Haven, CT: Yale University Press, 1932.

Dumézil, Georges, ed. "Soslan et l'Homme du Pays de Gum." In *Le Livre des Héros: Légendes sur les Nartes*, 78-81. Paris: Gallimard, 1965.

Edel, Elmar. *AltÄgyptische Grammatik*. Analecta Orientalia, nos. 34+39. Rome: Pontificium Institutum Biblicum, 1955+1964.

Emery, Walter B. *Archaic Egypt: Culture and Civilization in Egypt Five Thousand Years Ago*. New York: Penguin Books, 1961.

Finkelstein, Joel Jacob. "Mesopotamia." *Journal of Near Eastern Studies* 21 (April 1962): 73-92.

Fleming, Harold C. "Baiso and Rendille: Somali Outliers." *Rassegna di Studi Etiopici*, no. 21 (1964): 35-96.

Gadd, Cyril John. *A Sumerian Reading-Book*. Oxford: Clarendon Press, 1924.

Gardiner, Alan H. *Egypt of the Pharaohs: An Introduction*. New York: Oxford University Press, 1961.

———. *Egyptian Grammar*. 3rd ed. London: Oxford University Press, 1926.

Gelb, Ignace J. *The Assyrian Dictionary*. Chicago: University of Chicago, Oriental Institute, 1956-.

Gimbutas, Marija. *The Goddesses and Gods of Old Europe*. 2nd ed. Los Angeles: University of California Press, 1982.

Gleadow, Rupert. *The Origin of the Zodiac*. New York: Atheneum, 1969.

Gómez-Moreno Martinez, Manuel. "De Epigrafia Ibérica: El Plomo de Alcoya." *Revista de Filologia Española*, no. 9 (1922): 34-36.

Greenberg, Joseph H. "Some Universals of Grammar with Particular Reference to the Order of Meaningful Elements". In *Universals of Language*, ed. Joseph H. Greenberg, 73-113. 2nd ed. Cambridge, MA: MIT Press, 1966.

Guisepi, Robert A. "The Sumerian King List: Translation." *The History of Ancient Sumeria Including Its Cities, Kings and Religions*. Contribution by F. Roy Willis. Project by History World International. http://history-world.org/sumerian_king_list.htm. (Accessed September 4, 2010).

Hammond, Caleb D., Jr. *Hammond's Complete World Atlas*. New York: C. S. Hammond & Co., 1950.

Hayes, John L. *A Manual of Sumerian Grammar*. 2nd ed. Malibu, CA: Undena Publications, 2000.

Helck, Wolfgang. *Die Beziehungen Agyptens zu Vorderasien im 3 und 2 Jahrtausend V. Chr.* Wiesbaden, Germany: Otto Harrassowitz, 1962.

Gazetteer

Herodotus. *The Persian Wars*. Translated by George Rawlinson. IV. New York: Random House, 1942.

Hintze, Fritz. "Preliminary Report of the Butana Expedition 1958 made by the Institute for Egyptology of the Humboldt University, Berlin." Translated by Cicely Morgan. *Kush* 7 (1959): 171-196.

Hoffman, Michael H. *Egypt Before the Pharaohs: The Prehistoric Foundations of Egyptian Civilization*. New York: Knopf, 1979.

Homer. *The Iliad*. Translated by A.T. Murray. Loeb Classical Library. LCL 171. Cambridge, MA: Harvard University Press, 2001.

Honoré, Emmanuelle. "Earliest Cylinder-Seal Glyptic in Egypt: From Greater Mesopotamia to Naqada." In The International Conference on Heritage of Naqada and Qus Region, ed. H. Hanna, vol. I, 31-45. Naqada, Egypt: January 22-28, 2007. http://grepal.free.fr/articles/emmanuelle_honore_ico m_anglais.pdf. (Accessed September 15, 2010).

Hornemann, Friedrich. *The Journal of Frederick Horneman's Travels: From Cairo to Mourzouk, the Capital of the Kingdom of Fezzan, in Africa, in the Years 1797-8*. London: Darf, 1985.

Horowitz, Wayne. *Mesopotamian Cosmic Geography*. Mesopotamian Civilizations, vol. 8. Winona Lake, IN: Eisenbrauns, 1998.

Huntingford, George Wynn Bereton, ed. *The Periplus of the Erythraean Sea*. London: Hakluyt Society, 1980.

Ibn Khaldoun. *Histoire des Berbères et des Dynasties Musulmanes de l'Afrique Septentrionale*. Translated by M. Le Baron de Slane. vol. 4. Algiers: Imprimerie du Gouvernement, 1856. http://books.google.com/books?id=kyBO8X1WQd UC&pg=PA1&dq=Ibn+Khaldoun+Histoire+des+B erb%C3%A8res+et+des+Dynasties+Musulmanes+d e+Septentrionale+4+1856+l%E2%80%99Afrique+i nauthor:Ibn+inauthor:Khaldoun&hl=en&ei=tFaET OD2OYOClAf45KCQDg&sa=X&oi=book_result& ct=result&resnum=1&ved=0CCcQ6AEwAA#v=on epage&q&f=false . (Accessed August 31, 2010).

Jackson, Robert B. *At Empire's Edge: Exploring Rome's Egyptian Frontier*. New Haven, CT: Yale University Press, 2002.

Jordán Cólera, Carlos. "Celtiberian." *e-Keltoi Journal of Interdisciplinary Celtic Studies* 6. The Celts in the Iberian Peninsula (March 16, 2007): 749-850. http://www4.uwm.edu/celtic/ekeltoi/volumes/vol6/ 6_17/jordan_6_17.pdf. (Accessed May 5, 2009).

Junker, Hermann. *Bericht über die Grabungen der Kaiserlichen Akademie der Wissenchaften in Wien auf dem Friedhof in Turah,* Winter 1909-1910. Denkschrift der Kaiserlichen Akademie der Wissenschaften. vol. 56, no. 1. Vienna: Alfred Hölder, 1912.

Kamil, Mohamed Hassan. *Parlons Afar: Langue et Culture*. Paris: L'Harmattan, 2004.

Kobishchanov, Yuri M. *Axum*. Edited by Joseph W. Michels. Translated by Lorraine T. Kapitanoff. University Park, PA: Pennsylvania State University Press, 1979.

Krall, Jakob. *Beiträge zur Geschichte der Blemmyer und Nubier*. Denkschriften der Phil.-Hist. Classe der Kais. Akademie der Wissenchaften, vol. XLVI. Vienna: 1898.

Kramer, Samuel Noah. *The Sumerians: Their History, Culture, and Characters*. Chicago: University of Chicago Press, 1963.

Lambdin, Thomas O. *Introduction to Sahidic Coptic: A New Coptic Grammar*. Macon, GA: Mercer University Press, 1983.

Lepsius, Karl Richard. *Discoveries in Egypt, Ethiopia and the Sinai Peninsula, in the Years 1842-1845*. ed. Kenneth R. H. Mackenzie, 2nd ed. London: Richard Bentley, 1853.

_____. *Nubische Grammatik mit einer Einleitung über die Völker und Sprachen Afrikas*. Berlin: Verlag von Wilhelm Hertz, 1880.

Leslau, Wolf. *Concise Amharic Dictionary*. Los Angeles: University of California Press, 1976.

————. *Concise Dictionary of Ge'ez (Classical Ethiopic)*. Wiesbaden, Germany: Otto Harrassowitz, 1989.

MacAlister, Robert Alexander Stewart, ed. and translator. *Lebor Gabála Érenn, The Book of the Taking of Ireland*. vol. I. Dublin: The Irish Texts Society, 1938.

————. *Lebor Gabála Érenn, The Book of the Taking of Ireland: Index*. Compiled by Michael Murphy. Introduction, vol. VI. Dublin: The Irish Texts Society, 2008. http://www.ucc.ie./celt/LGintro.pdf. (Accessed January 7, 2010).

Manetho. *Manetho*. Translated by W. G. Waddell. Cambridge, MA: Harvard University Press, 1964.

Mattingly, David J. "The Laguatan: A Libyan Tribal Confederation in the Late Roman Empire." *Libyan Studies: Annual report of the Society for Libyan Studies*, 14 (1983): 96-108.

McCarus, Ernest N. and Adil I. Yacoub, eds. *Contemporary Arabic Readers*. Ann Arbor, MI: University of Michigan Press, 1963.

Menéndez Pidal, Ramón. *Primera Crónica General de España*. Madrid: Editorial Gredos, 1955.

Meyer, Kuno. *The Death-Tales of the Ulster Heroes.* Royal Irish Academy, Todd Lecture Series XIV. Dublin: Hodge, Figgs and Co., Ltd., 1906.

———, ed. "*Über die Älteste Irische Dichtung I: Rythmische Alliterierende Reimstrophen.*" Abhandlungen der königlichen Preussischen Akademie der Wissenschaften. Phil.-Hist. Klasse 6. Berlin: Verlag der königlichen Akademie der Wissenschaften, 1913.

Michelena, Luis. *Fonética histórica vasca.* 2nd ed. San Sebastián, Spain: Diputación Provincial de Guipúzcoa, 1976.

Midant-Reynes, Béatrix. "The Naqada Period." In *The Oxford History of Ancient Egypt,* ed. Ian Shaw, 44-60. Oxford: Oxford University Press, 2000.

Milstein, Mati. "Antiquities Under Fire." *Archaeology* 62, no. 3 (May/June, 2009): 31-33.

Moorehead, Alan. *The Blue Nile*. New York: Harper & Row, 1972.

————. *The White Nile*. New York: Harper & Row, 1971.

Morkot, Robert G. *The Black Pharaohs: Egypt's Nubian Rulers*. London: Rubicon Press, 2000.

Munro-Hay, Stuart C. *Ethiopia, the Unknown Land: A Cultural and Historical Guide*. New York: I. B. Tauris & Co, 2002.

Munzinger, Werner. *Ũeber die Sitten und das Recht der Bogos*. Winterthur, Switzerland: J. Wurster, 1859.

Musil, Alois. *[Maps of] Northern Arabia*. Oriental Explorations and Studies, nos. 1-4. New York: American Geographical Society, 1928.

Nashef, Khaled. *Die Orts und Gewässernamen der mittelbabylonischen und mittelassyrischen Zeit*. Repertoire Geographique des Textes Cuneiformes, vol. 5. Weisbaden, Germany: Ludwig Reichert Ferlag, 1982.

Naville, Edouard. "Les Plus Anciens Monuments Egyptiens." *Recueil de Travaux* XXIV (1902): 105-123.

Nesmenser. "The Temehu Tribes of Ancient Libya." By www.temehu.com, 2008. http://www.temehu.com/Temehu.htm. (Accessed December 27, 2008).

Oakes, Lorna and Lucia Gahlin. *Ancient Egypt: An Illustrated Reference to the Myths, Religions, Pyramids and Temples of the Land of the Pharaohs*. New York: Barnes & Noble, 2006.

Obenga, Théophile. *L'Afrique dans l'Antiquité*. Egypte pharaonique, afrique noire. Paris: Présence Africaine, 1973.

O'Connor, David. "The Locations of Yam and Kush and Their Historical Implications." *Journal of the American Research Center in Egypt* 23 (1986): 27-50.

Petrie Museum Of Egyptian Archaeology, Digital Egypt for Universities, University College London, 2001. "Chronology of the Naqada Period." http://www.digitalegypt.ucl.ac.uk/naqadan/chronology.html. (Accessed October 4, 2009).

Petrie, W. M. Flinders. *The Formation of the Alphabet.* British School of Archaeology Egyptian Studies Series, vol. III. London: Macmillan, 1912.

―――. *The Making of Egypt.* London: Sheldon Press, 1939.

―――. *The Royal Tombs of the Earliest Dynasties, Part 2.* Memoir of the Egypt Exploration Fund 21. Boston: Egypt Exploration Fund, 1901.

―――. *The Royal Tombs of the First Dynasty, Part 1.* Memoir of the Egypt Exploration Fund 18. London: Egypt Exploration Fund, 1900.

Phillips, Matt and Jean-Bernard Carillet. *Ethiopia and Eritrea.* 3rd ed. Oakland, CA: Lonely Planet, 2006.

Posener, Georges. *Princes et pays d'Asie et de Nubie: textes hiératiques sur des figurines d'envoûtement du Moyen Empire.* Brussels: Fondation Égyptologique Reine Élisabeth, 1940.

Pritchard, James B. *Ancient Near Eastern Texts Relating to the Old Testament.* 3rd ed. Princeton, NJ: Princeton University Press, 1969.

————, ed. *Atlas of the Bible*. Ann Arbor, MI: Borders Press/HarperCollins, 2003.

Reinisch, Leo. *Die Bilin-Sprache in Nordost-Afrika*. Sitzungsberichte der Phil.-Hist. Classe der Kais. Akademie der Wissenchaften, vol. XCIX, no. 2. Vienna: Adolf Holzhausen, 1881.

————. *Die ChamirSprache in Abessinien*. Sitzungsberichte der Phil.-Hist. Classe der Kais. Akademie der Wissenchaften, vols. CV+CVI, 573-697, 317-450. Vienna: Sohn, 1884.

————. *Die Somali-Sprache*. Südarabische Expedition Series. Kais. Akademie der Wissenchaften, vols. I-III. Vienna: Alfred Holder, 1900-02.

————. *Texte der Bilin-Sprache*. Leipzig, Germany: Grieben, 1883.

Roaf, Michael. *Cultural Atlas of Mesopotamia and the Ancient Near East*. New York: Facts on File, Inc, 2003.

Rose, Fiona A. "Text and Image in Celtiberia: The Adoption and Adaptation of Written Language into Indigenous Visual Vocabulary." *Oxford Journal of Archaeology* 22, no. 2 (May 2003): 155-175.

Saeed, John I. *Somali Reference Grammar*. Kensington, MD: Dunwoody Press, 1993.

Saggs, Henry William Frederick. *Civilization Before Greece and Rome*. New Haven, CN: Yale University Press, 1989.

Saghieh, Muntaha. *Byblos in the Third Millennium BC: A Reconstruction of the Stratigraphy and a Study of the Cultural Connections.* Warminster, United Kingdom: Aris & Phillips, 1983.

Sasse, Hans-Jürgen. "Dasenech." In *The Non-Semitic Languages of Ethiopia*, ed. M. Lionel Bender, 196-221. Committee on Ethiopian Studies, ed. John Hinnant, no. 5. East Lansing, MI: Michigan State University, 1976.

Schmidt, Peter R., Matthew C. Curtis, and Zelalem Teka, eds. *The Archaeology of Ancient Eritrea.* Trenton, NJ: Red Sea Press, 2008.

Schoff, Wilfrid, ed. *The Periplus of the Erythraean Sea -- Travel and Trade in the Indian Ocean by a Merchant of the First Century.* 2nd ed. New York: Longman Green, 1912. Reprint, New Delhi: Oriental Books Reprint Corp, 1974.

Schuchardt, Hugo E. M. "Berberische Studien." In *Wiener Zeitschrift für die Kunde des Morgenlandes,* 254-264, Band 22, Vienna: 1908.

Sethe, Kurt H. *Urgeschichte und älteste Religion der Ägypter.* Abhandlungen für die Kunde des Morgenlandes, vol. XVIII, no. 4. Leipzig, Germany: Deutsche Morgenlandische Gesellschaft, 1930. Reprint, Liechtenstein: Kraus Reprint, 1966.

Simons, Jan Jozef. *Handbook for the Study of Egyptian Topographical Lists Relating to Western Asia.* Leiden, Netherlands: E. J. Brill, 1937.

Strabo. *The Geography of Strabo: Literally Translated, with Notes.* Bohn's Classical Library, vols. I-III. Translated by Hans Claude Hamilton and W. Falconer. London: H. G. Bohn, 1854-57.

Tosco, Mauro. *The Dhasanac Language: Grammar, Texts, Vocabulary of a Cushitic Language of Ethiopia.* Cushitic Language Studies, ed. Hans-Jürgen Sasse, Band 17. Cologne, Germany: Rüdiger Köppe Verlag, 2001.

Tovar, Antonio. *The Ancient Languages Of Spain And Portugal.* New York: S. F. Vanni, 1961.

Trask, Robert L. *The History of Basque.* New York: Routledge, 1997.

Trigger, Bruce G., Barry J. Kemp, David O'Connor, and Alan B. Lloyd. *Ancient Egypt: A Social History.* Cambridge: Cambridge University Press, 1983. http://books.google.com/books?id=OiiUcYOHX74 C&pg=PA121&lpg=PA121&dq=%22Land+of+Cat tle%22+ancient+Egypt&source=bl&ots=ZnvfX6u_ 7Z&sig=1u1f2HIGbDYoG55rsNroTU-g_vQ&hl =en&ei=6AfWS7LqBYeg8ATd4vHCDw&sa=X&o i=book_result&ct=result&resnum=3&ved=0CAsQ6 AEwAg#. (Accessed April 26, 2010).

Tucker, Archibald N. and Margaret A. Bryan. *The Non-Bantu Languages of North-Eastern Africa.* New York: Oxford University Press, 1956.

Untermann, Jürgen and Dagmar S. Wodtko. *Monumenta Linguarum Hispanicarum* IV: Die tartessischen, keltiberischen und lusitanischen Inschriften. Weisbaden, Germany: Ludwig. Reichert, 1997.

Venture de Paradis, Jean-Michel. *Grammaire et Dictionnaire Abrégés de la Langue Berbère*. Paris: Imprimerie Royale, 1844.

von Dassow, Eva, ed. *The Egyptian Book of the Dead: The Book of Going Forth by Day*. San Francisco, CA: Chronicle Books, 1994.

Von der Way, Thomas. "Indications of Architecture with Niches at Buto." In *The Followers of Horus: Studies in Memory of Michael Hoffman*, eds. Renee Friedman and Barbara Adams, eds., 217-226. Egyptian Studies 2, Monograph 20. Oxford: Oxbow Books, 1992.

von Soden, Wolfram. *Grundriss der Akkadischen Grammatik*. Analecta Orientalia 33. 3rd ed. Rome: Editrice Pontificio Istituto Biblico, 1995.

Vrouyr, Norayr E. *Inscriptions Ourartéennes et Annales des Rois d'Assyrie*. 2nd ed. Anvers, Belgium: T. Vrouyr, 1944.

Watrin, Luc. "From Intellectual Acquisitions to Political Change: Egypt-Mesopotamia Interaction in the Fourth Millennium BC." *De Kêmi à Birît Narî*, 2 (2004-2005): 48-95. http://www.grepal.org/english/articles/luc_watrin_kbn.pdf. (Accessed September 15, 2010).

———. "The Relative Chronology of the Naqada Culture: A View from Buto, Ma'adi, Harageh and Gerzeh." In The International Conference on Heritage of Naqada and Qus Region, ed. H. Hanna, vol. I, 1-30. Naqada, Egypt: January 22-28, 2007. http://www.grepal.org/articles/luc_watrin_icom_anglais.pdf. (Accessed September 15, 2010).

White, Victor S., ed. *The Ships of Tarshish: The Phoenicians*. Wheathampstead, Hertfordshire, United Kingdom: Victor S. White, 2002.

Wikipedia Authors. "Arkiko." Wikipedia. http://en .wikipedia.org/wiki/Arkiko. (Accessed December 7, 2009).

———. "Bos aegyptiacus." Wikipedia. http://en .wikipedia.org/wiki/Bos_aegyptiacus. (Accessed June 10, 2010).

———. "Nandi People." Wikipedia. http://en .wikipedia.org/wiki/Nandi_people. (Accessed July 27, 2010).

———. "Northeastern Iberian Script." Wikipedia. http:// en.wikipedia.org/wiki/Northeastern_Iberian_script. (Accessed May 5, 2009).

———. "Protodynastic Period of Egypt." Wikipedia. http://en.wikipedia.org/wiki/Protodynastic_Period_ of_Egypt. (Accessed September 30, 2009).

———. "Qohaito." Wikipedia. http://en.wikipedia.org/ wiki/Qohaito. (Accessed December 7, 2009).

———. "Tiran Island." Wikipedia. http://en.wikipedia.org/ wiki/Tiran_Island. (Accessed December 7, 2009).

Wilberg, Friedrich Wilhelm, ed. *Claudii Ptolemæi Geographiæ Libri Octo: Græce et latine ad codicum manu scriptorum fidem.* Essen, Germany: G. D. Baedeker, 1838. http://books.google.com/books?id=j71AAAAAcAAJ&pg=PA59&lpg=PA59&dq=Wilberg+Ptolem&source=bl&ots=c5ecyfd_im&sig=8P_JxEnO9nhP0TpNBmPKafm3Ruc&hl=en&ei=TDSwS_GZLcP-8AanxvHGDQ&sa=X&oi=book_result&ct=result&resnum=8&ved=0CB0Q6AEwBw#v=onepage&q=&f=false. (Accessed March 9, 2010).

Woolley, Leonard. *Ur of the Chaldees: A Record of Seven Years of Excavation.* London: Ernest Benn, 1929.

Wyse, Elizabeth and Barry Winkleman. *Past Worlds Atlas of Archaeology.* London: HarperCollins, 1997.

Zaborski, Andrzej. "Cushitic Overview." In *The Non-Semitic Languages of Ethiopia*, ed. M. Lionel Bender, 67-84. Committee on Ethiopian Studies, ed. John Hinnant, no. 5. East Lansing, MI: Michigan State University, 1976.

Zorc, R. David and Madina Osman. *Somali-English Dictionary with English Index.* 3rd ed. Kensington, MD: Dunwoody Press, 1993.

Zyhlarz, Ernest. "Die Fiction der 'Kuschitischen' Völker." *Kush* 4 (1959): 19-33.

GAZETTEER

Where possible, each word has an anchor, an English translation in single quotes, a general latitude and longitude for the anchor, map numbers in bold and underlined or illustration numbers in regular text, and line number(s) in Botorrita III or Botorrita I-B, texts. For ethnonyms and areas or roads that are not points, coordinates are given for an anchor city.

WORD	Anchor 'English Trans.'	Latitude Longitude	Map Nos.	Text Line
Abalos	Siwa Oasis, Egypt, '[Temple] of Apollo'	29°15' N 25°30' E	**12**, 18	**III** 3.47
Abaniu	Semera city, Ethiopia, Danakil region, ethnonym for 'Afar / Afan people'	11°47' N 41°00' E	**1**, 16	**III** 3.25
(burdu) Abilikum	'(fort) Ebla, Syria'	35°52' N 37°02' E	**2**, **5**, **9**, 21	**III** 4.7
Aboiokum	'Abydos, Egypt'	26°11' N 31°55' E	**10**, 4	**III** 1.41
Abokum	Elephantine Island, Egypt, 'Elephant Land, from the Nile Bend to Djibouti'	24°05' N 32°53' E	**10**, 2, 6, 8, 12, 13, 15, 22	**III** 1.60, 2.9, 2.15, 2.60, 3.11, 4.14

Gazetteer

WORD	Anchor 'English Trans.'	Latitude Longitude	Map Nos.	Text Line
Aiankum	Sile, Egypt 'Northeast Egypt'	30°52' N 32°22' E	**12**, **16**, **17**	**I-B** 4, 7
Aiankum Tauro[120]	Cyprus, east Mediterranean coast, 'Bull's Eye Land'	35°30' N 32°30' E	**9**, **12**, **16**, **17**	**I-B** 7, 8
Ailokiskum	Eilat, Israel, ruins near Aqaba, Jordan, 'Aila of Kish'	29°32' N 35°00' E	**2**, **5**, **6**, **7**, **9**, 9, 10, 11, 19, 21, 25	**III** 2.22, 3.53
Akaina	Patras, Achaia, in Greece, ethnonym for 'The Achaeans, Greeks'	38°14' N 21°44' E	**12**, **16**, **17**	**I-B** 5
Akikum	'Aqiq, Sudan'	18°00' N 39°10' E	**11**, 7, 10, 11, 24, 26	**III** 2.12, 4.29
Akuikum[121]	'Agau Lands'		**1**, **11**, 24	**III** 4.28
Alasku	Cyprus, ancient Alashiya, 'The Island'	35°30' N 32°30' E	**12**, 2, 4	**III** 1.12
Alaskum	Aswan, Egypt, near the 1st Cataract, 'noble citadel of the island kingdom'	24°02'N 32°54'E	**11**, **14**, 4	**III** 1.37

---

[120] See *Alasku*.
[121] See *Akikum, Uiduskikum, Austunikum, Ataiokum, Kustikum.*

WORD	Anchor 'English Trans.'	Latitude Longitude	Map Nos.	Text Line
Alaskum	Dahlak Islands, Red Sea, 'Island Kingdom'	15°40' N 40°08' E	7	III 2.13
Albana[122]	'Arabs'		**9**, **13**, 1	III 0.1
Albinokum	Jauf, Arabia, 'Arabia'	29°30' N 39°00' E	**2**, **4**, **9**, **13**, 22, 25	III 4.17
Alikum	'Elim, Sinai'	29°05' N 32°59' E	**2**, **9**, **10**, 16, 19	III 3.30, 3.54
Alu	Soba, Sudan, 12 km to Khartoum, in 'Alodia'		**11**, 4, 11, 14, 18	III 1.43
Ama	Amman, Jordan, 'Amman'	31°00' N 35°00' E	**2**, **9**, 19	III 3.55
Anieskor	Gebel Sheikh Suleiman, Sudan, 'Mount Kor'	21°51' N 31°13' E	23	III 4.27
Antiokos	'Lord of the Antiu', people between the Nile and the Red Sea.		**5**, **10**, 14, 22	III 3.9, 4.13
Anu[123]	Aniba, Egypt, ethnonym for 'people in Lower Nubia'	22°40' N 32°01' E	**11**, **12**, **14**, 22	III 4.15

---

[122] See *Albinokum*.
[123] See glossary entry for further description.

WORD	Anchor 'English Trans.'	Latitude Longitude	Map Nos.	Text Line
Araiokum	Kerma, Sudan, 'Cataract Land'	19°36' N 30°24' E	**11**, 4	**III** 1.42, 1.43
(mailikum) Arkanta	in southern Iraq, '(kingdom) of Uruk'. Also an ethnonym for 'people of Uruk, Urukites'	31°18' N 45°40' E	**2**, **5**, **7**, **9**, **13**, 1, 9, 12, 14, 15, 18, 19, 22, 25	**III** 3.11, 3.12, 3.21, 3.44, 3.53, 4.20
Ataiokum	Begrawia, Sudan, Meroe, 'Incense Land'	16°54' N 33°44' E	**11**, **14**, 10, 11, 24	**III** 2.25, 2.30, 2.35, 4.32
Atauikum	Lalibela, Ethiopia, formerly Adefa, 'Adefa, Lasta'	12°02' N 39°02' E	**11**, 11	**III** 2.41
Ateskum	Şanlıurfa, Turkey, 'Edessa (Urfa)'	37°03' N 38°47' E	**9**, **10**, 21	**III** 4.11
Atokum	Sana'a, Yemen, 'Eastland'	15°24' N 44°14' E	**11**, **12**, **13**, **14**, 4, 7, 11, 12, 17, 24	**III** 1.35, 2.8, 2.46, 3.40
(burdu) Atokum	Aden, '(fort) Aden'	12°47' N 45°03' E	**13**, 6	**III** 1.54
Aualos	Manama, Bahrain, ethnonym for 'people of Bahrain'	26°12' N 50°38' E	**2**, **9**, **13**, 6	**III** 1.55

WORD	Anchor 'English Trans.'	Latitude Longitude	Map Nos.	Text Line
Auaskum	Jabal Habashi, Ta'izz, Yemen, 'Highlands'	13°28' N 43°53' E	<u>13</u>, 7	III 2.7
(burdu) Auikum	at Kharga Oasis, Egypt, '(fort) Hibis'	25°29' N 30°33' E	<u>10</u>, 3	III 1.26
Aunia	Aunu, ethnonym, 'an Aunu' associated with southerners			III 3.27
Aureiaku	Lalibela, Ethiopia 'birth place [of Blue Nile]'	12°02' N 39°02' E	<u>14</u>, 11	III 2.39
Austikum	Sokota, Ethiopia, in the Central Highlands, 'Lasta region on the High Plateau'	12°22' N 39°02' E	<u>11</u>, 3, 7	III 1.20, 2.14
Austunikum	Mogadishu, Somalia, 'down to Benadir (in ancient Ethiopia)'	2°05' N 45°30' E	<u>11</u>, 14	III 3.5
Austunikum	'Highlanders Land, (ancient Ethiopia)'		<u>11</u>, 24	III 4.31
Babokum	Aniba, Egypt, Wawat / Lower Nubia, 'Wawat'	22°40' N 32°01' E	<u>14</u>, 4	III 1.36

Gazetteer

WORD	Anchor 'English Trans.'	Latitude Longitude	Map Nos.	Text Line
Babos	Aniba, Egypt, Wawat / Lower Nubia, ethnonym for 'people of Wawat'	22°40' N 32°01' E	**14**, 20	**III** 3.56
Balaisokum	Tell el-Farama, Egypt, 'Pelusium'	31°03' N 32°32' E	**10**, 18	**III** 3.48
Balakos	'Failaka, Kuwait'	29°26' N 48°20' E	**2**, **9**, **13**, 22, 25	**III** 4.18
Bartiltun	Mersa Matruh, Egypt, 'Baretoun / Parætonium'	31°21' N 27°14' E	**10**, **12**, 12	**III** 2.50
Basaku	Basha, Ethiopia, 'the Basa Region'	12°02' N 37°37' E	10	**III** 2.32
Batokum	Tell el Rub'a, Egypt, 'Mendes'	30°57' N 34°34' E	**10**, 2	**III** 1.11, 1.19
Bentikum	Port Sudan, West Red Sea Coast, 'Baboon Land'	19°18' N 37°07' E	**3**, **4**, **11**, **12**, 8, 13	**III** 2.17, 2.58
(burdu) Bentilikum	Mogadishu, Somalia, 'the Benadir region or (fort) Benadir'	2°05' N 45°30' E	**11**, 14, 18	**III** 3.6, 3.7, 3.42
Berkantikum	'Barca, Libya'	32°30' N 20°50' E	**4**, **12**, **16**, **17**	**I-B** 3
Bertika	Suakin, Sudan, ethnonym for 'people of Berta'	19°06' N 37°20' E	**11**, 16	**III** 3.25

WORD	Anchor 'English Trans.'	Latitude Longitude	Map Nos.	Text Line
Beskokum	'Land of Bes'		16	**III** 3.27
(burdu) Betaskum	Siwa Oasis, Egypt, '(fort) Umm Ebeida'	29°11' N 25°33' E	**10**, 15	**III** 3.14
Beteriskum	'Petra, Jordan'	30°20' N 35°26' E	**2**, **9**, **13**, **16**, 12, 21	**III** 2.47
betikum	'the enemy lands'		25	**III** 4.34
Bibalos	Ocelis, Yemen, ethnonym for 'people from Mandeb Strait'	12°35' N 43°20' E	12	**III** 2.46
Bilibos	Kufra Oasis, Libya, at or near ancient Bilia, ethnonym for 'people from Bilia'	24°11' N 23°17' E	**12**, 3, 15	**III** 1.24
Bilinos	Lalibela, Ethiopia, ethnonym for 'Bilin people from the Lasta region'	12°02' N 39°02' E	**1**, **11**, 3	**III** 1.20
Bini Rusku	Phoinikon / Laqeita, Egypt, 'Phoenician *Rusku*'	25°53' N 33°07' E	**10**, **14**, 4, 8	**III** 1.38
(Koloutios) Binis[-]kum	Byblos, Lebanon, 'Phoenicia'	34°08' N 35°38' E	**3**, **4**, **9**, **10**, 14	**III** 3.8
(Tueidunos) Biniskum	Tell Judeideh, Syria, 'Phoenicia'	36°21' N 36°33' E	**3**, **4**, **9**, 19	**III** 3.50

Gazetteer

WORD	Anchor 'English Trans.'	Latitude Longitude	Map Nos.	Text Line
Bubilibor	Old Cairo, Egypt, 'Lord of Babal'	30°00' N 31°14' E	**14**, 23	III 4.22
Burikounikum	El Manzala, Egypt, 'Harbor Region'	31°10' N 31°57' E	**10**, 12	III 2.53
(ensikum) Ebursunos	Tell Brak, Syria, 'Khabur River empire'	36°46' N 41°00' E	**2**, **9**, 9, 19, 21, 25	III 3.52
Elkueikikum	Massawa, Eritrea, 'Arqiqo on mainland across from the island of Massawa, Red Sea coast'	15°32' N 39°27' E	**11**, 16	III 3.23
Elokum	Tell Atchana, Syria 'Alalakh'	36°19' N 36°29' E	**2**, **9**, 16	III 3.28
Eskutino	'person from Sokota, Lasta, Ethiopia'	12°36' N 39°20' E	**1**, **11**, 7	III 2.14
Esokum	'Issus, Turkey'	36°50' N 36°10' E	**16**, **17**	I-B 9
Esueiku	Gulf of Iskenderun, Turkey, 'Gulf of Issus'	36°30' N 35°40' E	**9**, **10**, 21	III 4.11
Kabelaikiskum	'Byblos, Lebanon'	34°08' N 35°38' E	**2**, **5**, **6**, **9**, 12	III 2.55
Kaburikum	Kalabsha, Egypt, 'Lower Nubia'	23°33' N 32°52' E	**11**, **12**, 4, 11, 14, 20	III 2.36, 3.10

WORD	Anchor 'English Trans.'	Latitude Longitude	Map Nos.	Text Line
Kabutu	'Coptus, Egypt'	26°00' N 32°49' E	**10**, 8, 22	III 4.14
Kadarokum	'Kadruka, Sudan'	19°22' N 30°24' E	**11**, 16	III 3.32
Kalaitos	'Chaldean'		**9**, 10, 22	III 2.33 4.5 4.12 4.16
Kalatokum	Charax Spasinu, Iraq, 'Chaldea'	30°53' N 47°34' E	**2**, **5**, **6**, **9**, 12, 22, 25	III 4.19
Kalisokum	'Klusma, Suez, Egypt'	29°59' N 32°32' E	**10**, 2, 7, 11, 12, 18, 21	III 2.44, 3.43, 3.45, 4.9
Kalmiku[m]	Khashm el-Girba, Sudan, 'Kemalke Ford'	14°58' N 35°55' E	**11**, **14**, 10	III 2.26
Kalos	Kellis, Dakhleh Oasis, Egypt, 'proper name, from Kellis'	25°12' N 29°04' E	**10**, **12**, 4	III 1.44
Kankaikiskum	Kish, Iraq, 'Sumer of Kish'	32°33' N 44°39' E	**2**, **9**, **13**, 6, 25	III 1.56, 4.35
Kara	Charax Spasinu, Iraq, 'city-state in Chaldea'	30°53' N 47°34' E	**9**, **13**, 22	III 4.19

WORD	Anchor 'English Trans.'	Latitude Longitude	Map Nos.	Text Line
Karbelos	Fada, Chad, ethnonym for 'Sand-dwellers of region near border of NW Sudan'	17°11' N 21°35' E	3	**III** 1.28
Karbilikum	Marib, Himyar, 'Desert Land / Sheba kingdom'	15°24' N 45°14' E	<u>13</u>, 17	**III** 3.39
Kares (ruaku)	'(the village of) Korosko, Sudan'	22°36' N 32°19' E	<u>11</u>, 11	**III** 2.37
Kari	Napata, 4th Cataract, 'district around Napata, Sudan'	18°32' N 31°49' E	<u>11</u>, <u>14</u>, 20, 24	**III** 3.59
(burdu) Karunikum	Tell Abu Sefa, Egypt, 'fort Sile'. Also name for NE Egyptian Delta, other names are Heroonopolis, and *Aiankum*	30°52' N 32°22' E	<u>10</u>, 2, 5, 18, 21	**III** 1.17, 3.47, 4.6
Kasilos	Al Jazirah, Yemen, peninsula due west of Sana'a on the coast and south of Kamaran Island. Ethnonym, for 'people from Al Jazirah, Yemen'	15°20' N 42°34' E	<u>13</u>, 7	**III** 2.8
Katunos	Ethnonym for 'Swamp dwellers, Egyptian Delta'		<u>12</u>, 12	**III** 2.53

WORD	Anchor 'English Trans.'	Latitude Longitude	Map Nos.	Text Line
Kaukirino	Keren, Eritrea, 'Keren Highlands'	15°47' N 38°27' E	**1**, **11**, 26	III 4.40
Keka	Byblos, Lebanon, 'Gigartus'	34°08' N 35°38' E	**9**, 12	III 2.55
Kinbiria	?Buri Peninsula, '?Birdland, Eritrea'	15°40' N 37°50' E	8, 13	III 3.4
Konikum	Megiddo, Israel, 'Canaan'	32°35' N 35°11' E	**2**, **9**, **10**, **12**, **13**, 9, 12, 16, 21	III 2.49, 3.26
Kontudos	Kurgus, Sudan, Ta Khont, south Nile River valley, ethnonym for 'people of the interior'	19°12' N 33°30' E	1	III 1.2
Korkos	'Kurgus, Sudan'	19°12' N 33°30' E	**11**, 11	III 2.37
Kortikos	'Lord of Khor, Qatar'	25°40' N 51°33' E	**2**, **9**, **13**, 6	III 1.55
Kounesikum	'Knossos, Crete'	29°08' N 25°10' E	**12**, **16**	I-B 1
Kuedontikum	'Kydonia, Crete'	35°31' N 24°01' E	**12**, **16**, 25	III 4.36
Kuinikum	Sennar, Sudan, Kueneion, 'South Land'	13°33' N 33°36' E	**6**, **11**, 10, 11	III 2.42

213

WORD	Anchor 'English Trans.'	Latitude Longitude	Map Nos.	Text Line
kuintitaku	'Deep South'		20	**III** 3.60
(burdu) Kulukamikum	Qohaito, Eritrea, '(fort) Koloe of Kam'	15°00' N 39°59' E	**11**, 7	**III** 2.10
kunikum	from Somali: *koonfer*, 'the southern kingdoms'			**III** 2.27
Kurmiliokum	'Kerma, Sudan'	19°36' N 30°24' E	**11**, 23	**III** 4.26
Kurmilokum	'Kerma, Sudan'	19°36' N 30°24' E	**11**, 20	**III** 3.57
Kustikum	Cheren / Keren, 'Eritrea'	16°00' N 38°00' E	**1**, **11**, 22, 24, 26	**III** 4.12, 4.13, 4.33 4.39
Lestera	Lalibela, Ethiopia, 'one [of the southerners of] Lasta (The Land) '	12°02' N 39°02' E	**1**, **11**, 1, 3, 7, 11	**III** 0.1
Letikum	'[Gortyn, Crete] on the Lethaeus River'	25°07' N 24°58' E	**12**, **16**	**I-B** 8
Litanokum	Tyre, Lebanon, 'Litani River Land'	33°16' N 35°12' E	**9**, 20	**III** 3.57
Litokum	'Lyttus, Crete'	30°08' N 25°23' E	**12**, **16**	**I-B** 1

WORD	Anchor 'English Trans.'	Latitude Longitude	Map Nos.	Text Line
Loudokum	Latakia, Syria, 'Laodikea province'	35°31' N 35°47' E	**12**, **16**, **17**	I-B 4
Loukaniko (uiriasku)	the Barka River which flows into the Red sea south of Suakin, Sudan		**12**, 7, 10	III 2.3
Loukanikum	Sollum, Egypt, 'Cattle Land, Kingdom of the Laguatan'	31°40' N 25°21' E	**3**, **4**, **5**, **6**, **10**, **12**, 2, 12, 15	III 1.14, 1.45, 1.46, 2.43, 3.12, 3.18
Lubinad	'by the Libyans'		**12**	I-B 3
Lubos	'Libyans'		**12**	I-B 1
Lukinos	'people of *Loukanikum*'		**12**	III 2.1
Makeskokum	Sile, 'Northern Egypt'	30°52' N 32°22' E	5, 21	III 1.48, 4.8
Matulokum	Damanhur, Egypt 'Metelis, Egypt'	31°03' N 30°28' E	**10**, **14**, 2	III 1.9
Melm	'Egyptian Berbers, in the River Kingdom'		14	III 3.9
Melman	Egyptians near Klusma, Suez, Egypt, 'locals, Egyptian Berbers'	29°59' N 32°32' E	**3**, **4**, **5**, **6**, **10**, 18	III 3.42, 3.46

Gazetteer

WORD	Anchor 'English Trans.'	Latitude Longitude	Map Nos.	Text Line
Melmando	Egyptians near Siwa Oasis, West Egypt, 'locals, Egyptain Berbers, Marmaridae'	29°15' N 25°30' E	**10**, 15	**III** 3.15
Melmandos	Egyptians from region of Northern Egypt, 'locals, Egyptian Berbers'	30°52' N 32°22' E	21	**III** 4.3
Melmanios	Kharga Oasis, South Egypt, 'Personal name of the king, one of the Egyptian Berbers'	25°00' N 30°30' E	**10**	**III** 1.27
Melmu	Gebel Uweinat, Libya, 'plundered *Melmu* Lands up to [the border] at the Uweinat', 'Egyptian'	21°55' N 24°59' E	**16**, **17**	**I-B** 2
Melmunos	Knossos, Crete, 'Egyptian Berbers from northeastern Egypt who attacked Knossos on Crete'	35°18' N 25°11' E	**12**	**I-B** 1
Melmunos	Sile, Egypt, ethnonym for 'Egyptians from Sile, *Aiankum*, who destroyed Ushu, Lebanon'	30°52' N 32°22' E	**12**	**I-B** 7

WORD	Anchor 'English Trans.'	Latitude Longitude	Map Nos.	Text Line
Mturiskum	Sile, 'Metcher, the double wall, Northern Egypt'	30°52' N 32°22' E	**10,** 21	III 4.5
Muturiskum	Memphis, Egypt, 'United Egypt (Vulture Cobra Land)'	29°51' N 31°15' E	**10,** 2, 6, 9, 12, 22	III 1.16, 1.58, 2.18, 4.16
Nouida	Naqada, Tukh, Egypt, 'Nubt, Gold City, Numidians'	25°56' N 32°45' E	1	III 0.1
Nouantubos	Petra, Jordan, ethnonym, 'of the Nabataeans'	30°20' N 35°26' E	**2, 13,** **16, 17**	I-B 6
Raiokum	Mit Rahina, Egypt, 'Memphis'	29°51' N 31°15' E	**10, 12,** 2, 9	III 1.10
Rusku	Phoinikon, Laqeita in Egypt, ethnonym for 'the Rusha'[124]	25°53' N 33°07' E	**10, 14,** 4, 8	III 1.39
Samikum	'Siwa Oasis, western Egypt'	29°15' N 25°30' E	**10, 12,** 2, 5, 15, 21	III 3.15
Sanios	Sana'a, Yemen, ethnonym for 'people of Sana'a'	15°24' N 44°14' E	**13,** 4	III 1.35
Sekanos	Shebka people at oases in Nubian Desert, Sudan		**12**	III 2.1

---

[124] See *Rusku* in the Glossary for further explanation.

Gazetteer

WORD	Anchor 'English Trans.'	Latitude Longitude	Map Nos.	Text Line
Seko	Shebka empire in oases in western Egypt		**12**, 2	**III** 1.13
Sikeia	Petra, Jordan, 'The Siq'	30°20' N 35°26' E	**2**, **9**, **16**, 12	**III** 2.47
Sleitiu	Sile, El Qantara, Egypt, ethnonym for 'people of Sile'	30°52' N 32°22' E	**10**, **16**, 5, 16, 21	**III** 1.17, 1.48, 3.33
Snadiuentos	Western Shendi, Sudan, ethnonym for 'people of Western Shendi'	16°41' N 33°22' E	**11**, 10	**III** 2.30
Statu	Emar / Meskene, Syria, 'Canaan, Syria and Palestine region'	36°02' N 38°04' E	**9**, 9	**III** 2.20, 3.26
Statulikum	Astata, Emar, Syria, 'Syria, Jordan, and possibly northern Arabia'	36°02' N 38°04' E	**2**, **9**	**I-B** 6
Statulu	Emar / Meskene, Syria, ethnonym for 'people of Syria and Palestine region'	36°02' N 38°04' E	**9**, 1, 16	**III** 1.3
Suaikinokum	'Suakin, Sudan'	19°06' N 37°20' E	**11**, **14**, 7, 13, 16, 17	**III** 3.25, 3.36

WORD	Anchor 'English Trans.'	Latitude Longitude	Map Nos.	Text Line
Suola	'Djibouti'	11°33' N 43°10' E	**1**, **11**, **14**, 13	**III** 3.2
Suoli[-]kum	Djibouti, 'Djibouti / Somalia'	11°33' N 43°10' E	**11**, 8, 17	**III** 3.37
Suostunos	Samos Island, Turkey, ethnonym for 'people of Cyclades Islands'	37°42' N 26°59' E	**12**, **16**	**I-B** 5
Suros	Amman, Jordan, ethnonym for 'people living between Elim, Sinai and Amman, Jordan'	31°57' N 35°56' E	**2**, **9**, 19	**III** 3.54
Tais	'Dessie, Ethiopia'	11°08' N 39°38' E	**14**, 10	**III** 2.31
Talukokum	Firka, 'Dal Cataract, Sudan'	20°54' N 30°35' E	**11**, 23	**III** 4.27
tar	Korosko, Egypt, North End, Arabic: *darb*, 'road'	22°36' N 32°19' E	**11**, 11	**III** 2.38
Tarkunbiur	Tarkhan or Kafr Tarkhan, Egypt, 'Tarkun City'	29°30' N 31°13' E	**10**, 12	**III** 2.45
Tauro	Kerunia, Cyprus, 'Bull, as in *Aiankum Tauro*, the Bull's Eye, Cyprus'	35°20' N 33°20' E	**12**	**I-B** 7, 8

WORD	Anchor 'English Trans.'	Latitude Longitude	Map Nos.	Text Line
Taskokum	'borderland, between Berbers and *Akuia,* perhaps near 5th Cataract'			**III** 2.1
(burdu) Teiuantikum	Medinet Habu, '(fort) Tjamet, Egypt'	25°43' N 32°36' E	<u>10</u>, 3	**III** 1.23
Teiuantikum	'countries west of Uruk, Western Lands'		16	**III** 3.21
Tekos	'proper name of someone from Taucheira, Libya'	32°32' N 20°34' E	<u>12</u>, 12	**III** 2.49
Teladokum	Tjel / Thar / Tanis, Egypt, 'Telad/Dela'	30°59' N 31°53' E	9	**III** 2.19
Telkaskum	Kellis, 'Dakhleh Oasis, Egypt'	25°32' N 29°04' E	<u>10</u>, <u>12</u>, 4, 5, 17, 18, 23	**III** 1.44, 3.38, 3.41, 4.24
Testios	'proper name of person from the Tibesti Mtns., Libya'	20°00' N 18°00' E	<u>12</u>, 13	**III** 3.1
Tetokum	'Korosko, the Nubian Desert region, Sudan'	22°36' N 32°19' E	<u>11</u>, <u>12</u>, 4, 11, 13, 14	**III** 1.31, 2.38
Tirikantanko	'in the middle of the Tiran Strait, Red Sea'	27°57' N 34°33' E	<u>10</u>, <u>13</u>, 21	**III** 4.10

WORD	Anchor 'English Trans.'	Latitude Longitude	Map Nos.	Text Line
Tirilokum	'Deire, Ethiopia, region on west coast of Mandeb Strait'	12°35' N 43°20' E	**11**, 7	**III** 2.11
Tiriu	Deire, on Mandeb Strait, west side, ethnonym for 'people of Deire'	12°35' N 43°20' E	**11**, 16	**III** 3.31
Tirtanikum	Dire Dawa, Ethiopia, 'Chercher Mtns. and Harar Province'	8°55' N 40°34' E	**3**, **7**, **11**, **13**, **14**, 1, 6, 13, 22	**III** 1.1, 3.3
Tirtanos	Bab el-Mandeb, 'ethnonym for Tirtanos people who controlled Mandeb Strait'	12°40' N 43°00' E	**11**, **13**, **14**, **16**, **17**, 5, 6, 12	**III** 2.46
(burdu) Tirtobolokum	Axum, Ethiopia, '(fort) Axum, exact location of fort uncertain'	14°07' N 38°44' E	**11**, 4, 5, 7, 20	**III** 1.47
Tirtobolokum	Axum, Ethiopia, 'All-Cities-Land, Metropolis'	14°07' N 38°44' E	**11**, 4, 5, 10, 12, 13, 16, 20	**III** 3.22, 3.29, 4.1
Tirtouios	Shambe, Sudd region, Sudan 'Marsh people'	7°00' N 31°00' E	**3**, 8	**III** 2.16
tolisokum	'clan territories [of the Turo empire]'		12	**III** 2.56

221

WORD	Anchor 'English Trans.'	Latitude Longitude	Map Nos.	Text Line
Totinikum[125]	? Tanis, Egypt		16	**III** 3.33
Toutinikum	Girga, Egypt, 'Thinis, ancient Egyptian capital'	26°20' N 31°54' E	**10**, **11**, 2, 6, 9, 11, 12, 18	**III** 1.7, 2.52, 3.44
tuatereskue[126]	area near the birthplace of the streams of the Blue Nile, marshy region east of Lake Tana, Ethiopia *aureiaku tuatereskue,* 'near the birthplace of the streams'		**14**, 11	**III** 2.40
tuateroskue	'in both directions'		16	**III** 3.24
Tueidunos	Tell Brak, Syria, 'proper name of Lord King of Khabur River people'	36°46' N 41°00' E	**2**, **9**, 9, 19	**III** 2.20 3.50
Turaios	Tyre, Lebanon, ethnonym for 'people of Tyre'	33°16' N 35°11' E	**2**, **9**, **12**, 20	**III** 3.57
Turaku	Tyre, Lebanon, 'the Tyre region'	33°16' N 35°11' E	**2**, **9**, **12**, 8, 9	**III** 2.20

---

[125] See *Teladokum.*
[126] See *Uiriraskum.*

222

WORD	Anchor 'English Trans.'	Latitude Longitude	Map Nos.	Text Line
Turanikum	Aqiq, 'Ptolemais Theron, Red Sea coast, Sudan / Eritrea'	18°00' N 39°10' E	**1**, **11**, 7, 11, 26	**III** 2.4, 4.38
Turenta	'of *Turanikum*'		10	**III** 2.25
Turikainos	Iken (modern Mirgissa), Sudan, ethnonym for 'people of Iken'	21°49' N 31°10' E	**11**, **14**, 20	**III** 4.2
Turikum	'West Red Sea coastal lowlands'		**11**, 13	**III** 3.4
Turo	'of *Turikum*', adj.		**11**, 15	**III** 2.57
Turos	ethnonym for 'people of *Turikum*'		**11**, 1	**III** 1.2
Turumokum	Khartoum, Sudan, 'Egypt and Sudan west of the Nile'	15°33' N 32°32' E	**3**, **11**, 3, 5, 6, 8, 12, 13, 18	**III** 1.24, 1.28, 1.51, 1.59, 2.16, 2.48, 3.1, 3.49
Ubokum	Gebel Uweinat, 'Uweinat, Libya'	21°55' N 24°59' E	**11**, **12**, **14**, **16**, 15	**III** 3.16
Uiduskikum	Kurgus, 'Bayuda region, Sudan, Ta Khont'	19°12' N 33°30' E	**11**, 4, 24	**III** 1.32, 4.30

WORD	Anchor 'English Trans.'	Latitude Longitude	Map Nos.	Text Line
Uikanokum	'Mycenae, Greece'	37°44' N 22°45' E	**12**, **16**	**I-B** 5
Uiriasku	'the river [Barka in E. Sudan]'		7, 10	**III** 2.3
Uiriaskum[127]	The [Nile] River Kingdom, from the Mediterranean Sea to Djibouti, to Mogadishu, from Yemen to regions in Loukanikum (Cattle Land) west of Egypt and Sudan. 'The River Kingdom'		**7**, **11**, **14**, 2, 3, 5, 7, 11, 13, 14, 15, 16, 17, 20, 21, 22, 23	**III** 1.8, 1.1, 1.2, 1.22, 1.27, 1.39, 1.49, 1.50, 1.53, 2.5, 2.28, 2.31, 2.32, 2.40, 3.3, 3.9, 3.19, 3.20, 3.31, 3.35, 3.55, 3.56, 3.58, 3.59, 4.4, 4.15, 4.22, 4.23

[127] See *Tetokum, Uiduskikum, Ubokum*.

224

WORD	Anchor 'English Trans.'	Latitude Longitude	Map Nos.	Text Line
Uiriraskum	'Urvuar, Lalibela, Ethiopia'	12°02' N 39°02' E	**11**, 11	**III** 2.34
(burdu) Uiskikum	Mouza, Yemen, North of Ocelis on East Red Sea coast, '(fort) Mouza'	14°36' N 43° 20' E	**13**, 4, 7	**III** 1.33, 2.6
Ukontad[128]	'by the [people of] Mycenae, Greece'		**12**	**I-B** 9
Ukulikum	Ocelis on east side of Bab el Mandeb (Mandeb Strait), 'Ocelis, Yemen'	12°35' N 43°20' E	**13**, 12	**III** 2.54
Usama	'Upper, Most High'		18	**III** 3.47
Useidu	'Ushu, Lebanon, mainland part of Tyre'	33°15' N 35°13' E	**2**, **9**, **12**, **16**, 8	**I-B** 7
Useidunos	Ushu, Lebanon, mainland part of Tyre, ethnonym for 'people of Ushu'	33°15' N 35°13' E	**9**, 8	**III** 2.15 **I-B** 5
Usidu	Luxor, 'Thebes, Egypt'	25°42' N 12°18' E	**10**, **11**, 3, 7, 23	**III** 2.9, 4.23
Ustitokum	Corresponds to Astitokum, 'Nile and / or Atbara River Land'		**11**, 10	**III** 2.24

---

[128] See *Uikanokum*.

APPENDIX A

GRAMMATICAL NOTES

§1 Introduction

1.1 As inscriptions go, the Botorrita III text with 518 words is quite long. Still as a basis for constructing a grammar, 518 words, constituting all the data available, is minimal.

1.2 There are other texts identified as Celtiberian, but there is more than one language represented among those texts. The language of Botorrita I, side A and probably Botorrita IV represent a language from a different non-Kushitic family of languages.

The language of Botorrita I-B, translated here in the chapter called Attack on the Bull's Eye, is the same language as the one in Botorrita III. Like Botorrita III, it uses what would be called a non-dual version of the writing system. This means that it makes no distinction between voiced (**b**, **d**, **g**) and voiceless (**p**, **t**, **k**) stops.

Even though this I-B text is very similar, there are differences. The symbol used for the letter **a** is not ⵔ , but ⊳. The symbol for the syllable **bo**, instead of ⵀ, is ⵋ , and the letter **r** is sometimes ⵔ , which is the same, and sometimes ◇, which is a little different. There are subtle differences in the spelling and use of the word *Melmu* and the use of the verb *letontu*.

226

These comments describe the grammar of the Botorrita III text. A description of the grammatical areas of Botorrita I-B that are different is given in Section 8 (§8) of this Appendix.

1.3 Although it is a bit of a stretch to write a formal, traditional grammar with so little data, I have followed the format Reinisch used for his grammars of Bilin and Chamir.[129] I hope that will make these notes more easily comparable to his works. They were a valuable resource in doing the translation. I believe the language of the Botorrita III text will turn out to be a very ancient ancestor of these languages. It is, by far, the oldest written example of a Kushitic language still available.

§2 Phonology

The Botorrita III writing system is a variant of the Iberian writing system. The Spanish scholar, Manuel Gómez-Moreno Martinez, in 1922, identified the values of the symbols.[130] The translation of the Botorrita III text provides confirmation for the accuracy of his analysis. The Botorrita III text has the following sounds and symbols:
a (Ⴔ), ba (Ⴈ), be (Ⴟ), bi (Ⴌ), bo (✳), bu (▢), d̲ (Ⴗ), e (Ⴊ), i (Ⴈ), ka (Ⴥ), ke (Ⴉ), ki (Ⴍ), ko (Ⴟ), ku (☉), l (Ⴊ), m (Ⴤ), n (Ⴈ), o (Ⴙ), r (Ⴓ), s (Ⴑ), ta (✕), te (Ⴘ), ti (Ⴒ), to (Ⴑ), tu (△), u (↑).

---

129 Reinisch, *Die Bilin-Sprache*; Ibid., *Die ChamirSprache*.
130 Gómez-Moreno Martinez, "De Epigrafia Ibérica," 34-36. The version of the writing system that he deciphered, like the Botorrita III writing system, does not distinguish between voiced and voiceless stops, that is, between b and p, t and d, k and g. Other later versions of the Iberian writing system have been described which do make a distinction; Wikipedia Authors, "Northeastern Iberian Script."

Appendix A: Grammatical Notes

2.1 There is no letter **p**. The letter **p** is also absent in native Bilin and Chamir words, and from native Basque words. Foreign words like 'Petra' and 'Pelusium' are written with **b,** in *Beteriskum* and *Balaisokum.*

2.2 The letters **r** and **l** are distinct. In those cases where the Egyptians use the letter **r**, and other languages use **l**, Botorrita III uses the letter **l**. Botorrita III has *mel* for 'king'. In Egyptian the word for 'king' is *mer* vs. Semitic which uses *mel.*

2.3 The Phoenician script and other related scripts have two signs, one for **s** (𐤔) and one for **sh** (M). The Botorrita III script only uses the M sign that would correspond to **sh**. This Botorrita III **sh** appears to correspond to **sh** when compared to other languages. For example, *Kus̱tikum* was probably pronounced 'Kushtikum'. For 'Kish', the text has *kis* (✓M). Cyprus, known in ancient times as *Alashiya*, is *Alasku*. I know of no language that completely lacks an **s**, but the differences between **s** and **sh** may have been predictable, allowing a single symbol to represent both sounds.

2.4 Unlike other languages that use the Iberian or related Phoenician scripts, which use *Ras*, 𐤓 ,a face looking sideways as the basis for **r**, the Botorritan **r** (𐤒) is like the Egyptian *hr* (🛇), a word meaning 'face' that shows the face looking forward. The pronunciation of *hr* for this sign suggests a voiceless, whispery **r**. Describing the Somali **r**, Saeed notes "the symbol **r** represents an alveolar roll… It is less voiced than the similar **r** in

Italian and Spanish, and is often voiceless word initially."[131]

2.5 There is no symbol for **h**. Other related languages in the region provide cognates for notable words that vary. In some dialects the word will have **h̲**, in others **s̲**, in still others the sound is dropped entirely.

This is relevant to *Austikum* (the High Plateau), a name for the Lasta region, whose first part corresponds to the Bilin word: *away*, 'high'. There is an Egyptian variant written: *H-s-t-KUM* and there are Ge'ez inscriptions from 5th century Axum that refer to the *Has* and *Hasat*.[132]

Reinisch notes, "As opposed to Bilin, Chamir has preserved **s** so where Bilin has *hab,* and Saho and Afar have *ab*, in Chamir, we find *sab*, in Demb. and Quara *Shab*, and in Agaumeder *s̲au,* all as variants of the word for 'to make, to do'."[133]

2.6 The sound of **d̲** is not English **d**, the stop, the voiced counterpart of **t**. Untermann in his romanizations of these Botorrita texts uses **d̲** for a sound like **th** in English 'then'. When Jordán Cólera writes Celtiberian words in the Latin alphabet, he uses **z** (Spanish *theta*) for this sound.[134] Most of the Kushitic languages have a retroflex **d̲**, made by touching the palate with the tongue curled back. This retroflex **d̲** may have been the original pronunciation of the **d̲** symbol.

---

[131] Saeed, Somali Reference, 17.
[132] Kobishchanov, *Axum*, 95, 252.
[133] Reinisch, *Die ChamirSprache*, vol. CV, 595.
[134] Jordán Cólera, "Celtiberian," 759, 804.

Appendix A: Grammatical Notes

2.7 Bilin and Chamir have a generous allocation of velar, uvular and laryngeal stops and fricatives, presumably reflecting long millennia of interactions with Semitic languages that make similar distinctions. Where the Botorrita III text has **k** (**ka, ke, ki, ko, ku,**) modern Chamir has **k, g, kh, gh, q, qh, ch**, and **j**.

2.8 The Botorrita III text has the labials **b, u** and **m**. Chamir has **b, f, w, m** and six varieties of **u**. Neither language has a dedicated symbol for **v**. The Botorrita III text uses **u** (↑) for **w** (*Uiriaskum* for *Wiriaskum*), for **b** (*Auikum* for Hibis), and sometimes for **m** (*Teiuantikum* for *Teimantikum*) and (*Nouida* for *Nomida*). For **f**, we find 'Failaka' and 'Phoenicia (Fenicia)' written with **b** as *Balakos* and *Biniskum*.

2.9 There are two examples where an unstressed vowel appears to have dropped when a suffix was added: *Sleitiu* from *Sile-it-iu* and *eskutino* from *e-Sokota-ino*.

2.10 *Eskutino* also displays an avoidance of initial consonant clusters seen in Somali: *iskutallab*, 'crucifix' from *saqala*, 'to crucify'. Foreign loan words in Botorrita III do not necessarily follow this pattern so we also find *skirtunos,* which may be an Egyptian loan that means 'captive'.

§3 Pronouns

3.1 First person singular
    3.1.1 First person subject 'I'
        The word *ia*, 'I', corresponds to the absolute form of the first person singular in Dhasanac which also

has *ia* meaning 'I'.[135] The pronoun only appears once in the text in the first line, 'One of the southerners from Lasta, I have prevented the Numidians...' (0.1). Bilin and Chamir have *yi* meaning 'my' and *yina* meaning 'our', but they use Semitic *an* for 'I'.[136]

3.1.2 First person singular possessive adjective

The word *i* means 'my, of mine' and corresponds to Chamir *yi* which is also a possessive adjective.[137] It occurs once in *likinos Ataiokum sa i* where it comes at the end of the noun phrase, after *sa*. It follows the head noun *likinos*. Here, it is an example of a possessive adjective that follows the noun in the NA pattern. It is translated here as 'of mine' in 'those Ethiopian princes of mine ...' (2.35), because English does not permit 'those my Ethiopian princes'.

3.2 First person plural possessive

The word *munika*, 'our' is a possessive adjective. Dhasenac has the pronoun *muuni*, 'we'.[138] This is the absolute form for inclusive 'we', i.e., 'we, including you', as in 'we will now all turn to the first page' as opposed to exclusive 'we', not including you, as in 'we will charge you a handling fee'. That allows us to infer that the ruler *Terkinos* directed his Proclamation inclusively to his subjects. For example, at the very end of line 4.37, 'for our provinces', he would mean for the provinces that are yours and mine.

---

[135] Tosco, *Dhasanac Language*, 212ff.
[136] Reinisch, *Die Bilin-Sprache*, 165; Ibid., *Die ChamirSprache*, vol. CV, 679-680.
[137] Ibid., *Die ChamirSprache*, vol. CV, 680.
[138] Tosco, Dhasanac Language, 568.

3.2.1 In Somali, possessive pronouns are converted into possessive adjectives by adding *-ka* (*-ga*).[139] Converting 'we' into 'our' may also be the purpose of the *-ka* at the end of *munika*. The word appears six times, always as *munika*. It precedes the noun it modifies in five cases and follows in the sixth. First, here are the five cases where it precedes.

1.6 *munika koitu koitina*, '<u>our</u> king of kings'.

2.51-52 *munika elkuakue*, 'as far as <u>our</u> king,'.

2.56 *munika tolisokum tirtun*, 'all are [now] <u>our</u> clan territories'.

3.34 *munika ensikum skirtunos*, 'in <u>our</u> conquered empire'.

4.37 *munika uerdaidokum*, 'for <u>our</u> provinces'.

3.2.2 The sixth example, where it follows, has a long string of possessive phrases. They may have affected its position.

1.50-53 *tiokenes uiriaskum uiroku turumokum miduku retukenos tirtanos <u>munikakue</u>*

can be translated

'*Tiokenes* of the River Kingdom, Great Lord of *Turumokum*, [rules] <u>as far as</u> the first of the Great kings of <u>our</u> *Tirtanos*'.

The ending *-kue*, 'near to, as far as' is a postposition suffix and is attached to *munika* so *munika* should be part of the postpositional phrase that precedes it.

3.3 <u>Third person plural</u>

The word *ste,* used just once in line 4.28, may correspond to the Egyptian pronoun *s-t*, which means 'they'. The line says *ste [---] akuikum*. The meaning of *ste* could be 'they' or 'these'. Since it only appears once,

---

[139] Saeed, *Somali Reference*, 166.

we can't eliminate the possibility that it is a noun, perhaps Egyptian *sote,* 'lord, king'.

Akuikum means 'Agau Land'. The kings who are in the list that follows this line are from Agau nations so this might be an introductory summary phrase, '<u>those</u> from the Agau kingdoms [who are under the jurisdiction of the king of Aqiq are]'.

3.4 <u>Third person plural possessive</u>
The word *taniokakue* may mean 'as far as what is theirs'. It has four morphemes: *tan-io-ka-kue.*

   3.4.1 *-kue* is the postposition that means 'near to, as far as'. In this phrase, which is part of a negated expression, it may mean 'not up to' or 'not beyond'.

   3.4.2 *-ka* is the suffix we saw with *munika* that turned a personal pronoun (meaning 'we') into a personal possessive adjective (meaning 'our'). Here its effect should be to turn *tanio,* 'they, these, those' into *tanioka*, 'their, theirs, their possessions'.

   3.4.3 *-io* is a plural marker. It is also a plural marker in Somali. Elsewhere in the Botorrita III text, we find it in *risati<u>o</u>ka*, 'the southerners' (0.1).

   3.4.4 *tan*, in Somali, is a feminine demonstrative adjective that is suffixed to a preceding noun, but it can also stand alone, as a pronoun, meaning 'this, these'.[140] In Chamir, *-tan* is a plural suffix, which can stand alone as a pronoun.[141] It should be feminine but Reinisch reported that his

---

[140] Ibid., 163.
[141] Reinisch, *Die ChamirSprache*, vol. CV, 673.

informants from Lasta used it freely for both genders. The word *tan* in *tanioka* appears exactly once in the text, 'One of the southerners from Lasta (Ethiopia), I have prevented the Numidians from conquering *taniokakue* (beyond [the limits] of their territory)' (0.1).

§4 Verbs

4.1 You can fill a whole book just listing the verb forms in a Kushitic language. The Botorrita III text gives us exactly 17 verbs. This may be a relief to those who are just not that into verb forms, but it will also place some limits on what we can understand about the language. The 17 verb forms with the line numbers where they appear are: *aias* (2.29), *aiu* (1.14, 1.43), *audanto* (0.1), *barnai* (1.59, 3.17), *belsu* (1.12, 1.21, 4.25), *(bi)* (3.46), *eskeninum* (0.1), *le* (1.17), *leton* (2.52), *letontu* (1.19, 1.25, 2.7, 2.24), *letontunos* (2.60), *litu* (1.57, 4.8), *saluta* (1.32), *sekilos* (1.7, 2.11, 2.23), *tarakuai* (0.1), *teudesi* (4.39), *tirs* (1.59), *tueidu* (1.5).

4.2 Past tense, third person singular

   4.2.1 Notice the ending *-u* on several of these verbs. In Chamir the suffix *-u* marks the third person singular in the perfect, i.e., past, tense.[142] Assuming that Botorrita III also uses *-u* to mark the third singular past that would give us the following: *aiu*, 'he was', *litu*, 'he conquered', and *tueidu*, 'he spoke'.

   4.2.2 In Somali, verbs with the suffix *-so* change in meaning, such that instead of *jooji*, 'to cause to

---

[142] Ibid., 622.

stop, halt', the verb becomes *joogso*, 'to stop oneself, come to a halt'.[143] I suspect that *-su* has the same effect on *belsu* so that instead of meaning 'he rules', it means 'it is ruled'. Instead of translating '*Austikum* rules the River Kingdom' (1.20-21), it is probably more correct to read that line as 'the River Kingdom is ruled by *Austikum*'.

In Chamir, there is a suffix *-sh* that causes a similar change in meaning.[144] Reinisch calls this a passive because it lends a sense of 'becoming' to the verb. *aias*, 'they become' may be an example of this in '[Those kings] *aias* (become) the kings of the River Kingdom [over] the districts of: Western Shendi... as far as the king of the Chaldeans' (2.28-2.33).

4.2.3 In Somali, the ending *-ay* (*-ai*) marks the first and the third person singular in the simple past (same as perfect for Chamir. The simple past is used for completed action in the past).[145] Root-changing verbs use this ending, mostly for Semitic loan words. We find that *bar-*, *barn-* translates as 'outside, go outside' in Egyptian, Semitic and Kushitic. It might fall into the loan word class. Assuming then that, in the example below, *barnai* is third person singular past, we will translate lines 1.58-59 as 'from *Abokum* (Elephant Land), *Muturiskum* (United Egypt) *barnai* (is excluded) '.

Another example of *-ai* used for the third person singular past is in 'a king of Cattle Land... [was] a

---

[143] Saeed, Somali Reference, 57.

[144] Reinisch, *Die ChamirSprache*, vol. CV, 618-619.

[145] Saeed, Somali Reference, 89.

commander of the Uweinat _barnai_ (which is outside of) the conquered empire' (3.12-17).

4.2.4 In Bilin, the suffix for the third person singular perfect is _-ux_.[146] The suffix _-ux_ corresponds to Botorrita III _-os_. In addition to verbs, it is also an adjective suffix and a suffix that marks the genitive on nouns. In all three of these uses, it corresponds to _-os_ in the Botorrita III text. We find this ending in _sekilos_ which means 'he hanged'.

4.2.5 Akkadian _tirs_, 'stretches, extends to' may be just a foreign loan word used as such.[147] An example is 'Abokum starts from Fort Aden... _Muturiskum_ (United Egypt) I exclude [from its territory, but] _tirs_ (it extends to) _Turumokum_' (1.54-59).

4.2.6 The Semitic word _saluta-_ is related to 'sultan' and translates as 'reigns, rules'. In Ethiopian Ge'ez _sallata_ means 'gain dominion, have power, have authority, exercise authority, become master, reign, rule'.[148] The word _sellut_ means 'who has power, who has dominion'. Lines 1.30-32 translate as 'the kings of the _Akuia_ kingdom saluta (rule) _Tetokum_.'. No contribution from Kushitic morphology is visible or needed.

4.2.7 In Somali, the verbs _ahay_, 'to be' and _leeyahay_, 'to have' are auxiliary verbs.[149] The verb form _le_ means 'he had' and is probably cognate with

---

[146] Reinisch, _Die ChamirSprache_, vol. CV, 593.

[147] von Soden, _Grundriss der Akkadischen_, 145sect.89c.

[148] Leslau, Concise Dictionary of Ge'ez, 50.

[149] Saeed, _Somali Reference_, 116-118; Bliese, "Afar," 143. See Afar verb for 'to have'.

Somali: *leeyahay*. It occurs once in *sleitiu karunikum le*, 'who <u>had</u> *Karunikum* of the *Sleitiu*' (1.17).

4.3 Causative

In Chamir, as in other Kushitic languages, there is a causative affix.[150] In Chamir, the affix is *-es*. Chamir can also use the suffix *-i* to indicate a verb is third person singular. If we apply these observations to *teud-es-i*, the verb means 'it was caused to be said / it was proclaimed / it was decreed'. In the Botorrita I-B text, we have *bintis* as the causative form of *bint*, 'to be burned'. The causative can be translated as 'cause to burn, destroy by burning down'.

4.4 Participle

In Untermann's Romanization of the Botorrita III text, the word (*bi*) appears in parentheses.[151] The symbol for *bi* (Γ) is rather simple. The parentheses seem to express uncertainty regarding if this was *bi* or a meaningless scratch on the plaque. If it is *bi*, it may be a verb cognate with Somali: *bi'i*, 'cause to be destroyed', from *ba*, 'spoil, defeat, obliterate'. It appears just once as *sura ensikum melman (bi)*, 'from the army of the <u>defeated</u> *Melman* empire to...' (3.46).

4.5 Future

Botorrita III *leton*, *letontu* and *letontunos* correspond to the Chamir verb *lat̲* which means 'to extend to, to stretch, to include', and *lit̲*, 'span, extent'.[152] In relative clauses, they can be translated as 'extending to' or

---

[150] Reinisch, *Die ChamirSprache*, vol. CV, 620, 625.
[151] Untermann and Wodtko, *Monumenta Linguarum*, 582.
[152] Reinisch, *Die ChamirSprache*, vol. CV, 626; Ibid., vol. CVI, 389, 445.

Appendix A: Grammatical Notes

'which extends to'.[153] You can see this in the following example, *stena muturiskum tirtu… retukenos ensikum letontu Batokum*, 'a king of all of United Egypt,… the kingdom of the Great King which <u>extended to</u> Mendes' (1.16-19). In main clauses, the form *letontu,* as a third person singular form, and perhaps *leton,* as a first person singular form, correspond to future forms in Chamir.

Some examples of possible future forms for these words are:
1.25 '[This new region] <u>will extend</u> to Fort Hibis'.
2.4-7 '…[in the domain] of the Great Chief of *Turanikum,* the king of the River Kingdom in the South, which <u>will extend</u> to the princes of *Uiskikum*'.[154]
2.52-53 'I <u>will extend</u> the Harbor kingdom of the Swamp dwellers to the king of the *Terkinos* at Thinis'.
2.58-60 'The province of *Bentikum* <u>will extend to</u> the borders of the Akuia empire in *Abokum* from the territories of the king of Djibouti'.

4.6 <u>Subjunctive of purpose</u>

The verb *audanto* is cognate with a Bilin verb *auti* that means 'to win, to conquer'.[155] The grammatical form is what Reinisch calls a "subjunctive of purpose". He gives some examples, two of which I repeat here. "*ni* (his) *fintir* (goats) *qualdo* (in order to see) *farux* (he went out)" or 'He went out in order to see his goats'.[156] *Qualdo* meaning 'in order to see' is in the subjunctive of purpose form. The Botorrita III verb *audanto,* as a

---

[153] In the language of the text, tense would not be marked in a relative clause like 'which extends to'. In English, this use of *letontu* may correspond to a participle, like 'extending' or 'including'. See §4.9.
[154] See §4.9.
[155] Reinisch, *Texte der Bilin-Sprache*, 10. Bilin: *autitux,* 'he conquered'.
[156] Ibid., Die Bilin-Sprache, 41.

238

subjunctive of purpose form, would mean 'in order to conquer', or 'for the purpose of conquering, invading'.

In this text, *audanto* is the only example of this verb form. Another example from Reinisch with several verbs in this form is "*Ta'anto, buqurto, zanzgito, hacacto, laqatto, sillaqsito*, kanal *zagarto*, ghaqual *waratto*, linensi *akabto*, nilik jarabugun ganjinat.*" This phrase can translated as, 'In order that she would grind meal [for me], cook polenta, bake bread, make coarse and fine meal, prepare beer, fetch wood and water, [and] watch-over the house, for-all-this I-need a slave'.[157]

4.7 Negation

Negation can be tricky, particularly in languages that allow double or triple negatives. Are those additional negatives just adding emphasis or are they expanding the scope of the negation? Grammars of Kushitic languages often provide complete and separate paradigms for positive and negative verb forms. There are two negative verb forms that appear in Botorrita III. Within those verb forms, there are examples of three common negative affixes -*k*- (or -*g*-, or -*ku*-,) -*in*- and -*m* (or -*um*).

The verb *tara-ku-ai*, 'cause-not-I-past', meaning something like 'I did not allow, I prevented', is cognate with the Somali verb: *taray*, 'to affect, to assist'. When we discussed *barnai* above, we mentioned a Somali paradigm where -*ay* (*ai*) is the first person singular past ending. Since *ia* ('I') precedes *tarakuai* in the Botorrita III text, we translate *ia tarakuai* as 'I prevented'.

---

[157] Ibid.

The second negative verb form is *eskeninum, which* means 'that they would not reach'. The word has three parts. The first is *esk-*, 'reach'. Note Amharic: *eska,* 'until', *asganna,* 'successful', and Chamir: *ash,* 'until'. The second part is *-kenin-*, 'they would not' as in Bilin: *-gininu-*.[158] This part is a negative subjunctive third plural, or negative jussive suffix. Third, is *-um*, 'that', the subordinating suffix, *-um* that marks verbal nouns and subordinate clauses, particularly those with a negative or subjunctive sense.[159] Put together they form the phrase 'that they would not reach'. 'They' are the would-be conquering Numidians.

The word *tarakuai,* 'I prevented' takes a subordinate clause as its object. That object clause has two subordinate phrases, which together answer the question, 'What did I prevent?'. The clause, 'that the Numidians who would conquer', acts as the subject of the larger object clause. The verb for the object clause is *eskeninum,* 'that they would not reach'. So the structure is 'I prevented + object clause'. Then object clause contains as its subject 'the conquering Numidians' and as its verb 'would not reach beyond their boundaries'. These are all in the first sentence in the text, 'One of the southerners from Lasta, I have prevented the Numidians from conquering beyond [the limits] of their territory' (0.1). Surely, life would be poorer without the negative subjunctive!

4.8 Ergative or not

There are many different kinds of ergative languages. In most of them transitive verbs are involved, often in perfect tenses. There is a subject case to mark the

---

[158] Ibid., *Die ChamirSprache,* vol. CV, 629-630, 689n1.
[159] Ibid., 636, 652-655; Kamil, *Parlons Afar,* 108-114.

subjects of intransitive verbs and the direct object of a transitive verb. The subject or agent of the transitive verb is in a different case, often called the absolute or ergative case.

Basque is considered an ergative language. There has been discussion and debate about whether the Kushitic languages are ergative.

 Like ergative languages, Kushitic languages often have different but parallel paradigms depending on whether the object of the verb is singular or plural. Saeed claims that Somali is a tone language and that differences in tone mark the difference between the subject and absolute cases.[160] These are difficult to observe when studying an ancient bronze plaque with no living native speakers. Reinisch does not report ergatives in Chamir or Bilin.

If you look carefully at the verb forms above, you will see that there is no clear evidence that the language of Botorrita III is or is not an ergative language.

The one clear example that says the language of Botorrita III is not ergative involves the verb *sekilos*, 'he hanged'. The verb is cognate with Ge'ez: *saqala*, Amharic: *saqqala,* 'to hang, to crucify', *masqal,* 'crucifix', Somali: *iskutallab,* 'crucifix'. This verb occurs three times, but only the first gives us a clear example of subject - transitive verb - object(s). '...our king of kings has hanged in Thinis, from the River Kingdom, the king of the army of Metelis, a king of Memphis, a chief of Mendes under whom the island (of Cyprus) is ruled, a king of the *Shebka* empire [who]

[160] Saeed, *Somali Reference*, 22-25.

was the commander of *Loukanikum*, the king of the
army of the River Kingdom, [and] a king of all of
United Egypt who had *Karunikum* of the *Sleitiu*, the
kingdom of the Great King which extended to Mendes'
(1.6-19).

The example above is good because it is clear that the
subject, and agent, must be the 'king of kings' and the
verb is singular, agreeing with the subject. If the verb
agreed with the six objects, it should be plural and is
not. In short, the evidence addresses the issues and
proves the point. Botorrita III is not an ergative
language. In our one clear example, the agent is the
grammatical subject of a transitive verb. Although we
only have one sentence, it provides evidence against
two kinds of ergatives. In Basque, every transitive
sentence is ergative. Clearly, our sentence shows we
don't have that kind of ergative. In Pashto, only
sentences with completed action, mostly in the past,
are ergative.This example also provides evidence
against this second kind of ergative. The verb in our
example describes a completed action, but still agrees
with the agent subject.

4.9 Relative clauses
The language of the Botorrita III text resembles
Chamir in that tense is not marked on the verb in a
relative clause. On Chamir, Reinisch points out,
"While Bilin has various forms for the present... and
perfect, Chamir has only a single form in relative
clauses, so that it is out of the meaning of the sentence
only that one can see what tense the verb in the relative
clause represents."[161] Both Chamir and the Botorrita III
text differ from Bilin and English in this respect. In

---

[161] Reinisch, *Die ChamirSprache*, vol. CV, 649-651, 649.

several sentences where the verb form *letontu* is used in a <u>relative clause</u>, the tense in the English translation is past, present or future as the meaning in English would require. Where that same verb form, i.e. *letontu*, is used as a <u>main verb</u>, the English translations are, appropriately, in the future tense. Examples in main clauses in the future tense were given above in §4.5. Examples with the verb in a relative clause are given below.

Past:

retukenos ensikum <u>letontu</u> batokum, 'the kingdom of the Great King which <u>extended</u> to Mendes' (1.18-9). This king is in a list of rulers who were hanged, so the description of the extent of his kingdom refers to a situation that requires a past tense in English.

Future:

medukenos turanikum elu uiriaskum launiku likinos uiskikum <u>letontu</u>, '...[in the domain] of the Great Chief of *Turanikum*, the king of the southern [part of] the River Kingdom, which <u>will extend to</u> the princes of *Uiskikum*' (2.4-7).
The text describes new boundaries that are being created, so future tense is needed in English to say they are coming into existence.

§5 Nouns

5.1 <u>Noun formation</u>
Nouns can be formed from verbs by adding *-anta*. If you take *arka*, 'to know' plus *anta*, it produces *arkanta* 'those who know, the wise ones'. *-ta* also forms nouns, as in *Turenta*, 'people of Turan' and *turtunta*, a foreign

word, perhaps 'controller', but also 'chief official at the court'.[162]

Nouns can be formed from adjectives or from other nouns with *-it* or *-at* meaning 'originating from' as in *ris-at-io-ka*, 'south originating from' or 'originating from the south'. The *-io* makes it plural, leaving 'people originating from the south' or 'the southerners'. If you look at *sleitiu* as *sile-it-iu*, you get 'people from Sile'.

Nouns can be formed from adjectives by adding the definite article suffix *-ku* as in:
> *midu-ku*, 'the First one',
> *uiro-ku*, 'the Great one',
> *kentis-ku*, 'the one in front, the foremost one',
> *launi-ku*, 'the one on the right, the south, the southern one' [if you face east, south is on the right hand side].

5.2   Compounds with *-enos* and *-kenos*
Medukenos, 'Great Chief', literally, 'the one with the big head', resembles Somali: *madax-ka-weyna*, 'head / chief, the-great-of', that translates as 'of the Great-Chief (emperor, president)'.[163]
Retukenos has a similar structure, as in *retu-ka-weyna*. The word '*retu*' may come from Egyptian: *retu*, 'man, men'. A better candidate might be Shilluk: *Reth*, 'Divine King'.[164] The parts of the word are 'king-the-

---

[162] Reinisch, *Die Bilin-Sprache*, 81-83, 85. Reinisch gives as an example "Am I my brother's keeper (*takawanta*)?" . Adding *-ta* to the verb 'keep' makes it 'keeper'.

[163] Saeed, Somali Reference, 121.

[164] Collins and Tignor, *Egypt and the Sudan*, 17. The text mentions "distinctive Shilluk institutions of political organization revolving around the Reth or Divine King." Shilluk speak a Nilo-Saharan language and live in southern Sudan along the Nile corridor.

great-of', so the word means 'Great King', 'of the Great King'.

Looking at *tiokenes*, it is a proper name from *tio*, 'wind god' as in *tio-ka-weyna-es*, 'the-great-wind-god's-one', the-great-wind-god's-person / follower'. Then with *tiokenesos*, you add the suffix -*os*. From the genitive case in Bilin, we get *tio-ka-weyna-es-os* or *tiokenes* plus the genitive plural, to form 'those of *Tiokenes*', or '*Tiokenes* followers'.

The name of Sargon of Akkad (2300 BC) in Akkadian was *sharru-ken*, 'king-great'.[165] His name in Sumerian was *lugal-gina*, 'king-great'. Sargon lived about a thousand years later than the Botorrita III text. The name in Sumerian and Semitic, unlike Kushitic, shows no awareness of the morphological pieces of this name. This word may originally be a Kushitic compound that was a loan word in Sumerian and in Semitic. Among the Celtiberians of Spain, *Madicenus* was a popular name, appearing on a Roman era funerary stele.[166] Also among the Phoenicians, as noted earlier, Matgenus was the father of Dido of Carthage.

5.3 Compound nouns

The word *kum* meaning 'land, or kingdom' is a noun. Therefore, all the placenames ending in *kum* (about 88) are, strictly speaking, compound nouns. It is never followed by a suffix.

---

[165] Horowitz, *Mesopotamian Cosmic Geography*, 70n31.
[166] Rose, "Text and Image in Celtiberia," 166-169.

Appendix A: Grammatical Notes

The other compound nouns are as follows:
ailo-kis-kum, 'Aila of Kish Land'
anies-kor, 'Mount Kor'
antio-kos, 'Antiu Lord'
Bilo-nikos, 'Lord-king'
bilos-ban, 'Enemy-lord, evil / abominable lord'
biurti-laur, 'noble island'
bubili-bor, 'Babal Chief'
eka-r-bilos, 'the leader's lord'
elau-kos, 'Elephant lord'
iunsti-bas, 'bowmen rebels'
kabelai-kis-kum, 'Hill of Kish Land'
kankai-kis-kum, 'Sumerian Land of Kish'
kenti-sum, 'foremost-leader'
korti-kos, 'Khor-lord', Khor in Qatar
kulu-kam-i-kum, 'Koloe in Kam Land'
kuinikum, 'South Land'
kuinti-taku, 'extreme south'
kunikum, 'the southern kingdoms'
melman-tama, '*Melman* Lord'
mut-uris-kum, 'Vulture Cobra Land', Egypt
snad-iuentos, 'Shendi West'
sten-iontes, 'king of the bowmen'
tarkun-biur, 'Tarkun City', Tarkhan
tirto-bolo-kum, 'all-city-land, ?Metropolis'
tirto-uios 'all-waters', [someone from] the Great
    Marsh, the Sudd (Somali: *biyo* "water")
tur-ikain-os, 'Fort Iken people'

5.4 Number
In several of the Kushitic languages, including Bilin
and Chamir, the base form of the noun is a collective,
unspecified for number. In Bilin, a collective noun can

246

be made specifically singular (or singulative) by adding *-ra*. In Chamir, the singular is *-a*.[167]
Examples of Chamir *-a* from the Botorrita III text are:

> *elkua*, 'a king' versus *elku*, 'kings'
> *stena*, 'a king' versus *stenu*, 'kings'
> *akuia*, 'a head, a chief' versus *akuios*, 'of the head / chief' (may also mean an Agau, one of the Agau or an *Akhou*, one of the *Akhou*)
> *buria*, 'a head, a chief'
> *aunia*, 'one of the Aunu'

An example in Botorrita III of a noun being made singular by adding *-ra*, as in Bilin, is *bolo-ra* meaning 'a town' or 'one town'.[168] The scope of *-ra*, which is attached to the last word in the noun phrase is over the whole noun phrase. The only other example of this in the Botorrita III text makes the noun phrase singular even though the noun it refers to is plural. The phrase *risatio-ka leste-ra* can translate as 'a southerner from Lasta', but *risatio-ka* means 'the southerners' and is plural. The translation 'one of the southerners from Lasta' (0.1) gives a clearer idea of the grammatical question at hand.

Many nouns in the text are foreign words with foreign plural suffixes. Plural suffixes cognate with other Kushitic languages like Somali and Dhasanac may be ancient, native Botorrita III plurals or may reflect a region-wide Kushitic *lingua franca* or trading language that was spoken widely under Kushitic speaking emperors. Some plural suffixes are:

---

[167] Reinisch, *Die ChamirSprache*, vol. CV, 671. Chamir: *bir*, 'blood'; *bir-a*, 'drop of blood'.
[168] Ibid., *Die Bilin-Sprache*, 87.

Egyptian: *-iu* as in *abaniu, sleitiu, tiriu.*[169]
Somali: *-ino* where the singular is *mailikum*, but
the plural is *mailik-INO-kum.*[170] Another
example is singular *elka*, but genitive plural
elk-INO-os or *elkinos*. Also *e-Sokota-INO* or
eskutino.
Somali: *-io* as in *risatio-ka, tanio-ka-kue.*[171]
Somali: *-man* as in *melman.*[172]
Dhasanac: *-ana* as in *lesana, albana.*[173]

5.5 Cases

Subject nouns are not marked for case. In Somali, the
definite article *-ku* can be used to mark the subject. In
Botorrita III *-ku* is used as a definite article, but is
often found inside of postpositional phrases in no
position to act as a subject.

Object case: There is just one potential example of an
object case suffix, direct or indirect in the text. In Bilin
-s usually marks objects, direct and indirect. The single
example of a potential dative (indirect object, **to** X) in
Botorrita III is *koitinas* in line 2.50-53 <u>koitinas</u> *terkinos*
toutinikum leton katunos burikounikum '**to** the <u>king</u> of
the *Terkinos* [people] at Thinis, I will extend the
Harbor Kingdom of the Swamp dwellers'.

Genitive case: This case is used to express possession
as well as other noun-noun relations. Nouns referring
to the possessor precede the noun that refers to the
thing possessed, so *Sleitiu Karunikum* means

---

[169] Gardiner, *Egyptian Grammar*, 61-62.
[170] Saeed, *Somali Reference*, 135. In Somali, Declension 6 adds *-oyin*
to form the plural.
[171] Ibid., 130-132.
[172] Ibid., 133.
[173] Tosco, *Dhasanac Language*, 83.

'Karunikum of the Sleitiu'. In Greenberg's terms, the word order for possessives is GN. Possessive nouns take *-r*, *-d* or *-os* in the singular and *-u* and *-os* in the plural, where *-os* corresponds to Bilin: *-ux*.[174] We find *elkinos* (*elk-INO-os*), 'of the kings'.

Other examples of genitives are:
> *bilir* turtunta, 'at the court <u>of the lord</u>'
> *tiriu uiriaskum turtunadkue*, 'to the court <u>of the</u>
> <u>Deire people</u> in the River Kingdom'
> *burdu auikum <u>melmanios</u> Uiriaskum*, 'fort Hibis
> <u>of</u> *Melmanios* of the River Kingdom'
> *munika <u>koitu</u> koitina*, 'our king <u>of kings</u>'

Other case-type relations like ablative and locative are expressed by postpositions and described in that section.

§6 Adjectives

6.1 Adjective position

Adjectives normally follow the noun (NA word order), except for the possessive adjectives. For the possessive adjectives, some precede the noun (*munika*, 'our', five examples). Some follow the noun (*i*, 'my', and one instance of *munika*, 'our').

Postpositions and adjectival suffixes belong to the noun phrase or verb phrase and normally follow or are attached to the last word in the phrase. The language of Botorrita III resembles other Kushitic languages and Basque in this respect.

---

[174] Reinisch, *Die Bilin-Sprache*, 95.

Appendix A: Grammatical Notes

6.2 Adjective formation
Some adjective forming suffixes are:
-*m*, *melm, mel* + *m*, 'local, Egyptian'
-*o*, *turo*, 'relating to *Turikum*', *seko*, 'relating to the
  Shebka kingdom', *tirtano*, 'relating to the
  Scorpion Clans, to *Tirtanikum*', *kaukirino*,
  'relating to the Keren Highlands', also
  eladuno, retukeno
-*i*, *bini*, 'Phoenician', 'people from *Biniskum*'
-*ino*, *eskutino, e-S[o]kut-ino*, 'someone from the
  Lasta town of Sokot*a̱*', *at-ino-os*, 'easterners'
  (for 'east', the text has three forms: *atinos* for
  'easterners', *atu* for 'eastern', and *atokum* for
  'eastland')
-*do*, *melmando*, 'belonging to the Melman'
-*os*, creates ethnonyms , comparable to Bilin -*ux*,
  akuios, atinos, aualos, babos, bilinos,
  ebursunos, kalaitos, karbelos, kasilos,
  katunos, kontudos, lukinos, melmandos,
  sanios, sekanos, statulos, suros, terkinos,
  tirtanos, tirtouios, tueidunos, turaios,
  turikainos, turos, useidunos[175]

6.3 Adjective conjugation
tirtu, 'all', singular, as in *stena Muturiskum tirtu*, 'a
  king of all United Egypt'
tirtun, 'all', plural, as in *munika tolisokum tirtun*,
  '[These are] all our tribal kingdoms'
tirtunos, 'all', genitive plural, as in *koitu kuinikum*
  tirtunos, '[they are] kings of all of the Southern
  Kingdom'

6.4 -*na, -no, -nos* used as demonstratives

---

[175] Ibid.

The suffix *-na* is used as a demonstrative meaning 'this, these' in both Chamir and Dhasanac.[176] When *-o* or *-os* follow *-n*, it can also be demonstrative. Some examples from the Botorrita III text are:

> *eladu-na*, 'these kings', *koiti-na*, 'this king'
> *burdu*, 'fort' and *eladu-n-o*, 'kings-this-adjective' combines for 'this royal fort'
> *eladunos*, *ela-du-n-os*, 'king-plural-these-genitive' forms 'of these kings'

6.5 *sa* as a demonstrative

Chamir uses the plural suffix *-zai* with other demonstratives as in *enzai*, 'these' and *ez-zai*, 'those'.[177] Reinisch gives an example from the language Agaumeder "*eni-sa*" meaning 'these'. He gives other examples from Chamir such as "*ienjan iuna-zan-za*", 'this woman'. The word *ienjan*, 'this' precedes the noun and *za,* also meaning 'this', follows. He points out an Egyptian parallel *an* for *en*, *ien* in Chamir. Recalling that Egyptian is a BEFORE language, one could guess that the Egyptian loan word is preceding the noun and the native Kushitic word is following the noun.

Our single example of *sa* meaning 'this, these' and following the noun phrase would support the idea that the original or at least earlier form of the demonstrative was just the postposition, without *ien* or *ienjan*. It occurs as *likinos ataiokum sa i kaburikum memun*, 'of those princes of mine in *Ataiokum* below *Kaburikum*' (2.35-36).

---

[176] Ibid., *Die ChamirSprache*, vol. CV, 683-684; Tosco, *Dhasanac Language,* 226.
[177] Reinisch, *Die ChamirSprache*, vol. CV, 682.

Appendix A: Grammatical Notes

6.6 Definite article

Both -*ku* and -*ka* are used as definite articles. All of the examples in the text that use the -*ka* form of the article are plural. The -*ka* that makes a pronoun possessive, as we saw above with *muni* / *munika* and *tanio* / *tanioka*, may be a different suffix. In other Kushitic languages like Somali, the suffix -*ka* / -*ga* that makes a pronoun possessive is used with all of the pronouns, singular and plural, but it is a little hard to be certain since only these two plural possessives occur in the text. All examples with -*ka* from the text are listed below:

risat-io-ka, 'the southerners'
bert-i-ka-kue, 'as far as the Berta people'
muni-ka, 'our'
tan-io-ka-kue, 'as far as theirs'

The examples of -*ku* in the text are singular, often adjectives turned into nouns, or collective nouns with the singulative suffix -*a*. Notice *tolokunos* where -*nos* is added to form a plural.

alas-ku, 'the island, Cyprus, Alashiya'
aurei-a-ku, 'the birthplace'
basa-ku, 'the Basa region'
esuei-ku, 'the gulf, the bay, the estuary'
kentis-ku, 'the foremost one, the one in front'
launi-ku, 'the right, the south'
midu-ku, 'the first one'
tolo-ku, 'the border'
tolo-ku-nos, 'those on the border'
tur-a-ku, 'the Tyre [region]'
uirias-ku, 'the river'

-ki is also used to mean 'his or theirs' and 'that or those'.
Somali also uses *-ki* in this way.[178] There are three
examples in Botorrita III. The first is *Elkuei-ki-kum*,
'of the king, his land', Royal Land, a word preserved in
the name 'Arqiqo'. Another is *Uidus-ki-kum*, 'Bayuda
people, their land', Bayuda Land. The third example is
Uis-ki-kum, 'Mouza people-their-land', Mouza Land.

6.7 Egyptian preposition that behaves like an adjective
The Egyptian preposition *khentis* means 'front,
upstream, south' and behaves as an adjective in
Botorrita III.[179]

1.39 *kentis-ku*, 'the southern part of the River
Kingdom'

2.2-3 *tirtanos kentis-kue*, 'as far as the southern
Tirtanos'

2.24-25 *ustitokum turenta kentis-kue*, 'In *Ustitokum*
down to (as far as) the southern *Turenta*'

3.3-4 *tirtanikum uiriaskum mel kinbiria kentis-kue*, 'as
far as *Tirtanikum*, south of the king of *Kinbiria* in
the River Kingdom'

3.56 *babos kentis-kue uiriaskum*, 'in the River
Kingdom from south of the *Babos* (people of
Wawat)'

3.58-4.2 *uiriaskum...steniontes turikainos bolora
kentis-kue*, 'in the River Kingdom... the king of
the bowmen as far as the southern town of the
Turikainos'

3.24 *kenti-sum tuateroskue*, 'is the foremost chief in
both directions', compound noun

---

[178] Saeed, *Somali Reference*, 160; Zorc and Osman, *Somali-English
Dictionary*.
[179] Budge, *Egyptian Hieroglyphic Dictionary*, 554; Gardiner, *Egyptian
Grammar*, 529sect.W-17.

§7 Postpositions

As the name indicates, postpositions occur at the end of their postpositional phrase. In a long phrase, the 'place to' or 'place from' is sometimes several lines before the postposition that describes the direction.

7.1.1 -anko, 'middle', like Bilin: anqay, 'middle'.[180]
    2.17 *elaukos bentikum* <u>roten-anko</u>, 'the Elephant Lord [rules] *Bentikum* from <u>the middle of the length</u> of the coast.'
    4.10 *koitina* <u>tirikant-anko</u>, '[becomes] the king, from <u>the middle of</u> the Tiran Strait'

7.1.2 -ar, 'to'.[181]
    2.58-60 *sekondos bentikum* <u>tolos-ar</u> *ensikum akuia abokum*, 'the province of *Bentikum* will extend <u>to the borders</u> of the Akuia empire in *Abokum*'

7.1.3 *auay*, 'over, high, up above'.[182] This is a common postposition but only appears in placenames in the text. *Austikum* (High Plateau), *Austunikum* (Highlanders Land), *Auaskum* (Highlands).

7.1.4 -id, 'of', genitive, 'under the authority of'.[183]
    4.28-29 *ste [---] akuikum* <u>elkue-id</u> *Akikum*, 'the lords of *Akuikum* [who] are <u>under the jurisdiction of</u> the king of Aqiq [are]'

---

[180] Reinisch, *Die Bilin-Sprache*, 102.
[181] Ibid.
[182] Ibid.
[183] Reinisch, *Die Bilin-Sprache*, 93, 99; Kamil, *Parlons Afar*, 195. The suffix -id, in this case, may be a form of Afar: *ixxo* (*iddo*), 'jurisdiction, authority'.

7.1.5 *ke*, 'in, within'.[184]

3.45 *toutinikum tolokunos ke*, 'those who are <u>within</u> the borders of Thinis'

7.1.6 *kekas ko*, 'in the middle of'.[185]

2.37-38 *kares ruaku korkos tar[--]tetokum kekas ko*, 'the road from Korosko village to Kurgis that passes <u>through the middle</u> of *Tetokum*'

7.1.7 *-ko-*, 'region, locality'.[186]

Found in *Beskokum, Makeskokum, Talukokum, Taskokum,* and *Loukaniko.*

7.1.8 *-kue*, 'as far as, near, up to, not beyond'.[187] It is

often used to delimit boundaries. Lists of boundaries often go from far to near, rather than from near to far. Depending on where in the list of new boundaries it appears, *-kue* sometimes needs to be translated as 'from, starting from' and at other times as 'up to, as far as'.
3.45-47 *kalisokum sura ensikum melman (bi) usama abalos-kue*, 'from the (defeated) army of the *Melman* empire at Klusma <u>up to</u> [the temple] of Apollo the Most High'

7.1.9 *l*, 'to'.[188]

1.1 *soisum albana skirtunos tirtanikum l*, '<u>to</u> that Arab leader [held] captive in *Tirtanikum*'

---

[184] Budge, *Egyptian Hieroglyphic Dictionary*, 813. Egyptian: ges, 'within'.

[185] Reinisch, *Die ChamirSprache*, vol. CV, 678; Lepsius, *Nubische Grammatik*, 429. Nubian: *gasko*, 'middle'. See §7.1.8.

[186] Resembles Somali: *kob*, 'region, land, locality'.

[187] Reinisch, *Die ChamirSprache*, vol. CV, 690. In Chamir: *gua*; Ibid., *Texte der Bilin-Sprache*, 6. In Bilin: *gaba* and *guae*.

[188] Reinisch, *Die Bilin-Sprache*, 100-101.

7.1.10 *me*, 'in'.[189] Corresponds to an Egyptian
preposition *m* () in meaning and use, but it is
used as a postposition.
1.7 *sekilos toutinikum me*, 'he has hanged in
Thinis'
1.22 *sekondos uiriaskum me*, 'a province [that will
be] in the River Kingdom'

7.1.11 *mem*, 'under, below'.[190]
1.11-12 *buria batokum belsu alasku mem*, 'a chief
of Mendes under whom the island (of Cyprus)
is ruled'
1.29 *likinos uerdaidokum mem*, 'Below the
princes of these districts [are]'

7.1.12 *ti*, 'to'.[191]
3.48-49 *eladuna balaisokum likinos turumokum
ti*, 'from the kings of Pelusium to the princes
of *Turumokum*,'

7.1.13 *ulta*, 'from, taken or transferred from'.[192]
1.25-28 *letontu mailikum burdu auikum
melmanios uiriaskum karbelos turumokum
ulta*, 'will extend to Fort *Auikum,*in the
kingdom of *Melmanios* of the River
Kingdom, from *Turumokum* of the Sand-
dwellers'

---

[189] Gardiner, *Egyptian Grammar*, 40sects.37-38.
[190] Edel, *AltÄgyptische Grammatik*, 391sect.760, no.6. Old Egyptian:
m-m, 'under'.
[191] Reinisch, *Die Bilin-Sprache*, 100.
[192] Horowitz, *Mesopotamian Cosmic Geography*, 70. From Akkadian.

7.2 Declension of postpositions
  7.2.1 *mem*, 'under, below', *memun*-, 'under + plural',
    memunos, 'under + genitive plural'.
      2.11-13 *tirilokum medukenos akikum memun*
        akuia alaskum memunos, 'The islands are
        under the chief of *Tirilokum,* who is under the
        Great-Chief of Aqiq'
      2.35-36 *likinos ataiokum sa[---]i kaburikum*
        memun, 'those princes of mine in *Ataiokum*
        below *Kaburikum*'

  7.2.2 *ulta*, 'from', *ultu*, 'from+ plural', *ultia*, 'from +
    singulative', *ultinos*, 'from + plural + genitive',
    ultatun, 'from + plural', *ultatunos*, 'from + genitive
    plural'.
      1.8-9 *ult-ia uiriaskum mel sura matulokum*, 'one
        from the River Kingdom, the king of the army
        of Metelis'
      1.23-24 *burdu teiuantikum bilibos turumokum ult-*
        u, '[ending at] Fort Tjamet from *Turumokum*
        of the *Bilibos* people'.
      2.47-48 *sikeia beteriskum sekontios turumokum*
        ultat-un, 'to the Siq at Petra are [taken] from
        the commander of *Turumokum*'
      3.6-7 *stenu bentilikum burdu bentilikum*
        ultatunos, 'of the kings of *Bentilikum* from
        those at Fort *Bentilikum*'
      3.54-55 *ailokiskum suros alikum ult-IN-os*
        amakue, 'the Syrians at Aila of Kish, those
        from Elim up to Amman'

7.3 Position
  Postpositions follow the last word in the noun phrase
  or verb phrase. In discussing number in nouns, we
  already looked at the singulative suffix -*ra* whose
  scope was the whole noun phrase in *risatioka leste-ra*,

Appendix A: Grammatical Notes

'<u>one of</u> the southerners from Lasta'. AFTER languages typically have subject-object-verb word order. In such languages, the verb is frequently the last word in the verb phrase. A postposition can follow or be attached to the end of a verb, as follows:

1.41-42 *aboiokum abulu <u>akuia-kue</u>*, '[he rules] <u>as far as</u> the *Akuia* cities of Abydos'

1.42-43 *araiokum alu <u>aiu-kue</u>*, '[To the south] Alodia was as far as [he ruled] in Cataract Land'

§8 Botorrita I-B Grammatical Notes

8.1 <u>Auxiliary verbs</u>

The word *aiu*, 'was' is used as a fairly regular auxiliary verb. As in other AFTER languages, the auxiliary follows the main verb, often coming at the end of the verb phrase. An example is 'The plundered *Melmu* land that was destroyed, which extends to the *Turo* Uweinat <u>was</u> destroyed by the Libyans' (I-B 2-3).

8.2 <u>Ablative of means, cause, reason</u>

In Bilin, the suffix -*d* marks a cause or reason.[193] In this text, -*d* seems to mark an agent, perhaps as a kind of cause. So *ubokum turo bintis lubina-d aiu* is 'which extends to the *Ubokum Turo* was destroyed <u>by</u> the *Lubina* (Libyans)' (I-B 3). Other examples are *Akaina-d*, '<u>by</u> the Achaeans' (I-B 5) and *Ukonta-d*, '<u>by</u> the Mycenaeans' (I-B 9).

8.3 <u>Plurals in -*na*</u>

There are two examples of plurals with the suffix -*na: lubi-na-d*, 'by the Libyans' and *akai-na-d*, 'by the Achaeans'.

---

[193] Reinisch, *Texte der Bilin-Sprache*, 100. Bilin: -*d* as ablative case of means, cause, or reason.

8.4 *uko-nta-d,* 'by the Mycenaeans'

Chadwick, in discussing the Mycenaean tablets from Pylos comments, "More significant are a group of tablets dealing with what they call the *o-ka.* Despite intensive study we are still not agreed upon the details, and in particular what an *o-ka* was: probably it was a kind of military unit, perhaps a command, though some have connected it with a word meaning 'merchant-ship'; but all are agreed that the context is military."[194] Reading this, I wonder if *o-ka* was an ethnonym, a variant of *uika, uko,* 'Mycenaean'.

---

[194] Chadwick, *Decipherment of Linear B*, 105.

APPENDIX B

BOTORRITA III: SIDE BY SIDE

0.1 *risatioka lestera ia tarakuai nouida audanto eskeninum taniokakue soisum albana*	0.1 One of the southerners from Lasta (Ethiopia), I have prevented the *nouida* (Numidians) from conquering beyond [the limits] of their territory. To that Arab leader
1.1 *skirtunos tirtanikum l*	1.1 [held] captive in *Tirtanikum* (Harar Province area, Ethiopia),
1.2 *kontudos turos* 1.3 *retukenos*	1.2-1.3 the Great King of the *Turos* (west Red Sea people) and the *Kontudos* (people of the interior in south Nile Valley, Sudan),
statulu 1.4 *medukenos*	1.4 the Great Chief of the *Statulu* (in Syria, Palestine),
koitina 1.5 *tueidu*	1.5 the king, has spoken.
uiroku 1.6 *munika koitu koitina*	The Great Lord, 1.6 our king of kings,
1.7 *sekilos toutinikum me*	1.7 has hanged in Thinis (in southern Egypt):
1.8 *ultia uiriaskum mel*	1.8 one from the River Kingdom, the king

1.9 *sura matulokum*	1.9 of the army of *Matulokum* (Metelis, Egypt),
1.10 *elkua raiokum*	1.10 a king of Memphis (in Egypt),
1.11 *buria batokum* 1.12 *belsu alasku mem*	1.11 a chief of Mendes 1.12 under whom the island (of Cyprus) is ruled,
1.13 *elkua ensikum seko*	1.13 a king of the *Seko* (shebka) empire
1.14 *sekontios loukanikum aiu*	1.14 [who] was the commander of *Loukanikum* (Cattle Land),
1.15 *sura uiriaskum mel*	1.15 the king of the army of the River Kingdom,
1.16 *stena muturiskum tirtu*	1.16 a king of all of United Egypt
1.17 *sleitiu karunikum le*	1.17 who had *Karunikum* (northern Egypt) of the Sile-ites,
1.18 *retukenos ensikum*	1.18 in the kingdom of the Great King which
1.19 *letontu batokum*	1.19 extended to Mendes.
1.20 *bilinos austikum* 1.21 *belsu uiriaskum*	1.21 The River Kingdom is ruled 1.20 by *Austikum* (Lasta region on the High Plateau, Ethiopia) of the Bilin people.
1.22 *sekondos uiriaskum me*	1.22 The [new] province [that will be] in the River Kingdom [ends at]
1.23 *burdu teiuantikum*	1.23 Fort Tjamet (Medinet Habu in Egypt at Thebes on the Nile),

1.24 *bilibos turumokum ultu*	1.24 from *Turumokum* (the region west of the Nile) of the *Bilibos* (Oebilia people from Bilia near the Kufra Oasis in Libya),
1.25 *letontu mailikum*	1.25 including
1.26 *burdu auikum*	1.26 Fort Hibis (in the Kharga Oasis),
1.27 *melmanios uiriaskum*	1.27 in the kingdom of *Melmanios* of the River Kingdom,
1.28 *karbelos turumokum ulta*	1.28 [beginning] from *Turumokum* (west of the Nile) [where] the Sand dwellers [live].
1.29 *likinos uerdaidokum mem*	1.29 Below the princes of these districts,
1.30 *koitu mailikum*	1.30 the kings of the Akuia kingdom rule
1.31 *akuios tetokum*	1.31 *Tetokum* (Nile Valley from 1st to 6th Cataracts).
1.32 *saluta uiduskikum*	1.32 In *Uiduskikum* (in the Bayuda region, 4th & 5th Cataracts on the Nile),
1.33 *burdu uiskikum lesana*	1.33 [they rule] as far as Fort Mouza in the lands
1.34 *uerdaidokum atu*	1.34 of the eastern district
1.35 *sanios atokum* 1.36 *niskekue*	1.35 of the king of the Sana'a people of Yemen.
babokum 1.37 *biurtilaur alaskum*	1.36-37 From Lower Nubia where the Bini Rusku [have] the noble citadel of the island kingdom,

Appendix B: Botorrita III - Text and Translation

1.38 *bini* 1.39 *rusku uiriaskum* *kentisku* 1.40 *or bilos likinoskue*	1.40 the Great Lord of the princes 1.38-39 of the Southern River Kingdom
1.41 *aboiokum* 1.42 *abulu akuiakue*	1.42 [rules] as far as the *Akuia* cities 1.41 of Abydos (in Egypt).
araiokum 1.43 *alu aiukue* *araiokum*	[To the south] 1.43 Alodia was as far as [he ruled] in Cataract Land. In Cataract Land,
1.44 *kalos telkaskum*	1.44 *Kalos* (a person) of the Dakhleh Oasis,
1.45 *eladuna loukanikum*	1.45 of the kings of *Loukanikum* (Cattle Land), [who was]
1.46 *medukenos loukanikum*	1.46 the Great Chief of *Loukanikum*,
1.47 *burdu tirtobolokum*	1.47 [is now held] at Fort *Tirtobolokum,* (metropolis of Axum in Ethiopia).
1.48 *sleitiu makeskokum*	1.48 From the Northern lands of the Sile-ites
1.49 *iunstibas uiriaskum*	1.49 to the River Kingdom with its rebel archers,
1.50 *tiokenes uiriaskum*	1.50 *Tiokenes* (a person) of the River Kingdom,
1.51 *uiroku turumokum*	1.51 the Great Lord of *Turumokum* (Egypt and Sudan, west of the Nile), [rules] as far as

264

1.52 *miduku retukenos* *tirtanos* 1.53 *munikakue*	1.52 the first of the Great Kings of our *Tirtanos* (Scorpion Clans, in Somalia and south Ethiopia).
uiriaskum 1.54 *burdu atokum*	1.53 The River Kingdom [starts] 1.54 at Fort Aden (Yemen),
1.55 *aualos kortikos*	1.55 which the Lord of Bahrain and Qatar, *Kaiaitos,*
1.56 *amu kankaikiskum*	1.56 from the nation of Sumer of Kish,
1.57 *kaiaitos litukue*	1.57 had conquered.
abokum 1.58 *muturiskum* 1.59 *barnai* *turumokum tirs*	1.59 I have excluded 1.58 United Egypt from *Abokum* (Elephant Land), [but] 1.59 it (*Abokum*) extends to *Turumokum* (west of the Nile).
1.60 *medukenos abokum* *turo*	1.60 The Great Chief of *Abokum Turo* (Elephant Land, Southern Egypt extended to Djibouti) [rules]
2.1 *sekanos taskokum* *lukinos*	2.1 the Loukanian (Cattle Land) *taskokum* (borderland) with the *sekanos* (shebka people),
2.2 *tirtanos* 2.3 *kentiskue*	2.2 as far as the southern *Tirtanos* (Somalis, Djiboutis, and southern Ethiopians).
loukaniko uiriasku	2.3 On the Loukanian river (the Barka River),
2.4 *medukenos turanikum*	2.4 the Great Chief of *Turanikum* (Eritrea), [is] the

Appendix B: Botorrita III - Text and Translation

2.5 *elu uiriaskum launiku*	2.5 king of the Southern River Kingdom. [His territory]
2.6 *likinos uiskikum* 2.7 *letontu*	2.7 will extend to 2.6 the princes of Mouza in Yemen, [who rule over]
auaskum 2.8 *kasilos atokum*	2.8 the people on the Al Jazirah [peninsula] of *Atokum* (Yemen) 2.7 off of the Highlands.
2.9 *usidu abokum titos*	2.9 [He rules] from the gates of Thebes (Waset) in Elephant Land,
2.10 *burdu kulukamikum* 2.11 *akuia sekiloskue*	2.10 as far as Fort Koloe of Kam (Qohaito, Eritrea), 2.11 where the chief was hanged.
tirilokum 2.12 *medukenos akikum* *memun* 2.13 *akuia alaskum* *memunos*	2.13 The (Dahlak Archipelago) islands are under the chief of *Tirilokum* (Deire on West side of the Mandeb Strait), 2.12 who is under the Great-Chief of Aqiq, [who is]
2.14 *terkinos austikum* *eskutino*	2.14 *Terkinos* (a person) of *Austikum* (Lasta region on High Plateau, Ethiopia) from Sokota.
2.15 *koitina abokum* *useidunos*	2.15 The king of the Lebanese from Ushu in *Abokum* (Elephant Land) [rules up to]
2.16 *tirtouios turumokum*	2.16 the Marsh people of southwestern Sudan.

2.17 *elaukos bentikum rotenanko*	2.17 The Elephant Lord [rules] Baboon Land from the middle of the [Red Sea] coast.
2.18 *elkuanos muturiskum*	2.18 Of the kings of United Egypt,
2.19 *terkinos teladokum*	2.19 *Terkinos* of *Telad* / Tjel (near Sile in northern Egypt)
2.20 *akuia statu turaku*	2.20 [is] the chief of the Tyre region of *Statu* (Canaan).
tueidunos 2.21 *medukenos eladunos* 2.22 *tirtukue ailokiskum* 2.23 *sekilos mailikum* 2.24 *letontu*	2.22 [His territory extends] as far as Tueidunos' 2.21 the Great chief of all the kings. 2.22 From Aila of Kish, 2.23 extending to the kingdom of those who were hanged,
ustitokum	2.24 down to *Ustitokum* (?Atbara River Land)
2.25 *turenta kentiskue ataiokum* 2.26 *koitina uerdaidokum kalmiku*	2.25 in [the region of] southern *Turenta*, the king of *Ataiokum*, (Meroe, Sudan), 2.26 in the district of the Kemalke Ford, [rules]
2.27 *elkuanos kunikum* 2.28 *launikue*	2.27 as far as the kings of the southern kingdoms.
uiriaskum 2.29 *koitu uerdaidokum aias*	2.28 [Those kings] become the kings of the River Kingdom, 2.29 [over] the districts of:
2.30 *snadiuentos ataiokum*	2.30 Western Shendi in *Ataiokum* (Meroe),

Appendix B: Botorrita III - Text and Translation

2.31 *tais uiriaskum*	2.31 *Tais* (Dessie, Ethiopia) in the River Kingdom,
2.32 *basaku uiriaskum*	2.32 the Basa [region] in the River Kingdom,
2.33 *kalaitos* 2.34 *koitinakue*	2.33 as far as the [territory of] the king of the Chaldeans.
uiriraskum 2.35 *likinos ataiokum* 2.36 *sa i kaburikum* *memun*	2.34 In *Uiriraskum* (Lalibela in Lasta, Urvuar), 2.35 those Ethiopian princes of mine, 2.36 below *Kaburikum* (Lower Nubia), [rule the territories along]
2.37 *kares ruaku korkos*	2.37 the road from Korosko village to Kurgis
2.38 *tar tetokum kekas ko*	2.38 passing through the middle of *Tetokum* (the Berber River Kingdom)
2.39 *aureiaku* 2.40 *tuatereskue*	down to 2.39 the birthplace [in Lasta] 2.40 of the rivers.
uiriaskum 2.41 *burdu atauikum*	In the River Kingdom,
2.42 *koitu kuinikum* *tirtunos*	2.42 the kings at 2.41 fort *Atauikum* (Adefa?), 2.42.[who have] all of the Southern Kingdom [now have taken]
2.43 *loukanikum tirtunos*	2.43 all [of the territories] in *Loukanikum* (CattleLand).
2.44 *toloku kalisokum* *atinos*	2.44 From the eastern border of Klusma (at Suez in Egypt)

2.45 *tarkunbiur*	2.45 to Tarkun City (Tarkhan, Egypt)
2.46 *bibalos atokum tirtano*	2.46 to the people at the Mandeb Strait in Yemen [controlled by the] *Tirtano* [people]
2.47 *sikeia beteriskum*	2.47 to the Siq at Petra (in Jordan), [these territories]
2.48 *sekontios turumokum ultatun*	2.48 were [taken] from the commander of *Turumokum* (Egypt and Sudan, west of the Nile), [who was]
2.49 *tekos konikum* 2.50 *bartiltun ekarbilos*	2.49 *Tekos* (a person) of Canaan. 2.50 [He was] the lord of the leaders at *Bartiltun* (Mersa Matruh, port in West Egypt),
2.51 *munika elkuakue*	2.51 as far as [the borders of] our king.
koitinas 2.52 *terkinos*	To the king of the 2.52 *Terkinos* (people) at
toutinikum leton 2.53 *katunos burikounikum*	Thinis, I will extend 2.53 the Harbor kingdom of the Swamp dwellers.
2.54 *eladuna ukulikum*	2.54 From the kings of Ocelis [at the Strait]
2.55 *keka kabelaikiskum*	2.55 to Gigartus near Byblos [in Lebanon],
2.56 *munika tolisokum tirtun*	2.56 all are [now] our clan territories
2.57 *eladuna ensikum turo*	2.57 of the kings of the *Turo* (clans) empire.
2.58 *sekondos bentikum*	2.58 The province of Baboon Land

Appendix B: Botorrita III - Text and Translation

2.59 *tolosar ensikum*	2.59 will extend to the borders of the Akuia empire
2.60 *akuia abokum letontunos*	2.60 in *Abokum* (Elephant Land) from
3.1 *testios turumokum* 3.2 *elku suolakue*	3.2 [the territories] of the king of Djibouti, 3.1 *Testios* of *Turumokum*,
3.3 *tirtanikum uiriaskum mel* 3.4 *kinbiria kentiskue*	3.3 from the king of *Tirtanikum* (Southern Ethiopia, Somalia), in the River Kingdom, to south 3.4 of *Kinbiria* (the Buri Peninsula, Eritrea),
turikum 3.5 *toloku koitinakue*	on the 3.5 border of the king of *Turikum* (Red Sea coast).
austunikum 3.6 *stenu bentilikum*	In *Austunikum* (Highlanders Land, Ethiopia) 3.6 of the kings of the Benadir region (around Mogadishu),
3.7 *burdu bentilikum ultatunos*	3.7 from those [held] at the fort of the Benadir region (around Mogadishu),
3.8 *koloutios biniskum* 3.9 *antiokos uiriaskum melm*	3.8 *Koloutios,* the Phoenician, [was] 3.9 the Lord of the Antiu (people between the Nile and the Red Sea) in the *Melman* part of the River Kingdom.
3.10 *eladunos kaburikum*	3.10 [His jurisdiction extended] over the kings of *Kaburikum* (Lower Nubia,),
3.11 *arkanta medukenoskue*	3.11 as far as the Great Chief of the *Arkanta* (Urukites).

abokum 3.12 *arkanta loukanikum*	In *Abokum* (Elephant Land), 3.12 of the Urukites, a king of Cattle Land,
3.13 *stena ensikum* *skirtunos*	3.13 the conquered kingdom, [was held]
3.14 *burdu betaskum*	3.14 at Fort *Betaskum* (Umm Ebeida, Siwa Oasis),
3.15 *koitu samikum* *melmando*	3.15 by the *Melman* kings of *Samikum* (Siwa Oasis in the *Melman* region).
3.16 *sekontios ubokum*	3.16 He was a commander of the Uweinat (in southeastern Libya),
3.17 *barnai ensikum* *skirtunos*	3.17 [which is] outside of the conquered empire.
3.18 *tetu loukanikum* 3.19 *stena*	3.18 *Tetu,* the Laguatan,
uiriaskum 3.20 *toloku*	3.19 [was] a king on the border [between] the River Kingdom,
uiriaskum 3.21 *arkanta*	3.20 [and] Uruk's part of the River Kingdom.
teiuantikum tirtunos	3.21 Over all of the Western Land,
3.22 *miduku* *tirtobolokum*	3.22 the first Lord of *Tirtobolokum* (the metropolis of Axum, Ethiopia),
3.23 *retukeno* *elkueikikum*	3.23 at the royal [domain] of Arqiqo (in Eritrea),
3.24 *kentisum* *tuateroskue*	3.24 is the foremost chief in both directions

3.25 *abaniu bertikakue*	3.25 as far as the Afan (people) [in the south] and the Berta (people) [in the north].
suaikinokum 3.26 *uiroku konikum* *statulos*	From Suakin (Sudan), 3.26 [he is] the Great Lord. over the *Statulos* (Canaanites) of Canaan.
3.27 *aunia beskokum*	3.27 This *Aunu* from the land of [the god] Bes,
3.28 *bilonikos elokum* *elkinos*	3.28 [is] the Lord-King of the kings of Alalakh (Syria).
3.29 *medukenos* *tirtobolokum*	3.29 This Great Chief at *Tirtobolokum* (the metropolis of Axum), [rules]
3.30 *akuios alikum*	3.30 from Elim (Sinai) of the Akuia,
3.31 *tiriu uiriaskum* 3.32 *turtunadkue*	3.31 up to the court of the Deire people (at the entrance to the Red Sea) in the River Kingdom,
kadarokum 3.33 *sleitiu totinikum*	3.32 as far as Kadruka (near the 3rd Cataract on the Nile) 3.33 to *Totinikum* (?Tanis near the Mediterranean Sea) of the Sile-ites
3.34 *munika ensikum* *skirtunos*	3.34 in our conquered empire.
3.35 *sekoutios uiriaskum* 3.36 *sura suaikinokum*	3.35 The [new] commander of the River Kingdom 3.36 army [is] the Suakin
3.37 *koitina suoli kum* 3.38 *bilir turtuntakue*	3.37 king from 3.38 the court of the lord of Somalia.

telkaskum 3.39 *elu*	3.39 [His domain is] from the ruler of the Dakhleh Oasis,
karbilikum 3.40 *terkinos atokum* *launikue*	3.40 to the *Terkinos* of southern *Atokum* (Yemen) in the Desert Land (Sheba kingdom).
3.41 *miduku telkaskum*	3.41 The first lord of the Dakhleh Oasis,
3.42 *melmantama bentilikum* 3.43 *markos kalisokum*	3.42 the *Melman* Lord, [is being held] in *Bentilikum* (Benadir region around Mogadishu), 3.43 at the central fortress there.
3.44 *arkanta toutinikum*	3.44 [He ruled] the *Arkanta* of Klusma (Suez),
3.45 *tolokunos ke kalisokum*	3.45 those who were within the borders of Thinis. [He ruled] from the army at Klusma
3.46 *sura ensikum melman (bi)*	3.46 of the (defeated) *Melman* empire
3.47 *usama abaloskue*	3.47 up to [the temple of] Apollo the Most High.
karunikum 3.48 *eladuna balaisokum*	3.48 In *Karunikum* (northern Egypt) [he ruled] from the kings of Pelusium [on the Mediterranean coast]
3.49 *likinos turumokum ti*	3.49 to the princes of *Turumokum* (west of the Nile).
3.50 *tueidunos biniskum*	3.50 *Tueidunos*, the Phoenician, [is]

Appendix B: Botorrita III - Text and Translation

3.51 *bilonikos ensikum*	3.51 the Lord-King of the Khabur River *ensikum* (empire)
3.52 *ebursunos mailikinokum* 3.53 *arkanta*	3.52 of the *Arkanta* (Urukite) *mailikinokum* (kingdoms).
ailokiskum	[*Tueidunos* rules] 3.53 the Syrians at Aila of Kish,
3.54 *suros alikum* 3.55 *ultinos amakue*	3.54-55 those from Elim (in the Sinai) up to Amman (Jordan).
uiriaskum 3.56 *babos kentiskue*	3.56 In the River Kingdom from south of the Lower Nubians,
uiriaskum 3.57 *turaios litanokum kurmilokum* 3.58 *launikue*	3.57 down to the *Turaios* (Tyre people) of *Litanokum*, (Litani Land, Lebanon) in the River Kingdom near Kerma (Sudan, 3rd Cataract)
uiriaskum 3.59 *kari*	3.59 to *Kari* (the Napata district, 4th Cataract) 3.58 in the River Kingdom,
uiriaskum 3.60 *kuintitaku mailikinokum*	3.60 the kingdoms of the River Kingdom in the Deep South [are ruled by]
4.1 *kainu tirtobolokum*	4.1 *Kainu* of *Tirtobolokum* (metropolis of Axum),
4.2 *steniontes turikainos*	4.2 king of the bowmen at
4.3 *bolora kentiskue*	4.3 the southern town of the *Turikainos* (people of Iken, 2nd Cataract).

melmandos 4.4 *tiokenesos uiriaskum*	4.4 The Melmandos led by *Tiokenes* of the River Kingdom) 4.8 conquered
4.5 *kalaitos mturiskum*	4.5 the Chaldeans of *Mturiskum* (Metcher / Egypt)
4.6 *burdu karunikum*	4.6 at the fortress of *Karunikum* (Northern Egypt) [and the]
4.7 *burdu abilikum* *eladuno* 4.8 *litu*	4.7 royal fortress of Ebla.
makeskokum	In the Northern Lands,
4.9 *medukenos kalisokum*	4.9 [as a result], the Great chief of Klusma,
4.10 *koitina tirikantanko*	4.10 [becomes] the king, from the middle of the Tiran Strait [in the Red Sea]
4.11 *esueiku ateskum*	4.11 to the Gulf of Issus in Edessa.
4.12 *kalaitos kustikum*	4.12 Of the Chaldeans of *Kustikum* (Eritrea),
4.13 *antiokos kustikum*	4.13 the Lord of the Antiu (people of Antat, between the Nile and the Red Sea) of *Kustikum* [ruled]
4.14 *kabutu abokum*	4.14 Coptos in *Abokum*, (Elephant Land)
4.15 *anu uiriaskum*	4.15 [and] the *Anu* (people in Lower Nubia) in the River Kingdom.

4.16 *kalaitos muturiskum* 4.17 *akuia albinokum*	4.16-4.17 This chief of the Chaldeans of *Muturiskum* (United Egypt), [ruled] *Albinokum* (Arabia) [and]
4.18 *balakos sekondos*	4.18 the province of Failaka (in Kuwait). [He ruled]
4.19 *kara kalatokum*	4.19 Charax Spasinu of Chaldea (southern Iraq), [and]
4.20 *arkanta mailikum*	4.20 the kingdom of Uruk
4.21 *eladunos albinokum*	4.21 of the kings of Arabia.
4.22 *bubilibor uiriaskum*	4.22 The Lord of Babal (Old Cairo) in the River Kingdom [rules]
4.23 *usidu uiriaskum*	4.23 Thebes in the River Kingdom.
4.24 *retukenos telkaskum*	4.24 [One] of the kings from the Dakhleh Oasis
4.25 *buria belsu*	4.25 [is] the chief [under whom] is ruled
4.26 *toloku kurmiliokum* 4.27 *anieskor talukokum*	4.27 Mount Kor (Gebel Sheikh Suleiman) from the Dal Cataract kingdom 4.26 to the border with Kerma.
4.28 *ste akuikum*	4.28 The lords of Agau Land
4.29 *elkueid akikum*	4.29 [who] are under the jurisdiction of [*Terkinos* from Sokota], the king of Aqiq, [are:]
4.30 *raieni uiduskikum*	4.30 [*Kainu*], the leader of Bayuda Land,

4.31 *urkala austunikum*	4.31 the Lion of the Highlanders Land (Abyssinia)
4.32 *tama ataiokum*	4.32 the lord of Ethiopia (Meroe),
4.33 *retukenos kustikum*	4.33 the Great King of Eritrea.
4.34 *bilosban betikum*	4.34 The evil lords of the enemy lands [are:]
4.35 *koitina kankaikiskum*	4.35 the king of Sumer of Kish,
4.36 *likinos kuedontikum*	4.36 the princes of Kydonia [in Crete].
4.37 *munika uerdaidokum*	4.37 For our provinces
4.38 *terkinos turanikum*	4.38 by *Terkinos* (the person) of *Turanikum* (Eritrea),
4.39 *teudesi kustikum*	4.39 decreed at *Kustikum* (Eritrea)
4.40 *kaukirino*	4.40 in the Keren Highlands.

GLOSSARY

Word definitions include the lines where the word
occurs in the side-by-side translation in Appendix B. Lines
from the Botorrita I-B text are indicated with 'I-B'.
References to areas in the grammatical notes in Appendix
A are prefaced by §.

ᕈ ᛁᛀᚼᚺᛢᕀ
a-ba-l-o-s-ku-e
Temple of Apollo near the Siwa Oasis in Western
Egypt. Alexander the Great consulted an Oracle at the
Temple of Apollo there.[195] Apollo was originally the
[Holy] Son in a family of north star gods. The name is
related to Hebrew Abel. His equivalent in Egypt is
Horus. Amon is another Egyptian god, who sometimes
overlaps with Horus. This particular temple is
sometimes called the Temple of Amon.[196] *-kue*, 'as far
as, near, up to'. Postposition, see §7.1.8.
3.45-47 '[He ruled] from the army at Klusma of the
(defeated) *Melman* empire <u>*Abaloskue*</u> (<u>up to [the
temple of] Apollo</u>) the Most High'.

ᕈ ᛁᛀᛀᚼ
a-ba-n-i-u
Afan / Afar - a Kushitic people of Dankalia.[197]
Dankalia stretches from the Red Sea coast in Eritrea to
the highlands of eastern Ethiopia. There is a reference
in 1214 AD by Ibn Said, an Arab geographer, who

---

[195] Strabo, *Geography of Strabo*, vol. III, 292.
[196] Cornell and Matthews, *Atlas of the Roman World*, 164.
[197] Bender, "Introduction," 2, 5, 66.

cites the Dankals, a group of Afar people living on the coast as far as Suakin, near modern Port Sudan.[198] *-iu*, plural suffix, see §5.4.

3.25 'as far as the *Abaniu* (Afan people) [in the south] and the Berta (people) [in the north]'.

ꝑ ⲅ𐌉ⲛⲟⲩ

a-bi-l-i-ku-m

Ebla - an ancient city / kingdom in Syria.[199]

4.6-7 'at the fortress of *Karunikum* (Northern Egypt) [and the] royal fortress of *Abilikum* (Ebla)'.

ꝑ ⲭⲛⲏⲟⲩ

a-bo-i-o-ku-m

Abydos - 8th nome, Upper Egypt, center of worship of Osiris.[200] City has tombs of PreDynastic rulers.

1.41-42 '[rules] as far as the *Akuia* cities of *Aboiokum* (Abydos)'.

ꝑ ⲭⲟⲩ

a-bo-ku-m

The Nile Valley, from the Nile Bend to the Buri Peninsula in Eritrea. The exact translation compares to the Egyptian for 'Elephant Land', Elephantine, which refers to a city and province near the 1st Cataract. During the time of the Old Kingdom, *Abokum* was just the first province, the region around the 1st Cataract, but it is used to refer to a larger and more expanded Southern Kingdom in the Botorrita III text.[201] It included Thebes, which would have been in the fourth

---

[198] Kamil, *Parlons Afar*, 16.

[199] Roaf, *Cultural Atlas of Mesopotamia*, 80.

[200] Baines and Malek, *Cultural Atlas*, 41; Budge, *Egyptian Hieroglyphic Dictionary*, 947; Gardiner, *Egyptian Grammar*, 550.

[201] Baines and Malek, *Cultural Atlas*, 41; Budge, *Egyptian Hieroglyphic Dictionary*, 947.

province later, and Coptus, controlled by Uruk, which is in the fifth province in the Old Kingdom. *Abokum Turo* is the domain of *Abokum* that is ruled by the *Turos*. It overlaps wiith the ancient kingdom of *Turikum*. The kingdom of *Turumokum* was west of the Nile. *Bentikum* and *Tirtanikum* were on its southern borders. Lebanese from Ushu (*useidunos*) also lived in *Abokum*.

1.57-59 'I have excluded United Egypt from *Abokum* (Elephant Land), [but] it (Elephant Land) extends to Turumokum (west of the Nile)'.

1.60-2.1 'The Great Chief of *Abokum* Turo (Southern Egypt) [rules] the Cattle Land *taskokum* (borderland) with the the shebka people'.

2.9 'from the gates of Thebes in *Abokum* (Elephant Land) as far as Fort Koloe of Kam'.

2.15 'The king of the Lebanese from Ushu [who are] in *Abokum* (Elephant Land)'.

2.58-3.5 'The province of Baboon Land will extend to the borders of the *Akuia* empire in *Abokum* (Elephant Land) from [the territories] of the king of Djibouti, Testios of Sudan… on the border of the king of *Turikum* (Red Sea Coast)'.

3.11-12 'In *Abokum* (Elephant Land), of the Urukites, a king of Cattle Land'.

4.13-15 'the Lord of the Antiu of *Kustikum* [ruled] Coptos in *Abokum* (Elephant Land), [and] the *Anu* (Nubians) in the River Kingdom'.

ᗡOʃHᛗ
a-bu-l-o-s
    city, cities, towns - Assyrian.[202]

---

[202] Vrouyr, *Inscriptions Ourartéennes*, 36.

Glossary

I-B 1-2 ' Libyan Knossos (in Crete) was destroyed by the Egyptian *Melmunos*, extending to Lyttus where they destroyed the *abulos* (towns) '.
See **I-B 4**, **I-B 8**, **I-B 9**.

ᛈ ⃝ᛙᛏ
a-bu-l-u
> cities, towns - Assyrian.[203]
> **1.41-2** '[He rules] as far as the *Akuia abulu* (cities) of Abydos'.

ᛈ ⃝ᛙᛏ
a-bu-l-u
> towns, cities - Assyrian.[204]
> **I-B 4-5** '[Because] the *abulu* (towns) of Laodikea of the Ushu (from Tyre) were destroyed by the Achaeans,'.
> See **I-B 8**.

ᛈᛰᛈᛉ⊙ᛣ
a-i-a-n-ku-m
> Egypt. 'Eye' land, from Semitic word *aian*, 'eye'. *Aiankum Tauro* is a name for Cyprus. The profile of the east Mediterranean coast resembles the head of a bull with Cyprus appearing as the eye, as in the 'eye' of the *Tauro* or 'bull'. The kingdom of Cyprus included cities like Byblos and Tyre on the Mediterranean coast. In the I-B text, *Aiankum* was also used for Egypt. According to Brugsch, "For the protection of the Eastern frontier, …Ramses III was the first who succeeded in protecting the entrance into Egypt from this side by building a new fortress near the Qasr Agerud, situated to the north-west of the Gulf of Suez, in the neighborhood of the 'great well'. The whole

---

[203] Ibid.
[204] Ibid.

282

country, to which the fortified place belonged, bore the appellation 'Aina or 'Aian, which continued till the time of Pliny in the slightly changed form of Aean. Under the Graeco-Roman dominion the particular nome to which Aean belonged was called the Heroopolitan nome after its capital".[205] Heroopolis corresponds to *Karunikum* in Botorrita III, the territory from Mendes in the Delta to Fort Sile where, the line of forts began, protecting the northeast Egyptian border along the road up the Mediterranean coast to Palestine. Heroopolis included the Suez region as well. In the Botorrita III text, the Suez region is *Kalisokum*.

I-B 4 '…all of the towns in <u>*Aiankum*</u> (<u>northeast Egypt</u>)'.

I-B 7 '*Melman (*Egyptian) *Aiankum* destroyed Ushu / Tyre, in the <u>*Aiankum Tauro*</u> (<u>eastern Mediterranean kingdom including Cyprus</u>)'.

I-B 8 'The cities of the <u>*Aiankum Tauro*</u> (<u>eastern Mediterranean kingdom including Cyprus</u>) were destroyed'.

ρ Ͷρ Ϻ

a-i-a-s

> become, shall be, inchoative form of verb 'to be'.[206] See §4.1, §4.2.2.
>
> **2.29-30** ' [Those kings] *aias* (become) the kings of the River Kingdom [over] the districts of: Western Shendi in Meroe,'.

ρ ͶιΗ√ϺΘϓ

a-i-l-o-ki-s-ku-m

---

[205] Brugsch and Seymour, *History of Egypt*, 252.

[206] Reinisch, *Die ChamirSprache*, vol. CV, 618.

Aila of Kish, Hebrew Eilat, ruins near modern Eilat, a resort in Israel, near Aqaba at the head of the Aelanitic Gulf (Gulf of Aqaba).[207]

2.22-24 'from *Ailokiskum* (Aila of Kish) to the kingdom of those who were hanged, down to *Ustitokum*'.

3.53 '[*Tueidunos* rules] the Syrians at *Ailokiskum* (Aila of Kish)'.

ρ Ν↑

a-i-u

he was. third person perfect, Somali: *aayu* from *yahay*, 'to be'.[208] See §4.1, §4.2.1.

1.14 '[who] *aiu* (was) the commander of Cattle Land,'.

ᐅΝ↑

a-i-u

was. See §8.1, §8.2.

I-B 2-3 'The plundered *Melmu* land, which extends to the *Turo* Uweinat *aiu* (was) destroyed by the Libyans'.

ρ Ν↑☉ᄂ

a-i-u-ku-e

was as far as. It was near, up to, third person, perfect, Somali: *aayu* from *yahay*, 'to be'.[209] -*kue*, 'as far as, near'. Postposition, see §7.1.8. See §4.1, §4.2.1.

1.42-43 '[To the south] Alodia *aiukue* (was as far as) [he ruled] in Cataract Land'.

ᐅ∧Ν Νᐅϟ

a-ka-i-n-a-d

---

[207] Strabo, *Geography of Strabo*, vol. III, 176n1; Baines and Malek, *Cultural Atlas*, 19; Wyse and Winkleman, *Past Worlds Atlas*, 241.
[208] Saeed, *Somali Reference*, 116.
[209] Ibid.

by the Achaeans. Greeks from Achaia, in Homer, "the chief tribe of the Greeks in Thessaly, Messene, Argos and Ithaca, mostly as a collective appellation of the Greeks before Troy".[210] See §8.2.

I-B 5 '[Because] the towns of Laodikea of the people of Ushu... were destroyed *Akainad* (by the Achaeans)'.

P ✓ⓞϒ

a-ki-ku-m

> Aqiq, also called Ptolemeis Theron, and *Turanikum*. Place where *loukaniko uiriasku* (the Barka River) flows into the Red Sea, in eastern Sudan.[211]
>
> **2.12** 'who is under the Great-Chief of *Akikum* (Aqiq)'.
> **4.28-29** 'The lords of Agau Land [who] are under the jurisdiction of the king of *Akikum* (Aqiq), are'.

P ⓞN P

a-ku-i-a

> a chief, one / some of the Agau people. Related to word for 'head', *ague* and *away*, 'over, upper' in several Kushitic languages, such as Chamir, Bilin, Dembea, and Agaumeder.[212] See §5.4.
>
> This word may correspond to *Akhou*, a line of ancient PreDynastic kings mentioned by Manetho.[213] The *Akhou* preceded the kings of the Old Kingdom.
>
> **2.10-11** 'as far as Fort *Kulukamikum* where he hanged the *akuia* (chief)'.
> **2.12-13** 'The (Dahlak Archipelago) islands are under the *akuia* (chief) of *Tirilokum*, who is under the Great-Chief of Aqiq,'.

---

[210] Autenrieth, *Homeric Dictionary*, 57; Barraclough, *Atlas of World History*, 66, 89.

[211] Hammond, *Complete World Atlas*, 98; Huntingford, *Periplus*, map1.

[212] Reinisch, *Die ChamirSprache*, vol. CV, 692n2.

[213] Manetho, *Manetho*.

2.20 '[He is] the *akuia* (chief) of the Tyre region in Canaan'.
See **2.60**, **4.17**.

ρ Ⲟ𐌽ρ ⲞᏝ
a-ku-i-a-ku-e

> as far as the chief (*Akuia, Akhou*?). -*kue*, 'as far as, near'. Postposition, see §7.1.8.
> **1.41-42** '[He rules] (as far as the) *Akuiakue* (*Akhou*) cities of Abydos'.

ρ Ⲟ𐌽ⲞᏉ
a-ku-i-ku-m

> Agau Land. Agau / Agew, sub-family of Kushitic languages, includes Bilin and Chamir.[214] See *akuia* above. In the text, *Akuikum* includes *Uiduskikum, Austunikum, Kustikum and Ataiokum* and is ruled from *Akikum*. See §3.3.
> **4.28** 'The lords of *Akuikum* (Agau Land)'.

ρ Ⲟ𐌽HM
a-ku-i-o-s

> of the Aku, of the chief, the lord, 'of the Agau'. See *Akuia, Akuikum*. See §5.4, §6.2.
> **1.30-31** 'the kings of the *Akuios* (of the *Akuia* / Agau / *Akhou*) kingdom rule *Tetokum*'.
> See **3.30**.

ρ Ꮭρ MⲞ
a-l-a-s-ku

> the island, Egyptian: *arasku*, 'Cyprus, island' in the Mediterranean that was part of *Batokum* (Egyptian Mendes).[215] -*ku*, 'the', definite article, see §6.6, §2.3.

---

[214] Bender, "Introduction," 3.
[215] Cornell and Matthews, *Atlas of the Roman World*, 164; Roaf, *Cultural Atlas of Mesopotamia*, 177.

1.11-12 'a chief of Mendes under whom *alasku* (<u>the island of Cyprus</u>) was ruled'.

𐦐 𐦏𐦐 𐦌⊙𐦟

a-l-a-s-ku-m

island kingdom. Based on context, probably describes 'the islands' of Lower Nubia south of Egypt in one place and 'the islands' of the Dahlak Archipelago in the Red Sea elsewhere.[216]

1.36-37 'From Lower Nubia where the Bini Rusku [have] the noble citadel of *alaskum* (<u>the island kingdom</u>)'.

2.11-13 '...*alaskum* (<u>the island kingdom, here may refer to the Dahlak Archipelago</u>) is under the chief of *Tirilokum*,'.

𐦐 𐦏𐦆𐦏𐦐

a-l-ba-n-a

Arabs, Kushitic: *arabas*, 'desert'. Egyptian: *aribi, arbin*.[217] See §5.4. See *albinokum*.

0.1 'To that *Albana* (<u>Arab</u>) leader [held] captive in *Tirtanikum*'.

𐦐 𐦏𐦏𐦈⊙𐦟

a-l-bi-n-o-ku-m

Arabia. Kushitic: '*arabas*, 'desert'. Egyptian: *aribi, arbin*.[218] Egyptian doesn't distinguish **l** and **r** consistently, but **l** is 𐦔, the lion, in some spellings. The word *albinokum*, 'Arabia' is written *a-l-bi-no-kum* with the lion for **l**. See *albana*.

4.16-17 'This chief of the Chaldeans of United Egypt [ruled] *Albinokum* (<u>Arabia</u>)'.

---

[216] Baines and Malek, *Cultural Atlas*, 54.

[217] Reinisch, *Texte der Bilin-Sprache*, 92; Budge, *Egyptian Hieroglyphic Dictionary*, 948.

[218] Ibid.

Glossary

See **4.21**.

ⲣ ⲓⲚⲰⲨ

a-l-i-ku-m

Elim, in the Sinai.[219]

3.30 'from the *Akuia* kingdom of <u>*Alikum*</u> (<u>Elim</u>)'.
See **3.54**.

ⲣ ⲓⲧ

a-l-u

Alodia, land between the White and Blue Nile.[220]
Alodia was south of Khartoum.
1.42-43 '[To the south] <u>*Alu*</u> (<u>Alodia</u>) was as far as [he ruled] in Cataract Land'.

ⲣ Ⲩ ⲣ ⲞⲒ

a-m-a-ku-e

As far as… Amman (capital of modern Jordan), *-kue*, 'as far as, up to, near'. Postposition, see §7.1.8.
3.50-55 '*Tueidunos*, the Phoenician… [rules] the Syrians of Aila of Kish, from Elim (in the Sinai) <u>*Amakue*</u> (<u>up to Amman</u>)'.

ⲣ Ⲩⲧ

a-m-u

nation, Arab loan word in Somali: *ummad*. For the Egyptians, the word meant Asiatics (foreigners).
1.56-57 '*Kaiaitos*, from the <u>*amu*</u> (<u>nation</u>) of Sumer of Kish,'.

ⲣ ⲚⲚⲒⲙⲆ ⲫ

a-n-i-e-s-ko-r

---

[219] Pritchard, *Atlas of the Bible*, 57.
[220] Kobishchanov, *Axum*, 83map1.

Mount Kor. hill, mountain, from Arabic: *anies*. Kor is a town north of the 2nd Cataract on the Nile. The modern name for this prominent hill near Kor is Mount Sheikh Suleimon or Gebel Sheikh Suleiman.[221]
4.26-27 '*Anieskor* (Mount Kor) from the Dal Cataract to the border with Kerma'.

ꝑ Ͷ𐐪ͰꚘM
a-n-ti-o-ko-s

Lord of the Antiu, Egyptian: *antiu* 𓈖 𓂝 𓂝 𓂝 people of the Antat, the region between the Nile and the Red Sea. *kos*, 'lord, king, client king'. A very early chronicle from the Old Kingdom records Egyptian kings celebrating the "Smashing of the Antiu" in an annual festival.[222]
3.8-9 '*Koloutios*, the Phoenician, [was] the *Antiokos* (Lord of the Antiu) in the *Melman* regions of the River Kingdom'.
4.13-14 'The *Antiokos* (Lord of the Antiu) of Eritrea [ruled] Coptos in Elephant Land'.

ꝑ Ͷ𐐪
a-n-u

people from region that was later named Lower Nubia. Naville quotes an inscription from Deir el Bahri where the god Tetun tells the queen he will tie up and behead the *Anu* of Nubia for her.[223]
4.12-15 'Of the Chaldeans of Eritrea, the Lord of the Antiu of Eritrea [rules] Coptos in Elephant Land and

---

[221] Baines and Malek, *Cultural Atlas*, 31, 41.
[222] Budge, *Egyptian Hieroglyphic Dictionary*, xxiii, 127, 958; Lepsius, *Nubische Grammatik*, 424; Breasted, *Ancient Records of Egypt*, 159.
[223] Naville, "Les Plus Anciens Monuments Egyptiens," 120.

the *Anu* (people in Lower Nubia) in the River Kingdom'.

ℙ φ ℙ ℵH☉Ɏ

a-r-a-i-o-ku-m

Cataract Land on the Nile. Nubian: *ar-e, arr-e,* cataracts on the Nile.[224] The *Aithiopes aroteres* of Pliny.[225] The *Araret* were one of 6 tribes that fought against the *Hr-Rusku* at Qusseir for King Pepi of the 6th Dynasty of the Old Kingdom.[226]

1.42-43 '[To the south] Alodia was as far as [he ruled] in *Araiokum* (Cataract Land)'.

1.43-46 'In *Araiokum* (Cataract Land), *Kalos* of the Dakhleh Oasis, one of the kings of Cattle Land, the Great Chief of Cattle Land,'.

ℙ φ ⋀ℵ✕

a-r-ka-n-ta

Uruk, ancient city in southern Iraq. Urukites, people from Uruk, Mesopotamians from Uruk. Akkadian: *Arkajjitu.*[227] Sounds like *Erkheye,* 'lapwings', a bird.[228] Chamir: *arq,* 'to know', *arq-ata,* 'wise one', *arq-nat,* 'wisdom'. Bilin: *-anta,* suffix forming verbal nouns.[229] See §5.1. Egyptian: *rekhyt,* a pun on lapwing, meant 'wise ones, fortune-tellers', but was also used to refer to northern Egyptians where it may have overlapped with the Berber word *argaz* that means 'man'.[230] In modern Chamir an *arqata* is still a fortune teller.

---

[224] Posener, *Princes et pays d'Asie et de Nubie,* 57.

[225] Schoff, *Periplus of the Erythraean Sea,* 64.

[226] Lepsius, *Nubische Grammatik,* 87.

[227] von Soden, *Grundriss der Akkadischen,* 85sect.56p.

[228] Gardiner, *Egypt of the Pharaohs,* 403.

[229] Reinisch, *Die ChamirSprache,* vol. CV, 663.

[230] Abdel-Massih, *A Reference Grammar of Tamazight,* 70.

3.10-11'[He ruled] the kings of *Kaburikum* as far as the Great Chief *Arkanta* (of Uruk).
3.11-12 'In Elephant Land of the *Arkanta* (Urukite), a king of *Loukanikum* (Cattle Land),'.
3.44 'the *Arkanta* (Urukites) of Klusma'.
3.50-53 '*Tueidunos*, the Phoenician, is the Lord King of the Khabur river empire of the *Arkanta* (Urukite) kingdoms'.
4.16-20 'This chief of the Chaldeans from *Muturiskum* (United Egypt) [ruled] Arabia [and] the province of Failaka (in Kuwait), Charax Spasinu of Chaldea, [and] the kingdom of *Arkanta* (Uruk)'.

ᛈ ᚷᛁᚺᛟᛉ
a-ta-i-o-ku-m

Meroe, Incense Land, Ethiopia. Likely source of the name 'Ethiopia'. The name may have been influenced by Adefa, an old name for modern Lalibela, in Lasta, in the Central Highlands of Ethiopia. The territory of *Ataiokum* is roughly that of Meroe, west of modern Ethiopia. It may also include people in the Cataract region of the Nile, the *Aithiopes aroteres* of Pliny. These latter people were frequently not ruled from Meroe or Ethiopia, although the narrator of the Botorrita III text claims them in line 2.35 below. The names *Ataiokum*, Ethiopia and Adefa may come from *atyob*, 'incense'.[231] Egyptian: *atef*, 'incense'.
2.22-26 'From Aila of Kish,... down to *Ustitokum* in [the region of] southern *Turenta*, the king of *Ataiokum* (Meroe), in the district of the Kemalke Ford [rules]'.
2.35-36 'of those princes of mine in *Ataiokum* (Meroe) below Lower Nubia'.
See **2.30**, **4.32**.

---

[231] Schoff, *Periplus of the Erythraean Sea*, 62, 64.

Glossary

ⲣ ⲭⲧⲛⲟⲩ

a-ta-u-i-ku-m

> may refer to a fortress at Adefa, modern Lalibela.
> **2.39-41** 'down to the birthplace of the rivers. In the
> River Kingdom, the kings at fort *Atauikum* (Adefa),
> [who have] all of the Southern Kingdom, [now have
> taken] all [of the territories] in Cattle Land'.

ⲣ ⲑⲙⲟⲩ

a-te-s-ku-m

> Edessa (modern Şanlıurfa) in Turkey.[232]
> **4.11** 'to the Gulf of Issus in *Ateskum* (Edessa, Turkey)'.

ⲣ ⲯⲛⲏⲙ

a-ti-n-o-s

> easterners, eastern, at-IN-os, Egyptian: *abt*, 'east'.[233]
> See *Atokum*. Ethnonym, and/or adjective or possessive,
> §6.2, §5.5, §5.4.
> **2.44** 'From the *atinos* (the eastern) border of Klusma'.

ⲣ ⲱⲟⲩ

a-to-ku-m

> East Land (Aden, roughly modern Yemen). Amharic:
> *watta*, 'rise, sunrise', Egyptian: *abt*, 'east'.[234] Note also
> Berber: *adhou*, 'wind, east wind'.[235]
> **1.35** 'of the king of the Sana'a people of *Atokum* (East
> Land, Yemen)'.
> **1.54** 'from Fort Atokum (Aden)'.
> **2.8** ' the islanders of Atokum (East Land, Yemen)'.

---

[232] Cornell and Matthews, *Atlas of the Roman World*, 151.
[233] Budge, *Egyptian Hieroglyphic Dictionary*, 18b, 19a.
[234] Ibid.
[235] Calassanti-Motylinski, *Grammaire, Dialogues et Dictionnaire Touaregs*, 304.

2.46 'to the Mandeb Strait (between the Red Sea and Gulf of Aden) in *Atokum* (East Land, Yemen) [controlled by the] *Tirtano* [people]'.
3.40 'to the *Terkinos* of southern *Atokum* (East Land, Yemen)'.

𐤐 △

a-tu

eastern, (modern Yemeni). Egyptian: *abt*, 'east'.[236] See adjective form, §6.2.
1.33-35 'as far as the fort of Mouza in the lands of the *atu* (eastern) district of the king of the Sana'a people of Yemen'.

𐤐 𐤕𐤐 𐤍𐤇𐤌

a-u-a-l-o-s

people of Bahrain, ethnonym for people from Awal, ancient name for Bahrain.[237] See §6.2.
1.55-56 'which the Lord of the *Aualos* (people of Bahrain) and Qatar, *Kaiaitos*, from the nation of Sumer of Kish, had conquered'.

𐤐 𐤕𐤐 𐤌☉𐤵

a-u-a-s-ku-m

Highlands in southern Yemen, ancient *Habashat*. Jabal Habashi is near Ta'izz, Yemen. Bilin: *auas*, 'high, upper'.[238] "In the Ethiopian texts of Ezana I's bilingual inscription, 'Habashat' is mentioned among the Arabian countries.... The Habashat of the Sabaean inscriptions is the district which belonged to the Ethiopians and was situated on the Arabian coast of the Red Sea".[239]

---

[236] Ibid.
[237] Dougherty, *Sealand of Arabia*, 173.
[238] Reinisch, *Texte der Bilin-Sprache*, 18.
[239] Kobishchanov, *Axum*, 64-65.

2.6-7 'will extend to the princes of Mouza in _Auaskum_ (Highlands, southern Yemen)'.

ꓑ ꓓꓰꓑ ꓠꕡ

_a-u-d-a-n-to_

conquering, invading, Bilin: _autitux_, 'he conquered'.[240] See §4.1, _-to_ participle ending.[241] See §4.6, _-anta_, 'agent', verbal noun.[242] See §5.1.

0.1 'One of the southerners from Lasta, I prevented the Numidians from _audanto_ (conquering) beyond [the limits] of their territory'.

ꓑ ꓓꓠꙨꓬ

_a-u-i-ku-m_

Hibis, capital of Kharga Oasis.[243]

1.26-27 'to Fort _Auikum_ (Hibis) in the kingdom of _Melmanios_ of the River Kingdom'.

ꓑ ꓓꓠꓠꓑ

_a-u-n-i-a_

an Aunu, an ethnic group. See also §5.4.

3.27 '_aunia_ (an Aunu) from the land of [the God] Bes'.

ꓑ ꓓ ꝙ ꓮ ꓠꓑ Ꙩ

_a-u-r-e-i-a-ku_

birth, beginning, Egyptian: _aur_.[244] _-ku_, 'the', definite article, see §6.6.

2.39-40 'the _aureiaku_ (birthplace) [in Lasta] of the rivers'.

---

[240] Reinisch, _Texte der Bilin-Sprache_, 10.
[241] Ibid., _Die Bilin-Sprache_, 41.
[242] Ibid., _Die ChamirSprache_, vol. CV, 663.
[243] Jackson, _At Empire's Edge_, 175ff.
[244] Budge, _Egyptian Hieroglyphic Dictionary_, 35.

ρ ↑ꟽꟻⴲꞶ
a-u-s-ti-ku-m

Lasta region on the High Plateau. In the Central
Ethiopian Highlands, a mountainous region near the
sources of the Blue Nile and the Atbara River, major
streams which both flow into the Nile. Lasta is the
traditional homeland of the Bilin, the name *Austikum* is
from Bilin: *auas*, 'high, upper'; *auaux-di*, 'highlands,
plateau'.[245] Lasta is also the homeland of the Chamir,
whose name for the region is *Kam*.[246] The name of the
prehistoric land of KUM is indicated by the mountain
range glyph (⌒⌒) on Gerzean pottery.[247] Later we see
Egyptian *h-s-t-KUM* (𓐮𓏺 ⌒⌒), 'mountain range land,
foreign land'.[248] The *Khastiu* who were one of the four
great tribes of the Sudan may also have come from
Austikum.[249] An inscription of an Axumite king from
the 6th century AD tells of a war against the rebellious
tribes of Aguezat and *Hasat*…The raids by the
Aguezat who were joined by the neighboring *Hasat*
(the *Hasa* or *Has* in other sources) preceded the war.
Vassal kingdoms of Axum on the Ethiopian plateau
include *Hasat*.[250] Around 1137 AD, a new dynasty, the
Zagwe, who were Agau Kushitic speakers, came to
power in Ethiopia. After a millennium of Semitic
rulers who were speakers of Ge'ez , the Zagwe,
deriving from the province of Bugna in Lasta, claimed
to restore the ancient traditional kings. The best known
of these kings was Lalibela. His capital city was called
Adefa (see *ataiokum* and *atauikum*.) This place, also

---

[245] Reinisch, *Texte der Bilin-Sprache*, 18.
[246] Ibid., *Die ChamirSprache*, vol. CV, 575.
[247] Hoffman, *Egypt Before the Pharaohs*, 292.
[248] Gardiner, *Egyptian Grammar*, 488.
[249] Budge, *Egyptian Hieroglyphic Dictionary*, 533-534.
[250] Kobishchanov, *Axum*, 95, 220, 252. See additional references to
Hasa, Hasat on 83, 96, 124, 132, 152, 214.

known as Roha or Warawar, was later named Lalibela after the king.[251] See *eskutino, lestera, kulukamikum, terkinos, uiriraskum.* See §2.5, §7.1.3.

1.20-21 'The River Kingdom is ruled by <u>*Austikum*</u> (<u>Lasta region, Ethiopia</u>) of the Bilin people'.

2.14 '*Terkinos* of <u>*Austikum*</u> (<u>Lasta region, Ethiopia</u>) from Sokota '.

ρ ↑ΜΔΝΝΘϒ

a-u-s-tu-n-i-ku-m

Ancient Ethiopia. Also, Land of the Highlanders. Name from Bilin: *auas*, 'high'; *auauxdi*, 'highland'; a variant of *Austikum* (High Land) *-un-*, plural marker.[252] In Chamir, the word for 'lion' is *absa,* plural *abisse.*[253] Perhaps the source of the name Abyssinia, is 'Lion Land'. The name Lalibela means Lion Lord.[254]

3.5-6 In <u>*Austunikum*</u> (<u>Highlanders Land, Ethiopia</u>) one of the kings of Benadir from those at the fort of Benadir (Mogadishu),'.

4.31 '[in a list of *Akuia* kings], the Lion of <u>*Austunikum*</u> (<u>Highlanders Land / Abyssinia - Lion Land</u>)'.

ΙϪΘϒ

ba-bo-ku-m

Wawat / Lower Nubia.[255] See also *turikainos.*

1.36-37 ' From Lower Nubia where the Bini Rusku have the noble citadel of the island kingdom '.

---

[251] Munro-Hay, *Ethiopia*, 22, 23.

[252] Reinisch, *Die Bilin-Sprache*, 87-89; Ibid., *Texte der Bilin-Sprache*, 18.

[253] Ibid., *Die ChamirSprache*, vol. CV, 671.

[254] Munro-Hay, *Ethiopia*, 194.

[255] Gardiner, *Egyptian Grammar*, 559; Baines and Malek, *Cultural Atlas*, 178-179, 227.

ba-bo-s

people of Wawat / Lower Nubia.[256] See §6.2, §6.7.
3.56 'from south of the *Babos* (people of Wawat) in the River Kingdom'.

ba-l-a-i-s-o-ku-m

Pelusium on Eastern Mediterranean coast of Egypt.[257]
3.48 'from the kings of *Balaisokum* (Pelusium)'.

ba-l-a-ko-s

Failaka Island in Kuwait, at head of Persian Gulf.[258]
4.18 'the province of *Balakos* (Failaka Island)'.

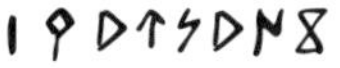

ba-r-a-u-d-a-n-ko

plundered.[259] Bilin: *wararux*, 'he robbed, invaded'. Chamir: *birbir, birbirdu, birbirata*, 'go on a raid, go robbing, robber, pirate' [260]
I-B 2 'The *baraudanko* (plundered) *Melmu* land that was destroyed, which extends to the *Turo* Uweinat'.

ba-r-n-a-i

exclude, out, outside of, Akkadian: *bar*, 'outside'.[261] *bar*, 'to leave'.[262] *barno*, 'to go out, leave'. See §4.1, §4.2.3.

---

[256] Ibid.
[257] Simons, *Egyptian Topographical Lists*, 176 list XXXI-#7.
[258] Roaf, *Cultural Atlas of Mesopotamia*, 79.
[259] Reinisch, *Texte der Bilin-Sprache*, 90.
[260] Ibid, *Die Chamir Sprache*, vol. CVI, 349
[261] Ibid., *Texte der Bilin-Sprache*, 627; Horowitz, *Mesopotamian Cosmic Geography*, 242; Gardiner, *Egyptian Grammar*, 564.
[262] Reinisch, *Die Bilin-Sprache*, 636.

1.59 'United Egypt *barnai*, (I exclude) from Elephant Land, [but] it extends to *Turumokum* (in the lands west of the Nile)'.

3.12-17 'a king of Cattle Land... [was] a commander of the Uweinat [which was] *barnai* (outside of) the conquered empire'.

ɪ ꟼ ꟻꜣꟼ

ba-r-ti-l-tu-n

Baretoun, Mersa Matruh, Egypt. Territory was ruled by Egypt or Libya off and on.[263] Appears to have been the capital of *Loukanikum*. Irish: *tun* is 'fort', giving 'the citadel of Partolan'. Roman: *Parætonium* meant 'the [ruined] walls, the ruins'. In Botorrita III times, it was still a working capital.

2.50 'the Lord of the leaders at *Bartiltun* (Mersa Matruh)'.

ɪꟻꟼ ☉

ba-s-a-ku

the Basa region. Located somewhere between Dessie, Ethiopia and Sennar, Sudan and west of the Atbara River.

-ku, 'the', definite article, see §6.6.

2.32 'the *Basaku* (the Basa region) in the River Kingdom'.

ɪ ꤄☉ꟲ

ba-to-ku-m

Mendes, Egyptian *Ba-tet*. Shrine of Osiris as *Ba*, a ram-headed god[264]. Herodotus says, "The Libyans call their kings, *'Battos'*"[265] The Libyans also worshipped a

---

[263] Cornell and Matthews, *Atlas of the Roman World*, 164.

[264] Budge, Egyptian Hieroglyphic Dictionary, 977

[265] Herodotus, *The Persian Wars*, 353.

ram-headed god, called *Ammon*. *Bityà* was also an Egyptian title meaning 'king of Lower Egypt'.[266]

1.11 'a chief of *Batokum* (Mendes, on a branch of the Nile in Lower Egypt)'.

1.16-19 'a king of all of United Egypt,… the kingdom of the Great King which extended to *Batokum* (Mendes, Egypt)'.

ꓜ ꓩ ꓟ ꓓ

be-l-s-u

is ruled. Inchoative, third singular.[267] See §4.1, §4.2.2. Resembles but differs grammatically from Akkadian: 'their Lord, he was their lord'.[268]

1.11-12 'a chief of Mendes under whom the island of Cyprus *belsu* (is ruled),'.

1.21 'The Nile Kindom *belsu* (is ruled) by… the Bilin people'.

See **4.25**.

ꓜ ꓠ ꓬ ꙮ ꓩ

be-n-ti-ku-m

Baboon Land (𓃥 𓈐). Egyptian: *bent* for 'baboon'. Greek: 'Land of the Dog-Headed Creatures'. Red Sea Coast in Eritrea, from roughly the Buri Peninsula in Eritrea to Djibouti.[269]

2.17 'The Elephant Lord [who rules] *Bentikum* (Baboon Land) from the middle of the [Red Sea] coast'.

See **2.58**.

---

[266] Manetho, *Manetho*, 4.

[267] Reinisch, *Die ChamirSprache*, vol. CV, 675; Saeed, *Somali Reference*, 57.

[268] von Soden, *Grundriss der Akkadischen*, 38sect.30f, 53sect.42g, 104sect.65b, 105sect.65f.

[269] Budge, *Egyptian Hieroglyphic Dictionary*, 219a; Huntingford, *Periplus*, map1.

Glossary

𐤗𐤍𐤕𐤉𐤍𐤀𐤅
be-n-ti-l-i-ku-m
    Benadir region, which extends along the Indian Ocean
    coast of Somalia, especially in the south, around
    Mogadishu. *Bandar* in Somali means 'port'. In Arabic,
    the word is *bender*.
    3.6-8 'One of the kings of *Bentilikum* (the Benadir
    region), from those at the fort of *Bentilikum* (the
    Benadir region), is *Koloutios,* the Phoenician'.
    See **3.42**.

𐤗𐤐𐤀𐤍𐤕𐤅
be-r-ka-n-ti-ku-m
    Barca, in Cyrenaica region of Libya.[270] In the I-B text,
    it is part of *Melman* Egypt. The Libyans destroy the
    town.
    I-B 3-4 'The town of *Berkantikum* (Barca, Libya), they
    burned down'.

𐤗𐤐𐤕𐤀𐤅
be-r-ti-ka-ku-e
    as far as the Berta people. Speak non-Kushitic
    language that is still spoken near Suakin, Red Sea port
    in East Sudan.[271] *-ka* as definite article, see §6.6. *-kue*,
    'as far as, near'. Postposition, see §7.1.8. In Chamir,
    berta means 'elephant'.[272] Strabo reports elephant
    hunting places all along the western Red Sea coast.[273]
    3.24-25 'the foremost leader in both directions (as far
    as) the Afan people [to the south] and the *Bertikakue*
    (the Berta people) [to the north]'.

[270] Cornell and Matthews, *Atlas of the Roman World*, 164.
[271] Hammond, *Complete World Atlas*, 98; Bender, "Introduction," 7;
    Tucker and Bryan, *The Non-Bantu Languages*, 80-81.
[272] Reinisch, *Die ChamirSprache*, vol. CVI, 350.
[273] Strabo, *Geography of Strabo*, vol. III, 194.

𐤓𐤌𐤆☉𐤙
be-s-ko-ku-m
> Land of Bes. A southern god from the region south of
> Egypt.[274] For -*ko*, meaning 'region', see §7.1.7.
> **3.27** 'an Aunu from *Beskokum* (the land of Bes)'.

𐤓✗𐤌☉𐤙
be-ta-s-ku-m
> Umm Ebeida, Siwa Oasis, western Egypt.[275]
> **3.14** 'at Fort *Betaskum* (Umm Ebeida)'.

𐤓◇𐤓𐤓𐤌☉𐤙
be-te-r-i-s-ku-m
> Petra in Jordan.The Romans called it *Arabia Petraea*.
> Biblical: *Petor* (Deuteronomy 23:5).[276] Capital of the
> Nabataeans in Roman times.
> **2.47** 'to the Siq at *Beteriskum* (Petra, Jordan)'.

𐤓𐤜☉𐤙
be-ti-ku-m
> enemy lands, land of abominable persons. Egyptian:
> *beti, betnu*.[277]
> **4.34** 'the evil lords of *betikum* (the enemy lands) [are:]'.

Γ
bi
> spoil, defeat, obliterate. Somali: *bi'i*, 'cause to be
> destroyed', from *ba*, 'spoil, defeat, obliterate'.[278] See
> §4.1, §4.4.2.

---

[274] Gardiner, *Egyptian Grammar*, 559; Baines and Malek, *Cultural Atlas*, 41; Oakes and Gahlin, *Ancient Egypt*, 171.
[275] Baines and Malek, *Cultural Atlas*, 50, 187.
[276] Ibid., 53; Finkelstein, "Mesopotamia," 85n42.
[277] Budge, *Egyptian Hieroglyphic Dictionary*, 208b, 227b, 228a.
[278] Saeed, *Somali Reference*, 50.

3.46 'the *bi* (defeated) army of the Melman empire at'.

bi-ba-l-o-s

possible ethnonym for people of the Bab el Mandeb (Mandeb Strait). From gateway people, Egyptian: *ber*, 'gateway', Coptic: *ebol*. Possibly living on Perim Island, near Ocelis, Strabo's Isle of Diodoros.The Strait is between the Red Sea and the Gulf of Aden.[279] See also *Elephas*, modern *Fel* or *Fellis* which means elephant in Arabic.[280] The *Tirtanos* were from the Djibouti hinterlands on the western side of the Strait. This reference to *Tirtanos* of *Atokum* (Yemen) seems to indicate control or at least a settlement on the eastern side of the strait in what is now Yemen in the southwest Arabian peninsula.

2.46 'to the *bibalos* (people of the Mandeb Strait) in Yemen [controlled by the] *Tirtano* [people]'.

bi-l-i-bo-s

Oebilia people from Bilia near the Kufra Oasis, which is part of the kingdom of *Turumokum* in modern southwestern Libya.[281]

1.22-24 'The [new] province [that will be] in the River Kingdom [ends at] Fort Tjamet (Medinet Habu in Egypt at Thebes on the Nile), from *Turumokum* (focused here in southwestern Libya) [in the lands] of the *Bilibos* (Oebilia people from Bilia near the Kufra Oasis)'.

---

[279] Budge, *Egyptian Hieroglyphic Dictionary*, 219b.

[280] Strabo, *Geography of Strabo*, vol. III, 200n4.

[281] Hornemann, *Journal of Frederick Horneman's Travels*, 122; Wilberg, ed., *Claudii Ptolemæi Geographiæ Libri Octo*, 279, 281.

ᒡ ᒐᑊᘉᑊᕼᗰ

bi-l-i-n-o-s

> an ethnonym for Bilin people. The Bilin, in modern
> times, live in the Keren Highlands in Eritrea and speak
> a Kushitic language. The tribe of Terqe is one of the
> two main groups in the Bilin nation. Their traditions
> say that about twelve generations ago (from the late
> 1800's), they used to live in Lasta in the Central
> Ethiopian Highlands, a region full of mountain ranges
> where the Nile River begins.
>
> **1.20-21** 'The River Kingdom is ruled by Lasta (in
> Ethiopia) of the *Bilinos* (Bilin people)'.

ᒡ ᒐᑊᘉ ᖴ

bi-l-ir

> of the lord. *-r*, genitive suffix, see §5.5.[282] Amharic:
> *bala*, 'possessor of'.
>
> **3.37-38** 'is at the court *bilir* (of the lord), [*Testios*], the
> king of Djibouti / Somalia'.

ᒡ ᒐᕼᑊᘉᔙᗰ

bi-l-o-n-i-ko-s

> the Lord-King. *nuguz*, 'king'.[283] Amharic: *negus*, 'king'.
> Basque: *nagusi*, 'boss'.
>
> **3.28** '[is] *bilonikos* (the Lord-King) of the kings of
> *Elokum* (Alalakh, Syria)'.
>
> See **3.51**.

ᒡ ᒐᕼᗰᒐᘉ

bi-l-o-s-ba-n

> evil lords. Egyptian: *b-n*, 'evil, abominable', Coptic:
> *bane*.[284]
>
> **4.34** '*Bilosban* (The evil lords) of the enemy lands'.

---

[282] Reinisch, *Texte der Bilin-Sprache*, 107; Ibid., *Die Bilin-Sprache*, 73.

[283] Ibid., *Die ChamirSprache*, vol. CV, 661.

[284] Budge, *Egyptian Hieroglyphic Dictionary*, 216b.

𐤓𐤀𐤁
bi-n-i

> Phoenicians from Lebanon and in Egypt, perhaps from *bina,* the phoenix bird.[285] See *Biniskum,* ethnonym, formed from adjective, see §6.2. 'the Phoenician Rus '. **1.37-40** 'From Lower Nubia where the <u>*Bini* *Rusku*</u> (the Phoenician Rus) have the noble citadel of the island kingdom'.

𐤓𐤀𐤁𐤉⊙𐤔
bi-n-i-s-ku-m

> Phoenicia.[286] Phoenix Land, Lebanon, Eastern Mediterranean coast. *Binashki* is mentioned in texts from Ebla in Syria that date to the Old Kingdom period in Egypt. A royal couple travels to their ancestral home in *Binas-ki* to perform a religious ritual.[287] A 'Phoenix Land' appears on the PreDynastic Libyan Palette. Egyptian placenames indicate Phoenicians in the southeast.The southern most point might be *Ras Benas* - Phoenician Head, near the Egyptian border. Note also Poeniconon / Phoinikon (Laqeita) mentioned as a stop on the road from Coptus on the Nile Bend to Berenike (a Red Sea port near Ras Benas).[288] Two personal names refer to leaders from this location.
> **3.8** '*Koloutios* of <u>*Biniskum*</u> (Phoenicia) '.
> *Kolodi* is the Nubian word for seven. He could be the seventh child or someone from the seven tribes of Lebanon.
> **3.50** '*Tueidunos* of <u>*Biniskum*</u> (Phoenicia)'.

---

[285] Ibid., 213b.
[286] Gleadow, *Origin of the Zodiac*, 177. For links between Egyptian Phoenicia, bennu-bird and phoenix.
[287] Archi, Piacentini, and Pomponio, *ARES II*, 179.
[288] Schoff, *Periplus of the Erythraean Sea*, 55.

Tell Judeidah is a site near ancient Alalakh in northern Syria in a region that may have been part of *Biniskum*. A people called the Teudjoi were at el Hibis on the Nile in Egypt.[289]

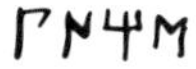

bi-n-ti-s

burned down, burned out, destroyed by burning down, perhaps conquered. Causative of Chamir: *bint*, 'to be burned'.[290] See §4.3.

I-B 1 'The Egyptian *melmunos* *bintis* (destroyed) Libyan Knossos'.

See **I-B 2, I-B 3, I-B 4, I-B 5, I-B 6, I-B 7, I-B 8, I-B 9**.

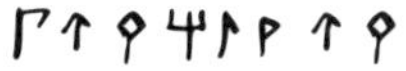

bi-u-r-ti-l-a-u-r

high citadel, Akkadian: *biritu*, 'citadel', *laur*, 'high, elevated'.[291]

1.37 'the *biurtilaur* (nobel shrine or citadel) of *Alaskum* (island kingdom), at Wawat, [between the First and Second Cataracts on the Nile].

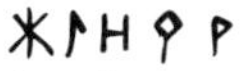

bo-l-o-r-a

a [particular] town, Somali: *buulo*, 'town, village'. Bilin: *-ra*, singulative suffix.[292] See §5.4.

3.58-4.3 'in the River Kingdom *Kainu* [rules]...as far as the southern *bolora* (town) of the people at the citadel of Iken'.

---

[289] Baines and Malek, *Cultural Atlas*, 121.

[290] Reinisch, *Die ChamirSprache*, vol. CV, 619.

[291] von Soden, *Grundriss der Akkadischen,* 69sect.54k, 210sect.115q.

[292] Reinisch, *Die Bilin-Sprache*, 87.

□𐤂𐤉𐤀𐤟𐤟

bu-bi-l-i-bo-r

lord of Babal. Egyptian: *Babar* (Babal), Old Cairo.[293]
See also *buria*, 'chief, lord'.
4.21-23 '*Bubilibor* (the Lord of Babal) [rules] *Usidu*
(Thebes) in the River Kingdom '.

□𐤟𐤟𐤟

bu-r-d-u

fort. Kassite: *bi-ir-ta*, Assyrian: *bi-ra-ti-shu*, 'their
forts'.[294] Also modern Turkish and Arabic: *burdj*.
1.23 '*burdu* (fort) *Teiuantikum* (the Western Land,
Tjamet, Medinet Habu in Egypt) '.
4.6 'at *burdu* (fort) *Karunikum* (combination refers to
Fort Sile)'. Fort Sile is the first and best known of a
chain of forts going north from Egypt along the eastern
Mediterranean shore to Gaza in what would be the
kingdom of *Karunikum*.
See **1.26, 1.33, 1.47, 1.54, 2.10, 2.41, 3.7, 3.14, 4.7.**

□𐤟𐤟𐤟

bu-r-i-a

a chief, a lord, a king, one of the lords, in Basque and
in Kassite.[295] See §5.4.
1.11 '*buria* (a chief) of *Batokum* (Mendes, Egypt)'.
See **4.25**.

□𐤟𐤟𐤟𐤟𐤟𐤟𐤟

bu-r-i-ko-u-n-i-ku-m

port or harbor kingdom, from *bur-*, also 19th nome of
Lower Egypt.[296]

---

[293] Budge, *Egyptian Hieroglyphic Dictionary*, 977.
[294] Balkan, *Die Sprache der Kassiten*, 109; Vrouyr, *Inscriptions
Ourartéennes,* 38.
[295] Balkan, *Die Sprache der Kassiten*, 104.
[296] Baines and Malek, *Cultural Atlas*, 166.

2.53 'the *Burikounikum* (the Harbor kingdom) of the Swamp dwellers'.

ᛒᛞ ᛩ ᛗᛏᛝᚺᛗ

e-bu-r-s-u-n-o-s

people of Khabur River region in Mesopotamia, also called Aborrhas River.[297]

3.51-52 'the Lord-king of the *Ebursunos* (people of the Khabur River) empire of the kingdoms of Uruk'.

ᛒᚠ ᛩ ᚠᛁᚺᛗ

e-ka-r-bi-l-o-s

lord of the leaders, *ekar*, Egyptian: *heq, heqa*, 'leader', -*ar*, Chamir genitive, see §5.5, *bilos*, 'lord'.[298]

2.50 '*ekarbilos* (the lord of the leaders) at Parætonium [on the Libyan border],'.

ᛒᛁᛈ ᛃᛏᛝᛈ

e-l-a-d-u-n-a

kings, of these kings, Ethiopian: *Ella Alada* 'lord of lords, lord of the princes, rulers'.[299] Suffix -*u* as genitive plural, Bilin.[300] -*na*, demonstrative, see §6.4, Dhasanac.[301]

1.44-46 '*Kalos* of the Dakhleh Oasis, *eladuna* (of the kings) of Cattle Land, [is] the great chief of Cattle Land'.

2.54 'From *eladuna* (the kings) of Ocelis (in Yemen) to Gigartus in Byblos'.

See **2.57, 3.48**.

---

[297] Strabo, *Geography of Strabo*, vol. III, 158.

[298] Budge, *Egyptian Hieroglyphic Dictionary*, 513a; Reinisch, *Die ChamirSprache*, vol. CV, 676.

[299] Kobishchanov, *Axum*, 82, 270, 276.

[300] Reinisch, *Die Bilin-Sprache*, 95.

[301] Tosco, *Dhasanac Language*, 226.

Glossary

ᛚᛁᛈ ᛂᛏᛂH
e-l-a-d-u-n-o
> royal, of the kings. See *eladuna*, adjective form, see
> §6.2, §6.4.
> **4.7** 'the *eladuno* (royal) fortress at Ebla'.

ᛚᛁᛈ ᛂᛏᛂHᛗ
e-l-a-d-u-n-o-s
> kings, of the kings, genitive plural. See §5.5, §6.4.
> **2.21** 'as far as *Tueidunos* the great chief of all the
> *eladunos* (kings)'.
> **3.10** '[He rules] *eladunos* (the kings) of *Kaburikum* as
> far as the Great Chief of Uruk.'
> **4.21** 'the kingdom of Uruk *eladunos* (of the kings) of
> Arabia,'.

ᛚᛁᛈ ᛏᚼᛗ
e-l-a-u-ko-s
> Elephant Lord, Berber: *elou* 'elephant'.[302] *kos*, 'lord,
> king, client king'
> **2.17** 'the *Elaukos* (Elephant Lord) [rules] Baboon Land
> from the middle of the length of the [coastline]'.

ᛚᛁᛌᛂHᛗ
e-l-ki-n-o-s
> kings, leaders, of the leaders. Amharic: *alaqa*, 'chief,
> leader, boss', *alga waras*, 'crown prince'. See §5.4,
> §5.5.
> **3.28** '[is] the Lord-King *elkinos* (of the kings) of
> Alalakh'.

ᛚᛁᛣ
e-l-ku

---

[302] Calassanti-Motylinski, *Grammaire, Dialogues et Dictionnaire
Touaregs*, 83.

of the kings, princes. Amharic: *alaqa*, 'chief, leader, boss', *alga*, 'throne', *alga waras*, 'prince'. See §5.4.
3.2-3 '[the territories of] *Testios* of Khartoum, <u>*elku*</u> (<u>of the kings</u>) of Suola, Djibouti, '.

ᒣᑊᘈ ᑭ
e-l-ku-a
> a (particular) king, see *elku*. For *-a* suffix as singulative, see §5.4.[303]
> **1.10** '<u>*Elkua*</u> (<u>one of the kings</u>) of Memphis (in Egypt). See **1.13**.

ᒣᑊᘈ ᑭ ᘈᒣ
e-l-ku-a-ku-e
> a (particular) king, see *elkua*. See *-kue*, 'as far as, near', postposition, see §7.1.8.
> **2.51-52** 'He was the lord of the leaders at *Bartiltun elkuakue* (<u>as far as our king</u>).'

ᒣᑊᘈ ᑭ ᘍᕼᙢ
e-l-ku-a-n-o-s
> kings, leaders, see *elkua*.[304]
> **2.18** 'the <u>*elkuanos*</u> (<u>kings</u>) of United Egypt'. See **2.27**.

ᒣᑊᘈᒣᘍᕽ
e-l-ku-e-i-d
> under the jurisdiction of the king, see *elkua*, plus *-id*, postpostion, see §7.1.4. Bilin: *id*, 'from'.[305] *-id* may be a form of Afar: *ixxo* (*iddo*), 'jurisdiction, authority'.[306]
> **4.28-29** 'The lords of Agau Land [who] are <u>*elkueid*</u> (<u>under the jurisdiction of the king</u>) of Aqiq'.

---
[303] Reinisch, *Die ChamirSprache*, vol. CV, 671, 673.
[304] Ibid., *Die Bilin-Sprache*, 95-96.
[305] Ibid., 99.
[306] Kamil, *Parlons Afar*, 195.

ㄴㅏⵔㅇㄴ✓ㅇⵅ
e-l-ku-e-ki-ku-m

 royal kingdom (land of the king) at Arqiqo, Eritrea.
Arqiqo is on the mainland across from the island of
Massaua on the Red Sea coast. The royal kingdom
may have been somewhat larger, but Arqiqo preserves
the name.[307]
 3.23 'at the royal *elkuekikum* (kingdom) [at Arqiqo]'.

ㄴㅏHㅇⵅ
e-l-o-ku-m

 Alalakh, Syria, on the Orontes River, ancient ruins
existed before the Late Uruk period (3500-3200 BC)
and after.[308]
 3.28 '[is] the Lord-King of the kings of *Elokum*
(Alalakh)'.

ㄴㅏⵔ
e-l-u

 king, lord, ruler. *Ella*, 'lord' (*Allah*, 'lord, he who').[309]
 2.5 '*elu* (king) of the southern [part of] the River
Kingdom'.
 See **3.39**.

ㄴⵏㅐⵏㅇⵅ
e-n-s-i-ku-m

 empire, kingdom. Akkadian: *ensi*, 'governor, client
king'.[310] Kassite: *Iansi*, 'king'.[311] Egyptian: *nesu*, 'king'
is transcribed in Mesopotamian cuneiform by *in-si*.[312]

---

[307] Huntingford, *Periplus*, 187; Wikipedia Authors, "Arkiko."

[308] Roaf, *Cultural Atlas of Mesopotamia*, 53, 64.

[309] Munro-Hay, *Ethiopia*, 308; Kobishchanov, *Axum*, chap.V, 276, 308n66.

[310] Roaf, *Cultural Atlas of Mesopotamia*, 225.

[311] Brinkman, *Political History of Post-Kassite Babylonia*, 202n1225.

1.13 'a king of the Shebka *ensikum* (empire)'.
3.13 'a king of Cattle Land from the conquered
ensikum (empire)'.
3.51-3.52 'the Lord-king of the Khabur River *ensikum*
(empire) of the kingdoms of Uruk'.
See **1.18, 2.57, 2.59, 3.17, 3.34, 3.46, 3.51**.

ⱕⲙⲕ ⲚⲚⲚⲦⲰ

e-s-ke-n-i-n-u-m

> that they would not reach, Amharic: *eska*, 'until',
> *asganna*, 'successful'. Chamir: *ash*, 'until' + Bilin: -
> *gininu*, negative subjunctive third plural, negative
> jussive + 'that' -*m*, subordinating suffix.[313] See §4.1,
> §4.7.
> **0.1** 'One of the southerners from Lasta (Ethiopia), I
> have prevented the [would be] conquering Numidians
> *eskeninum* (that they would not reach) beyond [the
> limits] of their territory'.

ⱕⲙⲞⲨⲚⲎ

e-s-ku-ti-n-o

> from Sokota, city of Lasta in Central Ethiopian
> Highlands. See also §2.9, §2.10, §5.4, §6.2.[314]
> **2.14** '*Terkinos Eskutino* (from Sokota) on the High
> Plateau'.

ⱕⲙⲎⲞⲰ

e-s-o-ku-m

> Issus, city at head of Gulf of Issus (now Gulf of
> Iskenderun) near the border between Turkey and
> Syria.[315]

---

[312] Budge, *Egyptian Hieroglyphic Dictionary*, 391a.
[313] Reinisch, *Die ChamirSprache*, vol. CV, 629-630, 636, 652-655,
  689n1; Kamil, *Parlons Afar*, 108-114.
[314] Munro-Hay, *Ethiopia*, map1.
[315] Cornell and Matthews, *Atlas of the Roman World*, 151map.

Glossary

I-B 9 '[and included] _Esokum_ (Issus), which was [also] destroyed'.

ᒷ�436O
_e-s-u-e-i-ku_

Bay or Gulf of Issus on the Mediterranean Sea near the border between Turkey and Syria.[316] -_ku_, 'the', definite article, see §6.6. Somali: -_ku_ suggests this is the Gulf and not the city. Modern name is the Gulf of Iskenderun. Perhaps the original word was a variant of Basque: _itsasso_, 'sea' or a predecessor of English: 'estuary'.

4.9-4.11 'as a result, the Great Chief of Klusma becomes the king from the middle of the Tiran Strait on the Red Sea to _esueiku_ (the Gulf of Issus) in Edessa'.

Ͷρ
_i-a_

'I', first person pronoun, as in Dhasanac.[317] See §3.1.
0.1 'One of the southerners from Lasta, _Ia_ (I) have prevented the Numidians from'.

ͶↃͶᛄⵉᛄ
_i-u-n-s-ti-ba-s_

rebel archers, Nubians, Egyptian: _iunsti_, 'archer', _bash_, 'rebel', _beshtiu_, 'rebels'.[318]
1.49 'to _iunstibas_ (the rebel archers) of the River Kingdom'.

ⵏⵝↃρ ͶⵌͷO⑁
_ka-be-l-a-i-ki-s-ku-m_

---

[316] Ibid.
[317] Tosco, _Dhasanac Language_, 212ff.
[318] Gardiner, _Egyptian Grammar_, 552; Budge, _Egyptian Hieroglyphic Dictionary_, 224.

Byblos, Lebanon. 'Hill of Kish', *kabelai* reflects
Semitic: Gebel / Jebel, 'hill', archeological excavations
show a shrine on a central hill with Mesopotamian
architecture and pottery.[319] Egyptian: *keben*,
'Byblos'.[320] Mentioned in the Bible as Gebal.[321]
2.55 'to Gigartus in *Kabelaikiskum* (Byblos)'.

𐤊𐤀𐤐𐤍𐤀𐤅
ka-bu-r-i-ku-m

Lower Nubia, region on the Nile River between the 1st
and 2nd Cataract. The Egyptians called Lower Nubia
Qebh Heru, meaning "The Springs of Horus". The
term was also used as a name for Upper Egypt. Some
ancient Egyptians may have viewed this region as the
source of the Nile, or at least the beginning of their
Nile.[322]
2.35-36 'of those princes of mine in *Ataiokum* below
Kaburikum (Lower Nubia)'.
3.9-11 'the Lord of the Antiu of the *Melman* part of the
River Kingdom. [He ruled] over the kings of
Kaburikum (Lower Nubia) as far as the Great Chief of
Uruk'.

𐤊𐤀𐤁𐤃
ka-bu-tu

Coptos, a city and province on the Nile Bend, 5th
Nome, Coptic: *Kbtw*, Egyptian: *Gebtu*.[323]
The boundaries of *Abokum* (Elephantine, Elephant
Land) varied over time. At one point in the 4th

---

[319] Saghieh, *Byblos in the Third Millennium BC*, 119.

[320] Budge, *Egyptian Hieroglyphic Dictionary*, 1047.

[321] Ezekiel 27:9 (NIV). See note equating Gebal to Byblos.

[322] Budge, *Egyptian Hieroglyphic Dictionary*, 1043; Gleadow, *Origin of the Zodiac*, 167.

[323] Budge, *Egyptian Hieroglyphic Dictionary*, 1043; Baines and Malek, *Cultural Atlas*, 14, 111.

Dynasty, Old Kingdom, when the boundaries of the nomes / provinces were marked relative to the length of the Nile, *Abokum* was the 1ˢᵗ nome and Coptus was in the 5ᵗʰ nome. At the time of this text, *Abokum* is much larger with its northern boundary stretching up to, and beyond, Coptus.

4.14 '*Kabutu* (Coptos) in Elephant Land'.

ᛚ᛫ᚠ ᚠ H☉ᛉ
ka-d-a-r-o-ku-m
Kadruka, on Nile, around 3ʳᵈ Cataract.[324]
3.32-33 'from *Kadarokum* (Kadruka) to Tanis of the Sile-ites near the Mediterranean Sea'.

ᛚᛈ ᚠ ᛈᛰᛘ
ka-i-a-i-to-s
a person, proper name. Lugal (king) Kitun / Kidul, last king of Uruk before it was destroyed in 3200 BC.[325] He ruled for 36 years. He followed Melamanna / Melam-ana / Melmanios.
1.55-57 'Fort Aden which the Lord of Bahrain and Qatar, *Kaiaitos*, from the nation of Sumer of Kish, had conquered'.

ᛚᛈᛈᛏ
ka-i-n-u
proper name, might mean 'man', 'men'. Kunama (a language spoken in Ethiopia and Eritrea): *ina kena (ka-ina)*, 'this man'.[326]
4.1 '*Kainu* (a person) of the metropolis of Axum'.

---

[324] Baines and Malek, *Cultural Atlas*, 186.
[325] Crawford, *Sumer and the Sumerians*, 18; Kramer, *The Sumerians*, 329; Guisepi, "The Sumerian King List".
[326] Reinisch, *Die ChamirSprache*, vol. CV, 682n6.

ΛⲢⲢ ⲚШⲘ

ka-l-a-i-to-s

Chaldeans from Mesopotamia, Lowlanders from anywhere, imperialists of the Libyan: *kaldi / geldi,* 'empire'. The term may have been triply ambiguous since the Chaldeans of Southern Iraq would also have been 'Lowlanders, those from the coast'. On the 'imperialist' meaning from *geldi*, during this Uruk Expansion period, the Mesopotamians may have been just as imperialistic as the Libyans, the Egyptians and the Ethiopians.

Contributing to this ambiguity, note that in lines 4.16-4.20, the lord of the Chaldeans of Egypt is also the lord of [Mesopotamian] Chaldea, and the lord of the kingdom of Uruk, just north of Chaldea. Amharic: *qwalla*, 'low country, is between sea-level and 5,000 ft. elevation'. Inhabitants of the Egyptian Delta region are also 'Lowlanders'. In the *Book of Invasions*, the *Cal* province of Egypt is the Delta region between Memphis and the harbor kingdom on the coast.[327] It is used as an ethnonym in Eritrean Bilin: *Kelau, Kelauti,* 'Lowlanders'.[328] See *Turikum* and discussion of *Troglodutike* as '*Turo Kalodutike*' meaning 'coastal lowlands, lowland plain, coastal empire'. The Celtiberians also used *Calaito*s as a personal name.[329] There is a Latin version on the funeral stele of *Madicenus Calaetus*.[330] See §6.2.

2.33 'as far as the king of the *Kalaitos* (Chaldeans)'.

4.5 'the *Kalaitos* (Chaldeans) of *Mturiskum* (*Egypt*)'.

4.12 'Of the *Kalaitos* (Chaldeans) of *Kustikum* (Eritrea),'.

---

[327] Best, Bergin, and O'Brien, *Book of Leinster*, line 614.

[328] Reinisch, *Texte der Bilin-Sprache*, 18.

[329] Jordán Cólera, "Celtiberian," 831.

[330] Rose, "Text and Image in Celtiberia," 168.

4.16 'Of the *Kalaitos* (Chaldeans) of *Muturiskum* (United Egypt),'.

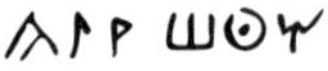

ᐱᚱᑊ ��
ka-l-a-to-ku-m
Chaldea in southern Iraq, southwest Iran.[331]
4.19 'Charax Spasinu of *Kalatokum* (Chaldea),'.

ᐱᚱᑊᛏᛗᚻᛟᛘ
ka-l-i-s-o-ku-m
Qulzum / Klusma, 'the beach', town near, just north of
Suez.[332]
2.44 'from the eastern border of *Kalisokum* (Klusma)'.
3.41-45 'the *Melman* Lord [held]... at the central
fortress of Benadir [ruled] the *Arkanta* of *Kalisokum*
(Klusma). [He ruled] those who were within the
borders of Thinis, from the army at *Kalisokum*
(Klusma) of the (defeated) Melman empire up to the
[temple] of Apollo, the Most High'.
4.9 'the Great Chief of *Kalisokum* (Klusma)'.

ᐱᚱᛁᛊᚾᛟ
ka-l-m-i-ku[m]
the Kemalke Ford, crossing of the Atbara River near
Kassala.[333]
2.25-26 'down to [the region of] southern *Turenta*,
[where] the king of Meroe, (in Sudan) in the district of
Kalmiku[m] (the Kemalke Ford), [rules]'.

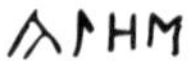

ᐱᚱᛁᚻᛗ
ka-l-o-s
proper name, also ethnonym, from Kellis, city in the
Dakhleh Oasis, in Egypt.[334]

---

[331] Barraclough, *Atlas of World History*, 57.
[332] Baines and Malek, *Cultural Atlas*, 166.
[333] Kobishchanov, *Axum*, map1.

1.44 '*Kalos* (a person) of the Dakhleh Oasis, one of the kings of *Loukanikum* (CattleLand), the Great Chief of *Loukanikum,* [is now held] at the fortress of Axum'.

Λ𡥠Λ𡥠✓ΜⵙⲨ

ka-n-ka-i-ki-s-ku-m

> Sumer of Kish, *kankai* from Sumerian *ka-na-ag2*, meaning 'the country', but particularly, 'The Country', i.e., Sumer.[335] The whole name translates as 'the Sumerian country of Kish land' or 'Sumer of Kish'.
> **1.55-57** 'Fort Aden which the Lord of Bahrain and Qatar, *Kaiaitos*, from the nation of *Kankaikiskum* (Sumer of Kish), had conquered'.
> **4.34-35** 'The evil lords of the enemy lands [are:] the king of *Kankaikiskum* (Sumer of Kish), and the princes of Crete'.

Λ𐤒𐤓

ka-r-a

> Predecessor city of Charax Spasinu in Chaldea (southern Iraq). Romans called it Charax, Characene.[336]
> **4.16-19** 'The chief of the Chaldeans of United Egypt, [rules] Arabia, the province of Failaka. [He rules] *Kara* (Charax Spasinu) in Chaldea [and] the kingdom of Uruk'.

Λ𐤒𐤓𐤉ΗΜ

ka-r-be-l-o-s

> Sand-dwellers.[337] Ethnonym for people living in the desert region near the western border of Sudan. See §6.2.

---

[334] Jackson, *At Empire's Edge*, 204ffmap4.

[335] Hayes, *Manual of Sumerian Grammar*, 248.

[336] Barraclough, *Atlas of World History*, 57; Hammond, *Complete World Atlas*, 78.

1.28 'from *Turumokum* (in the lands west of the Nile) where the *Karbelos* (Sand dwellers) live'.

ᛟ ᛩ ᚷ ᛁᛅᛟᛨ
ka-r-bi-l-i-ku-m

desert land.[338] Himyar or Sheba in Arabian Peninsula. Kharibael and Karib'il were titles, sometimes taken as names of the kings (and queens) of Himyar and Sheba in the southern Arabian Peninsula. Himyar and Saba (Sheba) are both northeast of Sana'a, capital of Yemen.[339]

3.39-40 '[His domain is] from the ruler of the Dakhleh Oasis, to the *Terkinos* of southern Yemen in *Karbilikum* (Desert Land / Sheba kingdom)'.

ᛟ ᛩ ᛚᛘ
ka-r-e-s

Korosko. *kares ruaku*, 'the village of Korosko' (*ruak-ku*), Somali: *rug*, 'village'.[340] There is a famous road across the desert that avoids the Nile cataracts and begins at Korosko. This road was traveled by envoys of the Old Kingdom, Egyptian kings and Lepsius used it in the 1840's.[341]

2.37-38 'the road from *Kares* (Korosko) village to Kurgis that passes through the middle of *Tetokum* (the Nubian Desert)'.

ᛟ ᛩ ᛁ
ka-r-i

---

[337] Budge, *Egyptian Hieroglyphic Dictionary*, 1024.
[338] Ibid., 1025.
[339] Kobishchanov, *Axum*, map1.
[340] Baines and Malek, *Cultural Atlas*, 41, 179.
[341] Lepsius, *Discoveries in Egypt, Ethiopia and the Sinai Peninsula*, 129; O'Connor, "The Locations of Yam and Kush," 27-50.

district around Napata, 4th Cataract.[342]

3.58-59 'In the River Kingdom, at _Kari_ (the Napata district) in the River Kingdom'.

ᚠᚡᛏᚾᚾᚥᚤ
_ka-r-u-n-i-ku-m_

northeastern Egypt. Followers of Horus (Kar) Land. Land of the Falcon clan. This is the Botorrita III pronunciation of _Heru An Kum,_ the Egyptian name for the region in northeastern Egypt along the coast to Gaza in the north and sometimes to Suez in the south. The name is preserved in the Greek word _Heroopolis / Heroonopolis_, which was used in Greek and Roman times for a city and province in the Suez Canal region.[343] _Karunikum_ included Fort Sile and _Aiankum_ but was much larger. It corresponds to _Herind_ and _Heriu_ in the early sections (_Nemed, Partolon_) of the _Book of Invasions_ where it includes Memphis and all of the north on both sides of the Nile.[344]

1.16-19 'a king of all of United Egypt, who had _Karunikum_ (northern Egypt) of the Sile-ites, the kingdom of the Great King which extended to Mendes (in the Egyptian Delta)'.

3.47-49 'In _Karunikum_ (northern Egypt) [he ruled] from the kings of Pelusium [on the Mediterranean coast] to the princes over the regions west of the Nile'. See **4.6**.

ᚠᛗᚾᛁᚻᛗ
_ka-s-i-l-o-s_

---

[342] Budge, _Egyptian Hieroglyphic Dictionary_, 1046b.

[343] Strabo, _Geography of Strabo_, vol. III, 294. Strabo says, "When you sail from _Heroopolis_ (Suez) along the _Troglodutike_ (West Red Sea coast)…."

[344] Best, Bergin, and O'Brien, _Book of Leinster_, lines 475-476, 490-497, 613-615, 619-620.

ethnonym for people of Al Jazirah, Yemen, which is a peninsula due west of Sana'a on the coast and south of Kamaran Island. From Somali / Arabic: *gazira, jezira,* 'peninsula, island'. See §6.2.

2.8 'the *Kasilos* (people of Al Jazirah) of *Atokum* (Yemen)'.

ᚠᚮᚾᚺᛗ

ka-tu-n-o-s

ethnonym for Egyptian Delta people, Swamp dwellers, from Egyptian: *khat,* 'swamp'.[345] The town of el Khata'na in the Delta.[346] See §6.2. Middle Irish: *Ghathlaigib, Gaedelaib,* 'people of the marshes of Heriu'[347]

2.53 'the *Burikounikum* (the Harbor kingdom) of *Katunos* (the Swamp dwellers)'.

ᚠᛏᚠᚠᚾᚾᚺ

ka-u-ki-r-i-n-o

the Keren Highlands, literally, 'stony heights'. Egyptian: *qa,* 'to be high', 'exalted'.[348] Egyptian: *qau,* 'height of the ridges of the land above the river'.[349] Somali: *qau,* 'cliff, steep rock wall'.[350] Chamir: *kiriŋa,* 'stone'.[351] Keren / Cheren is a place in Eritrea.[352] Adjective form, see §6.2.

4.39-40 'decreed at *Kustikum* (Eritrea) in the *Kaukirino* (Keren Highlands)'.

---

[345] Budge, *Egyptian Hieroglyphic Dictionary*, 76a, 76b, 526.
[346] Baines and Malek, *Cultural Atlas*, 41.
[347] Best, Bergin and O'Brien, *The Book of Leinster*, 6, 7, lines 171, 221.
[348] Budge, *Egyptian Hieroglyphic Dictionary*, 760.
[349] Ibid., 762.
[350] Reinisch, *Die Somali-Sprache*, 267.
[351] Ibid., *Die ChamirSprache*, vol. CV, 670.
[352] Hammond, *Complete World Atlas*, 81; Munzinger, *Ũeber die Sitten und das Recht der Bogos*, map.

⟨

ke

> within, around, near, by, on. Postposition, see §7.1.5.
> Egyptian: *ges*, 'near, by, on both sides'.[353]
> **3.45** 'from those who are *ke* (within) the borders of
> Thinis'.

⟨ ∧

ke-ka

> Gigartus, in Lebanon, near Byblos; "Gigartus" in
> Strabo is a "fortress for robbers near Byblos".[354]
> **2.55** 'to *Keka* (Gigartus) near Byblos, Lebanon'.

⟨ ∧M 𝕏

ke-ka-s ko

> in the middle of. Postposition, see §7.1.6. Egyptian:
> *ges*.[355] Nubian: *gasko*, 'middle'.[356]
> **2.37-38** 'the road from Korosko village to Kurgis that
> passes through *kekas ko* (the middle of) the Nubian
> desert'.

⟨ ⱫⱭM☉

ke-n-ti-s-ku

> the chief, the Foremost one.[357] From Egyptian: *khentis*,
> 'before, hence, first and foremost'. See §5.1, §6.7, *-ku*,
> 'the', definite article, §6.6.
> **1.38-40** ' the Great Lord of the princes of *kentisku* (the
> southern) part of the River Kingdom'.

⟨ ⱫⱭM☉Ⱶ

ke-n-ti-s-ku-e

---

[353] Budge, *Egyptian Hieroglyphic Dictionary*, 813.
[354] Strabo, *Geography of Strabo*, vol. III, 170.
[355] Budge, *Egyptian Hieroglyphic Dictionary*, 813.
[356] Lepsius, *Nubische Grammatik*, 429.
[357] Budge, *Egyptian Hieroglyphic Dictionary*, 554.

upstream, which would be south, southern. From Egyptian: *khentis*, 'before, hence, first and foremost', see §6.7.[358] *-kue*, 'as far as, near'. Postposition, see §7.1.8.

2.2-2.3 '(as far as) the *kentiskue* (southern) *Tirtanos*'. See **2.25**, **3.4**, **3.56**, **4.3**.

⟨ 𐎐𐎃𐎎𐎚𐎛

ke-n-ti-s-u-m

foremost leader. Egyptian: *khentis*, 'foremost' + Amharic: *shum*, 'leader, lord, master'. See §6.7.

3.24-25 'is *kentisum* (the foremost chief) in both directions as far as the Afan people [in the south] and the Berta people [in the north]'.

𐎋𐎐𐎁𐎗𐎛𐎀

ki-n-bi-r-i-a

(?) Buri Peninsula, Somali: *ga'an*, 'peninsula'.[359] Another possibility is that this word may be related to a long list of similar words in Kushitic languages, mostly meaning 'bird'. In Somali, 'bird' is *shimbir*, in Baiso, *kimbiri*, in Afan / Afar, *kimmiro*, in Galab, *kimirre*, in Rendille, *chimbir*, in Galla, *shimpirre*, in Konso, *hambir-deta*, and in Gidole, *hambira*.[360] This word could be a place-name meaning 'Birdland,' somewhere in southern *Turikum*, but, if so, I haven't found it. The Buri Peninsula is known for its birds, particularly ostriches, as well as other wildlife, and it is located in *Turikum*.

3.3-4 'Baboon Land extends… from the king of *Tirtanikum* in the River Kingdom, to just south of

---

[358] Budge, *Egyptian Hieroglyphic Dictionary*, 554; Gardiner, *Egyptian Grammar*, 529sect.W-17.

[359] Huntingford, *Periplus*, map4.

[360] Fleming, "Baiso and Rendille," 40.

Kinbiria (the Buri Peninsula, Eritrea) near the border of the king of *Turikum*'.

ꚉꙀꚗꙀꝐ

ko-i-ti-n-a

 this particular king, Chamir: *gutya, gueta,* 'lord, owner'.[361] Amharic: *geta,* 'lord, master, owner', *-na* as demonstrative, see §6.4.

 1.4-5 'the Great Chief of the *Statulu*, the *koitina* (king), has spoken'.

 1.6 'The Great Lord, our *koitina* (king) of kings,'.

 See **2.15, 2.26, 3.37, 4.10, 4.35**.

ꚉꙀꚗꙀꝐ Ꙩꝇ

ko-i-ti-n-a-ku-e

 from, as far as, this particular king, see *koitina. -kue,* 'as far as, near'. Postposition, see §7.1.8.

 2.33-34 '*koitinakue* (as far as the king) of the Chaldeans'.

 3.4-5 '(near) the border of *koitinakue* (the king) of *Turikum*'.

ꚉꙀꚗꙀꝐ Ꙧ

ko-i-ti-n-a-s

 to the king. See *koitu, -s,* see §5.5.

 2.51-52 ' *koitinas* (to the king) of the *Terkinos* people at Thinis, I will extend the Harbor Kingdom of the Swamp dwellers'.

ꚉꙀ△

ko-i-tu

 kings, of kings, *-u,* see §5.5, Bilin genitive plural.[362] *gutya, gueta,* 'Herr, lord'.

 1.5-6 'The Great Lord, our king *koitu* (of kings)'.

---

[361] Reinisch, *Die ChamirSprache*, vol. CV, 594.
[362] Ibid.; Ibid., *Die Bilin-Sprache*, 95.

1.30 'the _koitu_ (kings) of the _Akuia_ kingdom'.
See **2.29**, **2.42**, **3.15**.

ꡆ ꞵ HꞴꝴHꟿ
_ko-l-o-u-ti-o-s_

> personal name is the most likely translation, a person
> from _Biniskum_. The _Koloutios_ may also have been a
> Lebanese tribe or a group of seven tribes. Nubian:
> _kolodi_, 'seven'.[363] 'Seven' had many associations. As
> discussed in the Background section, on the Libyan
> Palette, _Biniskum,_ a kingdom on the Eastern
> Mediterranean coast, is shown with seven client
> kingdoms. See §6.2.
> **3.8** 'is _Koloutios_ (a person), the Phoenician'.

ꡆ ꞴꞴꙨꝴ
_ko-n-i-ku-m_

> Canaan, 'Kinahhi'.[364]
> **2.49** '_Tekos_ of _Konikum_ (Canaan)'.
> **3.26-28** '[The narrator is] the Great Lord over the
> _Statulos_ of _Konikum_ (Canaan). This Aunu from the
> land of Bes is the Lord-King of the kings of Alalakh'.

ꡆ ꞴꙵꝴHꟿ
_ko-n-tu-d-o-s_

> ethnonym for people of the interior, from the south
> Nile Valley, Sudan. Upper Egypt, the interior,
> Egyptian: _pe-khunnu, pe-kh-n-t_, "The regions
> bordering on Egypt, from the 1st Cataract to the south
> of Mount Barkal, bore the general appellation of Ta-
> Khont, of 'the Land of Khont', the capital of which…

---

[363] Lepsius, _Nubische Grammatik_, 347.
[364] Pritchard, _Atlas of the Bible_, 46, 66; Helck, _Die Beziehungen
Agyptens_, 279.

was Napata".[365] See §6.2.

1.2-3 'the great-king of the *Turos* (on the western Red Sea coast) and the <u>*Kontudos*</u> (people of the interior),'.

𐤏 𐤟 𐤏𐤌
ko-r-ko-s
> Kurgis, on the southern end of the Korosko-Kurgis Road across the Nubian Desert, is south of the 4th Cataract.[366]
> **2.37-38** 'the road from Korosko village to <u>*Korkos*</u> (<u>Kurgis</u>) that passes through the middle of the Nubian Desert'.

𐤏 𐤟 𐤛𐤏𐤌
ko-r-ti-ko-s
> Lord of Khor, the capital, in Qatar.[367]
> **1.55-57** 'which the <u>*Kortikos*</u> (<u>Lord of Khor in Qatar</u>) and the [Lord] of Bahrain, *Kaiaitos*, from the nation of Sumer of Kish, had conquered'.

𐤏𐤉𐤍𐤋𐤉𐤍⊙𐤅
ko-u-n-e-s-i-ku-m
> Knossos in Crete.[368]
> **I-B 1** 'The [Egyptian] *Melmunos* destroyed <u>*Kounesikum*</u> (<u>Knossos</u>) of the Libyans'.

⊙𐤋𐤉𐤇𐤍𐤉⊙𐤅
ku-e-d-o-n-ti-ku-m
> Kydonia in Crete.[369]Old Irish: *Tor inis Chetni,* 'the island fortress of Kydonia', Mag Cetni, Mag Ceitne.[370]

---

[365] Brugsch and Seymour, *History of Egypt*, 329; Brugsch, *Dictionnaire Géographique,* 1398.

[366] Baines and Malek, *Cultural Atlas*, 186.

[367] Roaf, *Cultural Atlas of Mesopotamia*, 98.

[368] Cornell and Matthews, *Atlas of the Roman World*, 164map.

[369] Ibid.

Glossary

4.36 'the princes of *Kuedontikum* (Kydonia)'.

ᐤᴎᴎᐤ⍑
ku-i-n-i-ku-m

> South land, Somali: *koonfur*, 'south'. Perhaps *Kueneion*.[371]
>
> **2.42** 'the kings at Fort *Atauikum* who have all of *Kuinikum* (the Southern kingdom)'.

ᐤᴎᴎ⍦✕ᐤ
ku-i-n-ti-ta-ku

> Deep South. Somali: *koonfur*, 'south' compares to *kuinti-*. Somali: *takti*, 'extremist', Amharic: *taqaran*, 'extreme'. *-ku*, 'the', definite article, see §6.6.
>
> **3.60** 'the kingdoms of *Kuintitaku* (the Deep South) [are ruled by]'.

ᐤ⍓⊼⍑ᴎᐤ⍑
ku-l-u-ka-m-i-ku-m

> Land of Koloe of Kam, the fortress may have been at Qohaito in modern Eritrea. Kam is another name for Lasta, the homeland of the Chamir in the Central Highlands of modern Ethiopia.[372] The two places are not distant and we do not know what the boundaries of Kam were. Kam is possibly also the Kam of Bau K-m, Bau Q-m, Bau G-m, a country from whence the worship of the goddesses and gods, Hathor, Shu / Tiu, and Tefnut was introduced into Egypt.[373] Bau-K-m may correspond to the province of Bugna near Lake Tana in Lasta. In the 12th century AD, a dynasty of Kushitic speaking Agau, called the Zagwe, and

---

[370] Best, Bergin and O'Brien, *The Book of Leinster*, 20,23, lines 634, 636, 737.The Story of Nemed.

[371] Huntingford, *Periplus*, map1.

[372] Reinisch, *Die ChamirSprache*, vol. CV, 575.

[373] Budge, *Egyptian Hieroglyphic Dictionary*, 977.

originating from Bugna, claimed descent from the most ancient of kings.[374] The town of Koloe / Coloe corresponds to modern Qohaito / Kohaito in Eritrea, north of Axum.[375] It is just north of Matara on a map in Munro-Hay.[376] On the Libyan Palette, the fortress of Lion Land (Kam) has three kingdoms and a large fortress. The fortress may be Fort Koloe of Kam.
2.10-11 'as far as the fort of *Kulukamikum* (Koloe of Kam) where the chief was hanged'.

ᎤᏬᏃᏰᏋ

ku-n-i-ku-m
> the southern kingdoms. Somali: *koonfer*, 'south'.
> **2.25-28** 'the king of *Ataiokum* in the district of the Kemalke Ford (on the Atbara River) [rules] as far as the kings of *kunikum* (the southern kingdoms) [and]'.

ᎤᎤᏋᏃᏋᏃᎯᏬᏋ

ku-r-m-i-l-i-o-ku-m
> Kerma, Sudan, 3rd Cataract on Nile.[377]
> **4.26** 'to the border with *Kurmiliokum* (Kerma)'.

ᎤᎤᏋᏃᎯᎯᏬᏋ

ku-r-m-i-l-o-ku-m
> Kerma, Sudan.[378]
> **3.55-58** 'as far in the southern River Kingdom as the people from Tyre of Litani Land (Lebanon) [settled in] *Kurmilokum* (Kerma)'.

---

[374] Munro-Hay, *Ethiopia*, map; Wikipedia Authors, "Qohaito."
[375] Kobishchanov, *Axum*, 35map3.
[376] Munro-Hay, *Ethiopia*, 43-48.
[377] Budge, *Egyptian Hieroglyphic Dictionary*, 1028; Baines and Malek, *Cultural Atlas*, 186.
[378] Ibid.

ⵙⴰⵟⵙⴰⵢ

ku-s-ti-ku-m

Eritrea. Gash River region to Red Sea coast.[379] See §2.3.

4.12-13 'Of the Chaldeans of *Kustikum* (Eritrea), the Lord of the Antiu of *Kustikum* (Eritrea) [rules] Coptus in southern Egypt'.

See **4.33, 4.39**.

ⵏ

l

to, into. Postposition, see §7.1.9, Chamir: *-l*, 'by, to, into'.[380]

0.1-1.1 '*l* (To) that Arab leader [held] captive in the Djibouti / Harar Province area'.

ⵏ ⵒ ⵟⵏⵏⵙ

l-a-u-n-i-ku

the right, the south (on the right hand side facing east), Chamir: *lau*, 'right (hand)'.[381] See §5.1. *-ku*, 'the', definite article, see §6.6.

2.5 'king of *launiku* (the Southern) River Kingdom, which'.

ⵏ ⵒ ⵟⵏⵏⵙⵞ

l-a-u-n-i-ku-e

as far as the southern, see *launiku*. *-kue*, 'as far as', postpostion, see §7.1.8.

2.27-28 '(as far as) the kings of *launikue* (the southern) kingdoms'.

See **3.40, 3.58**.

---

[379] Budge, *Egyptian Hieroglyphic Dictionary*, 1047.
[380] Reinisch, *Die ChamirSprache*, vol. CV, 689.
[381] Ibid., 609.

ᚱᛖ

l-e

> he has. Verb form, Somali: *leh*, 'to have, possess'.[382]
> Afar: *le*, 'has'.[383] See §4.1, §4.5.
> **1.17** '*le* (he has) northern Egypt of the Sile people'.

ᚱᛖᛗᛈ ᚾᛈ

l-e-s-a-n-a

> fields, territories, lands, plural of *les*, see §5.4.
> Dhasanac: *lesanu*, 'fields, lands'.[384]
> **1.33-36** 'as far as Fort Mouza in *lesana* (the lands) of
> the Eastern district of the king of the Sana'a people of
> Yemen'.

ᚱᛖᛗᛟ ᚠ ᛈ

l-e-s-te-r-a

> one of the (southerners) from Lasta. *-ra*, singulative,
> see §7.3, 'one of', Bilin, *-ra*, suffix that makes a noun,
> that is unspecified for number, singular.[385] See §5.4.
> Dhasanac also has a singulative but uses a different
> ending. See *les*. The name Lasta may just have meant
> 'the Land', comparable to Ta Mela as a name for Egypt.
> **0.1** '(One of) the southerners from *Lestera* (Lasta) I
> have prevented the Numidians from conquering
> beyond [the limits] of their territory'.

ᚱᛖᛗᛏᚾᚺᛗ

l-e-s-u-n-o-s

> land, field, territory. Dhasanac: *lesanu*, 'fields,
> lands'.[386]

---

[382] Saeed, *Somali Reference*, 116-118.
[383] Bliese, "Afar," 143.
[384] Tosco, *Dhasanac Language*, 257; Sasse, "Dasenech," 200, 203, 205.
[385] Reinisch, *Die Bilin-Sprache*, 87.
[386] Tosco, *Dhasanac Language*, 257.

I-B 2 'The plundered *Melmu lesunos* (land) that was destroyed,'.

I-B 6 'They destroyed the *lesunos* (land) of the *Tirtanos* of *Statulikum*'.

ᚹᚦᚻᚩᚼ

l-e-ti-ku-m

> Gortyn, in Crete on the Lethaeus River.[387]
>
> **I-B 8** 'The cities of the eastern Mediterranean were destroyed, including the towns of *Letikum* (Gortyn) which were'.

ᚹᚦᛰᛘ

l-e-to-n

> I will extend, extend. Future, first person singular, Chamir: *lat*, 'to extend'.[388] See §4.1, §4.5.
>
> **2.52-53** '*Leton* (I will extend) the Harbor kingdom of the Swamp dwellers to the king of the *Terkinos* at Thinis'.

ᚹᚦᛰᛘᛩ

l-e-to-n-tu

> he / it will extend, will include. Verb, future, third person singular. Also used in relative clauses where tense is not specified. [389] See §4.1, §4.5, §4.9.
>
> **1.18-19** 'the kingdom of the Great King which *letontu* (extended) to *Batokum* (Mendes, Egypt)'.
>
> **1.25** '[This new region] *letontu* (will extend to) Fort Hibis'.
>
> See **2.7**, **2.24**.

In Botorrita I-B, *letontu* shows no change in form for singular or plural. The meaning is still 'extending to',

---

[387] Strabo, *Geography of Strabo*, vol. II, 199.

[388] Reinisch, *Die ChamirSprache*, vol. CVI, 389.

[389] Ibid., vol. CV, 626; Ibid. vol. CVI, 389, 445.

'including', 'continued on to'. In no case is *letontu* used as a main verb and there are no clear examples where the sense is future.

I-B 1-2 'The Egyptian *Melmun* destroyed Knossos of the Libyans, *letontu* (<u>extending to</u>) Lyttus where they destroyed the towns'.

I-B 2-3 'The plundered *Melmu* land that was destroyed, which *letontu* (<u>extends to</u>) the *Turo* Uweinat was destroyed by the Libyans'.

I-B 4-6 'the towns in Laodikea (Syria) of the *Useidunos* (people from Tyre) were destroyed by the Achaeans (Greeks), [who] *letontu* (<u>expanded [the fighting])</u> by burning out the people of the Cyclades Islands in Mycenae'.

I-B 6-7 'They (the Greeks) destroyed the lands of the *Tirtanos* of *Statulikum letontu* (<u>reaching down to</u>) the *Nouantubos*'.

I-B 8-9 'The cities of the *Aiankum Tauro* were destroyed, *letontu* (<u>including</u>) the towns of Gortyn which were destroyed by the Mycenaeans, *letontu* (<u>including</u>) Issus, which was [also] destroyed'.

ᚾᚳᚹᛜᚾᚻᛗ
l-e-to-n-tu-n-o-s

  will extend, verb with participle and adjectival suffixes. See *leton* and *letontu*, §4.1, §4.5.

  2.58-60 'The province of Baboon Land *letontunos* (<u>will extend</u>) to the borders of the Akuia empire along the Red Sea coast from Djibouti'.

ᚾᛂᚴᚾᚻᛗ
l-i-ki-n-o-s

chiefs, heads, princes, rulers, of the princes. Genitive plural, Ge'ez: *liq*, 'chief, head, ruler, king, prince, archbishop'.[390] (Ge'ez is a Semitic language, the religious language of Ethiopian Christians, related to Amharic and Tigrinya.)

1.29 'Below the *likinos* (princes) of these districts [are]'.

See **2.6, 2.35, 3.49, 4.36**.

ｌＮＶＮＨＭＯﾄ

l-i-ki-n-o-s-ku-e

of the princes. See *likinos*. *-kue*, 'as far as, near, from'. Postposition, see §7.1.8.

1.36-40 '(From) Lower Nubia where the *Bini Rusku* [have] the noble citadel of the island kingdom, the Great Lord *likinoskue* (of the princes) of the southern part of the River Kingdom...'.

ｌＮＸＮＨＯＶ

l-i-ta-n-o-ku-m

Land of the Litani River (in Lebanon, between Tyre and Sidon).[391]

3.56-57 'in the southern River Kingdom up to the Tyre people from *Litanokum* (Land of the Litani River) who are settled in Kerma'.

ｌＮШＯＶ

l-i-to-ku-m

Lyttus in Eastern Crete.[392]

I-B 1 'The Egyptian Melmun destroyed Knossos of the Libyans extending to *Litokum* (Lyttus)'.

ｌＮ△

---

[390] Munro-Hay, *Ethiopia*, 43-48.
[391] Pritchard, *Atlas of the Bible*, 58.
[392] Cornell and Matthews, *Atlas of the Roman World*, 164map.

l-i-tu

conquered. Chamir: *litaq, lataq*, 'to conquer'.[393] Bilin: *lataqux*, 'he won'.[394] Akkadian: *litatu*, 'victory'.[395] See §4.1, §4.2.1.

4.4-8 'the Melmandos led by *Tiokenes* of the River Kingdom *litu* (conquered) the Chaldeans of Egypt at the fortress of Northern Egypt [and the] royal fortress of Ebla'.

ʃℕ△☉ⵂ

l-i-tu-ku-e

conquered. Chamir: *litaq, lataq*, 'to conquer'.[396] Bilin: *lataqux*, 'he won'.[397] Akkadian: *litatu*, 'victory'.[398] *-kue*, 'starting from, up to, as far as, near'. Postposition, see §7.1.8.

1.57 'The River Kingdom starts from) Fort Aden (in Yemen), which the Lord of Bahrain and Qatar, *Kaiaitos*, from the nation of Sumer of Kish, *litukue* (conquered)'.

ʃH↑ⵏH☉ⵣ

l-o-u-d-o-ku-m

Laodikea / Latakia, coastal province of Syria.[399]

I-B 4-5 'The towns in *Loudokum* (Laodikea) of the *Useidunos* (people of Tyre) were destroyed by the Achaeans,'.

ʃH↑ⵉℕℕⵋ

l-o-u-ka-n-i-ko

---

[393] Reinisch, *Die ChamirSprache*, vol. CV, 589.

[394] Ibid., *Texte der Bilin-Sprache*, 242.

[395] von Soden, *Grundriss der Akkadischen*, 95sect.61m.

[396] Reinisch, *Die ChamirSprache*, vol. CV, 589.

[397] Ibid., *Texte der Bilin-Sprache*, 242.

[398] von Soden, *Grundriss der Akkadischen*, 95sect.61m.

[399] Hammond, *Complete World Atlas*, 77.

the Barka River, flows into the Red Sea south of
Suakin, ancient Aqiq may have been at the mouth of
this river. Ptolemeis Theron was also in this region.
Adjective form of Loukanikum. Loukanian, see
Loukanikum. For *-ko*, meaning 'region', see §7.1.7.
2.3 'on the *Loukaniko* (Barka) river, the Great Chief of
Turanikum is the king of the Southern River Kingdom'.

ᛏHᛏ⅄ᛃᛃᛣ⅄

l-o-u-ka-n-i-ku-m

Cattle Land, *Loukanikum* would have included Egypt,
Libya, and Sudan. It was controlled by Berbers,
possibly the Laguatan, whose name appears in history
much later, in Roman times. In the time of the I-B text,
Syria and Palestine were part of its empire, but not
during Botorrita III times. Its capital would have been
Bartiltun (Mersa Matruh) where *Tekos* of Canaan was
based. *Loukanikum* may have been a Kushitic pun on
the name of the Berber Laguatan confederation[400]. In
Kushitic, *Loukanikum* would mean 'Cattle Land' from
Chamir: *luwa*, 'cow', plural *lūkŭe*, 'cattle'. Also, the
hieroglyphic sign for the Tjekker, a name for the

Libyans, resembles the glyph for a leg (𝕁). The
hieroglyphic name may have been a pun on Chamir:
lūk, 'leg'.[401] An Egyptian statue from the 5th Dynasty
was found with the title 'governor of the land of cattle'.
The Farafra Oasis, which would have been within the
kingdom boundaries, was also known as Cattle
Land.[402] Ancient Egyptian cattle were a distinctive

---

[400] Mattingly, "The Laguatan", *Libyan Studies*, 96-108
[401] Reinisch, *Die ChamirSprache*, vol. CVI, 389, 431. "If I had been the
one who stole them, so I would have given your *lūkŭ-t* (cattle)
back". -Trans.
[402] Trigger et al, *Ancient Egypt*, 121.

breed that may have originated in North Africa. Rock art all across North Africa from the fifth millennium BC depicts cows and herds of cattle[403]. Also relevant may be Lukhu / Ru<u>h</u>u, the god of the phallus of Osiris. In later times a different part of the body of Osiris was assigned to each of the 42 provinces of Egypt.

1.14 'a king of the shebka empire who was the commander of *Loukanikum* (Cattle Land),'.

1.45-47 'In Cataract Land, *Kalos* of the Dakhleh Oasis, one of the kings of *Loukanikum* (Cattle Land), [was] the Great Chief of *Loukanikum* (Cattle Land). [He is now held] at Fort *Tirtobolokum* (somewhere nearAxum)'.

2.43-49 'In *Loukanikum* (Cattle Land), all [of the territories] from the eastern border of Klusma (at Suez in Egypt) to... to the people of the Mandeb Strait in Yemen [controlled by the] *Tirtano* to the Siq at Petra, [are taken] from the commander of *Turumokum*, [who was] *Tekos* of Canaan,'.

3.12-3.14 'In Elephant Land, one of the Urukites, a king of *Loukanikum* (Cattle Land), from the conquered empire [was held] at the fort of Umm Ebeida, by the *Melman* kings of the Siwa Oasis. He was a commander of *Ubokum,* which is outside of the conquered empire'.

3.17-3.20 '[He was] *Tetu, Loukanikum* (the Laguatan), who was the king [in a region on] the border of the River Kingdom with the Urukite part of the River Kingdom.'.

ᛗᛏᚵᛉᛈ ᛋ
l-u-bi-n-a-d

---

[403] Wyse and Winkleman, *Past Worlds Atlas*, 94, 95.

by the *Lubina*, *Lubina* are the Libyans, *-na* as a plural suffix, §5.4 as in *albana*, *-d*, as an ablative of cause or reason.[404] See §8.2.

I-B 3 'The plundered Egyptian land, which extends to the *Turo* Uweinat, was destroyed *Lubinad* (by the Libyans)'.

ᛗᛏᚸᛗ

l-u-bo-s

Libyans. In Egyptian, where distinctions between *l* and *r* are unreliable, we find *lub* and *rub* for Libyans. Amharic has *leba* meaning 'thief' which might refer to pirates, but these people seem to come from Libya.

I-B 1 'The Egyptian *Melman* have destroyed Knossos of the Libyans'.

ᛗᛏᚏᛝᚺᛗ

l-u-ki-n-o-s

people of *Loukanikum* (CattleLand), *Loukanian*, Laguatan Berbers. This is a people whose territory was conquered, according to the Proclamation.

1.60-2.2 'The great chief of *Abokum Turo* [rules] the *Lukinos* (Cattle Land) borderland with the shebka people as far south as the *Tirtanos*'.

ᛘᛔᚺᛝᚏᚺᚻᛘ

m-a-i-l-i-ki-n-o-ku-m

kingdom, plural, See *mailikum*, §5.4.

3.52 'the Lord-king of the Khabur river *ensikum* (empire) of the *mailikinokum* (kingdoms) of Uruk'.

3.60 'the *mailikinokum* (kingdoms) of the Deep South'.

ᛘᛔᚺᛝᚻᛘ

m-a-i-l-i-ku-m

---

[404] Reinisch, *Die Bilin-Sprache*, 100.

kingdom, *mel* (king) becomes *mail* + *kum*. This is a common Semitic word. See §5.4.

1.22-26 'The new province in the River Kingdom [which ends] at the fortress of the Western Land,... includes the fortress at Hibis from the *mailikum* (kingdom) of *Melmanios* '.

1.30 'the kings of the Akuia *mailikum* (kingdom) rule *Tetokum* (the Nubian Desert)'.

See **2.23, 4.20.**

ⲧⲣ ⲋ ⲙⲝⲟⲧ

m-a-ke-s-ko-ku-m

the Northern Lands, Northern Egypt and Libya, Egyptian: *m-h,* 'north'.[405] For *-ko*, meaning 'region', see §7.1.7.

1.48 'from *Makeskokum* (the Northern Lands) of the Sile people'.

4.8 'In *Makeskokum* (the Northern Lands, Northern Egypt and Libya), the Great Chief of Klusma'.

ⲧⲣ ⲡⲝⲙ

m-a-r-ko-s

center, central part of town, central fortress, from Arabic: *marqaz*

3.43 'the *markos* (central fortress) of Benadir'.

ⲧⲣ ⲟⲓⲏⲟⲧ

m-a-tu-l-o-ku-m

Metelis, capital of the seventh province of Lower Egypt, near modern Damanhur, ruins possibly at Tell el Ahmar.[406]

1.9 'king of the army of *Matulokum* (Metelis)'.

---

[405] Budge, *Egyptian Hieroglyphic Dictionary*, 1001.
[406] Baines and Malek, *Cultural Atlas*, 167.

Glossary

ᛏᛈ

m-e

in, at. Also as predicate 'is, are', used as a postposition, §7.1.10, but it resembles the Egyptian preposition: *m* (🏛), 'in', which may also be used as a predicate.[407] Bilin has parallels.[408]

1.7 'Those hung *me* (at) Thinis '.

1.22 'the provinces of the River Kingdom *me* (are)'.

ᛏᛈᛋᛏᛣ ᚾᚺᛗ

m-e-d-u-ke-n-o-s

Great Chief, Emperor, ranks above kings, Somali: *madax-weyna,* 'great chief', from *madax,* 'head / chief' and *weyna,* 'great', currently used to translate 'president of the republic'. See §5.2. The name of Sargon of Akkad (2300 BC) in Akkadian was *sharru-ken* (king-great). His name in Sumerian was *lugal-gina* (king-great). See *retukenos* (great king). Among the Celtiberians of Spain, this was a popular name, comparable perhaps to Caesar. It appears on a stele from Burgos below a Don Quijote-like figure with horse and lance. The Latin inscription says '*Madicenus Calaetus ambati f(ilius) an(norum) LV*' 'Madicenus Calaetus, son of Ambatus, [lived] to 55 years'. The stele is believed to date to the Flavian Period of the Roman era (1st century BC).[409] In the Botorritan language, the name would be spelled *Medukenos Kalaitos* - Great chief of the Lowlanders, of the Chaldeans.

1.4 '*medukenos* (the Great Chief) of the *Statulu*'.

See **1.46, 1.60, 2.4, 2.12, 2.21, 3.29, 4.9.**

ᛏᛈᛋᛏᛣ ᚾᚺᛗ☉ᛈ

---

[407] Gardiner, *Egyptian Grammar*, 40sects.37-38.

[408] Reinisch, *Die Bilin-Sprache*, 119sect.194.

[409] Rose, "Text and Image in Celtiberia," 166-169.

m-e-d-u-ke-n-o-s-ku-e
> as far as the Great Chief, Emperor. See *medukenos*.
> *-kue*, 'as far as, near'. Postposition, see §7.1.8.
> **3.11** '[He ruled over] the kings of *Kaburikum*
> *medukenoskue* (as far as the Great Chief) of Uruk'.

𐤌𐤋𐤉

m-e-l
> king, at ancient temple of Hercules at Tyre in Lebanon,
> Hercules' title is *mel kart*, 'king of the city'.[410] This
> corresponds to Egyptian *mer* which means 'King' as a
> title for the Scorpion King, and for the kings on the
> Libyan Palette, but was also used in bureaucratic titles,
> so in Egyptian, *mer khart* meant 'king of the city of the
> dead, director of the cemetery'.[411] In the Proclamation
> text, a *mel sura* 'king of the army' may be a general.
> **1.8** '*mel* (king) of the army of Metelis from the River
> Kingdom'.
> See **1.15, 3.3**.

𐤌𐤋𐤉𐤌

m-e-l-m
> local (to Egypt), Egyptian, adjective based on ancient
> name for Egypt, Ta Mera / Ta Mela.[412] Note Berber:
> *tamurt*, 'country, land'. [413]Adjective forming suffix *-m*,
> see §6.2, as in Chamir.[414] Root as in Somali: *meel,*
> 'place, land, location'.
> **3.9** 'Lord of the Antiu in *Uiriaskum Melm* (in Egyptian
> Berber colonies in the River Kingdom)'.

---

[410] Pritchard, *Atlas of the Bible*, 101.
[411] Budge, *Egyptian Hieroglyphic Dictionary*, 312.
[412] Ibid., 1050.
[413] Venture de Paradis, *Grammaire*, 124.
[414] Reinisch, *Die ChamirSprache*, vol. CV, 664.

Glossary

ᕗᒿᐱᕗ ᕇ ᐅ
m-e-l-m-a-n
>locals, native Egyptians, Somali: *-man* is a plural
>marker. See §5.4. See *melm* above. The *melman* are
>likely predecessors of the Blemmyes who fought with
>the Greek and Roman Empires, also predecessors, if
>not ancestors, of the Marmaridae who lived in the
>Western Oases and Libya.[415] In the Botorrita I-B text,
>as *melmu* and *melmunos* they rule all of Egypt, a
>territory that includes Barca in the Libyan Cyrenaica. It
>extends to the Gebel Uweinat on the southwest border
>of modern Egypt.
>**3.46** 'the defeated army of the <u>*Melman*</u> (Egyptian
>Berber) kingdom'.

ᕗᒿᐱᕗ ᕇ ᐅᕉH
m-e-l-m-a-n-d-o
>in the *Melman* region. *-do*, Adjective suffix, see §6.2.
>See *melm, melman.*
>**3.15** '*the melmando* (<u>*Melman*</u>) kings of *Samikum* (Siwa
>Oasis, which is in the Melman region)'.

ᕗᒿᐱᕗ ᕇ ᐅᕉHᙏ
m-e-l-m-a-n-d-o-s
>people of the Melman region. See *melman, melmando*
>above, §6.2.
>**4.4-5** 'The <u>*Melmandos*</u> (people from the Melman
>region) under *Tiokenes* of the River Kingdom
>conquered the Chaldeans'.

ᕗᒿᐱᕗ ᕇ ᐅᐊHᙏ
m-e-l-m-a-n-i-o-s

---

[415] Budge, *Egyptian Hieroglyphic Dictionary*, 204, 998; Strabo,
Geography of Strabo, vol. III, 294; Jackson, *At Empire's Edge.*

personal name, Melamanna, 2nd to the last king of Uruk, one of the Egyptian Berbers, one of the locals. See §5.5, *melm, melman*.

1.27 'the fortress of *Auikum* (el Hibis in the Kharga Oasis) in the kingdom of *Melmanios* (a person) of the River Kingdom'.

ᛑᛚᛂᛑᚪᛀᛏᚷᛑᚪ

m-e-l-m-a-n-ta-m-a

Melman Lord. See *melm, melman, tama*.

3.42 '*Melmantama* (the Melman Lord) [held] at the central fortress of *Bentilikum* (Benadir region around Mogadishu)'.

ᛑᛚᛂᛑᛏ

m-e-l-m-u

locals, Egyptian Berbers, Marmaridae, Blemmyes. Somali: *meel*, 'place, land'. See *melm, melman*.

I-B 2 'The plundered *Melmu* (Egyptian) lands extend to *Ubokum Turo*'.

ᛑᛚᛂᛑᛏᛀᚻᛗ

m-e-l-m-u-n-o-s

of the Egyptians. See *melmu, melman*. *-nos,* genitive plural, see §4.2.4.

I-B 1 'The *Melmunos* (Egyptians) have destroyed Knossos (on Crete) of the Libyans'.

I-B 7 'The *Melmunos* (Egyptians) of *Aiankum* have destroyed Ushu of the *Aiankum Tauro* (describes an attack from Fort Sile in Egypt on Lebanese Tyre / Ushu just up the coast)'.

ᛑᛚᛂ

m-e-m

below, under, postposition, see §7.1.11, §7.2.1, Old Kingdom Egyptian preposition: *m_m* 'under'.[416]
1.12 'the lord of *Batokum* (Mendes) *mem* (under [whom]) the *Alasku* (Alashiya, the island of Cyprus) is ruled'.
1.29 '*mem* (below) the princes of these districts'.

Ⲯ ⳑ Ⲯ ⳑ Ⲛ

m-e-m-u-n

below, under, postposition, see §7.2.1, which can be conjugated like a verb, see *mem* above.
2.12 '*memun* (under) the Great-Chief of *Akikum* (Aqiq)'.

Ⲯ ⳑ Ⲯ ⳑ Ⲛ Ⲏ Ⲙ

m-e-m-u-n-o-s

below, under, postposition, see §7.2.1, Bilin adjective ending, see *mem*, see *memun*.
2.13 'the [Dahlak Archipelago] islands *memunos* (are under) the chief of *Tirilokum* who is under the Great Chief of Aqiq, *Terkinos* of Sokota in *Austikum*'.

Ⲯ Ⲛ ⳑ ⳑ ☉

m-i-d-u-ku

the First [lord], the king, Somali: *mid,* 'one, first'.[417] *-ku* 'the', definite article, see §6.6. See §5.1.
1.52 '*miduku* (the first) of the great kings of our *Tirtanos*'.
3.22 'Over all of the Western Land, *miduku* (the First) [Lord] at *Tirtobolokum* (Metropolis of Axum)'.
See **3.41.**

Ⲯ Δ ⳑ Ⲛ Ⲙ ☉ Ⲯ

m-tu-r-i-s-ku-m

---

[416] Edel, *AltÄgyptische Grammatik*, 391sect.760, no.6.
[417] Saeed, *Somali Reference*, 143.

Egypt. *Metcher* (🦅𓈖⌢𓊖), place bounded by a double wall, the northern border of Egypt towards Palestine was strongly fortified.[418]

4.5 'the Chaldeans of *Mturiskum* (Egypt)'.

ᛌᛏᛟᛉᛉᛘ
m-u-n-i-ka

> we, inclusive, our, Dhasanac: *muuni*, 'we, (inclusive) our'. Absolute form of the pronoun.[419] See §3.2. In Somali, possessive adjectives are formed by adding *-ka*, the definite article, to the pronoun.[420] See §6.6.
>
> **1.6** 'the Great [Lord], *munika* (our) king of kings'.
> **2.56** 'these are all *munika* (our) tribal territories of the kings of the Turo empire'.
> **4.37** 'to *munika* (our) provinces, by *Terkinos* of *Turanikum*, this is decreed in *Kustikum*, in the Keren Highlands'.
> See **2.51, 3.34.**

ᛌᛏᛉᛉᛘᚭᛚ
m-u-n-i-ka-ku-e

> as far as our, see *munika*, *-kue*, 'as far as, near'. Postposition, see §7.1.8.
>
> **1.50** '*Tiokenes* of the River Kingdom, the Great Lord of *Turumokum*, [rules] (as far as) the first of the Great kings of *munikakue* (our) Scorpion Clans'.

ᛌᛏᚦᛉᛘᚭᛌ
m-u-tu-r-i-s-ku-m

> United Egypt, Vulture Cobra Land, Egyptian: *mut-uris-kum* (🦅𓆓𓈖), 'Land (*kum*) of Upper Egypt protected by the Vulture goddess, *Mut*, and Lower

---

[418] Budge, *Egyptian Hieroglyphic Dictionary*, 338.
[419] Tosco, *Dhasanac Language*, 568.
[420] Saeed, *Somali Reference*, 166.

Egypt protected by the *uris* / uraeus of the Cobra goddess'.

1.16 'the king of all of *Muturiskum* (United Egypt)'.

1.57-59 '[the new borders of the] River Kingdom [begin] at Fort Aden… from Elephant Land I exclude *Muturiskum* (northern Egypt), but it stretches to *Turumokum*, (the lands west of the Nile)'.

2.18-19 'One of the kings in *Muturiskum* (United Egypt), *Terkinos* of *Teladokum*'.

4.16 17 'This chief of the Chaldeans of *Muturiskum* (United Egypt), [rules] *Albinokum* (Arabia), the island of Failaka in Kuwait, Charax Spasinu in Chaldea, and the kingdom of Uruk of the kings of Arabia'.

ᚿᚿᛗᚼ ☉ᛚ
n-i-s-ke-ku-e

as far as the king, Egyptian: *nesu* (⸺ 𓅆𓅿), 'king', corresponds to cuneiform *ensi*, 'king, governor', as well as to Egyptian: *soten, stena* (𓇓𓏤⸺𓈖) meaning 'king'.[421] In Mesopotamian Kassite, it is *nishakku*, 'mayor, high priest, chief seer'.[422] In Bilin, there is Bilin: *nasaux*, 'masculine', as in *duquara nasaux*, 'male jackass' vs. *duquara ussari*, 'female jackass'.[423] *-kue*, 'as far as, near'. Postposition, see §7.1.8.

1.34 '(as far as) Fort Mouza of *niskekue* (the king) of the Sana'a people in the lands of the eastern district of Yemen'.

ᚿᚺᛏᛞᚿᚨᚼᛗ
n-o-u-a-n-tu-bo-s

---

[421] Gardiner, *Egyptian Grammar*, 575; Budge, *Egyptian Hieroglyphic Dictionary*, 391.

[422] Brinkman, *Political History of Post-Kassite Babylonia*, 300n1970.

[423] Reinisch, *Die Bilin-Sprache*, 86.

Nabataeans, people of Jordan and Northern Arabia, who had their capital at Petra in Roman times.[424] Numidians, related to Berbers allied with Carthage. See 2.47 for reference to Petra, *Beteriskum*. May be related to the *Nouida* in Botorrita III, possibly from *Nubt*, a town in the Naqada region at the Nile Bend in Egypt. In the *Book of Invasions*, Nemed dies of the plague in Aila in the Numidian region near the Litani river. The *Nouantubos* would have lived in the region around Aila, which is not far from Petra.

I-B 6 'They have destroyed the lands of the *Tirtanos* of *Statulikum* reaching down to the *Nouantubos* (northern Arabians)'.

ᚾᚻᛏᚾᛋᛕ

n-o-u-i-d-a

Numidian Berbers. They may have held *Nubt*, center for ancient Naqada, PreDynastic competitors of Thinis. Historical Numidia was in North Africa, Tunisia and eastern Algeria. Numidian Berbers were allied with Carthage. The Romans have left accounts of their interactions with the Numidians. Some of the Numidian inscriptions in a Berber language have been preserved. Descendants of the eastern *Nouida* may have moved west when Phoenicians from Tyre established their colony at Carthage. The word also resembles words meaning 'troublemakers' in Old Kingdom Egyptian: *nbd̲*, 'perverse one, foreign enemy', Amharic: *nawt*, 'disturbance, rebellion, commotion', Bilin: *nabanta*, 'scoundrel'.[425]

---

[424] Cornell and Matthews, *Atlas of the Roman World*, 157map, 161.
[425] Reinisch, *Texte der Bilin-Sprache*, 107: Ibn Khaldoun, *Histoire des Berbères*, 511.

Glossary

0.1 'A southerner from Lasta, I prevented the conquering _nouida_ (Numidians) from reaching beyond the limits of their territory'.

H ⸢ ⸣ HM
o-r [-] bi-l-o-s
    Great Lord, title.
    1.40 'The _or bilos_ (Great Lord) of the princes of the Southern River Kingdom'.

  ⸢ ⸣
r-a-i-e-n-i
    leaders, Somali: _ray_ (Arabic loan word), 'leader'; Arabic: _ra'is,_ 'head, president'.
    4.30 '_raieni_ (leaders) of _Uiduskikum_ (Bayuda region in Sudan, 4th and 5th Cataracts on the Nile)'.

  ⸢ ⸣
r-a-i-o-ku-m
    Mit Rahina, remains of Ancient Memphis.[426] Less likely is Rayan in Egypt, southwest of Fayyum.[427] or

    Old Egyptian: *r-'3-w-kum* (⟨⟩), '(?) Turah'.[428]
    1.10 'a king of _Raiokum_ (Memphis) [was hanged]'.

  ⸢ ⸣
r-e-tu-ke-n-o
    royal, pertaining to the king from _retu-ka-weyna-o_, literally 'king-the-great-adjective suffix'. Egyptian _retu_, 'man, men', Shilluk: _Reth,_ 'Divine King'.[429] Somali:

---

[426] Baines and Malek, _Cultural Atlas_, 136-137.
[427] Jackson, _At Empire's Edge_, 239map4, 256.
[428] Edel, _AltÄgyptische Grammatik_, 54.
[429] Collins and Tignor, _Egypt and the Sudan_, 17. From text, "distinctive Shilluk institutions of political organization revolving around the Reth or Divine King". Shilluk speak a Nilo-Saharan language and live in southern Sudan along the Nile corridor.

weyna, 'great', Somali: *ka,* 'the'. Adjective suffix *-o,* see §6.2.

3.23 'at the *retukeno* (royal) [domain of] *Elkueikikum* (Arqiqo, Eritrean Red Sea Coast)'.

ꟼ ᚼᐃ ᚼᚺᛗ

r-e-tu-ke-n-o-s

king-the-great-of, of the great man, of the great king. *retukenos - retu-ka-weyna-os* – Egyptian: *retu,* 'man, men', Shilluk: *Reth,* 'Divine King'.[430] Sumerian: *lugal* meaning 'king' is literally 'great man', *lu*-'man', *gal*- 'great'. Genitive or adjective.[431] See §5.2.

1.3 '*retukenos* (the great-king) of the Turos, of the Kontudos'.

See 1.18, 1.52, 4.24, 4.33.

ꟼ ᚼᛗꟼ ᚼᚺᐱ

r-i-s-a-ti-o-ka

the southerners, Egyptian: 𓃝𓄿𓏤 resa-t-u – 'south', 𓃝𓇋𓈖𓏏𓀀 resi-u– 'southern tribes, peoples in the South'.432 See §5.1, §5.4. Somali: *-io-* noun plural, *-ka* 'the', definite article.[433] See §6.6.

0.1 'One of *risatioka* (the southerners) from Lasta, I prevented the conquering Numidians from reaching beyond the limts of their territory'.

ꟼ ᚺᛜᚼꟼ ᚼᚷ

r-o-te-n-a-n-ko

in the middle of the length/extent, *roten* –'length, extent' from Amharic: *rezmat,* 'length'; *anko,* 'in the

---

[430] Collins and Tignor, *Egypt and the Sudan*, 17.

[431] Ibid.; Reinisch, *Die Bilin-Sprache*, 95, 96.

[432] Budge, *Egyptian Hieroglyphic Dictionary*, 431b.

[433] Saeed, *Somali Reference*, 130-133, 160-163.

middle of,' postposition, see §7.1.1. Bilin: *anqay,* 'in the middle of', postposition.[434]

2.17 'The Elephant Lord [rules] *Bentikum* from *rotenanko* (the middle of the length of) the [coastline]'.

𓏞 𓏏 𓏞 ☉

r-u-a-ku

the village (*ruak-ku*), Somali: *rug,* 'village, settlement'. *-ku -* 'the', definite article, see §6.6.

2.37 '*kares ruaku* (the Korosko village) to *Korkos* (Kurgis) road [which runs] through the middle of *Tetokum* (the Nubian Desert)'.

𓏞 𓏏𓅓☉

r-u-s-ku

the Rusha people or the Rus, Rushu, or Rusku people, living in the Red Sea Hills of Egypt from the southern Egyptian border north to Abydos. This may be an early reference to the Etruscans. There is an early Old Kingdom inscription that refers to the *Hr-Rusha-kum* who fought with Pepi, a 6th Dynasty, Old Kingdom king near Qusseir.[435] Perhaps the text is referring to the

R-u-sh-a (⬭𓃒▭—), ruled by the *Hr-Rushakum*

(𓊹⬭𓃒▭—𓈗), translated as 'Overlord of the Rusha Lands'.[436] Egyptian and Bilin: *At-,* 'land, tribe' gives *At-rusku / Etrusku,* 'tribe of the *Rusku*', *ku,* 'the', definite article, see §6.6.

1.36-37 'From Lower Nubia where the *Bini Rusku* (the Rusha) have the noble citadel of the island kingdom'.

---

[434] Reinisch, *Die Bilin-Sprache,* 102.

[435] Edel, *AltÄgyptische Grammatik,* 456; Krall, *Beiträge zur Geschichte der Blemmyer,* 23.

[436] Budge, *Egyptian Hieroglyphic Dictionary,* 495. Other spellings of this word can be found in Budge under *Heriusha.*

ᛘ ᛈ ᛀ
s-a [ ] i

    this, these, see §6.5, Chamir uses the plural suffix *zai*
with demonstratives as in *enzai* – 'these' and *ez-zai* –
'those'. Reinisch gives an example from Agaumeder
eni-sa meaning 'these'. He also gives examples from
Chamir such as *ienjan iuna-zan-za* –'this woman'
where *ienjan* - 'this' precedes the noun and *za*, also
meaning 'this' follows.[437]

    2.36 'below *Kaburikum*, <u>sa</u> (these) Ethiopian princes of
mine who rule the Korosko-Kurgis road'.

ᛘ ᛈ ᛀᛏᚷ
s-a-l-u-ta

    rules, a verb, Somali: *salliday, ku sallid,* 'to force,
compel, subject', see §4.1, §4.2.6.

    1.32 ' the kings of the *Akuia* kingdom <u>saluta</u> (rule)
Tetokum'.

ᛘ ᛈ ᚤᛀᚢᚤ
s-a-m-i-ku-m

    Siwa Oasis, west of the Nile, the Semui, 𓃒 𓃒 the
Two Bulls, the Sun and the Moon, were worshiped
there.[438] The region had ties to Libya (see *Ubokum*)
and to the *Melman*. The Roman era Marmaridae had a
kingdom in western Egypt that controlled the Siwa
Oasis. They also lived in the Libyan Uweinat, which is
Ubokum in the Botorrita III text. The king of *Ubokum*
was held captive at *Samikum*.[439]

    3.15 'a king of Cattle Land, the conquered kingdom
[was held] at the fortress of *Betaskum* (Umm Ebeida,

---

[437] Reinisch, *Die ChamirSprache*, vol. CV, 682.

[438] Budge, *Egyptian Hieroglyphic Dictionary*, 1009-1010.

[439] Baines and Malek, *Cultural Atlas*, 21, 53, 54, 187; Jackson, *At
Empire's Edge*, 239map4.

Glossary

Siwa Oasis) by the Melman kings of *Samikum* (Siwa Oasis) [He was] the commander of *Ubokum*, which is outside of the conquered kingdom'.

ℳℙ ℕℳℋℳ
s-a-n-i-o-s

people of Sana'a, capital of modern Yemen.[440]
1.35 'from the fortress of *Uiskikum* (Mouza) of the king of the *sanios* (Sana'a people) in the eastern lands of *Atokum* (Yemen)'.

ℳℒ⋀ℕℋℳ
s-e-ka-n-o-s

people of the *shebka*, Berbers, North Africans, Berber *asaka* 'land, country'.[441] The word 'shebka' describes a geologic feature, in North Africa, which is a flat plain, often high in salt. After a rain, the plain becomes a marsh or a shallow lake. The oases in Western Egypt often depend on local shebka.
2.1 'as far as the great chief of Abokum Turo [who rules] the Cattle Land *Taskokum* (borderland) with *the Sekanos* (shebka people) as far south as the Tirtanos'.

ℳℒ√ℐℋℳ
s-e-ki-l-o-s

those hung, Amharic: *seqlat,* 'hanging, crucifixion', *saqqala,* 'to hang, to crucify', Somali: *iskutallab,* Christian crucifix. Also, *sileq* in Chamir as a transposed version of Amharic: *siqel,*' to hang, hang up'.[442] See §4.1, §4.2.4, §4.8.
1.7 '*sekilos* (those hung) at Thinis'.
2.23 'from Aila of Kish extending to the kingdom of *sekilos* (those who were hanged)'.

---

[440] Hammond, *Complete World Atlas*, 81.
[441] Venture de Paradis, *Grammaire*, 124.
[442] Reinisch, *Die ChamirSprache*, vol. CV, 612.

350

ᛗᛖᚄ�079ᚻᛗᏫᛚ
s-e-ki-l-o-s-ku-e
> from, as far as... those who were hanged. See *sekilos*,
> §4.1, §4.2.4. *-kue* - 'as far as, near'. Postposition, see
> §7.1.8.
> **2.9-11** ' (from) the gates of Thebes to the fortress of
> *Kulukamikum* (Koloe of Kam) where the Chief
> *sekiloskue* (was hanged).'.

ᛗᛖᛪ
s-e-ko
> shebka, Libyan, North African, Berber, see Sekanos.
> Adjective form, see §6.2.
> **1.13** 'a king of the *Seko* (shebka) empire'.

ᛗᛖᛪᚾ9ᚻᛗ
s-e-ko-n-d-o-s
> province, region, settlements, Akkadian: *shakinu* – 'to
> settle, to sit'.[443]
> **1.22** 'The *sekondos* (provinces) of the River Kingdom
> are'.
> See **2.58, 4.18.**

ᛗᛖᛪᚾᛘᚻᛗ
s-e-ko-n-ti-o-s
> commander.[444]
> **1.14** 'he was the *sekontios* (commander) of
> *Loukanikum* (CattleLand)'. See **2.48, 3.16, 3.35.**

ᛗᚾᛤᚾᛂ
s-i-ke-i-a

---

[443] von Soden, *Grundriss der Akkadischen*, 17sect.12d.
[444] Dougherty, *Sealand of Arabia*, 126; Roaf, *Cultural Atlas of
Mesopotamia*, 102; Vrouyr, *Inscriptions Ourartéennes,* 37.

The Siq, entrance to Petra, narrow ravine with monuments.[445]

2.47 'All of [the territories that belonged to] Loukanikum from Suez to Tarkhan (in Egypt) to Ocelis on the Mandeb Strait to *Sikeia* (the Siq) at Petra (in Jordan) [was taken] from the commander of *Turumokum, Tekos* of *Konikum*'.

ᛗ√ ? ᐃᛈHᛗ

s-ki-r-tu-n-o-s

captives, subjects, offerings / sacrifices, the conquered, Akkadian: *suhhurtu-* throwing back enemies.[446] Egyptian:, *shrt*, ' to overthrow', *skr*, ' prisoner-of-war'.[447] *sqer*, 'to fight', *sqeru*, 'prisoner'.[448] Nubian: *oshkirin*, 'slave'.[449] Somali:, *saxariir*, 'torment', see §2.11.

1.1 'to that Arab leader [held] *skirtunos* (captive) in *Tirtanikum* (Chercher Mountain region in Ethiopia)'. **3.13** 'a king of *skirtunos* (the conquered) kingdom'. See **3.17, 3.34**.

ᛗᛉᛚᛈᛡᛏ

s-l-e-i-ti-u

people of Sile, a fortress near modern el Qantara, the first of a series of forts that followed the eastern Mediterranean coast, and the road, north to Gaza.[450] *-iu* - plural suffix, see §5.4. See §2.10, §5.1.

---

[445] Wyse and Winkleman, *Past Worlds Atlas*, 185.
[446] Horowitz, *Mesopotamian Cosmic Geography*, 72; von Soden, *Grundriss der Akkadischen*, 76sect.55n.
[447] Gardiner, *Egyptian Grammar*, 228, 540.
[448] Budge, *Egyptian Hieroglyphic Dictionary*, 702.
[449] Lepsius, *Nubische Grammatik*, 120.
[450] Baines and Malek, *Cultural Atlas*, 44; Pritchard, *Atlas of the Bible*, 50. Map includes the series of forts.

1.17 'a king of all Egypt, he had *Karunikum* of the *Sleitiu* (people of Sile) '.

 1.48 'From *Makeskokum* (in the Northern Lands) of the Sleitiu (people of Sile) to the rebel bowmen in the River Kingdom'.

3.33 'to Totinikum (Tanis) of the *Sleitiu* (people of Sile) in our conquered kingdom'.

ᛗᛈᛈ ᛋᚱᛏᛐᛈᛦᚺᛗ
s-n-a-d-i-u-e-n-to-s

    snad - Shendi, Sudan, *iuentos* - Western, on Nile south of Meroe, in Butana region, and north of Khartoum.[451]
    2.30 ' [over] the districts, of *Snadiuentos* (Western Shendi) in *Ataiokum*, of Dessie in the River Kingdom and the Basa region in the River Kingdom'.

ᛗᚺᛈᛗᛏᛦ
s-o-i-s-u-m

    leader, Egyptian: *seshem* –'to lead', *seshem neteru* – 'leader of the gods'.[452]
    0.1-1.1 'To that Arab *soisum* (leader) [held] captive in *Tirtanikum…*'

ᛗ᙭ᚱ
s-ta-tu

---

[451] Hintze, "Preliminary Report of the Butana Expedition 1958," 173map.

[452] Budge, *Egyptian Hieroglyphic Dictionary*, 622-623.

Canaan, Syria, Asia, enemy territory for the Egyptians. Egyptian: Stt ☖⛆◠〰 'Asia'.[453] Although they were enemies of the later Egyptians, in our text, *Terkinos*, the narrator, is the *Medukenos*, the Great Chief of the *Statulu*. Excavations at Emar on the Euphrates Bend in Syria revealed a kingdom of Astata, which may have given its name to these perennial Egyptian enemies. **2.19-20** '*Terkinos* of *Teladokum* [is] the chief of the Tyre region of *Statu* (Canaan), as far as *Tueidunos*'.

ⵎ╳△ⵏHⵎ
s-ta-tu-l-o-s

Canaanites, Asiatics, enemies of the Egyptians, people in Palestine and Syria who were subject to the *Terkinos*, genitive form.
3.26 '[the narrator] is the Great Lord of the *Statulos* (Canaanites) of Canaan'.

ⵎ╳△ⵏↂ
s-ta-tu-l-u

men of *Statu* (Canaan), Sumerian: *lu*-'man'.[454]
1.3 'the Great-Chief of the *Statulu* (people of the Eastern Mediterranean coast)'.

ⵎ╳△ⵏNↂⵖ
s-ta-tu-l-i-ku-m

Land of the *Statu* perhaps named for kingdom of Astata, remains of which were found at Emar in Syria at the Euphrates Bend. From ancient times, this was an Egyptian name for Asiatic foreigners, mostly enemies. Also, see *statu*.
I-B 6 'They have destroyed the lands of the Tirtanos of *Statulikum* (Syria) reaching down to the Nouantubos'.

---

[453] Gardiner, *Egyptian Grammar*, 593.
[454] Gadd, *Sumerian Reading-Book*, 187.

ᛗᛩ

s-te

> they, those. Egyptian: *s-t*-'they'.[455] See §3.3.
> **4.28** '<u>Ste</u> (Those) [lords]…. of AgauLand, [who are vassals] of the king of Aqiq'.

ᛗᛩᛔᛈ

s-te-n-a

> king, Egyptian: s-t-n ⚬⚬⚬, 'king of Upper Egypt'.[456] See §5.4.
> **1.16** 'a *stena* (king) of all of Muturiskum (Egypt)'.
> **3.13** 'a *stena* (king) of the conquered kingdom'.
> **3.19** 'Tetu, a *stena* (king) of Cattle Land'.

ᛗᛩᛔᛝᚼᛔᛩᛗ

s-te-n-i-o-n-te-s

> king of the Bowmen; Egyptian: *sten,* 'king'; Egyptian: *iwnt* ⚬⚬ 'bow', *iontes,* 'bowmen, archers, Nubians'.
> **4.2** '*steniontes* (king of the archers) of *Turikainos* (people of the Fort at Iken)'.

ᛗᛩᛔᚠ

s-te-n-u

> of the kings, genitive plural. See *stena.*
> **3.6** '*stenu* (of the kings) of *Bentilikum* (the Benadir region around Mogadishu)'.

ᛗᚠᛈ ᚾᛨᛔᚼᛩᚤ

s-u-a-i-ki-n-o-ku-m

> Suakin, Red Sea port city, eastern Sudan.[457]
> **3.25** 'At *Suaikinokum* (Suakin), [he is] the Great Lord.'

---

[455] Gardiner, *Egyptian Grammar*, 98.

[456] Ibid., 616.

[457] Hammond, *Complete World Atlas*, 98; Huntingford, *Periplus*, map1.

Glossary

3.36 'the [new] commander of the River Kingdom army [is] the *Suaikinokum* (Suakin) king'.

ᛗᛏᚺᛝᛈ ⵙᛚ
s-u-o-l-a-ku-e
    as far as Djibouti / Solate.[458] *-kue* - 'as far as, near'.
    Postposition, see §7.1.8.
    3.2-4 ' (as far as) *Testios* of *Turumokum,* the king of *Suolakue* (Djibouti)'.

ᛗᛏᚺᛝᚾ-ⵙᛩ
s-u-o-l-i [-] ku-m
    Djibouti, Somalia.[459]
    3.37 'the king of *Suoli kum* (Somalia)'.

ᛗᛏᚺᛗⵔᚾᚺᛗ
s-u-o-s-tu-n-o-s
    unknown, possibly S[a]mostunos, residents of Cyclades Islands just north of Crete, sometimes under the jurisdiction of Samos.
    I-B 5 'They burned out the *Suostunos* (people of the Cyclades) of Mycenae'.

ᛗᛏ ⵡ ᛈ
s-u-r-a
    army, Bilin:, *sura,* 'weapon'; Ge'ez: *sarwe,* 'army, military detachments', based on an Inscription of 5th century AD Axumite king.[460]
    1.9 'the king of the *sura* (army) of *Matulokum* (Metelis in Egypt)'.
    1.15 'the king of the *sura* (army) of the River Kingdom'.

---

[458] Kobishchanov, *Axum*, map1.
[459] Huntingford, *Periplus*, map1.
[460] Kobishchanov, *Axum*, 208.

3.36-37 'the commander of the River Kingdom *sura* (army) is the king of *Suaikinokum* (Suakin)'.
3.46 'the {(?) defeated} army of the Melman kingdom'.

s-u-r-o-s

Syrians, *shur-*'salt flats, desert', *Shuros* in Sinai at Elim and at Tyre.[461]
3.54 'the *Suros* (Syrians) at Aila of Kish from those at *Alikum* (Elim in the Sinai) up to Amman (in Jordan)'.

ta-i-s

Dessie on lake Hayq in North Central Ethiopia.[462]
2.31 '*Tais* (Dessie) in the River Kingdom'.

ta-l-u-ko-ku-m

Dal Cataract on the Nile.[463] For *–ko*, meaning 'region', see §7.1.7.
4.27 '*Anieskor* (Gebel Sheikh Suleiman) in *Talukokum* (the Dal Cataract kingdom)'.

ta-m-a

Lord. Egyptian: *Tem*, *Temu*  'the first living Man-God, creator of heaven and earth, created *Shu* / *Tiu* and *Tefnut,* (gods of *Bau Kem,*) his first consort was *Ausausit*. *Tem-Asar* was a god of Heroonopolis.[464]
3.42 '*Melman tama* (lord) [held] at the central fortress of *Bentilikum (*Benadir region around Mogadishu*)*'.

---

[461] Pritchard, *Atlas of the Bible*, 35, 57.
[462] Hammond, *Complete World Atlas*, 98; Munro-Hay, *Ethiopia*, map1.
[463] Baines and Malek, *Cultural Atlas*, 41.
[464] Budge, *Egyptian Hieroglyphic Dictionary*, 834.

Glossary

4.32 '*tama* (lord) of *Ataiokum* (Meroe)'.

ᚷ ... ta-n-i-o-ka-ku-e

ta-n-i-o-ka-ku-e

possessions-their-as far as, Somali: tanaad, 'become rich, wealthy', see §3.4. -io – plural, see §5.4. -ka, possessive adjective marker, see §6.6. -*kue* - 'as far as, near'. Postposition, see §7.1.8.
0.1 'One of the southerners from Lasta, I prevented the conquering Numidians from reaching *taniokakue* (beyond the [limits] of their territory)'.

ta-r

ta-r

road, Arabic: *darb*, 'road'; Bilin: *darib*, 'road'.[465] Somali: *dariiq*, 'road'.
2.38 'the Korosko village to Korkos (Kurgis) *tar* (road) [runs] through the middle of *Tetokum* (the Nubian Desert)'.

ta-r-a-ku-a-i

ta-r-a-ku-a-i

I did not allow, I did not cause, I prevented, Somali: *taray*, 'to cause, affect', §4.1. Bilin: –k,-g,-ku – negative marker, §4.7, Somali: –*ai*, first person singular past for root changing verbs.[466] See §4.2.3.
0.1 'One of the southerners from Lasta, *tarakuai* (I prevented) the conquering Numidians from reaching beyond the limits of their territory'.

ta-r-ku-n-bi-u-r

ta-r-ku-n-bi-u-r

Tarkun City (Tarkhan) in Egypt, south of Memphis.[467]

---

[465] Reinisch, *Die Bilin-Sprache*, 101.
[466] Saeed, *Somali Reference*, 89.
[467] Baines and Malek, *Cultural Atlas*, 31.

2.45 '*Tarkunbiur* (Tarkun City)' (in a list of places in *Loukanikum*)'.

ХΜ⅄☉Ϟ
ta-s-ko-ku-m

Border land, frontier land. Egyptian: *tash* –'boundary, frontier'. For *–ko*, meaning 'region', see §7.1.8.
2.1 'as far as the great chief of Abokum Turo, [who rules] the Cattle Land *Taskokum* (borderland) with the *Sekanos* (shebka people) as far as the southern *Tirtanos*'.

Хϯ◇Н
ta-u-r-o

'Bull', as in the constellation Taurus', the word was used as part of the name of Cyprus, *Aiankum Tauro* – 'the Bull's Eye land'. *Ushu*, the mainland portion of Tyre in Lebanon, is described as being in the *Aiankum Tauro*.
I-B 7 '*The Melmunos* of *Aiankum* have destroyed Ushu of the *Aiankum Tauro* (Eye of the Bull Land)'.
I-B 8 'They continued destroying the cities of the *Aiankum Tauro* (Eye of the Bull Land)'.

◇Νϯρ Νᴪ☉Ϟ
te-i-u-a-n-ti-ku-m

the Western Land, Egyptian: *Ta-imn-t-kum* ⸗⸗⸗, 'the Western Land'. 'The fortress of the Western Land', sometimes written *Tjamet*, is Medinet Habu, across from Thebes, by the entrance to the Valley of the Kings, guarding the Westerners, the dead, those who have gone west.
1.23 'the burdu (fortress) of *Teiuantikum* (the Western Land)'.

3.21 'of all *of Teiuantikum* (the Western Land, perhaps the lands west of Mesopotamia)'.

Ϙ Ȝ ᛗ

te-ko-s

> a personal name, also an ethnonym meaning 'the Libyan', other names for Libyans were Tjeker and Takhsi, Libyan colonists who lived in ancient Canaan. Botorrita I-B describes the Greek and Egyptian (Melmu) invasion of the Libyan-controlled Eastern Mediterranean. The name *Tjekker* is from the Libyan city of Taucheira. Strabo mentions the Teucrians.[468]
> **2.49** '*Tekos* of *Konikum* (Canaan)'.

Ϙ ᛁ ᚱ ᛋ ᚻ ☉ ᛦ

te-l-a-d-o-ku-m

> Tjel near Sile in northern Egypt, another name for Tanis.[469] Old Irish: *Deled, Deleid, Dela* – the king of *Deled* fights against the people of Nemed when they attack Tyre'[470]
> **2.19** ' *Terkinos* of *Teladokum* (Tjel)'.

Ϙ ᛁ ᛚ ᛗ ☉ ᛦ

te-l-ka-s-ku-m

> the Dakhleh Oasis, in Egypt, west of the Nile.[471]
> **1.44** '*Kalos* of *Telkaskum* (Dakhleh Oasis)'.
> **3.39** 'as far as the ruler of *Telkaskum* (Dakhleh Oasis) [in the west], up to the *Terkinos* of *Karbilikum* in southern Yemen [in the east]'.
> **3.41** 'the First [Lord] of *Telkaskum* (Dakhleh Oasis) '.

---

[468] Cornell and Matthews, *Atlas of the Roman World*, 164; Pritchard, *Atlas of the Bible*, 47, 66-67.

[469] Baines and Malek, *Cultural Atlas*, 53.

[470] Best, Bergin and O'Brien, *The Book of Leinster*, 20, line 633.

[471] Ibid., 54, 187.

4.24 'of the great-king of _Telkaskum_ (Dakhleh Oasis)'.

ⵀ ⵓ ⵝⵀⵎ
_te-r-ki-n-o-s_

> Personal name, also ethnonym for people of narrator of text. Perhaps ancestors of Terqe who led the Bilin from Lasta to the Keren Highlands. Bilin tribe of _Terqe qur_, descendants of Terqe.
> **2.14** '_Terkinos_ of Sokota in _Austikum_ (Lasta)'.
> **2.19** ' _Terkinos_ of _Teladokum_ (Tjel, Tanis, North Egypt)'.
> **2.52** 'To the king of the _Terkinos_ at Thinis, I will extend the Harbor Kingdom of the Swamp dwellers'.
> **3.40** 'the _Terkinos_ in southern _Atokum_ (Yemen)'.
> **4.38** 'by _Terkinos_ of _Turanikum_ (Aqiq, Ptolemais Theron on Red Sea Coast)'.

ⵀⵎⵟⵀⵎ
_te-s-ti-o-s_

> Personal name, also was an ethnonym for Tibou from the Tibesti region in southern Libya.[472] Egyptian: _T3_
>
> _Sti_ ⵀⵓ ⵀ ⵀ ⵀ , 'Nubia, the Bow people'.[473]
> **3.1-4** '_Bentikum_ extends …from [the territories] of the king of Djibouti, _Testios_ of _Turumokum_, from this king of _Tirtanikum_ in the River Kingdom, to just south of the Buri Peninsula, on the border of the king of _Turikum_'.

ⵀⵡⵀⵓ
_te-to-ku-m_

---

[472] Hammond, _Complete World Atlas_, 93; Baines and Malek, _Cultural Atlas_, 12.
[473] Gardiner, _Egyptian Grammar_, 593.

Upper Nubia, Nubian Desert region plus adjacent regions on the Nile River.[474] Berber: *that* means 'river' so this word could have meant 'riverland'.[475]

1.31 'the kings of the *Akuia* kingdom rule <u>*Tetokum*</u> (River Kingdom)'.

2.38 'the Korosko village to *Korkos* (Kurgis) road [runs] through the middle of <u>*Tetokum*</u> (River Kingdom)'.

❤△
te-tu

Tetu, proper name, 'people', genitive plural. Berber: *that* 'river'.Somali: *dad,* 'people', Also the name of a god, Tetun. Naville quotes an inscription from Deir el Bahri where the god Tetun tells the queen he will tie up and behead the Anu of Nubia for her.[476]

3.18 '<u>*Tetu*</u> of *Loukanikum*'.

❤↑↗ᒪⴅᴎᴎ
te-u-d-e-s-i

decreed, proclaimed, caused to be spoken, *te.ide* - 'decree'.[477] Bilin: *te'idadsi, ti'idad,* 'command'.[478] *Teudot Lachish* –'Letters of Lachish, collection of letters in Hebrew'. See §4.1, §4.3.

4.39 '<u>*teudesi*</u> (proclaimed) in the Keren Highlands of *Kustikum*'.

Ψ
ti

---

[474] Baines and Malek, *Cultural Atlas*, 44, 179.

[475] Basset, *Le Dialecte de Syouah*, 57.

[476] Naville, "Les Plus Anciens Monuments Egyptiens", 120.

[477] Zyhlarz, "Die Fiction der 'Kuschitischen' Völker," 26.

[478] Reinisch, *Die Bilin-Sprache*, 39, 96, 183; Pritchard, *Atlas of the Bible*, 322.

to. Postposition, see §7.1.12, Bilin: *ti,* 'to'.[479]
3.49 '*ti* (to) the princes of *Turumokum'.*

tis

these.
I-B 8 '*tis* (these) cities of *Aiankum Tauro* they continued to destroy'.

ti-o-ke-n-e-s

Tiokenes of the River Kingdom, proper name, is the new lord of *Turumokum. Tiu,*  or , is a wind god, one of the gods the Egyptians borrowed from *Bau Kam* (see *kulukamikum*). Later, *Tiu* merged with the Egyptian god Shu. Kharga Oasis is *Kenem Tiu.*[480]. See §5.2.
1.50 'As far as *Tiokenes* of the River Kingdom, the Great Lord of *Turumokum.* He rules up to the first of the Great Kings of our *Tirtanos*'.

ti-o-ke-n-e-s-o-s

Of Tiokenes, possessive form, *-os* corresponds to Bilin *-ux*,[481]
4.4 'The Melman forces *Tiokenesos* (of Tiokenes) of the River Kingdom conquered the Chaldeans of Egypt…'

[479] Reinisch, *Die Bilin-Sprache*, 100.
[480] Budge, *Egyptian Hieroglyphic Dictionary*, 795; Baines and Malek, *Cultural Atlas*, 41.
[481] Reinisch, *Die Bilin-Sprache*, 95-96. Reinisch discusses use of *-ux* as genitive or adjective.

ti-r-i-ka-n-ta-n-ko

Gulf and Strait of Tiran, (modern name is Gulf of Aqaba, Arabia). There is also an island of Tiran.[482] *-anko* – 'middle', §7.1.1, Bilin: *-anqay,* 'middle'.[483] **4.10** 'The Great Chief of Klusma [becomes] the king *tirikantanko* (from the middle of the Gulf of Tiran) to [the Gulf of] Issus in *Ateskum (*Edessa / Urfa in Turkey)'.

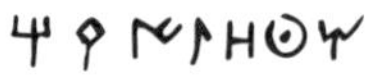

ti-r-i-l-o-ku-m

Deire, 'the neck', town on the western shore of the Mandeb Strait, opposite Ukulikum (Ocelis) on the eastern side. Land of the Dir, Dire Dawa, southeast Ethiopia, *Dir* – Somali tribe, see *tiriu, -il* adverb of place.[484] *Gundar-il* - 'in Gondar', *-o,* Somali plural. **2.11** '*Tirilokum* (the kingdom of Deire) is under the Great Chief of Aqiq'.

ti-r-i-u

People of Deire, 'the neck', a place on the western side of the Mandeb Strait, opposite Ukulikum (Akila, Ocelis) on the eastern (or Yemeni) side.[485] The Dir people, a Somali tribe. DireDawa, a city in southeast Ethiopia, means the 'Way of the Dir', that is, on the road to the Strait.[486] *-iu* - plural suffix, see §5.4. **3.31** 'from the *Akuia* of the Sinai to the court of the *Tiriu* (Deire people) of the River Kingdom'.

---

482 Musil, *Northern Arabia*; Wikipedia Authors, "Tiran Island."
483 Reinisch, *Die Bilin-Sprache*, 102.
484 Reinisch, *Die ChamirSprache*, vol. CV, 662, 692.
485 Strabo, *Geography of Strabo*, vol. III, 192-193.
486 Munro-Hay, *Ethiopia*, map1, 177, 180.

ʕ ቀ ᛙ

ti-r-s

> stretching, extending to, Akkadian: *tirs.*[487] See §4.1,
> §4.2.5.
>
> **1.59** 'excluding *Muturiskum* (Egypt) but <u>*tirs*</u> (<u>extending
> to</u>) *Turumokum* (Sudan, West of the Nile)'.

ʕ ቀ ╳ᛘᛘ☉ᛣ

ti-r-ta-n-i-ku-m

> The Chercher Mountain region of Harar province in
> Ethiopia, southwest of Djibouti.[488] Corresponds to
> 'Scorpion Land' from Egyptian: *chart /tchart.*[489] It may
> also have been 'Ancestor land', from Egyptian:
> *tchertiu.* See *Tirilokum, tirtano.*
>
> **1.1** 'to that Arab leader [held] captive in <u>*Tirtanikum*</u>
> (Scorpion Land)'.
>
> **3.2-4** '*Bentikum* extends…from[the territories] of the
> king of Djibouti, *Testios* of *Turumokum*, from this king
> of <u>*Tirtanikum*</u> (<u>Scorpion Land</u>) in the River Kingdom,
> to just south of the Buri Peninsula, on the border of the
> king of *Turikum*'.

ʕ ቀ ╳ᛘH

ti-r-ta-n-o

> relating to *Tirtanikum.* Adjective, see §6.2. In
> Egyptian, Chart/*Tchart* was a mythological
> scorpion.[490] Berber also has *teguirdoumt,* 'scorpion[491].
> The *Tirtanos* of *Tirtanikum* may have taken it as their
> symbol. The Roman era geographer Strabo, speaking

---

[487] von Soden, *Grundriss der Akkadischen*, 145sect.89c.

[488] Phillips and Carillet, *Ethiopia and Eritrea*, map of Eritrea and
Ethiopia.

[489] Budge, *Egyptian Hieroglyphic Dictionary*, 899, 909, 1057-1069,
1062; Kobishchanov, *Axum*, 45, 82.

[490] Budge, *Egyptian Hieroglyphic Dictionary*, 899.

[491] Venture de Paradis, *Grammaire*, 155.

of a Red Sea people, perhaps the Afan in the Danakil region just north of the Chercher Mountains, says, "Above these people is situated a desert tract with extensive pastures. It was abandoned in consequence of the multitudes of scorpions and tarantulas, called tetragnathi (or four-jawed), which formerly abounded to so great a degree as to occasion a complete desertion of the place long since by its inhabitants."[492]
2.46 'Mandeb Strait people from Tirtano Yemen'.

ti-r-ta-n-o-s

people of Tirtanikum, Scorpion clans.
1.52 'the Great Lord of *Turumokum* [rules] as far as the First [Lord] of the Great kings of our *Tirtanos* (Scorpion Clans)'.
2.2 'as far as the great chief of Abokum Turo, [who rules] the western Cattle Land Taskokum (borderland), with the shebka people as far south as the Tirtanos (Scorpion Clans)'.
I-B 6 'They have destroyed the lands of the Tirtanos (Scorpion Clans) of *Statulikum* reaching down to the *Nouantubos'*.

ti-r-to-bo-l-o-ku-m

Metropolis at Axum in Ethiopia. *tirto* – 'all', *bolo* - 'town', so 'all cities' or 'metropolis'. The name is translated by Greek μητρόπολιν *metropolin* in The Periplus (written in the 1st century AD), which speaks of the 'Metropolis of the Axumites'. References in the Botorrita III text place this city between Suakin and Dankalia and close to Arqiqo.[493]

[492] Strabo, *Geography of Strabo*, vol. III, 198.
[493] Huntingford, *Periplus*, 90.

1.47 'the great-chief of *Loukanikum* [held] at the fortress of *Tirtobolokum'* (Axum)'.
3.22 '[Over] all of the WesternLand, the First [Lord] at *Tirtobolokum* (the Metropolis of Axum)'.
3.29-31 ', this great chief of *Tirtobolokum* (Axum) [rules] from the Akuia Sinai to the court at Deire in the River Kingdom ....'
4.1 '*Kainu of Tirtobolokum* (Axum), the king of the Bowmen, of the *Turikainos* (people of Iken, near the 2nd Cataract)'.

Ⴘ Ⴚ Ш↑Ⴖ нⲘ
ti-r-to-u-i-o-s
Marsh people, from *tirto* 'all' and Somali: *biyo* 'water'. people from the region of all the water, the Sudd in southern Sudan.
2.16 '*Tirtouios* (the Marsh people) of [southern] *Turumokum* (Sudan)'.

Ⴘ Ⴚ ◿
ti-r-tu
all, the whole. Adjective, see §6.3, Egyptian: *aterti,* 'all', *tertiu, terti, tcher.* [494]
1.16 'a king of *tirtu* (all) *Muturiskum* (United Egypt)'.
I-B 4 'They destroyed *tirtu* (all) of the towns in *Aiankum*'.

Ⴘ Ⴚ ◿Ⴘ ⸢
ti-r-tu-ku-e
as far as all. *tirtu*-'all'. Adjective, §6.3. *-kue* - 'as far as, near'. Postposition, see §7.1.8.
2.20 -23 'as far as *Tueidunos*, the Great chief of *tirtu* (all) the kings'.

---

[494] Budge, *Egyptian Hieroglyphic Dictionary*, 40, 908.

Glossary

ተ ዖ ∆ᑊ
ti-r-tu-n
> all. Adjective plural, §6.3.
> 2.56 '*tirtun* (all) our *tolisokum* (tribal lands)'.

ተ ዖ ∆ᑊHᛊ
ti-r-tu-n-o-s
> all those. Adjective used as noun in genitive, see §6.3.
> **2.42** ' the kings at Fort *Atauikum* have *tirtunos* (all) of the Southern Kingdom
> **2.43** In *Loukanikum (*CattleLand*)* *tirtunos* (all) [of the territories] from the eastern border...'.
> **3.21** 'Over *tirtunos* (all) of the Western Lands'

ተᚹᛊ
titos
> gate, door, threshold. *Tait*.[495] Homer mentions Thebes as 'a city of one hundred gates'.[496]
> **2.9** 'from the *titos* (gates) of *Usidu* (Thebes) in *Abokum* (southern *Egypt*)'.

ᚹᑊᑊᛊH◉ᕿ
to-l-i-s-o-ku-m
> tribal lands, clan territories. Somali: *tol,* 'clan, race, family'
> **2.56** 'all our *tolisokum* (tribal lands)'.

ᚹᑊH𐤎
to-l-o-ku
> the border, Ge'ez: *dawal*, 'territory boundary', Inscription on a boundary stone from Matara,

---

[495] Ibid., 819.
[496] Homer, *The Iliad*, book 9, line 383.

Ethiopia.[497] Dhasanac: *tol,* 'foreign', *tollu,*
'foreigners'.[498] *-ku* - 'the', definite article, see §6.6.
2.44 'from the *toloku* (<u>the</u> border) of Klusma with the
Easterners '.
3.5 'from this king on *toloku* (<u>the</u> border) of *Turikum*'.
3.20 '*toloku* (<u>the</u> border) of the River Kingdom'.
4.26 'a lord of the great-chief of *Telkaskum* (the
Dakhleh Oasis) ruled *Anieskor* in the Dal Cataract
region to *toloku* (<u>the</u> border) of Kerma'.

ШⲢⲎⲞⲢⲎⳘ
to-l-o-ku-n-o-s

> those on the border. *-ku* - 'the', definite article, see
> §6.6. *tolo* – 'border'. *–nos*, 'those, of those', see §6.4.
> **3.45** '*tolokunos* (<u>those who are</u>) within (<u>the borders</u>) of
> Thinis'.

ШⲢⲎⳘⲢ ⳋ
to-l-o-s-a-r

> ' to the borders, borders on',", see §7.1.2.
> **2.58-3.2** 'the province of *Bentikum* (Baboon Land) will
> extend *tolosar* (to <u>the borders</u>) of the *Akuia* empire in
> *Abokum* (Elephant Land) from [the territories] of the
> king of Djibouti, *Testios* of *Turumokum*'.

ШⲎⲚⲚⲞⳓ
to-ti-n-i-ku-m

> Tanis, also called Tjel. See *Teladokum*. This word
> resembles *Toutinikum* (Thinis) but the context requires
> a city in the north.
> **3.33** 'Sile people of *Totinikum* (one expects Sile people
> in the north, not as far south as Thinis, so perhaps this
> is *Tanis* in the Eastern Delta)'.

---

[497] Kobishchanov, *Axum*, 257.
[498] Tosco, *Dhasanac Language*, 556.

Glossary

ШꞭꙎꝰꝪꝪӨꝰ
to-u-ti-n-i-ku-m

> Thinis, capital of 8th nome, which contains Abydos. It
> was the Capital of Egypt during the first 2 dynasties of
> the Old Kingdom. According to Manetho, the fourth
> dynasty of the PreDynastic *Akhou* also had their capital
> at Thinis.[499]
>
> Egyptian: ⸺ ◠ ∿ ○ 𓀀 𓏏 𓎡 ⌇ To-t-n-no-u-
> 'M'3T-TN-KUM.[500]
> **1.7** 'Those who were hung at *Toutinikum* (Thinis) '.
> **2.52** 'I will extend the Harbor kingdom of the Swamp
> dwellers (in the Delta) to the king of the *Terkinos* at
> *Toutinikum* (Thinis)'.
> **3.44** 'the Arkanta of Klusma, those who are within the
> borders of *Toutinikum* (Thinis) '.

ΔꝦＱꝰꞭꝪӨꞭ
tu-a-te-r-e-s-ku-e

> river, lake region as far as, Egyptian: *atur, atr* –'river,
> lake ', *tu* '=-'mount, region'.[501] *-kue* - 'as far as, near'.
> Postposition, see §7.1.8.
> **2.40** '(as far as) the birthplace of *tuatereskue* (the river
> region)'.

ΔꝦＱꝰꞪꝪӨꞭ
tu-a-te-r-o-s-ku-e

> limits, borders, Egyptian: *ater* –'limit'.[502] *-kue* - 'as far
> as, near'. Postposition, see §7.1.8.

---

[499] Manetho, *Manetho*, 5.
[500] Budge, *Egyptian Hieroglyphic Dictionary*, 1057; Baines and Malek,
Cultural Atlas, 16.
[501] Budge, *Egyptian Hieroglyphic Dictionary*, 97, 99.
[502] Ibid., 100.

3.24 'the foremost leader *tuateroskue* (as far as the border) with the Afan people, as far as the Berta people'.

ᐊᏂᑎ

tu-e-i-d-u

speaks, Bilin: *duw,* 'speak', *duwina,* 'say it', *duwiri,* 'I will say'.[503] See §4.1, §4.2.1.

1.5 'the king *tueidu* (speaks)'.

ᐊᏂᑎᐧHᛘ

tu-e-i-d-u-n-o-s

personal name for someone from *Biniskum*, 'Phoenicia', on the Eastern Mediterranean coast.

2.20 -23 'as far as *Tueidunos* the Great chief of all the kings'.

3.50 ' *Tueidunos*, the Phoenician, the Lord King of … the Khabur River empire '.

ᐊᏇᏡᛘ

tu-r-a-i-o-s

Ethnonym for people of Tyre in kingdom on the Litani River of Lebanon. Here they seem to have a settlement or trading colony in Sudan near the 3rd Cataract on the Nile.[504]

3.57 'down to the *Turaios* (Tyre people) of *Litanokum* in the River Kingdom at Kerma'.

ᐊᏇᏡ☉

tu-r-a-ku

the Tyre region, *-ku* - 'the', definite article, see §6.6.

2.19-20 '*Terkinos* of *Teladokum* [is] the chief of *turaku* (the Tyre region) of *Statu* (Canaan).'

---

[503] Reinisch, *Texte der Bilin-Sprache*, 19.
[504] Pritchard, *Atlas of the Bible*, 58.

Glossary

△ የ ↑ ΝΝΘϒ

tu-r-a-n-i-ku-m

Ptolemais Theron, Aqiq on the Red Sea coast where the Barka River flows into the Red Sea.[505]Eritrea.

2.4 '[the domain] of the Great-Chief of *Turanikum* (Eritrea), the king of the Southern River Kingdom will extend to the princes of Mouza, the islanders off of the Habashat) of Yemen, from the gates of Thebes in Abokum (S. Egypt),as far as the fortress of *Kulukamikum* (Koloe of Kam) where the chief was hanged'.

4.38 'for our provinces, by *Terkinos* of *Turanikum* (Eritrea), proclaimed in the Keren Highlands of *Kustikum*'.

△ የ Ⴑ𝝢Χ

tu-r-e-n-ta

region where people from *Turanikum* live. Bilin: -*ta*, noun forming suffix. See §5.1.

2.25 'down to *Astitokum* in the region of the southern *Turenta* (part of Turanikum),where the king of *Ataiokum* in the district of the Kemalke Ford...'.

△ የ Ν⋏𝝢𝝢ΗΜ

tu-r-i-ka-i-n-o-s

Citadel of Iken / Aken, modern Mirgissa.[506] -*os* - 'people of' Iken, see §6.2. *tur* - 'citadel, fort'.[507]

4.2-3 'a king of the bowmen at the southern town of the *turikainos* (Fort Iken people)'.

---

[505] Ibid.

[506] Baines and Malek, *Cultural Atlas*, 41, 133-134, 186; Budge, *Egyptian Hieroglyphic Dictionary*, 965; Jackson, *At Empire's Edge*, 284n17.

[507] Budge, *Egyptian Hieroglyphic Dictionary*, 851.

△ ၉ ℕ☉🜨
tu-r-i-ku-m

Western coast of Red Sea and the hinterlands from the Nile Bend in Egypt to the Buri Peninsula in Eritrea. Under *Terkinos* of *Turanikum*, the borders of *Turikum* are set to match the borders of *Abokum Turo* and the borders of *Turanikum*. This is also the *Troglodutike* or *Turo Kelaututike* (*Turo* Lowlands, coastal plain, *Turo* empire) mentioned in the Periplus of the Red Sea.[508] Amharic: *qwalla,* 'low country, between sea-level and 5,000 ft. elevation', Berber: *geldi,* 'empire, kingdom'. *Turikum* is very ancient. The I-B text (from the early 5th millennium BC) mentions *Ubokum Turo*. The story of Fenius Farsaid in the *Book of Invasions* has him go to *Turikum* to work as a scribe. If that took place during the First *Akhou* Dynasty, it would go back to the 9th millenium BC.

3.4-5 '*Bentikum* extends …from this king of *Tirtanikum* in the River Kingdom, to just south of the Buri Peninsula on the border of the king of *Turikum* (western Red Sea coast kingdom) '.

△ ၉ H
tu-r-o

pertaining to, or ruled by *Turikum or Turanikum*. Adjective, see §6.2.

1.60 'the Great-Chief of *Abokum Turo*'.

2.57 'all our tribal kingdoms of the kings of the *Turo* empire'.

I-B 3 ' The plundered *Melmu* land that was destroyed, extending to the Turo Uweinat, was destroyed by the Libyans'.

△ ၉ HℳM

---

[508] Huntingford, *Periplus*, 82.

tu-r-o-s

> people of Turikum.
> **1.1** 'to that Arab leader [held] captive in Tirtanikum,
> the great-king of the *Turos* and *Kontudos,* the Great
> Chief of the *Statulu,* the king, has spoken'.

ᐃ ᕙ ᐊᑎ ᕐ ᔅᐤᒃ
tu-r-tu-n-a-d-ku-e

> as far as the court. *Turtanu* is a court official, *turtunad*
> is likely to be the court, the administrative center.
> *turtanu-*'the chief official, Assyrian: chief official of
> late Assyrian court, often translated as marshal or
> Grand Vizier'.[509] Chamir-*nat,* forms abstract nouns.[510]
> -*kue* - 'as far as, near'. Postposition, see §7.1.8.
> **3.32** 'the Great Chief at *Tirtobolokum* (Metropolis of
> Axum) from the *Akuia* of *Alikum, turtunadkue* (as far
> as the court) of the *Tiriu* of the River Kingdom'.

ᐃ ᕙ ᐊᑎ᙭ᐤᒃ
tu-r-tu-n-ta-ku-e

> the Chief official, the controller. In Assyrian, this was
> a title of the chief official of the late Assyrian court.[511]
> Bilin: -*ta,* noun forming suffix. See §5.1. -*kue* - 'as far
> as, near'. Postposition, see §7.1.8.
> **3.38** 'the commander of the army of Uriaskum is the
> king of Suakin *turtuntakue* (from the court) of the
> lord of Djibouti/Somalia'.

ᐃ ᕙ ᐱᔑᕨᐤᕨ
tu-r-u-m-o-ku-m

> Egypt and Sudan, west of the Nile.[512] May include
> parts of Chad. One spot on its western border was near

---

[509] Baines and Malek, *Cultural Atlas,* 227.
[510] Reinisch, *Die ChamirSprache,* vol. CV, 663.
[511] Baines and Malek, *Cultural Atlas,* 227.
[512] Ibid., 12-13; Moorehead, *The Blue Nile,* 10.

the Kufra Oasis in southeast Libya. The name *Turumokum* is preserved in the placename UmDurman, a large fortified city near Khartoum, the Mother of Citadels, where the White Nile and the Blue Nile merge to form the main branch of the Nile. The mountain, Jabal Turum, is found in the Nuba Mountains in Kordofan, Sudan, as well as a tribe called the Turum.

1.24 'from the *Bilibos* (Oebilia people from Bilia near the Kufra Oasis) of [northwest] *Turumokum* (lands west of the Nile)'.

1.28 'from *Turumokum* where the Sand-dwellers live'.

1.51-52 'the Great Lord of *Turumokum* (lands west of the Nile) [rules] as far as the first of the Great Kings of our Tirtanos'.

1.59 'Abokum (Elephant Land) extends to *Turumokum* [which is west of the Nile]'.

2.16 'to the *Tirtouios* (Marsh people) of *Turumokum* (South Sudan)'.

2.48-50 'are [taken] from the commander of *Turumokum*, [who was] *Tekos* (a person) of Canaan, [who was] the lord of the leaders at Parætonium (capital of *Loukanikum*, port in West Egypt),'.

3.1 '[the territories] of *Testios* of *Turumokum* (a person from the Tibesti Mountain area in southern Libya),'.

3.49 'to the princes of *Turumokum* (lands west of the Nile)'.

↑✳☉𝕐

u-bo-ku-m

Uweinat, in Southern Libya, south and west of the southwest corner of Egypt.[513] A region in Libya to the southwest of Egypt.

---

[513] Hammond, *Complete World Atlas*, 98; Baines and Malek, *Cultural Atlas*, 12-13.

3.16 'a king of the conquered kingdom [who was held] at the fortress of *Betaskum* (Umm Ebeida, Siwa Oasis), [controlled by] the Melman kings of *Samikum* (Siwa Oasis) [was] the commander of *Ubokum* (Uweinat), which was outside of the conquered kingdom '.
I-B 3 ' The plundered *Melmu* land that was destroyed, extending to the *Turo Ubokum* (Uweinat), was destroyed by the Libyans'.

u-e-r-d-a-i-d-o-ku-m

district, province, ward. Amharic: *warada,* 'district, province'.[514] *woreda,* 'district', Egyptian: *waret,* 'governmental departments'.[515]
1.29 'below the princes of these *uerdaidokum* (provinces) [are] the kings of the Akuia kingdom...'
See 1.34, 2.26, 2.29, 4.37.

u-i-d̲-u-s-ki-ku-m

Bayuda region in Sudan, Napata, Egyptian: *Ta Khont,* ' the interior'.[516] See *–ki* – 'his, theirs', see §6.6.
1.31-32 'In *Uiduskikum* (Bayuda land), they rule as far as the king of Sana'a in Yemen'.
4.30 'the leader of *Uiduskikum* (Bayuda land)'.

u-i-ka-n-o-ku-m

Mycenae, a kingdom in Greece, residence of Agamemnon, who led the forces that attacked Troy.[517]

---

[514] Munro-Hay, *Ethiopia*, 288.
[515] Budge, *Egyptian Hieroglyphic Dictionary*, 156b.
[516] Baines and Malek, *Cultural Atlas*, 13.
[517] Autenrieth, *Homeric Dictionary*, 194; Barraclough, *Atlas of World History* , 66.

I-B 5 'They burnt out the *Suostunos* of Uikanokum (Mycenae)'.

u-i-r-i-a-s-ku

the river, Egyptian: *weresh,* 'river'.[518] Rendille: *wor,* 'river'. Somali: *war,* 'swamp, marsh, quagmire'.[519] Bilin: written as *warraba* , pronounced *worraba,* 'river', plural *warraf.*[520] Chamir: *wirba* (*uirba*), 'river'.[521] *-ku* - 'the', definite article, see §6.6.

2.3 'From the Loukanian Uiriasku (River) (the Barka River) the domain of the Great Chief of Aqiq will extend [east] to the princes of *Uiskikum(*Mouza in Yemen)'.

u-i-r-i-a-s-ku-m

[Nile] River Kingdom, Egyptian: *wr-r-sh-MR-KUM,*

 *Ueresh*, '[Nile] River country'.[522] Rendille: *wor,* 'river', Somali: *war,* 'swamp, marsh, quagmire'.[523] Bilin: written as *warraba* and pronounced *worraba,* 'river', plural *warraf.*[524] Chamir: *wirba* (*uirba*), 'river'.[525]

1.8 'from *Uiriaskum* (the River Kingdom), the king of the army of *Matulokum (*Metelis, Egypt*)*'.

1.21 '*Uiriaskum* (the River Kingdom) is ruled by the *Bilinos of Austikum* (Lasta) '.

---

[518] Brugsch, *Dictionnaire Géographique*, 1401.
[519] Fleming, "Baiso and Rendille," 69.
[520] Reinisch, *Die Bilin-Sprache*, 17, 92.
[521] Ibid., *Die ChamirSprache*, vol. CV, 595.
[522] Brugsch, *Dictionnaire Géographique*, 1401.
[523] Fleming, "Baiso and Rendille," 69.
[524] Reinisch, *Die Bilin-Sprache*, 17, 92.
[525] Ibid., *Die ChamirSprache*, vol. CV, 595.

1.39 'up to the Great Lord of the princes of the southern part of *Uiriaskum* (the River Kingdom)'.

1.53 '*Tiokenes of Uiriaskum* (the River Kingdom), the Great Lord of *Turumokum,* [rules] as far as the First [Lord] of the great kings of our *Tirtanos*'.

2.28 'the kings of *Uiriaskum* (the River Kingdom), [who are] over the districts of Western Shendi in *Ataiokum*'.

2.31 '*Tais* (Dessie, Ethiopia) *of Uiriaskum* (the River Kingdom)'.

2.32 'the Basa region (in Meroe region) of *Uiriaskum* (the River Kingdom)'.

2.41 '*In Uiriaskum* (the River Kingdom) the kings at Fort *Atauikum* (?Adefa)who have all of the southern kingdom'.

3.3 'from this king of *Tirtanikum* south of *Kinbiria* in *Uiriaskum* (the River Kingdom)'.

3.9 'the lord of the Antiu in *Uiriaskum* (the River Kingdom) *Melm*'.

3.19-20 ' on the border of *Uiriaskum* (the River Kingdom) with *Arkanta Uiriaskum*'.

3.31 'as far as the court of the *Tiriu* (Deire/Dir people) of *Uiriaskum* (the River Kingdom)'.

3.35 'the [new] commander of the *Uiriaskum* (the River Kingdom) army [is] the *Suaikinokum* (Suakin) *king* '.

3.54-56 'In *Uiriaskum* (the River Kingdom) from south of the *babos* (people of *Wawat*) '.

3.57 ' as far in southern *Uiriaskum,* (the River Kingdom,) as the *Turaios* (Tyre people) of *Litanokum,* (Litani Land, Lebanon) in Kerma (Sudan, 3rd Cataract)

3.59 '*kari* (the Napata district) in *Uiriaskum* (the River Kingdom)'.

4.22 'the lord of Babal (?Old Cairo) has *Usidu* (Thebes) in *Uiriaskum* (the River Kingdom)'.

4.23 'in *Uiriaskum* (the River Kingdom) one of the kings of the Dakhleh Oasis is the chief who rules Mount Kor to the Kerma border'.
    See **1.15, 1.22, 1.27, 1.49, 2.5, 4.4, 4.15**.

↑N ϙN ϙ ρ M☉ϒ
u-i-r-i-r-a-s-ku-m
    Warawar, Urvuar name for the Lalibela region in Lasta, from notes by a Venetian written in 1523.[526] Capital city of the 12th century Zagwe dynasty, see Austikum.
    2.34 ' In *Uiriraskum* (*?* Warawar), those Ethiopian princes of mine who are below *Kaburikum*'.

↑N ϙ H☉
u-i-r-o-ku
    the Great [Lord], Egyptian: *wr* 𓄿 'great'.[527] *ur* [*wr, uir*] was a title meaning commander. *-ku* - 'the', definite article, see §6.6. See §5.1.
    1.5 'the king speaks, *uiroku* (the Great Lord), our king of kings'.
    1.51 ' *uiroku* (the Great Lord) of *Turumokum*'.
    3.26 'Of Suakin [he is] *uiroku* (the Great Lord)'.

↑NM↗☉ϒ
u-i-s-ki-ku-m
    Mouza in Yemen or Moskha, port in Oman SW Arabian Peninsula.[528] for *–ki*, 'his', see §6.6.
    1.33 'the fortress of *Uiskikum* (Mouza) in the eastern province of the king of the people of Sa'na in Yemen'.
    2.6 'the king of the south of the River Kingdom, up to the princes of *Uiskikum* (Mouza) including *Auaskum* (the Highlands, *Habashat*)'.

---

[526] Munro-Hay, *Ethiopia*, 23, 189, 195.
[527] Brugsch and Seymour, *History of Egypt*, 254.
[528] Budge, *Egyptian Hieroglyphic Dictionary*, 996; Huntingford, *Periplus*, map 1.

↑𝚇ᴎ✕𝟋
u-ko-n-ta-d

> by the Mycenaeans, by the *ukonta* of *uikanokum*, see
> *uikanokum*.
> **I-B 9** 'The town of Gortyn was destroyed <u>*ukontad*</u> (by
> the Mycenaeans)'.

↑ⵙ𝖨ᴎⵙᵞ
u-ku-l-i-ku-m

> Okelis (Ocelis), port in Yemen at or near the Mandeb
> Strait, separating the Red Sea from the Gulf of
> Aden.[529]
> **2.54** 'from the kings of <u>*Ukulikum*</u> (Ocelis) to Gigaskert
> at Byblos'

↑𝖨✕
u-l-ta

> from, Akkadian: *ultu*, 'from'.[530] Postposition, see
> §7.1.13, §7.2.2, can be declined like a noun.
> **1.28** ' <u>*ulta*</u> (from) *Turumokum* where the Sand-dwellers
> live'.

↑𝖨✕ⴷᴎ
u-l-t-a-tu-n

> who were from. Postposition, see §7.2.2.
> **2.48** ' <u>*ultatun*</u> (taken from) the commander of
> *Turumokum*'.

↑𝖨✕ⴷᴎHᴍ
u-l-ta-tu-n-o-s

> from among those. Postposition, see §7.2.2.
> **3.7** 'a commander of *Bentilikum* <u>*ultatunos*</u> (from
> among those) at the fortress of *Bentilikum*'.

---

[529] Huntingford, *Periplus*, map1.
[530] Horowitz, *Mesopotamian Cosmic Geography*, 70.

𐤉𐤉𐤉𐤉
u-l-ti-a
> one from. Postposition, see §7.2.2.
> **1.8** 'Of those hung in Thinis, <u>*ultia*</u> (<u>one from</u>) the River Kingdom was the king of the army of *Matulokum* '.

𐤉𐤉𐤉𐤉𐤉𐤉
u-l-ti-n-o-s
> those from. Postposition, see §7.2.2.
> **3.55** 'the Syrians at Aila of Kish, <u>*ultinos*</u> (<u>those from</u>) Elim in the Sinai up to Amman in Jordan'.

𐤉𐤉△
u-l-tu
> from. Postposition, see §7.2.2.
> **1.24** '<u>*ultu*</u> (<u>from</u>) the *Bilibos* of *Turumokum*'.

𐤉𐤉𐤉𐤉𐤉
u-r-ka-l-a
> lion, Akkadian: *ur.gu.la* – 'Leo, constellation Leo'.[531]
> **4.31** '<u>*urkala*</u> (<u>the lion</u>) of *Austunikum* (Highlander Land, Abyssinia).

𐤉𐤉𐤉𐤉
u-s-a-m-a
> the highest, epithet of god, great. Arabic: '*aẓim, 'aẓama* – 'great, the Highest'. See *abaloskue*.
> **3.47** 'as far as the [temple] of Apollo, <u>*Usama*</u> (<u>the Most High</u>) '.

𐤉𐤉𐤉𐤉𐤉𐤉
u-s-e-i-d-u

---

name for Ushu, mainland part of Tyre in Lebanon.[532]
The Tyre part of the city was on an island just off of
the coast.

I-B 7 The *Melmunos* of *Aiankum* destroyed <u>Useidu</u>
(<u>Ushu</u>) in the *Aiankum Tauro'*.

ፐMԱℕ⅄ፐℕHM

u-s-e-i-d-u-n-o-s

of the people of Ushu, mainland-based part of ancient
Tyre.[533]

2.15 'the king <u>Useidunos</u> (<u>of the Ushu people</u>) in
Abokum (Elephant Land)'.

I-B 5 ' the cities of Laodikea <u>Useidunos</u> (<u>of the Ushu</u>
<u>people</u>) were destroyed by the Achaeans'.

ፐMℕ⅄ፐ

u-s-i-d-u

Thebes, Waset, in the Nile Bend region of Egypt.

2.9 'the gates of <u>Usidu</u> (<u>Thebes</u>) in *Abokum*.

4.23 '<u>Usidu</u> (<u>Thebes</u>) in the River Kingdom'.

ፐMᲧШ⊙⅄

u-s-ti-to-ku-m

Astitokum, Land of the <u>Asta</u>, the Nile. In Nubian, the
Nile was the Astapus. The Atbara River, which starts
in Lasta / *Austikum*, flows into the Nile. It was
formerly called the Asta-bara – branch of the Nile.[534]
In the context of the text, the kingdom it refers to
appears to be Meroe, whose eastern border would
sometimes have been the Atbara River. Budge
translates *Asti* as 'the two Egypts, Upper and Lower'.[535]

---

[532] Baines and Malek, *Cultural Atlas*, 177.
[533] Ibid.
[534] Sethe, *Urgeschichte und älteste Religion der Ägypter*, 91n6;
    Moorehead, *The Blue Nile*, 10, 278.
[535] Budge, *Egyptian Hieroglyphic Dictionary*, 962.

As an Egyptian term and to the extent that it meant 'Lands along the Nile', this may also be correct.
2.24 'In _Ustitokum_ (in the Atbara River region) down to the region of the southern _Turenta,_ the king of Meroe in the district of the Kemalke Ford...'.

INDEX

Abaniu, 5, 6, 69, 152, 153
Abokum, 36, 118, 128
Agau, 5, 6, 16, 59, 158, 247
Aian, 168, 175
Aiankum, 123, 139, 168,
   169, 171, 172, 180
Aila, 12, 25, 55, 57, 75, 175
Ailokiskum, 10, 123
Akhou, 14, 15, 16, 17, 35,
   110, 118, 131, 247
Akuia, 5, 6, 16, 17, 85
Antiu, 25, 65, 81, 97
Apollo, 139
Aqiq, 133, 136
Arkanta, 30, 31, 33, 73,
   123, 167
Aunu, 35, 247
Austikum, 5, 134, 157, 158,
   229, 235
Baboon Land, 20, 63, 107
Bahrain, 8, 9, 13, 81, 144
Basque, 145, 147, 153, 228,
   241, 249
Bilin, 5, 6, 114, 116, 154,
   158, 227, 228, 229, 230,
   231, 232, 236, 238, 240,
   241, 245, 246, 247, 248,
   249, 250, 254, 258
Bini Rusku, 105
Biniskum, 20, 102, 104,
   124, 149, 250
Botorrita, 91, 92, 93, 96, 97,
   101, 102, 104, 105, 106,

110, 154, 178, 182, 226,
   227, 234
Calaetus, 97
Celtiberia, 91, 94
Celtiberian, 96, 110, 148,
   226
Chamir, 6, 114, 147, 154,
   157, 158, 227, 228, 229,
   230, 231, 232, 233, 234,
   237, 240, 241, 246, 247,
   251
Coptus, 32
Crete, 87, 140, 162
Dahna, 143
Danaan, 143, 174
Dhasanac, 116, 155, 230,
   232, 247, 251
Djibouti, 6, 134, 135, 154
Egypt, 3, 6, 7, 8, 13, 15, 16,
   17, 32, 96, 97, 100, 101,
   105, 116, 130, 141, 146,
   168, 169, 181, 250
Elephantine. See Abokum
ensi, 146
Ensikum, 75, 124, 126, 129,
   141, 146
Eritrea, 3, 5, 7, 81, 89, 114,
   128, 134, 135, See
   Kustikum
Ethiopia, 5, 6, 32, 114, 134,
   164
Etruscan, 105, 106

Ge'ez, 148, 165, 236, 241, 295

Great Chief, 6, 104, 148

Jordán Cólera, 96, 97, 102, 229

Kaiaitos, 8, 13, 49, 95

Kalaitos, 7, 79, 81, 97, 124

Karunikum, 16, 17, 32, 34, 79, 129, 169

Keren, 3, 5, 89, 114, 134, 135, 154, 250

Kushitic, 4, 6, 16, 101, 110, 114, 116, 146, 147, 152, 154, 155, 158, 178, 226, 227, 234, 235, 239, 241, 245, 246, 247, 249, 251, 252

Kustikum, 5, 81, 89, 128, 133, 135, 164, 228

Kuwait, 124, 144

Laguatan, 21, 30, 32, 41, 67, 93, 141, 149

Lasta, 5, 6, 32, 34, 110, 114, 116, 135, 137, 154, 157, 180, 229, 234, 247, 250

Libyan, 147, 180

Lion Land, 20, 32, 34, 157

Lugal Kitun, 8, 149

Macehead, 31, 34

Manetho, 14, 15, 16

Marmaridae, 93

Matgenus, 104, 245

medukenos, 6, 148, 244

Melamanna, 8, 9, 130

melman, 129, 246, 248, 255

Melmanios, 3, 8, 130

Melmu, 180

Metropolis, 107, 164, 246

Muturiskum, 7, 16, 17, 34, 81, 97, 118, 130, 250

Nouida, 5, 17, 30, 32, 39, 126, 130, 144, 175, 230

Nubian, 153

Petra, 61, 114, 130, 143, 144, 173, 228

Petra, the Siq, 124, 125

Petrie, 35, 36, 100, 101, 107

Phoenician, 99, 100, 101, 102, 104, 105, 106, 228, 250

PreDynastic, 14, 15, 17, 35, 131

Sargon, 245

shebka, 140

Shilluk, 148

Sokota, 158, 178

Somali, 5, 6, 7, 101, 104, 109, 129, 135, 148, 154, 228, 230, 232, 233, 234, 236, 237, 239, 241, 244, 246, 247, 252, 253

Sousse, 92, 93

Thinis, 6, 10, 16, 17, 35, 36, 73, 110, 130, 131

Tiokenes, 79, 149, 245

Tirtobolokum, 77, 107, 136, 149, 164

Turanikum, 5, 6, 36, 106, 136, 149, 159

Turkana, 5, 35, 155, 165

Untermann, 229

Uruk, 3, 7, 8, 9, 12, 13, 14, 15, 34, 97, 106, 123, 124, 128, 149, 162, 182

Uweinat, 67, 139, 141, 173, 178